Ecological Economics and Finance

"This handbook and the philosophy behind its creation represent an integrated approach to placing nature and humanity at the heart of economics and finance. Erudite, complex without being overly opaque, and above all stimulating, it is destined to become a key text as we move towards reclaiming economics and finance as anthropocentric social sciences."

—Brian M. Lucey, Professor of Finance, *Trinity College Dublin, university of Dublin*

"Many economists still dream of an economic world which, following natural laws, would spontaneously converge towards a general market equilibrium, if we let it. The time for dreaming has given way to the nightmares of financial crises, growing social inequalities, and global warming that leaves us no choice but to act. This book is an introduction to the real workings of the economy, a much more complex and uncertain world, where money and finance can justify other political choices. It opens the way to understanding the challenges of the 21st century."

—Edwin Le Héron, Professor of Economics, *Sciences Po Bordeaux—Centre Émile Durkheim CNRS 5116*

"Rethinking money and debt through the prism of the common good rather than guilt, defending a truly sustainable approach to finance, reconsidering the crushing weight of short-term profitability in financial models... This book takes a serious and competent approach to the renewal of economic thinking, so that it can no longer be an obstacle but a support in tackling the major challenges of the 21st century, starting with climate change. This book is an essential contribution to the development of humanist and ecological economic thinking. It is written by top-quality researchers from the French branch of SDSN, gathered around the talented Thomas Lagoarde-Ségot."

—Nicolas Dufrêne, *Senior civil servant and Director of the Institut Rousseau*

"Our new age of sustainable development calls for a new age of economics and finance textbooks as well. Bravo to the contributors to this exciting and pioneering book, demonstrating important new ways to re-think the financial system and its ethical foundations to align with the Sustainable Development Goals and the Paris Climate Agreement."

—Jeffrey D. Sachs, *President of the UN Sustainable Development Solutions Network, University Professor at Columbia University, USA*

Thomas Lagoarde-Ségot
Editor

Ecological Economics and Finance

An Introduction to Sustainable Monetary and Financial Systems

Second Edition

Springer

Editor
Thomas Lagoarde-Ségot
Kedge Business School
Talence, France

ISBN 978-3-031-71248-7 ISBN 978-3-031-71249-4 (eBook)
https://doi.org/10.1007/978-3-031-71249-4

Cover credit: Yaorusheng|Getty Images

This Palgrave Macmillan imprint is published by the registered company Springer Nature Switzerland AG
The registered company address is: Gewerbestrasse 11, 6330 Cham, Switzerland

If disposing of this product, please recycle the paper.

Preface

Presentation

To facilitate the achievement of the 17 Sustainable Development Goals (SDGs), in 2014 the United Nations endowed themselves with a specific vehicle: the Sustainable Development Solutions Network. Under the presidency of professor Jeffrey Sachs, this network (present in over 50 countries) set up in France in 2018 where it brought together, on a voluntary basis, some thirty researchers and actors aware of the new climate and social challenges. From the very first meetings of this working group, the consensus was that university teaching in these disciplines needed to evolve to meet the objectives of the Paris Agreements.[1]

The book you are holding in your hands, which was written between 2019 and 2023, is a product of this working group. Conceived as an interdisciplinary dialogue between economics and management sciences, it contains two parts. The first, entitled 'The Monetary Economy', re-examines the functioning of a monetary production economy from the perspective of sustainable development. The second, entitled 'Financial Actors and Practices', describes the economic and financial players involved in sustainable development, their ecosystems and their instruments.

The aim of this text is to enable higher education teachers to alternate the use of the 'macroscope' and the 'microscope' in new economics and management courses that give pride of place to intellectual pluralism, diversity and the demands of sustainability—without sacrificing methodological rigor. Whether you're a teacher, a student, or simply a citizen wishing to better understand the workings of the monetary and financial system, we hope you enjoy reading!

[1]This observation was confirmed in 2020 with the publication of the Veblen Institute's report, "*Ten years after the financial crisis, how to teach finance?*", coordinated by Laurence Scialom, Yamina Tadjeddine and Stéphanie Servet.

Use

This textbook can be used as a main resource in courses with an economics or management focus, following the suggested sequencing, or as a complementary resource. The table below gives some examples of courses taught at KEDGE Business School in the 2020's and using this textbook as their main resource. Taking these courses did not require any methodological prerequisites. To encourage interactive learning, each chapter also contains learning objectives and an 'Activities' section, grouped together with questions and case studies.

A Few Examples of Use

Course Title	Ecological Macroeconomics	Sustainable Monetary Systems	International Finance	Ecological Finance
University level	Undergraduate	Postgraduate	Postgraduate	Postgraduate
Hourly volume	30 h	30 h	30 h	30 h
Corresponding chapters	1–8	3–9 and 11–13	3–4 and 8–11	12–24

Thanks

It would have been very difficult to finalize this book without the support and encouragement of our friends. Our special thanks go to Eve de la Mothe Karoubi and Andrija Erac of SDSN France, Aurélien Decamps and Jean-Christophe Carteron of Sulitest, Christian Walter, Bernard Paranque, Olga Battaïa, Frantz Maurer, Dorian Simon-Meslet, Anne-France Piteau, Coralie Reslinger, Luis Reyes-Ortiz, Ramzi Klabi and Alban Mathieu of KEDGE Business School. Our warm thanks also go to our eminent colleague and mediator Roland Pérez (Université de Montpellier), and to all members of the *Finance et Communs* mailing list, to the *Association française d'économie politique* (AFEP), to the *Réseau international de recherche sur les organisations et le développement durable* (RIODD) and to the *Association pour le développement des études keynésiennes* (ADEK). Finally, we would like to thank Wyndham Packet Hain, economics editor at Palgrave-Macmillan, for his confidence in the first English edition of this book, as well as Pauline Monclin, Mireille Raskin and Claudia Mericskay at De Boeck for their editorial support, their kindness and their efficiency.

Talence, France Thomas Lagoarde-Ségot

Contents

Part II Financial Actors and Practices

Contributors

Sharam Alijani The American University of Paris, Paris, France

Nicolas Aubert CERGAM, Aix-Marseille Université, Marseille, France

Nicolas Bédu ART-Dev, Université de Montpellier, Montpellier, France

Rachelle Belinga California State University, Los Angeles, CA, USA; MINES Paris Tech, Paris, France

Héloïse Berkowitz LEST, CNRS, Aix Marseille Université, Aix en Provence, France

David Bourghelle Université de Lille, Lille, France

Isabelle Chambost Conservatoire National des Arts et Métiers, Paris, France

Jérôme Courcier ESG Senior Advisor, KPMG, Courbevoie, France

Thibault Cuénoud Excelia Business School, La Rochelle, France

Charles Daussy NEOMA BS, Mont-Saint-Aignan, France

Raphaël Didier Université de Lorraine, Metz, France

Elias Erragragui Al Akhawayn University, Ifrane, Morocco

Caroline Granier Chaire Energie Et Prospérité, Paris, France

Xavier Hollandts KEDGE BS, Talence, France

Catherine Karyotis The American University of Paris, Paris, France

Thomas Lagoarde-Ségot KEDGE Business School (KEDGE BS), Talence, France

Laurence Le Poder KEDGE Business School, Talence, France

Marc Lenglet NEOMA Business School, Mont-Saint-Aignan, France

Jean-François Ponsot Université Grenoble Alpes, Grenoble, France

Christophe Revelli KEDGE Business School, Marseille, France

Laurence Scialom Université Paris Nanterre, EconomiX UMR, Nanterre, France

Blanche Segrestin MINES Paris Tech, Paris, France

Antoine Souchaud NEOMA Business School, i3-CRG, École Polytechnique, CNRS, Institut Polytechnique de Paris, Palaiseau, France

Yamina Tadjeddine Université de Lorraine, CNRS, BETA, Nancy, France

Part I
The Monetary Economy

1 Economics, Finance and Reality

Thomas Lagoarde-Ségot

Putting Things into Perspective

According to the United Nations, some 4.7 million hectares of forest disappear every year. Yet these forests are only included in national accounts when the trees are cut down, i.e., when they are destroyed. Since this destruction generates monetary income, it is not counted as a loss, but as an increase in well-being (via higher GDP).

To describe this paradox, ecological economics pioneer Herman Daly (1938–2022) used the metaphor of a biologist who would attempt to analyze a dog's organism on the basis of its cardiovascular system alone, while ignoring its digestive system. The cardiovascular system is certainly important, but without a digestive system that connects it to its environment, the dog will die very quickly, either of starvation or constipation.

Similarly, economic and management indicators treat the economic and financial system as if it were disconnected from its environment, whereas it is integrated into a fragile whole that surrounds and supports it. This whole includes society, of course, but also the Earth system (which includes the atmosphere, biosphere, hydrosphere and geosphere). So, before studying economics and finance, it may be useful to take a step back and consider the nature of our object of study. This will enable us to acquire more relevant knowledge in order to act more responsibly.

Learning Objectives

- Situating the economic and financial system within the Earth system
- Understanding the role of economic theories and financial indicators
- Measuring the importance of *pluralism* in the social sciences

1.1 The Economy Is the Sub-Part of a Whole

The Earth System

On December 24, 1968, American astronaut William Anders took an incredible series of photos of the Earth from the Moon. In these photos, our planet, home to billions of human beings (as well as ants, bears and jellyfish), appears for what it is: a tiny blue ball, lost in the immense

T. Lagoarde-Ségot (✉)
KEDGE BS & SDSN France, Talence, France
e-mail: thomas.lagoardesegot@kedgebs.com

T. Lagoarde-Ségot (ed.), *Ecological Economics and Finance*, https://doi.org/10.1007/978-3-031-71249-4_1

darkness of an expanding universe. Scientists estimate the diameter of the observable Universe at 93 billion light-years (about 880,000 billion kilometers).

If you were propelled randomly through the Universe, you'd probably find yourself in a void of darkness and cold—the average temperature being –270 degrees Celsius. In the distance, a faint glimmer flickers. A star? No, a galaxy. According to astrophysicists, there are between 100 and 200 billion galaxies in the Universe. One of them, the Milky Way, is thought to contain between 200 and 400 billion stars. One of these—a dwarf star—is the Sun. Surrounding the Sun is a tiny speck of dust: our common home, the Earth (Fig. 1.1).

On Earth, the oceans, atmosphere, land and living organisms function as an integrated whole: the Earth system made up of four open, interconnected systems: the *atmosphere*, *geosphere*, *hydrosphere* and *biosphere.*

The *atmosphere* is a protective envelope of gases about a hundred kilometers thick. Composed of a subtle, fragile balance of nitrogen, oxygen and carbon dioxide, it filters out the deadly ultraviolet rays emitted by the Sun and destroys most celestial objects liable to hit the Earth (turning them into shooting stars). The atmosphere also reflects back to Earth the Sun's rays, which would otherwise bounce off into space. This *greenhouse effect* maintains temperatures on Earth that are compatible with life. Finally, the atmosphere redistributes heat and humidity across the Earth's surface, absorbing water through evaporation and then releasing it in the form of rain, snow or other precipitation.

The *geosphere* is the solid mineral part of the Earth. It is constantly undergoing the effects of erosion, tectonic forces and underground volcanic activity.

The hydrosphere contains water in all its forms: oceans, seas, water vapor, ice caps, ice crystals, glaciers, lakes, rivers, streams, atmospheric humidity and permafrost.

Finally, the biosphere is a thin strip some twenty kilometers thick that covers almost the

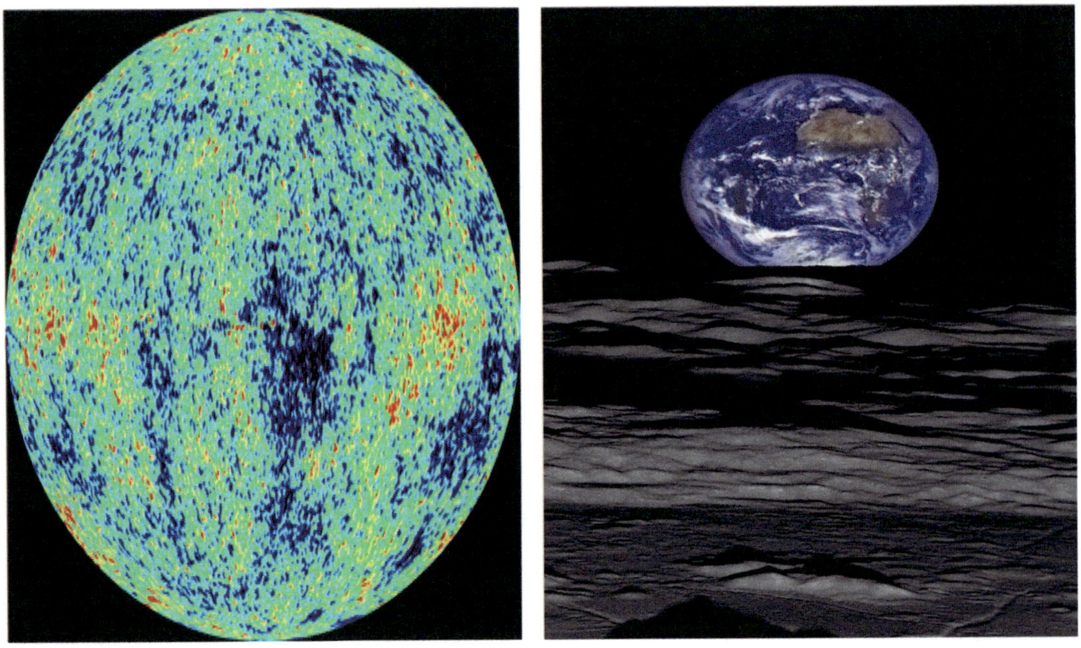

Fig. 1.1 Big bang and Earthrise (*Note* The image on the left represents the "cosmological background radiation", the first light released by the Universe, 380,000 years after the big bang. The image on the right is a photograph from the Earth Rise series, taken on December 24, 1968, during the Apollo 8 mission)

entire surface of the Earth. This thin, fragile layer is home to life and all the substances produced by living organisms, some of which are useful for life (e.g., humus).

Situating the Economy

The biosphere, with its estimated 9 million living species, functions on the basis of *photosynthesis*. Indeed, certain living organisms (such as plants and plankton) are capable of producing organic molecules from solar energy, water and minerals. These organic molecules then enter a chain of interdependent organisms (such as fish, insects, vertebrate animals or human beings).

The solar energy thus "canned" by photosynthesis circulates between species along the food chain, then accumulates as *biomass* when living beings die, putting their constituent elements back into circulation. At each stage, some of this energy is dissipated in the form of heat.

Since the first bacteria appeared some 3.85 billion years ago, millions of species have succeeded one another in the biosphere. Some have reigned unchallenged (like the megalodon of the prehistoric oceans), before becoming extinct. In this long evolutionary process, our ancestor *Homo Sapiens* only appeared very recently, around 200,000 years ago.

Like any other species, we need to capture a sufficient flow of solar energy stored in the biosphere to survive. Our earliest ancestors, nomadic hunter-gatherers, took what they needed directly from the biosphere. During the Paleolithic period, crises of scarcity decimated the human population as soon as its caloric needs exceeded the flow of energy extracted by hunting and gathering.

At the beginning of the interglacial period, however, climatic conditions became more favorable and, for reasons that are still obscure, in many parts of the world agriculture and animal husbandry appeared simultaneously. Around 12,000 years ago, man thus discovered that, instead of drawing directly on nature, he could work to improve it. This led to a demographic explosion in areas where plants with high calorific value were domesticated (e.g., wheat, rice, maize and sorghum).

Gradually, our ancestors were able to produce more food than they needed to survive. As the emergence of a *production surplus* enabled certain individuals to be exempted from the work involved in food production, society came to be divided into social classes. In exchange for a share of the food surplus, new social classes produced new services for the community: administration, the clergy, writing (whose primary function was in fact to keep an accounting record of the surplus) and metal extraction (often used to manufacture weapons to defend the surplus) (see Fig. 1.2).

The production surplus facilitated the development of civilizations, but it also gave rise to new threats. From then on, crises of *scarcity* (which nevertheless remained recurrent) were superimposed by new, more complex crises: *social* crises, generally resulting from misallocation of the surplus.

The *Bisecular Fluctuation*, which began around 1346, and during which Europe lost almost half of its population, is a striking example. Historians believe that this event was triggered by a combination of biospheric events (the spread of the Black Death microbe) and atmospheric conditions (the persistence of long, cold winters during the Little Ice Age of the Middle Ages), and by an inefficient allocation of surplus production.

In feudal society, almost all surplus production was transferred to the aristocracy and the clergy, via heavy taxes in kind or labor. This surplus was then allocated to costly wars (such as the Crusades and the Hundred Years' War). The European population, weakened by malnutrition, then collapsed under the aggression of another species (the bacillus *Yersinia Perstis*). It took around two centuries for the demography to recover.

It should now be apparent that the economy, social rules, and the Earth system are interconnected. The economy is a *sub-system* nested within the more complex biosphere system, which itself belongs to the Earth system (see

Fig. 1.2 The Neolithic revolution (*Note* The image on the left shows a plowing scene in ancient Egypt (Sennedjem tomb, XIIIth century BC). The image on the right is a photograph of the Sphinx of Giza. The construction of the Sphinx, a religious and political monument, probably consumed a large part of Egypt's *production surplus*)

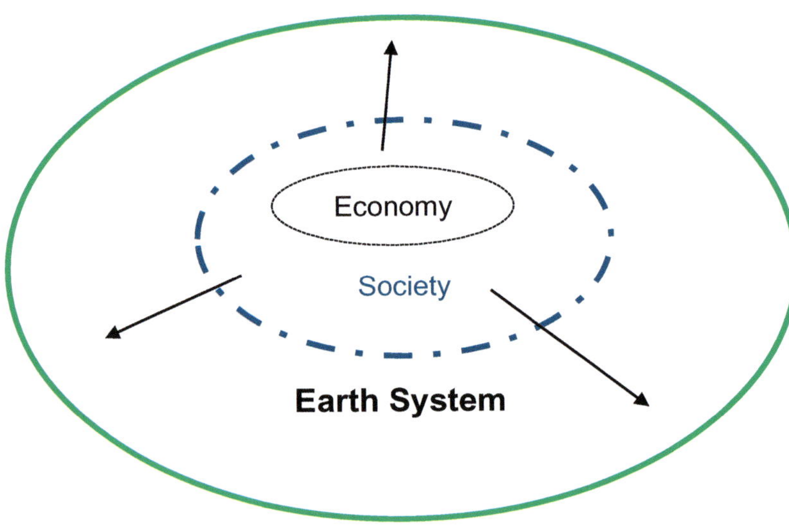

Fig. 1.3 The economy a sub-system nested within society and the Earth System. (*Note* the economy is a *compartment* of the social subsystem, itself *embedded* in the Earth-system. One fallacy consists of think of the relationship between the economy, society and nature as an interface between different systems, when these are an *integrated* whole)

Fig. 1.3). Within the economy, energy flows in the opposite direction to monetary flows. While the source of energy flows lies in the biosphere (in permanent interaction with the Earth system), their direction and intensity are determined by the social rules and technical methods available at each historical period. According to the great Hungarian economist Karl Polanyi (1886–1964) the economy can be thought of as an "instituted process of interactions between man and his environment" (1983, p. 45).

Illustration: The Monetary and Financial System

The global economy is driven by signals from a gigantic computer network of financial balance sheets, interconnected via thousands of bank computers. And for many economic agents and political decision-makers, the information provided by this network coincides with reality.

The perspective developed in the previous section may, however, lead us to consider things differently. Indeed, every monetary flow—whether a payment in the real economy or a financial transaction—is the counterpart of an energy flow, extracted from the biosphere and circulating in the opposite direction.

Take the case of a banker working in New York or Tokyo. Although she is not directly involved in material production, the economy gives her access to the flows of energy required for her varied consumption needs. At the end of each month, her employer transfers money to her bank account (in exchange for her work, which consists precisely of handling monetary symbols). However, money only acquires value insofar as it can be exchanged for real goods and services. And these must be produced in the first place. The banker's consumption requires other individuals to extract the production surplus (for example, the employees of the bank's borrowing firms). In our globalized economy, production often falls to the countries of the Global South, which produce goods and raw materials that are then shipped to the rich countries that consume them. This process consumes material and energy resources and generates greenhouse gas emissions that interact with the Earth system.

Of course, we're used to seeing the economic and financial system as the first-order system. But if we adopt a truly ecological perspective, the hierarchy is reversed: the Earth system appears as the all-encompassing system. Within it lie two *instituted* sub-systems (i.e., dependent on established social rules): the productive system and the financial system (see Fig. 1.4).

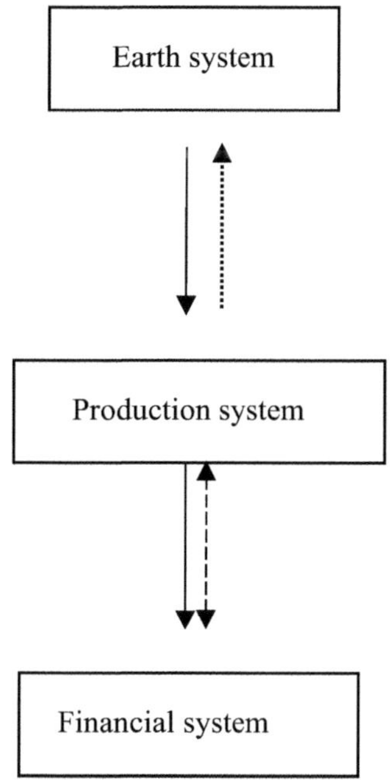

Fig. 1.4 The financial, production and Earth systems (*Note* A solid line represents a flow of energy from the biosphere. A dotted line represents a flow of waste and human emissions. A hatched line represents a monetary flow)

1.2 The Impact of the Great Industrial Acceleration

On the scale of human history, 250 years of capitalism are equivalent to less than two minutes in a 24-hour day. During this short period, humans have radically disrupted the Earth system which, nonetheless, encompasses and sustains their species. The exponential growth of industrial development indicators mirrors the disruption of the Earth system—causing the sixth mass extinction of biodiversity (see Figs. 1.5 and 1.6).

According to scientific consensus, the expansion of the economic sphere beyond *planetary limits* is generating an unpredictable cascade of interconnected biospheric, atmospheric, hydrospheric and geological shocks. By impacting our economies, these planetary shocks diminish human well-being and destabilize our societies. With the signing of the Paris

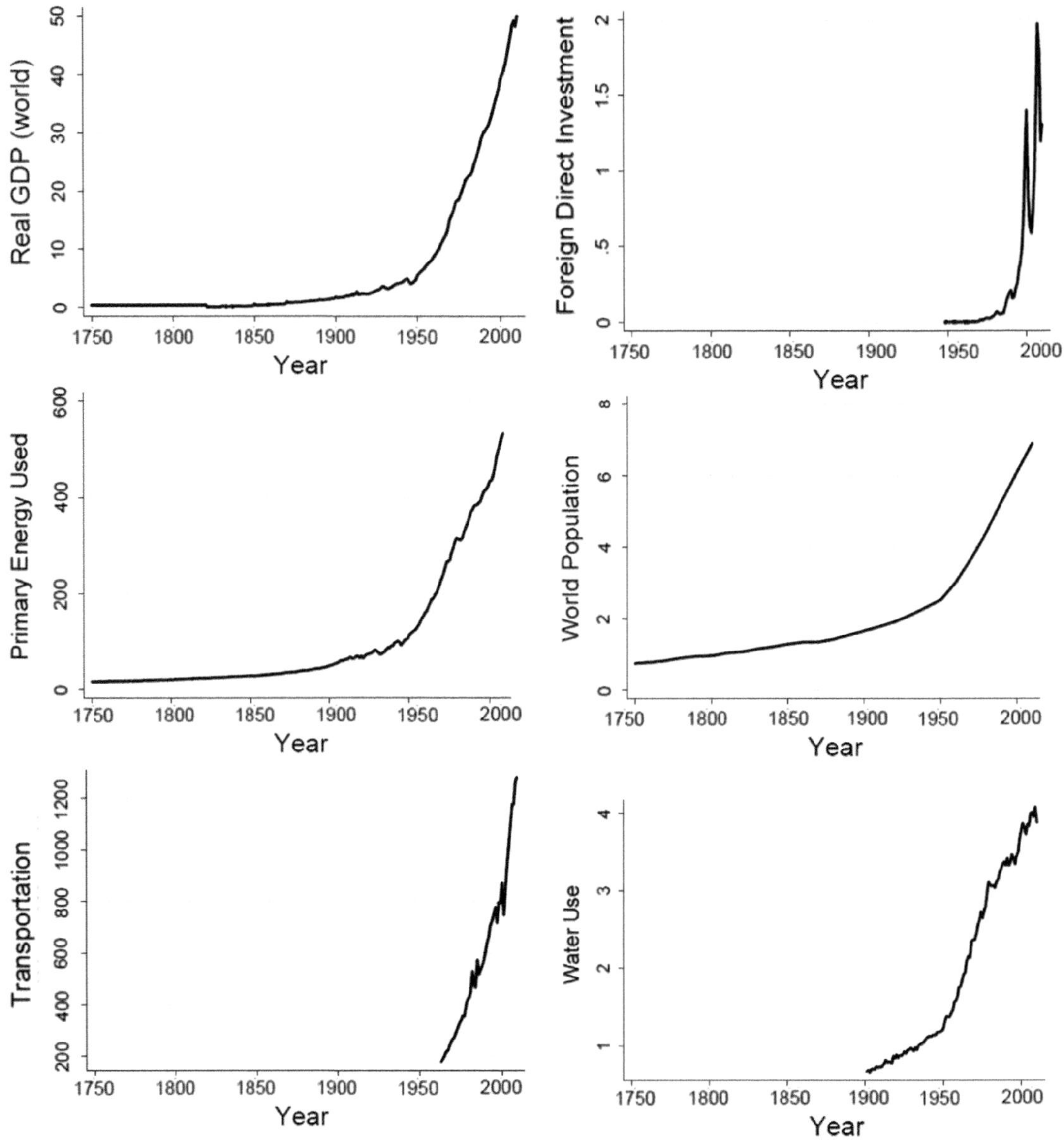

Fig. 1.5 The Great Acceleration: global socio-economic indicators, 1750–2013

Agreements in 2015, the United Nations therefore endorsed the need to fork out toward a new decarbonized, inclusive and democratic socio-economic model, which would embed the economic system within planetary limits, while reducing development inequalities.

This project undoubtedly involves going beyond the economic steering indicators we have inherited. Foremost among these indicators is the economic growth rate, which measures the annual increase in gross domestic product (i.e., the quantity of final goods and services consumed over the course of a year). In the second half of the 20th century, the overwhelming majority of economists saw high economic growth as a goal in itself. More recent models, however, weigh the gains of endless economic growth against its ecological costs, and highlight its ambiguous impact on human well-being.

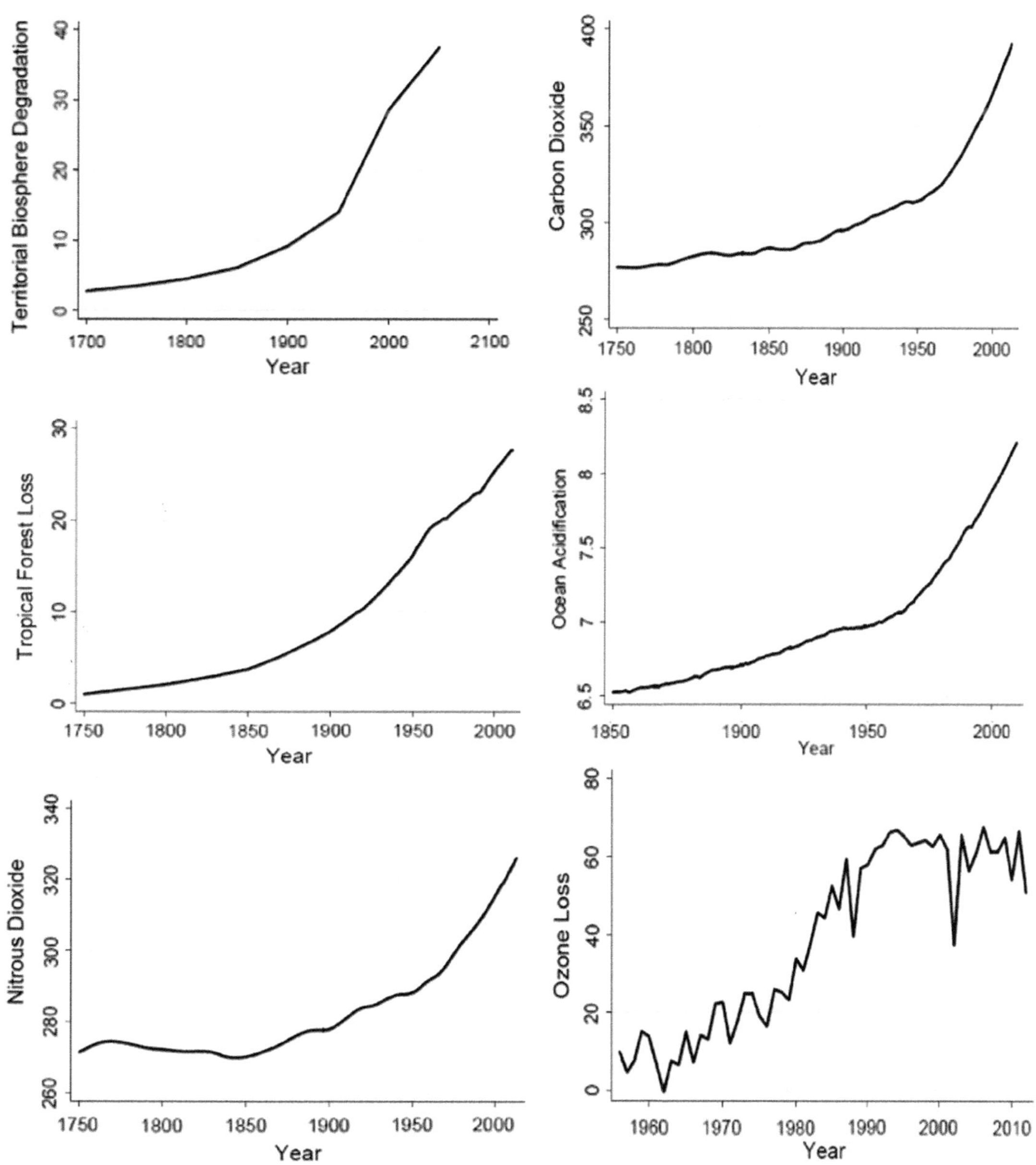

Fig. 1.6 The great acceleration: Earth system, 1750–2013 (*Source* Steffen et al. [2015]. Full data, variable definitions and calculations are available at www.igbp.net)

For instance, pioneers of the ecological economics movement Herman Daly and Joshua Farley (2005) have developed a very simple model that highlights the possibility of anti-economic growth. This model, inspired by the work of neoclassical economist William Jevons (1835–1882) on the labor market, is shown in Fig. 1.7.

On this graph, the marginal gain from economic growth (the upper curve) represents the welfare derived from the consumption of an additional unit of goods or services. However, this marginal gain diminishes over time as the economy grows and GDP increases. This is because the first few points of economic growth

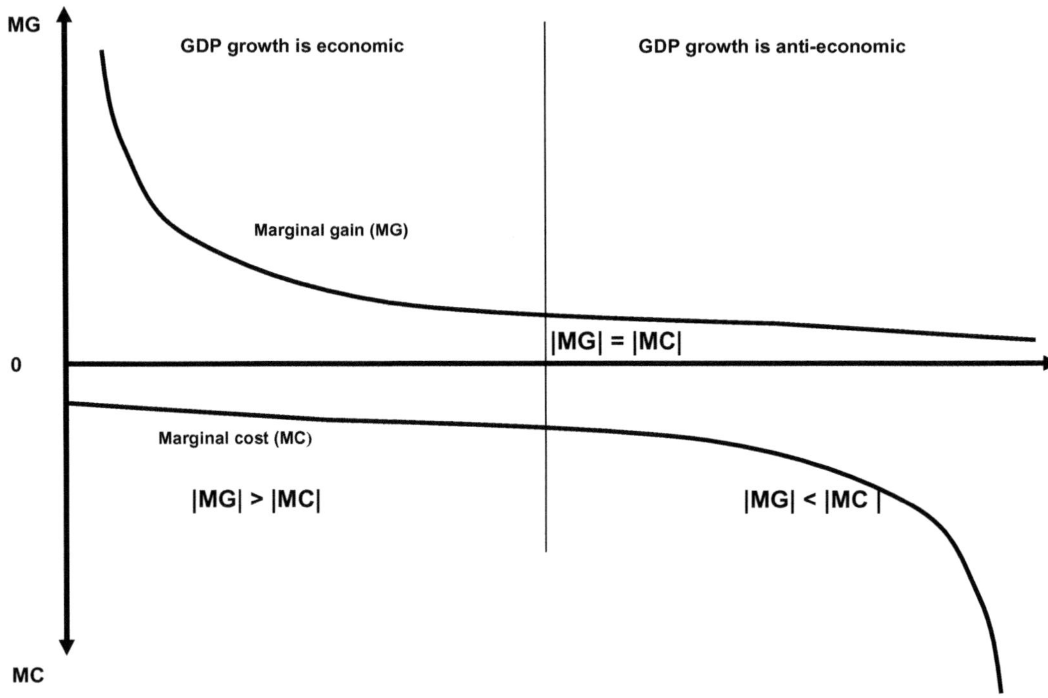

Fig. 1.7 The Daly-Farley model (2005) (*Source* adapted from Daly, H. E. and Farley, J., 2005. *Ecological Economics. Principles and Applications*, p. 20. Island Press, USA)

satisfy primary needs (e.g., heating, running water, food). But beyond a certain threshold, an additional point of growth only enables us to satisfy secondary needs (for example, ordering sushi online).

The *marginal cost* of economic growth (the lower curve) represents the ecological and social cost of one additional point of growth. This cost may be considered zero, or even negative, during the initial stages of economic development, but it increases considerably over time and takes on an exponential dynamic as planetary limits are crossed.

Considering these two curves allows us to identify two scenarios: to the left of the vertical line, the marginal gain from economic growth remains higher than the marginal cost. Within this zone, GDP growth can truly be described as economic, since it corresponds to a net increase in collective well-being. To the right of the vertical line, on the other hand, the marginal cost of economic growth exceeds its marginal gain. In this case, economic growth ceases to measure wealth and becomes, on the contrary, an indicator of collective ruin.

Like all models, this one naturally raises more questions than it answers. One of its most interesting implications is that it leads us to rethink economic growth. Our economy, driven by an indicator (GDP) which is no more than an accounting construct, functions *as if* it were disconnected from the Earth system. What's more, this indicator may signal an increase in well-being, whereas in reality, the opposite is happening. This double confusion leads to the emergence of *systemic risk:* our collective decisions seem perfectly rational, yet when put together, they lead to increased general insecurity and instability.

For ecological economists such as Kate Raworth (2017), prosperity in the 21st century will require respecting planetary boundaries, while inventing new macroeconomic indicators to ensure human flourishing at the global scale.

If followed by concrete action, events such as the signing by the 191 member states of the

United Nations of the Paris Agreements (2015) endorsing the 17 Sustainable Development Goals (SDGs) could be significant steps in this direction.

1.3 Understanding Economic Theories

Theories: Reflections or Drivers of Social Behavior?

This reasoning on indicators can also lead us to reconsider economic and financial theories inherited from the 20th century. For example, the neoclassical theory of finance, developed by Chicago School authors such as Nobel Prize winner Eugene Fama (b. 1939), analyzes the financial sector through the prism of a hypothetical selfish, rational individual, who has direct access to all relevant information and makes investment decisions via a mathematical utility function. Assuming the absence of market rigidities, it is then possible to demonstrate mathematically that only unbridled financial markets would make it possible to discover the fundamental value of goods and services, and reveal it to all in the form of a vector of equilibrium prices coinciding, of course, with the optimum of collective well-being.

It has to be said, however, that this theoretical representation is ill-equipped to explain events such as repeated financial crises, persistent international macroeconomic imbalances, widening social inequalities and the crossing of planetary boundaries.

Authors belonging to the critical management studies movement, such as Donald MacKenzie (b. 1950), argue, for example, that the purpose of neoclassical theory is not to describe reality, but rather to set it in motion. According to these authors, neoclassical financial theory is not ideologically neutral (see Fig. 1.8). Beneath its impressive mathematical veneer, which contributes to a false impression of neutrality and objectivity, lies a toxic mix of *scientism* (by applying the procedures of Newtonian physical science to the social sciences) and *neoliberal ideology*. It follows that the hegemony of neoclassical theory in economics departments and business schools has considerably deteriorated *the* quality of management practices over time, by providing a pseudo-scientific justification for

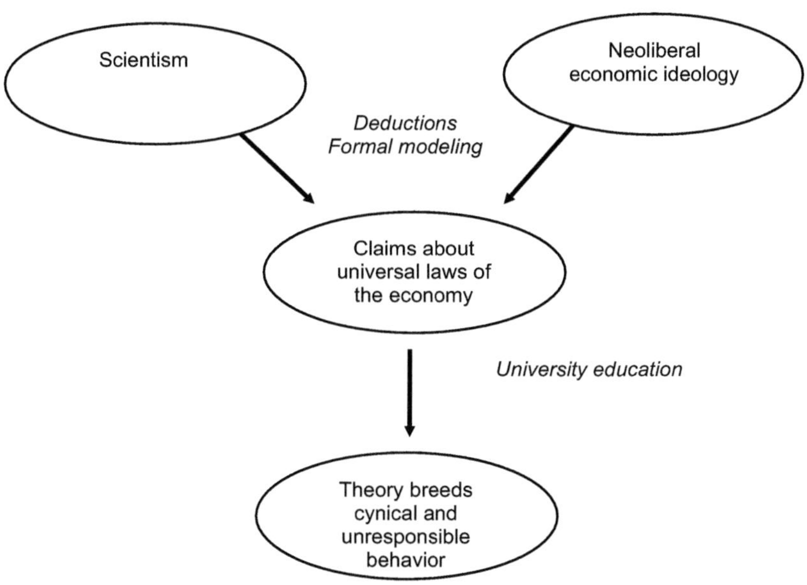

Fig. 1.8 How finance theory drives social behavior (*Source* adapted from Ghoshal, S. "Bad management theories are destroying good management practices", *Academy of Management Learning and Education*, 2005, 4, pp. 75–91)

cynical and dangerous behavior. The hegemony of neoclassical theory coincides with a marked increase in the frequency and severity of financial crises.

In conclusion, economic theories give us access to a world of shared meaning and thus enable us to coordinate our actions. But they can also play a perverse role, concealing conflicts of interest and power relations under a hypocritical veil of *scientificity*.

The Need for Pluralism in Economics

Nowadays, many authors (and students) deplore the consequences of *monism* in economics. Monism is an intellectual attitude that recognizes only one view as legitimate.

And yet, the many ramifications of economic thought testify to its richness and diversity. As shown in Fig. 1.9, economic science can be represented as comprising an *orthodox* core (structured around the neoclassical school and other peripheral schools, such as New Keynesian macroeconomics, game theory and other approaches based on imperfect competition and information asymmetries), and a host of so-called *heterodox* approaches (post-Keynesian economics, ecological economics, feminist economics, economic geography, socio-economics, critical management studies, evolutionary economics, Austrian economics, Marxian economics, critical realism…). Some branches of economic thought (such as economic history, behavioral finance, comparative economics or experimental microeconomics), and of course many economists, borrow simultaneously from these different approaches.

This manual adopts a resolutely *pluralist* perspective. Pluralism, as opposed to monism, simply means respecting the legitimacy of different theoretical approaches.

This diversity broadens the scope of the discipline, making it more complex, more agile, and therefore better able to grasp the complexity of the real world. Far from detracting from

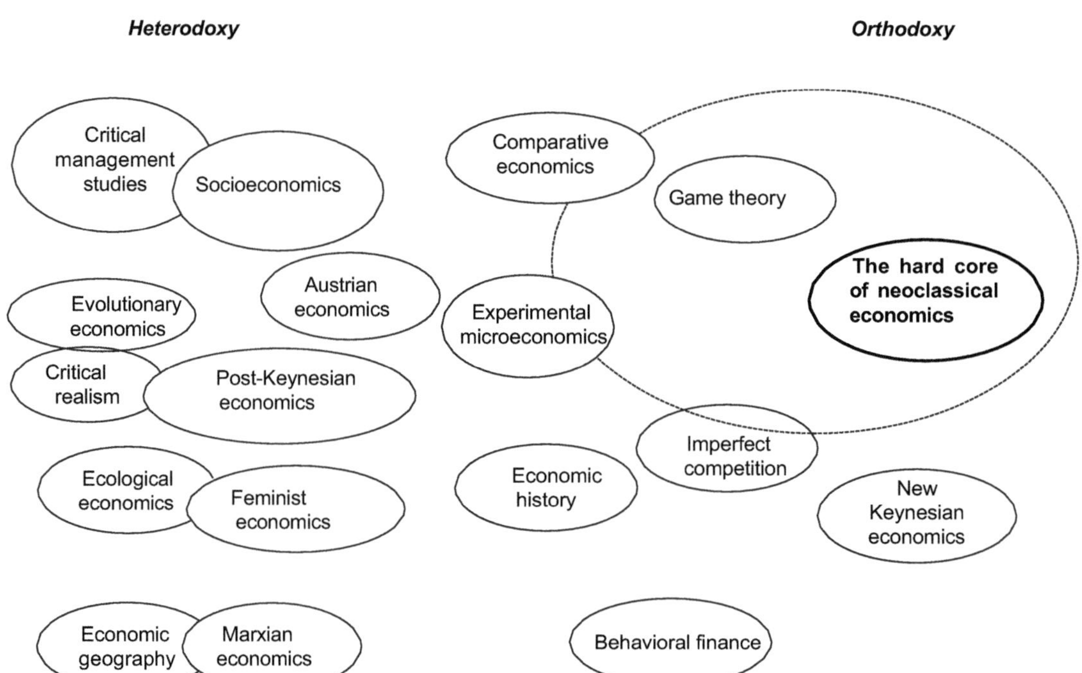

Fig. 1.9 Some currents of thought in economics (*Source* adapted from Labrousse A. (2017), "Le pluralisme, source de rigueur et de découvertes scientifiques", in Coriat et al. (2017), Paris, Croquant, pp. 41–55 (untranslated).)

the scientific character of economics, pluralism is a precious heritage and resource as we grapple with the "economic problems of our generation" (Alfred Marshall, 1842–1924).

1.4 Conclusion

- The Earth system connects and encompasses four open, interconnected systems: the *atmosphere*, the *geosphere*, the *hydrosphere* and the *biosphere*;
- The economy is a sub-system of the biosphere and contains instituted interactions between humans and the Earth system;
- Great industrial acceleration and the overstepping of "planetary limits" are producing unprecedented risks on a planetary scale;
- The pluralism of economic schools of thought can help us to think through the complexity of this new context and to find solutions.

Activities

Questions for Discussion

1. Choose two currents of economic thought and list their differences and similarities. What would be the best attitude to adopt in order to understand the world, given the disagreements and differences in viewpoints observed?
2. Consider the 17 Sustainable Development Goals (SDGs). How could you contribute to these goals through your future professional life? What obstacles, if any, would you encounter?

Mini-case: Planetary Limits

1. Read the scientific article by Rockström et.al (2009) given as a bibliographic reference, define the concept of "planetary limits", then describe each limit.
2. Go to the Stockholm Resilience Center website (https://www.stockholmresilience.org/) and describe the current position of the Earth System in relation to these planetary limits.
3. Visit the doughnut economics website (https://www.kateraworth.com/doughnut/). To what extent does this new economic model offer new economic prospects? Discuss its limitations and the obstacles to its implementation.

Reference

Rockström, J., Steffen, W., Noone, K., et al. (2009). A safe operating space for humanity: A safe operating space for humanity. *Nature, 461*, 472–475. https://doi.org/10.1038/461472a

2 Understanding Economic Diversity

Thomas Lagoarde-Ségot and Laurence Le Poder

Putting Things into Perspective

On their trip to the USSR in 1988, journalists Nina and Jean Kéhayan[1] humorously observed that, while the centrally planned Soviet economy had sent a man into space, it couldn't keep grocery stores stocked with sausages. It's true that, to date, all attempts to completely eliminate markets from economic and social life have failed. This observation, however, does not necessarily imply that the market economy is a natural system, nor that markets should absorb the whole of society. In fact, the earliest known historical documents (from the Persian Gulf, dating from the third dynasty of Ur, between 2112 and 2004 BC) tend to describe a highly centralized, administered economy. Much later, the collapse of the 1930s sounded the death knell for the illusion of the 'great self-regulating market' (Karl Polanyi, 1944)—that is, an economy regulated solely by market forces. And today, economic diversity is the rule throughout the economies of high-income democratic countries. What are the market structures commonly observed in the economy? What are the main categories of organizations ensuring social provisioning? What are the motivations underpinning economic transactions? These are the main questions addressed in this chapter.

Learning Objectives

- Identifying different market structures
- Understanding institutional diversity
- Understanding economic diversity

2.1 The Diversity of Market Structures

The most famous market structure is probably that of pure and perfect competition. The cornerstone of the neoclassical school developed in the 19th century by Stanley Jevons (1835–1882), Carl Menger (1840–1821) and Léon Walras (1834–1910), this market structure describes an idealized situation in which

[1] Nina and Jean Kéhayan, *Le Chantier de la Place Rouge*, Éditions du Seuil, 1988 (untranslated).

T. Lagoarde-Ségot (✉)
KEDGE BS & SDSN France, Talence, France
e-mail: thomas.lagoardesegot@kedgebs.com

L. Le Poder
KEDGE BS, Talence, France
e-mail: laurence.lepoder@kedgebs.com

T. Lagoarde-Ségot (ed.), *Ecological Economics and Finance*, https://doi.org/10.1007/978-3-031-71249-4_2

large number of firms (identical and too small to influence the market) compete on prices and sell a single product to consumers (also identical, and too small to influence the market). In this market structure, *entry barriers* (i.e. economic or institutional conditions preventing the entry of competing firms) are non-existent. New competitors can enter the market, and others can leave it, without frictions.

Far from this idealized vision, market structures encountered in the real economy are more often *monopolies*, *oligopolies* and *monopsonies*.

A *monopoly* describes a situation in which a single company has succeeded in erecting barriers that enable it to control both prices and production. It may own all the resources needed for production (e.g. railways in the rail transport sector), or the intellectual property of the factors of production (e.g. software in the IT sector), enabling it to set market prices. A variant of the monopoly is the *cartel*, in which a group of producers have agreed on prices and production, so that each member company of the cartel behaves, in effect, monopolistically. The Organization of Petroleum Exporting Countries (OPEC), for instance, operates very much like a cartel.

In an *oligopoly,* a small number of dominant companies have set barriers to entry and enjoy significant market power. For example, mergers and acquisitions have enabled a conglomerate of firms to gain so much from economies of scale that no new entrants may challenge its dominant position. Product *differentiation*—via marketing, advertising or various labels (such as wine appellations or business school accreditations)—is an important channel by which firm may erect entry barriers. Today, a considerable part of the economy (in fields as varied as energy, finance, tobacco, IT, publishing, air transport, etc.) operates on an oligopolistic basis. In the USA, for example, the top 100 companies account for around 50% of total value added. In industry, commerce, hospitality and technology, the 'winner takes all' company model has become dominant.

The mirror image of monopoly and oligopoly is the *monopsony*, famously described by economist Joan Robinson (1903–1983). In a monopsony, a single company buys the entire market's production, and imposes its conditions on producers. Today, the retail sector is clearly monopsonic. Large retailers (such as Wal-Mart, Carrefour and Amazon) have significant market power over ther suppliers—which lowers consumer prices, yet squeezes wages and aggregate demand.

To understand why real-world markets are so rarely pure and perfect, post-Keynesian economists underline the role of *uncertainty* and *power.* Indeed, small businesses have no way of predicting future market trends or the behavior of their competitors, which exposes them to risk. A rational strategy, therefore, is to acquire market power by buying out their competitors. In the words of economist Nina Shapiro (1948–2019), "to survive in the market, you must have market power" (Shapiro, 1995, p. 38).

Today, corporate power tends to extend beyond the strictly economic sphere. Large multinational corporations directly influence laws and regulations (see Box 2.1). This may explain why their effective tax rate is much lower than that applied to ordinary citizens or small businesses. Other multinationals use charities and foundations (such as the Bill and Melinda Gates Foundation) as vectors of political influence.

Box 2.1: Southern Pacific Railroad

Source: MichaelVi—stock.adobe.com

Source: Mark Rasmussen—stock.adobe.com

Note On the left, an old *Southern Pacific Railroad* advertising poster. On the right, a reproduction of the U.S. Constitution of 1776.

The story of the *Southern Pacific Railroad* is emblematic of the transformation of corporations into political actors. In 1881, the California state government imposed a tax on railroad ownership. Lawyers for the U.S. railroad countered by arguing that the tax violated the Fourteenth Amendment to the U.S. Constitution. This amendment, adopted at the end of the Civil War to protect the civil rights of former African-American slaves, guarantees "all persons the equal protection of the law". It was argued that the *Southern Pacific Railroad* being a legal entity, it should not be subject to 'discriminatory' taxation. The case set a precedent, as the U.S. Supreme Court subsequently frequently invoked the Fourteenth Amendment to curb attempts to regulate markets (such as laws limiting working hours or urban zoning). Between 1868 and 1912, for example, the U.S. Supreme Court invoked the Fourteenth Amendment in 28 lawsuits concerning the rights of African-Americans, compared with 312 lawsuits concerning businesses.[2]

Finally, *monopolistic competition* is a market structure where entry barriers are low, but where each company faces a stable demand and enjoys market power. The majority of small businesses (such as garages and hair salons) operate in this type of market.

2.2 The Diversity of Organizational Models

A second type of diversity refers to the types of goods produced in the economy. As shown in Table 2.1, a good is *rival* if its consumption reduces the quantity still available for consumption. A good is *exclusive* if it is possible to prohibit (or limit) its consumption by others. Crossing these two characteristics, four categories of goods appear: *private goods* (which are rival and exclusive), *club goods* (which are non-rival and exclusive), *public goods* (which are non-rival and non-exclusive) and *common goods* (which are rival and non-exclusive).

A diversity of enterprises is required to supply the economy with these various categories of goods. At the most general level, an enterprise is an "organization where a set of transactions takes place between stakeholders involved in the production of goods and services" (Reardon et al., 2018).

[2] See https://www.theatlantic.com/business/archive/2018/03/corporations-people-adam-winkler/554852/.

Table 2.1 Four categories of goods

	Exclusive	Non exclusive
Rival	*Private goods*: houses, cars, corporate bonds...	*Common goods*: forests, pastures, ponds, valleys, fishing resources, air, climate…
Non-rival	*Club goods*: toll roads, libraries, telephone networks…	*Public goods*: security, education, health, financial stability…

Here, the term *organization* indicates that an enterprise can take on a wide variety of forms, according for instance to its size (from self-employment to a large multinational), its purpose (profit-making or non-profit), or its legal status (such as a cooperative, a B-corporation, a LLC, or a publicly listed firm). The term *stakeholder* indicates that social groups with sometimes divergent interests are involved in its operations: employees (and their families), customers, users, taxpayers, creditors, shareholders, suppliers, public authorities, etc.

To apprehend the diversity of organizations, one can break down the economy into three main institutional sectors: the private sector, the public sector and the third sector (see Fig. 2.1).

The for-profit sector, located in the north-west quadrant of the diagram, supplies most private goods to the economy. The organizations operating in this sector are very diverse, yet they are embedded in the *monetary economy of production*—a system in which the 'rule of the game' is to accumulate money. The expression (1) takes up the famous formula of the capital accumulation cycle (used by Karl Marx, John Maynard Keynes or Thorstein Veblen) to describe this process:

$$C - M - P - M' - C' \text{ with } C' > C \quad (2.1)$$

In this cycle, a profit-seeking entrepreneur exchanges an initial monetary capital (*C*)—which may be borrowed from other entrepreneurs, or made available by a bank—for various intermediate goods (*M*) required for production (materials, capital goods, land, human labor). During the production phase (*P*), the entrepreneur combines these various inputs and has the workers produce a new commodity of his choice (*M'*). The sale of this new commodity enables her to obtain new monetary capital ($C' > C$), the difference between (*C'*) and (*C*) being equal to his profit. The latter is obtained through the pricing of goods, an operation by which businesses add a mark-up to their production costs (the so-called *cost-plus* mechanism).[3]

The public sector, located in the northeast quadrant of the diagram in Fig. 2.1, comprises enterprises controlled, either directly or indirectly, by the state, and supplying most *public goods* to the economy. These goods (such as universal healthcare and education) are essential to social provisioning, but as their production is unprofitable, they cannot be produced in sufficient quantities by profit-seeking organizations. In her book "The Entrepreneurial State" (2013), economist Mariana Mazzucato (b. 1968) underscored the importance of the public sector by focusing on technological progress. She showed that technological innovation often requires a prior expansion of fundamental knowledge (for example, in physics or mathematics). However, investment in fundamental research entails a significant risk of failure, and often cannot be made profitable in the short term. Only state-owned organizations (such as universities or research institutes), which are not subject to the constraint of monetary accumulation (Eq. 2.1), are in a position to take these game-changing entrepreneurial risks.

In a similar vein, for François Perroux (1903–1987), the State is the only economic agent

[3] Market price fluctuations therefore depend not only on supply and demand but also on companies' cost structures and pricing. If prices are stable, then production costs are stable (e.g. in the service sector)—and conversely, when prices are volatile, so are production costs (e.g. in the energy sector) (Lavoie, 2022).

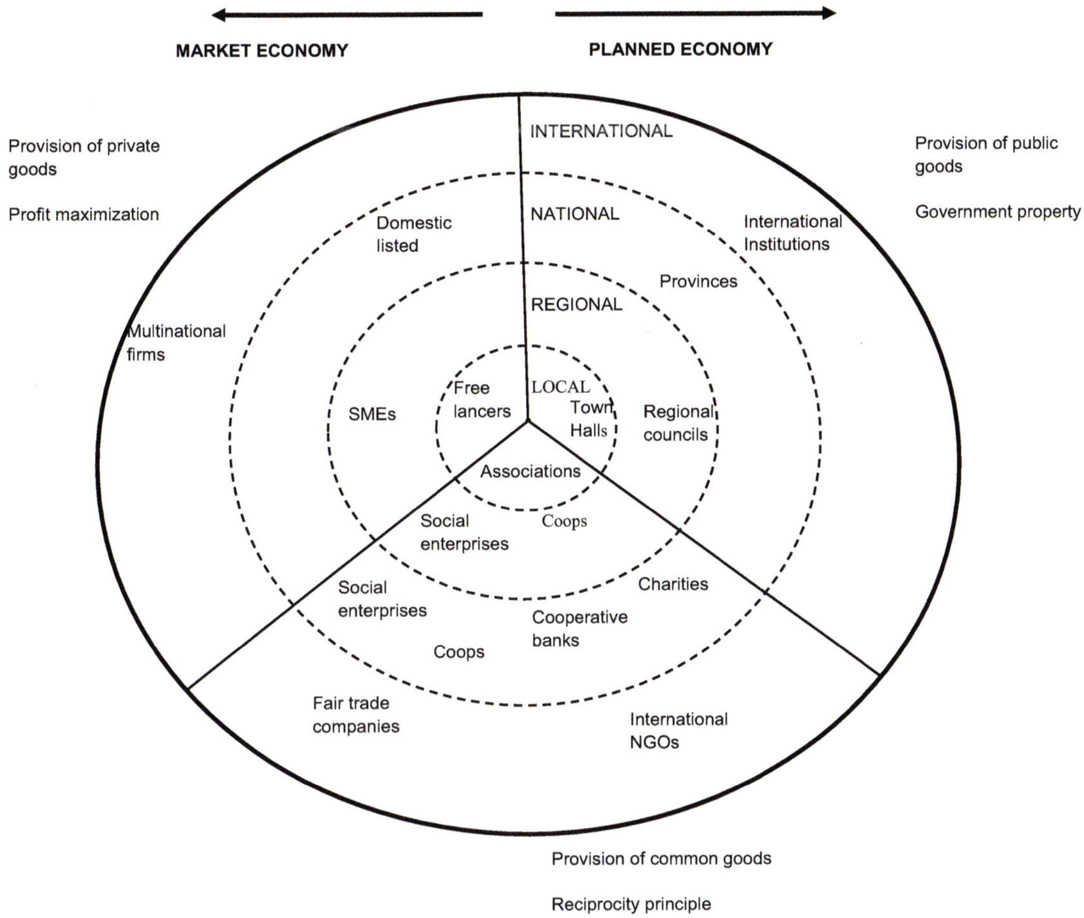

Fig. 2.1 A three-tiered economic system

capable of driving productive combinations that are inaccessible to private enterprise for reasons of immediate profitability. Examples include the coordination of mining and electricity in the 20th century, or the coordination of rail, bicycle and bus transport networks nowadays.

Finally, there are cases in which state control is necessary to limit the abuse of dominant positions by private companies. Since state-owned companies are not intended to make a profit, they are able to offer goods and services at a price equal to or lower than that of private monopolies, oligopolies or monopsonies. On a more political level, the nationalization—total or partial—of companies can help to remove activities that are important from the point of view of the general interest from the abusive influence of overly powerful private interests, monopolies or major financial powers.

Finally, the third sector, located in the southern quadrant of the diagram in Fig. 2.1, includes private, yet not for profit organizations supplying most common goods (and club goods) to the economy. The governance and functioning of these enterprises have long been poorly understood by economists. It was only relatively late that they were elucidated by Nobel Prize-winning economist Elinor Oström (1933–2012). According to Oström, proper management of the commons (lakes, rivers, fisheries, irrigation systems, forests, etc.) requires the community of users to establish access rights and to

Table 2.2 Property as a bundle of rights

Rights	Full ownership	Property without right of sale	Rights of use and management	Right of use
Right to access	X	X	X	X
Righ to establish governance rules	X	X	X	
Right to exclude	X	X		
Right to sell the resource	X			
Examples	Corporate stock	Club membership	Creative commons license	Natural resources

set up specific governance structures to enforce these rights. In the case of the commons, ownership tends to be broken down into a *bundle of* rights: the right to use a resource, the right to set its management rules, the right to exclude others from accessing it, and the right to sell it (see Table 2.2).

Cooperative enterprises, whose origins date back to the declaration of the International Cooperative Alliance in 1895, are key players in the third sector. A cooperative is a democratic enterprise, founded on values of responsibility, solidarity and transparency, whose mission is to provide services to its members. The cooperative movement finds its intellectual roots in utopian socialism, whose leading exponents in the 19th century included Robert Owen, Louis Blanc, Charles Fourier and Pierre-Joseph Proudhon[e]. Influenced by humanist philosophy and social Christianity, these thinkers, who were not hostile to the market *per se*, asserted the need to place capital under the control of society. Cooperatives are private organizations operating in markets, but their purpose is to serve a social objective shared by their members. To describe their institutional logic, we could adapt formula (1) as follows:

$$\begin{aligned} &\varphi - C - M - P - M' - C' - \varphi' \\ &\text{with } C' > C \text{ and } \varphi' > \varphi \end{aligned} \tag{2.2}$$

where the Greek letter φ (*Philia*) measures the cooperative's contribution to its social objectives. Like any private company, a cooperative must make a profit ($C' \geq C$); but profit is merely a tool for achieving the mission defined by its members ($\varphi' > \varphi$).

2.3 The Diversity of Exchange Regimes

A third way of shedding light on economic diversity is to consider organizations from the point of view of economic transactions. To do so, one can rely upon the distinction between the *use value* and *exchange value* of commodities developed by David Ricardo (1772–1823). In an economy, any commodity simultaneously has two values:

- a *use value*, which measures the satisfaction derived from its consumption. For example, the use value of a sheet of paper is to use it to read, write or make origami;
- an *exchange value*, which measures a value relative to that of other goods, expressed in money. For example, if a ream of paper is worth 2.50 euros and a kilogram of bread is worth 5 euros, the exchange value of a ream of paper is equal to 500 grams of bread.

The demand for a commodity may be motivated by access to its *use value* (the satisfaction one expects to derive from its consumption) or its *exchange value* (the monetary gain one expects to earn by selling the commodity). These two values often fluctuate in the same direction, but tend to reach different levels. For instance, the use value of a kilogram of bread may increase if you're fasting, although its exchange value (its price) remains the same. Exchange can therefore be motivated by access to either exchange value or use value. This observation reveals five types of circulation regimes in the economy: gift,

Table 2.3 Exchange regimes

Exchange regime	Features
Gift	A gift is unilateral. It creates neither obligations nor rights for the transferor and the recipient Ex: donation, inheritance
Reciprocity	Reciprocity is a double relationship involving neither synchronization nor obligation for both parties Ex: carpooling
Exchanges, including:	Exchanges imply a cause-and-effect relationship and an obligation
Non-market exchange	Price considerations do not motivate the exchange, which is based on other motivations Ex: public health systems, fair trade
Non-capitalist market exchange	The buyer is solely motivated by accessing the *use value* of the commodity Ex: daily consumption (restaurant, taxi…)
Capitalist market exchange	The buyer is motivated by access to the *exchange value* of the commodity E.g.: acquisition of a company, acquisition of financial security, hiring of an employee

Source Lagoarde-Ségot and Paranque (2018)

reciprocity, non-market exchange, non-capitalist market exchange and capitalist market exchange (see Table 2.3).

Every economic agent is involved in various circulation regimes, motivated alternately by the search for use value or exchange value. Let's illustrate this with an example. When you arrive at university in the morning, you go to the administration building to pay your tuition fees; you are both motivated by the *use value* (understanding the world) and *exchange value* of your university education (your diploma will increase your bargaining power on the job market).

Then you invite a friend for coffee, which you pay for using your bank card. You've signed up for a charity program with your bank, which rounds up the transaction price to the next decimal place and sends the difference by bank transfer to the NGO of your choice. This is a *gift*. What's more, the acquisition of this cup of coffee is motivated by access to *use value* (it is a *non-capitalist market exchange*).

It's also worth noting that by buying your friend this coffee, you're entering into a *reciprocal* relationship. In fact, she may buy you a drink this evening (at a different price from the coffee you've just bought).

Finally, you may have earned the money with which you just paid for this coffee through a summer job, for example in a small tiling business. The relationship between you and your employer was based on a capitalist market exchange (you sold him your labor power in exchange for a wage). At the same time, your employer may have obtained the sites you worked on through relationships of reciprocity. Another craftsman (a plumber, for example) may have recommended your employer to one of his customers. Finally, let's imagine that, after completing your studies, you set up a company which, after a few years, is bought out by an investment fund. Such a transaction is clearly a *capitalist market exchange* based on the pursuit of *exchange value*. The diversity of exchange regimes can be found everywhere in the real economy.

2.4 Conclusion

- Monopoly, monopsony, oligopoly and monopolistic competition are frequently observed market structures in the economy.
- The production of private goods, public goods and common goods requires several types of enterprises, belonging to the private sector, the public sector and the third sector.
- Economic transactions involve various circulation regimes based on the search for the exchange value or use value of goods.

Activities

Questions for Discussion

1. In what market structures do the various companies you interact with operate? To which institutional sector do they belong? In which exchange regimes could you situate your various economic transactions during a typical day?
2. In your opinion, are natural resources (water, forests, oceans) private goods, public goods, club goods or common goods? What implications could you draw from this regarding a desirable global stewardship of these resources?
3. According to you, is there an ideal organizational model to address the challenges of sustainable development?

Mini-case: The Cooperative Sector

1. Visit the website of the International Cooperative Alliance (https://www.ica.coop/fr). After browsing the site, explain why cooperative enterprises are different from both state-owned and capitalist enterprises.
2. Visit the World Cooperative Monitor website (https://monitor.coop/en). Download the latest report on the state of the cooperative sector worldwide, then give a presentation describing its size, the main players, their countries of origin and their sector of activity.
3. Choose a cooperative enterprise and present its history, mission, governance, and contribution to sustainable development objectives.

References

Lagoarde-Ségot, T., & Paranque, B. (2018). Finance and sustainability: From ideology to Utopia. *International Review of Financial Analysis, 55*, 80–92.

Lavoie, M. (2022). *Post Keynesian economics. New foundations* (744 pp). Edward Elgar Publishing.

Mazzucato, M. (2013). *The entrepreneurial state. Debunking public vs private sector myths* (261 pp). Anthem Press.

Polanyi, K. (1944). *The Great Transformation: The political and economic origins of our time* (360 pp). Beacon Press.

Reardon, J., Ladi, M. A., & Cato, M. S. (2018). *Introducing a new economics. Pluralist, sustainable and progressive* (364 pp). Pluto Press.

Shapiro, N. (1995). Markets and mark-ups: Keynesian views. In *Keynes, knowledge and uncertainty*. Edward Elgar.

What is Money?

3

Raphaël Didier and Thomas Lagoarde-Ségot

Putting Things into Perspective

Money can be compared to the oil in the engine of the modern economy. Without a sufficient quantity of money, the economic engine seizes and is often beyond repair; conversely, too much money can cause the economic engine to flood. In this case, the engine must be purged to run again. But while very few social institutions are as essential to the functioning of the economy as money, the latter is paradoxically very difficult to define. Certainly, the collective imagination associates money with precious metals (such as gold or silver) or, today, with lines of computer code. Yet it would be impossible to define money by reference to its physical properties alone. Let's take a simple analogy. If you present a pebble to someone and claim that it contains limestone, they can test your claim by pouring hydrochloric acid over it: if your pebble contains limestone, it will effervesce on contact with the acid. But it may also turn out to be just a piece of plastic. Unlike pebbles however, coins cannot be defined by their physical properties. We tend to consider an object to be money only because we know that others also consider it to be so. So money is as much a *social fact* as an economic one. But how can collective trust in money be established? What are the most important functions of money? How is it issued, and destroyed? Which factors establish its value? These are some of the issues addressed in this chapter.

Learning Objectives

- Knowing and ranking the different functions of money
- Learning lessons from monetary and financial history
- Applying double-entry bookkeeping to economic analysis
- Understanding the role of States in the monetary system

3.1 The Economic Status of Money

My participation in the monetary economy (for example, as a consumer or borrower) in no way prevents you from getting involved too. Money is therefore a *non-excludable* good. And, given that

R. Didier
Université de Lorraine, Metz, France
e-mail: didierraphael@wanadoo.fr

T. Lagoarde-Ségot (✉)
KEDGE BS & SDSN France, Talence, France
e-mail: thomas.lagoardesegot@kedgebs.com

T. Lagoarde-Ségot (ed.), *Ecological Economics and Finance*, https://doi.org/10.1007/978-3-031-71249-4_3

Fig. 3.1 Money as a unit of account (*Note* The image on the left shows Egyptian hieroglyphs. The image on the right is a Mesopotamian cuneiform tablet. In Mesopotamia (3500 BC), the unit of currency was the silver shekel. A silver shekel weighed the same as a bushel of barley, and each shekel was divisible into 60 minas, each equivalent to a ration of barley. But shekels hardly circulated at all. Debts (notably to the Temple) were denominated in shekels but could be settled in a variety of goods: furniture, goats, lapis-lazulis, and so on)

the quantity of money in circulation is relatively stable in the short term, the quantity of money I hold is no longer available to you. Money is therefore a *rival good*. By virtue of these two characteristics, money can be categorized as a *common good* (in the same way as natural resources, such as forests or oceans). Perhaps this explains why, as we shall see in this chapter, all attempts to privatize money throughout history have ended in resounding failure, and have also led to serious political and social unrest.

The Origins of Credit and Debt

Our immediate intuition would suggest that the financial system developed from the monetary economy, itself arising from barter. However, we have no historical trace of any barter economy from which money would have emerged.[1] The translation of Egyptian hieroglyphs and Mesopotamian cuneiform documents dating back to around 3500 BC suggests that the first exchanges were based on a credit system. So, in a way, finance preceded the invention of money. This reversal of perspective has fundamental implications for our understanding of money and its mechanisms (Fig. 3.1).

Let's take a fictitious example to illustrate how credit can enable trade without money. Let's imagine we've been transported back in time to pre-Roman Gaul, at the time of the Ligurians. You're a Greek fisherman from Massalia, longing for fresh tomatoes after a long period at sea. I'm a farmer from Entremont, north of Aquae Sextiae, and I'd like to eat cured sardines. How are we going to trade, in the absence of money ?

First, we'll probably negotiate an exchange rate (tomatoes for sardines). Then you'll agree to deliver a given quantity of sardines to me and, in return, I'll agree to deliver tomatoes to you. As my tomatoes are perishable (more perishable, in any case, than your cured sardines), you'll probably prefer to have them delivered at regular intervals (for example, one crate a week).

In exchange for your sardines, I'll give you an IOU with my signature engraved on a stick that reads: "On presentation of this stick, Thomas di Rafael will deliver a crate of

[1] Readers interested in this question may wish to refer to the major work *Debt: 5,000 Years of History*, by David Graeber (2011). For specific case studies on the emergence of money in different historical and social contexts, see *Introducing Money*, by Mark Peacock (2013). For francophone readers, we can also recommend Jean-Michel Servet's text, *La Fable du troc* (1994).

Table 3.1 Transaction stage 1

Me		You	
Assets	Liabilities	Assets	Liabilities
Sardines	Tomatoes (debt)	Tomatoes (credit) ~~Sardines~~	

tomatoes". You thus become my *creditor* and I your *debtor*.

Let's now look at the position of our respective balance sheets. As Table 3.1 shows, your sardines are now an asset on my balance sheet. However, this asset is offset by a liability of the same value: my debt (in tomatoes). In return, the sardines disappear from the assets side of your balance sheet, this loss being offset by a new asset: my IOU (in tomatoes).

This example highlights a universal fact: whenever a transaction is not carried out on the spot, but comprises three distinct phases (contract, delivery and payment), it implies the simultaneous creation of a *debt* and a *credit*. An IOU is in fact a two-sided accounting item, corresponding to both an asset (for you, the creditor) and a liability (for me, the debtor).[2] The debtor is obliged to transfer an asset to the creditor (in our example, a series of tomato crates) on a specific date. Conversely, the creditor gains a new financial asset (the IOU) whose value is strictly equal to that of the debtor's new liability, and which will be extinguished at the time of payment. Should the debtor default on his or her debt (for example, if I die), the creditor's assets (and the corresponding liability) will disappear simultaneously.

The principle of debt/credit allows us to envisage a coherent system of exchange without money. Imagine, for example, that you deliver your sardines to me in exchange for my IOU, denominated in tomato crates and engraved on a stick. Then, as you pass a tavern, you suddenly get the urge to buy a barrel of brandy. Having sold your sardines, the only asset you can offer in payment is my IOU stick. Before agreeing to the exchange, the tavern-keeper might inquire about the issuer of this stick (is he creditworthy?). Let us suppose that he's reassured to learn that I'm the issuer, as I enjoy a certain social prestige in the community. And he might know me personally: just last week, I delivered a large quantity of tomatoes to him in exchange for an IOU in Cervoise beer (which he engraved on a bone). He therefore accepts the deal. Then, the following week, he visits me and gives me back my stick-IOU. However, instead of delivering tomatoes, I give him back his bone-IOU, and we break them both (we're even). This fictitious example shows that credit is the natural vector of commerce, as it allows for trade even in the absence of physical money (which appeared in Lydia in the seventh century BC).

Money as a Unit of Account

Unfortunately, this idealized credit-based exchange system would, sooner or later, face the problem of loss of trust. Suppose, for example, that I refuse to deliver the tomatoes (or that my tomatoes are rotten). You'll probably demand a compensation. But in what merchandise, since tomatoes are no longer an option? And for how much? We're now in a dispute, and trust has given way to mistrust and perhaps even animosity, with threats of violence.

To restore confidence and to ensure the continuity of trade, it is necessary to introduce a new actor: a political authority. The latter can impose a common *unit of account* (often a metal) in which relative prices for different goods and services are expressed. Let's imagine that a crate of tomatoes is equivalent to two crates of onions, their values being equal when expressed in grams of silver. Table 3.2 shows the new position of our respective balance sheets.

The unit of account imposed by the political authority (silver) has enabled us to establish a rate of exchange between tomatoes and onions, to settle our dispute and thus restore confidence

[2] Francophone readers interested in the moral aspect of debt may refer to Nathalie Sarthou-Lajus, "La dette, le devoir, la faute" (pp. 95–112), in: N. Sarthou-Lajus, *L'éthique de la dette* (1997) (242 p.).

Table 3.2 Transaction stage 2

Me		You	
Assets	Liabilities	Assets	Liabilities
	~~Tomatoes (debt)~~	~~Tomatoes (credit)~~	
	Onions (silver value, debt)	Onions (silver value, credit)	

in the payment system. Compensation was paid in onions but could have been paid in any commodity with an official silver value (nails, eggplants, hours of work, etc.).

Money and Political Sovereignty

The above example illustrates that the primitive function of money, a creation of political authority, was to provide a *unit of account* for quantifying social relations. Traces of money as a unit of account can be found in official documentation from the Ur III dynasty (2112–2004 BC) and the Paleo-Babylonian period (2004–1595 BC). These archaeological texts, among the earliest written documents known to mankind, also describe a centralized economy organized around the Palace, in which the unit of account played an eminently political role, linked to the distribution of the surplus. The official unit of account made it possible to measure the value of taxes (which were mainly paid in kind), and thus to transfer part of the agricultural surplus to the political authority[3] (see Chapter 1).

The primitive money-unit of account thus takes on the aspect of a *public good*, making it possible to express the value of all debts in a common standard. From the outset, money has also been the expression of *monetary sovereignty*, defined as the sovereign's ability to impose a common standard to measure the universal value of debts (and credits).[4] Throughout history, dominant nations have imposed their own monetary unit of account for calculating prices, measures, taxes, fines and war tributes levied on defeated nations (Box 3.1).

Nowadays, monetary sovereignty is expressed on coins and banknotes—fiduciary money in the broadest sense (from the Latin *fides*: confidence)—which bear the name of the issuing institution guaranteeing the value of the currency and, where applicable, the national symbols helping to maintain confidence in the currency. For example, the US dollar bears the signature of the Secretary of the US Treasury and the name of the US Central Bank on the front. On the reverse is the famous official national motto of the United States, adopted by Congress in 1956: *In God We Trust*, and an unfinished pyramid of 13 steps, surmounted by the eye of Providence in a triangle.[5]

Box 3.1: The Athenian tetradrachm

In ancient Greece, the first silver coins appeared in the seventh century BC on the small island of Aegina, bearing the

[3] Peacok (2013, pp. 49–68) provides a detailed description of historical knowledge in this field.

[4] It was Jean Bodin, in the sixteenth century, who first theorized the links between sovereignty ("the absolute and perpetual power of a republic") and money.

[5] At the base of the pyramid are the Roman numerals MDCCLXXVI (1776), the date of the declaration of independence. Two other Latin references can be found: *ANNUIT COEPTIS* ("He approves our undertaking") and a quote from Virgil *NOVUS ORDO SECLORUM* ("New order of the centuries").

effigy of the sea turtle. The choice of animal motifs rather than human representations on coins was constant in the Greek world. A city seeking to extend its domination and unify its lands would impose its monetary and weighting system on defeated cities. So, when the famous silver *tetradrachm*, adorned with an owl on the reverse, became the dominant currency of the Mediterranean basin in the fifth century BC, it was above all a sign of sovereignty asserting itself through monetary reforms. The choice of silver as the reference metal can be explained by the existence of silver mines in Laurion, some fifty kilometers from Athens.

Collin, B. and Lecomte-Collin, V., 2000, *Histoire de la monnaie—Du troc à l'euro*, pp. 24–25 (untranslated).

Source By Marie-Lan Nguyen (2011), CC BY 2.5, https://commons.wikimedia.org/w/index.php?curid=11407401

3.2 Understanding Modern Money

The modern currency we use every day has two main characteristics. Firstly, in addition to its function as a unit of account, it also serves as an intermediary for trade and as a store of value. Secondly, since the collapse of the Bretton Woods system in 1973, it is no longer based on any fixed parity with metal.[6] Its nature is therefore purely *fiduciary*. And yet, unlike many metallic currencies, it fulfills all its functions perfectly.

Following in the footsteps of German economist Georg Knapp (1905), *Modern Money Theory* (MMT) economists Randall Wray (b. 1953) and Stephanie Kelton (b. 1969) have recently come up with an explanation for this paradox.

For these authors, money becomes the intermediary of exchange as soon as the state identifies it as the only means of payment accepted in the settlement of a specific compulsory debt it imposes on society: taxation. Since state money is the only instrument for recording and paying taxes, there is an incompressible demand for it, which in turn guarantees public confidence in its status as an instrument of exchange.

This explains why state currencies dominate private currencies. Suppose, for example, that a private organization, such as an airline, offers to issue its IOU as a means of payment, such as *Air Miles*. The use of this private IOU as a means of payment is limited to a restricted circle of organizations and individuals, in this case, the *Air Miles* partners.

But when the state imposes a compulsory debt on society, denominated and payable in a unit of account of its choice (such as the euro), this unit of account immediately enjoys a special status (everyone needs it to pay taxes). This helps explain why we prefer to receive our salaries in euros rather than *Air Miles*: as everyone needs euros to pay taxes, we are guaranteed that euros will be accepted for other payments. Taxation is the foundation of the modern monetary system, which is why MMT economists often use the expression "*taxes drive money*".

The MMT perspective implies that a sufficiently credible political authority can always succeed in imposing any currency as an exchange intermediary, be it metal, paper or lines of computer code. Only one condition is necessary: the chosen currency must be both *issued in payment of public expenditure* and *accepted for the payment of taxes.* The foundations of a modern monetary system can then be summed up in the following sequence:

1. The State identifies a unit of account (such as the dollar or the euro) and simultaneously imposes a tax denominated in this unit of account. This creates an incompressible demand for this unit of account within the private sector.

[6] The reason why human societies chose a precious metal as their standard of value remains obscure. As Keynes noted as early as 1924, gold (which he called a 'barbarous relic') has served for millennia as an unconscious symbol of power and stability, validating a posteriori the magical properties that the ancient Egyptian clergy attributed to yellow metal.

2. The State puts this unit of account—which then becomes money—into circulation through public spending in the private sector. This new currency (coins, banknotes and bank reserves) then appears as a liability on the consolidated balance sheet of the State (nowadays, the Central Bank and the Treasury), and as an asset on the consolidated balance sheet of the private sector (households and businesses), which holds it as a financial asset.
3. Whenever a private-sector agent pays a tax, the corresponding amount of money is withdrawn from circulation, and a corresponding debt liability to the state is erased.

This explanation helps us to understand the link between monetization and taxation in different historical contexts (as illustrated in Box 3.2).

Box 3.2: Imperialism, Colonial Taxation and Monetization

In the nineteenth century, the European colonial powers, seeking to exploit the labor and resources of their colonies to accelerate their own industrial development, were faced with frequent local labor shortages. Indeed, colonized populations had no reason to work for (generally very low) monetary wages, since the subsistence economy provided for their needs, and peasants who accepted salaried work had every interest in returning to their fields at harvest time, which regularly dried up the supply of labor for colonial projects.

The colonizers' solution was to introduce new taxes, payable in *colonial currency*. The effect of these taxes was to force people to leave the subsistence economy to work in plantations, mines, administration, etc., in order to acquire the colonial currency needed to pay the tax. The monetization of indigenous economies by colonial taxation led traditional societies to enter the capitalist world, contributing to the transformation of the traditional peasantry into a new class of salaried workers.

In addition to the low wages paid (often below the subsistence level), the tax schedule imposed by the colonialists plunged many peasants into poverty and considerably reduced their life expectancy. For example, in India in the 1930s, colonial taxes were due just after the harvest period, when agricultural prices were at their lowest (due to abundant supply on the market). Farmers were then forced to sell most of their harvest at a discount, often drawing on their subsistence stock and fuelling the fall in prices. Later in the year, faced with malnutrition, they often had to sell their land (or go into debt to wealthier farmers) to buy back agricultural produce (at a higher price). The creation of the colonial tax and monetization thus had the indirect effect of expropriating peasants from their ancestral lands (which they were often forced to sell to colonialists in order to obtain the currency needed to pay the tax).

Peacock, Mark (2013), Chapter 8: "Monetization in colonial contexts: famine, class and markets in 'development' strategies". Introducing Money, Routledge, 224 pp.

Dupon Jean-François, "Les immigrés indiens de la Réunion. Evolution and assimilation of a population". In: *Cahiers d'outre-mer*. N° 77–20e year, January-March 1967. pp. 49–88 (untranslated).

This reasoning leads to a reversal of perspective regarding the economic function of taxation. Seen through the prism of MMT, the view that states finance their spending through taxation is somewhat misleading. The causality is reversed: to be able to *collect* money through taxation, the state must first have *issued* it through deficit spending in the private-sector.

A public deficit is not a borrowing from the private sector, but a net monetary creation. Conversely, the payment of taxes in no way corresponds to the financing of public spending, but to a process of monetary destruction. In addition

Fig. 3.2 Modern currency (*Source* Jenny Thompson—stock.adobe.com; *Note* British banknote bearing the effigy of the Queen of England and the inscription "I promise to pay the bearer on demand the sum of five pounds".)

to anchoring public confidence in money, taxation also helps to regulate the quantity of money in circulation.

To summarize, one should not interpret the government's budget balance as if it were that of a *money user,* whereas its structure, which is fundamentally different, is that of a *money issuer.* For MMT economists, public debt is a negligible statistical residual measuring the stock of money issued by the State via its deficit in previous periods, and not yet removed from circulation through taxation (Fig. 3.2).

3.3 Conclusion

- Credit precedes money, and of all the functions of money, the most important is that of the *unit of account.*
- Monetary sovereignty is generally inscribed on coins and banknotes. These means of payment mention the issuing institute, which guarantees the value of the currency, and feature various symbols which can maintain confidence in the currency.
- In a modern monetary system, the currency in circulation is a liability of the state, held as an asset by the private sector. Public confidence in money is based on taxation, which also helps regulate the supply of money.

Activities

Questions for Discussion

1. To what extent can we say that *credit precedes trade*?
2. Can bitcoins and Air Miles be considered as currencies?
3. Can the euro be considered a currency in the same way as the US dollar?
4. Identify countries where several currencies are in circulation. Why is this the case?
5. According to MMT economists, what is the monetary function of taxes?

Mini-case: The Lady of Saint-Cannat

Read these two versions of the monetary fable entitled *The Lady of Saint-Cannat*:

Version 1

We're in the Provencal village of Saint-Cannat. One Friday morning, a young woman turns up at the village hotel. She books a room for the night and, as she has no luggage, leaves a 50 euro bill as a deposit. She then set off to visit the surrounding countryside. The owner takes the opportunity to settle a debt of 50 euros he owed the pastry chef for the cake delivered for his daughter's communion. The pastry chef then spends the 50-euro bill to buy flour from the miller… who in turn uses it to get his flat tire repaired at the garage… who buys 50 euros worth of fruit and vegetables from the market gardener… and as it's already midday, the latter goes to lunch at the hotel with a colleague for 50 euros. Just as the market gardener pays his bill and hands it over to the hotelier, the young woman returns from her walk and announces that she is canceling her reservation. The hotelier gives her back her banknote. She tore it up: it was a fake.

Version 2

We're in the Provencal village of Saint-Cannat. One Friday morning, a young woman turns up at the village hotel. She books a room for the night and, as she has no luggage, leaves a 50 euro bill as a deposit. She then set off to visit the surrounding countryside. The owner immediately goes to Ikea and spends 50 euros to buy a new bed base, as the bed in the young woman's room needs replacing. Ikea includes the 50 euros in its monthly turnover. Today is payday. After work, Franky, an Ikea employee, goes to the hotel in Saint-Cannat to have an aperitif with his friends and spends 50 euros. Just as Franky is settling his bill and handing it over to the hotelier, the young woman returns from a walk and announces that she is canceling her reservation. The hotelier gives her back her banknote. She puts it back in her purse.

Now answer the following questions in a few lines:

1. How does this fable illustrate the nature of money?
2. In which of the two versions does the economic well-being of locals appear to be higher? Use simplified balance sheets to support your answers.
3. By way of transposition, do you think our monetary system is compatible with sustainable development objectives? Do you think it would be necessary to put new currencies into circulation? If so, what could be the objectives of these currencies, and how could their value be guaranteed? To answer these questions, you may wish to look for information online on complementary local currencies.

4 Exploring Monetary Systems

Raphaël Didier and Thomas Lagoarde-Ségot

Putting Things into Perspective

Economists don't generally speak of money in the broad sense, but rather of *monetary aggregates*. These monetary aggregates are all denominated in one unit of account (the euro) and are classified according to their *liquidity*, i.e. how quickly they can be converted into bills and coins. In 2023, monetary aggregates in the eurozone were defined as follows:

M0: banknotes, coins, bank accounts held by commercial banks with the Central Bank;

M1: banknotes, coins and sight deposits managed by financial institutions in the eurozone;

M2: M1 + term deposits up to two years and deposits redeemable at notice up to three months;

M3: M2 + repurchase agreements, money-market fund units and debt securities with maturities of up to two years.

As the table below shows, these monetary aggregates have increased significantly in the eurozone from 1980 to 2020.

R. Didier
Université de Lorraine, Metz, France
e-mail: didierraphael@wanadoo.fr

T. Lagoarde-Ségot (✉)
KEDGE BS & SDSN France, Talence, France
e-mail: thomas.lagoardesegot@kedgebs.com

T. Lagoarde-Ségot (ed.), *Ecological Economics and Finance*, https://doi.org/10.1007/978-3-031-71249-4_4

Eurozone monetary aggregates (millions of euros) 1980–2020.

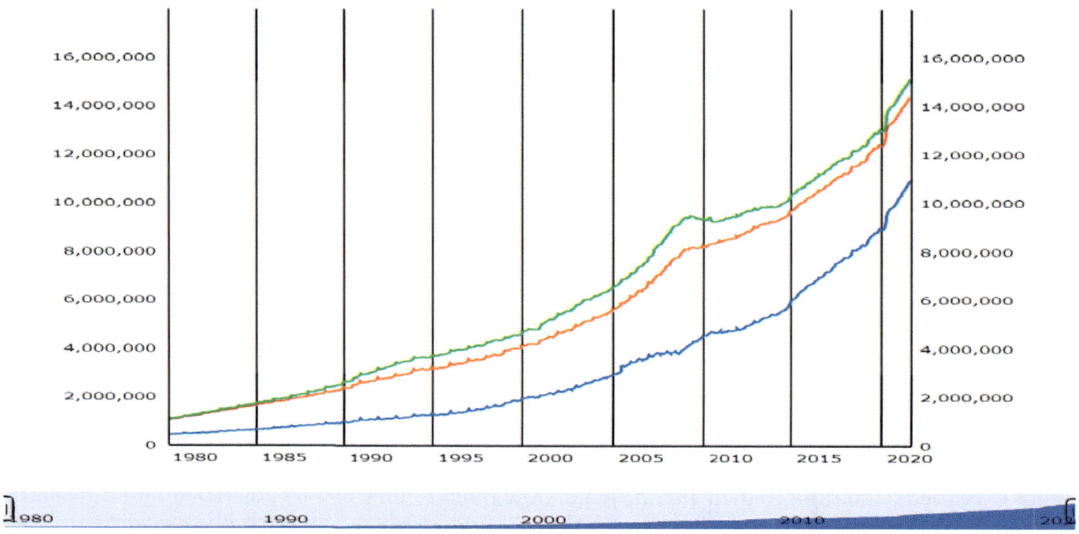

Source European Central Bank (https://sdw.ecb.europa.eu/).

With the exception of the monetary base (M0), the money represented on this graph is not created by the State or the Central Bank, but by *commercial banks*. So it's the banks' power to create money (and the various disputes that arise from it) that we'll be concentrating on in this chapter.

Learning Objectives

- Using double-entry bookkeeping to analyze money creation
- Analyzing interbank clearing mechanisms
- Understanding the role of the Central Bank
- Discovering monetary initiatives and contestations

4.1 Money and the Payment System

Modern Money: Bank Debt

You probably have a bank account in which you have a deposit, the amount of which is recorded as an *asset* on your personal balance sheet. However, this same deposit also appears as a *liability* on your bank's balance sheet: you can demand payment (i.e. conversion into banknotes) at any time. A bank deposit is therefore an acknowledgment of debt that appears simultaneously on the *liabilities* side of the bank's balance sheet and on the *assets* side of its holder's balance sheet. This is clearly illustrated by the simplified balance sheets below (see Table 4.1)[1]:

Table 4.1 Simplified balance sheets for a bank and its customer

Bank		Customer	
Assets	Liabilities	Assets	Liabilities
Loans	**Deposits**	Financial securities	Loans
Central bank reserves	Net wealth	**Deposits**	Net wealth
Banknotes and coins		Banknotes and coins	

[1] In a balance sheet, the following equality holds: Assets = Liabilities + Net wealth. Net wealth (NW) is a residual variable appearing on the liabilities side of the balance sheet.

Table 4.2 Bank lending and money creation

Bank		Company	
Assets	Liabilities	Assets	Liabilities
Loan = 100,000 euros	Deposit = 100,000 euros	Deposit = 100,000 euros	Loan = 100,000 euros

The balance sheets of modern banking sectors show trillions of euros worth of bank deposits on their liabilities side. According to the European Central Bank, the value of sight deposits (appearing on banks' liabilities and their depositors' assets) was 2,410 billion euros in 2023.[2] This scriptural money, registered on bank accounts and used in transactions, is a debt of the banking sector to the public.

Credit and Money Creation

Every bank loan is a money-creation operation. For example, suppose your company negotiates a credit line of 100,000 euros with its bank. When the contract is signed, four new accounting entries are made: a new deposit is simultaneously entered on the assets side of your company's balance sheet and on the liabilities side of your bank's balance sheet. The money supply therefore increases by 100,000 euros. In return for this new deposit, a new loan appears on the assets side of the bank's balance sheet, and on the liabilities side of your company's balance sheet (see Table 4.2).

Modern banking institutions therefore have a power to create money *ex nihilo*.[3] Like any social construct, this system is of course subject to criticism and contestation. As the Nobel Prize-winning economist Maurice Allais (1911–2010) put it: "In essence, the current creation of money *ex nihilo* by the banking system is identical (…) to the creation of money by counterfeiters (…). The only difference is that those who benefit are different".

The Limits of Banking Power to Create Money

Nevertheless, the power of banks to create money is, in practice, limited by several factors. The first, linked to the economic cycle, concerns the estimated solvency of borrowers: if your company defaults on its loan, the bank's net wealth will fall accordingly. An excessive money creation can therefore weaken banks' balance sheets and threaten the stability of the monetary system. This is why international prudential regulations (such as the Basel III accords) now provide a certain degree of control over lending activities.

Secondly, the repayment of a loan destroys an equivalent amount of credit currency. As the simplified balance sheets below show (see Table 4.3), four accounting entries disappear when your company repays its loan.

It's easy to see why bank credit is so vital: it allows money to flow into the economy. This money circulates, in return for the production and consumption of various goods and services, and finally flows back when a loan is repaid. The money supply is therefore endogenous, in the sense that it results from banks' and companies' expectations of the future state of the economy. Economists belonging to the 'circuitist' movement, notably the Italian Augusto Graziani (1933–2014) and the Frenchman Alain Parguez (1940–2022), have extensively analyzed the economy from a monetary perspective.

[2] The latest data are available on the European Central Bank website: https://sdw.ecb.europa.eu/.

[3] This was not always the case. For example, the British *Bank Charter Act* of 1844, strongly influenced by David Ricardo, limited the issue of money by banks to their gold holdings. This system, which led to a number of banking crises (in 1846, 1857 and 1866), came to a definitive end with the outbreak of the First World War. For a more detailed analysis, see Makoto Itoh and Costas Lapavitsas (1999, pp. 4–24), *Political Economy of Money and Finance*.

Table 4.3 Credit repayment and monetary destruction

Bank		Company	
Assets	Liabilities	Assets	Liabilities
~~Loan=100,000 euros~~	~~Deposit=100,000 euros~~	~~Deposit=100,000 euros~~	~~Loan=100,000 euros~~

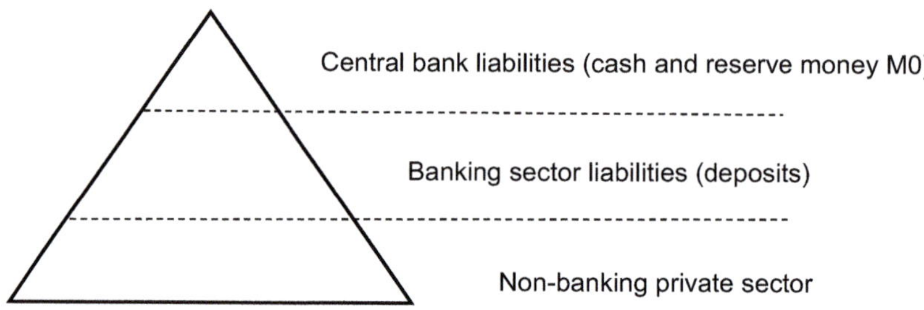

Fig. 4.1 The pyramid-shaped payment hierarchy (*Note* There are far more liabilities at the bottom of the pyramid than at the top: modern monetary systems operate on a leveraged basis, based on a relatively small amount of reserve money.)

How the Monetary System Works

In our modern economies, money essentially takes the form of bank deposits (bank liabilities) denominated and convertible into cash (government liabilities) (Chapter 3). These two categories of liabilities serve as means of payment for non-financial agents, who use them to settle their own debts. As shown in Fig. 4.1, these various monetary liabilities can be positioned according to their degree of separation from the balance sheet of the central bank.

The bottom layer of the pyramid contains non-bank liabilities, issued by households and productive companies, and held as assets by other households, companies and banks (e.g. supplier credits). These liabilities can only be canceled out by the transfer of a liability to the top layer of the pyramid (bank deposit or cash).

All these liabilities are *denominated* and *convertible* into currency (i.e. government liabilities). The State, via the Central Bank, is at the top of the payments hierarchy: in fact, only its own liabilities (bank reserves) are *non-convertible*[4].

The pyramid shape calls for two comments. Firstly, there are more liabilities at the bottom of the pyramid than at the top. In this sense, the entire monetary system leverages central bank debt. Secondly, the credibility of liabilities increases the higher up the pyramid you go: the probability of a government defaulting on its non-convertible liabilities is almost nil; the probability of a bank failure is low, and the probability of a business or household failure is much higher.

Interbank Clearing

Suppose your company, a customer of bank A, uses its loan (see Table 4.2) to pay an invoice to a supplier, a customer of bank B, by bank transfer. As deposits are bank liabilities, bank B will only accept this transaction if bank A simultaneously transfers an asset of equivalent value.

[4]This is particularly true in the case of a floating currency (such as the euro or the U.S. dollar); by contrast, in the case of a fixed exchange rate regime, a foreign currency (such as the U.S. dollar in currency board regimes like Hong Kong's) or a precious metal (such as gold in the case of the Bretton Woods system) stands at the top of the payments hierarchy.

Table 4.4 Interbank clearing

Bank A		Bank B	
Assets	Liabilities	Assets	Liabilities
Reserves: –100,000 euros	Deposit: –100,000 euros	Reserves: +100,000 euros	Deposit: +100,000 euros

In the absence of a central bank, this asset necessarily takes the form of an IOU issued by Bank A and may be backed by a precious metal (such as gold). Such a *free banking* system is, however, highly unstable. Indeed, any rumor of Bank A's fragility may lead Bank B to refuse the transfer in order to protect its net worth, thereby threatening the integrity of the payment system (see Box 4.1).

Box 4.1: The American free banking experience

Between 1837 and 1863, banks in the U.S. (as well as some insurance and even railroad companies) issued their own bills, pledged against their gold and silver reserves, and the exchange rate between these different currencies fluctuated with the reputation of their issuer. However, East Coast banks frequently rejected bills issued by Western frontier banks as unreliable. In the absence of a mechanism to guarantee the face value of bank deposits, banking crises were endemic (and many depositors were ruined). For their part, banks passed on the risk of default to their customers, charging higher interest rates on loans. It wasn't until 1913 and the creation of the Federal Reserve that the instability of the American payment system disappeared. This historical example testifies to the progress made by the invention of central banks, which make exchanges more fluid and secure by guaranteeing the *liquidity of* the payment system.

Source Peacock (2016).

Nowadays, interbank clearing is based upon the transmission of a special asset: *reserve money*.

Table 4.5 Interbank clearing

Central bank	
Assets	Liabilities
	Bank A's reserve account: –100,000 euros Bank B's reserve account: +100,000 euros

This asset is issued by a public institution (the Central Bank) which has a monopoly on it, as part of its mandate to maintain the integrity of the payment system. Reserve money is recorded as an asset of the banks and a liability of the Central Bank.

Banks have an account with the Central Bank, in which they hold reserve money in the form of sight deposits. They cannot lend these reserves to the public, and do not need them to grant loans; however, they use them daily for interbank transaction purposes.

Your company now pays its supplier by transferring 100,000 euros to its account at Bank B. Bank B's balance sheet features a new deposit liability balanced by a new central bank reserve asset, which Bank A (your company's bank) will have transferred to it at the same time (Table 4.4).

This transfer of interbank reserves takes place by means of a book entry in the Central Bank's balance sheet, which debits Bank A's reserve account and credits Bank B's. The impact of this operation on the Central Bank's balance sheet is as follows (Table 4.5):

If bank A does not have the necessary reserves, it can easily obtain them, for example, by selling a financial asset (such as a Treasury bond) on the interbank market. It can also borrow from other banks (domestic or foreign), or directly from the Central Bank, which has unlimited power to create reserve money under its mandate. In the latter case, balance sheets evolve as follows (Table 4.6):

Table 4.6 Interbank clearing

Bank A		Central bank	
Assets	Liabilities	Assets	Liabilities
Reserves: +100,000 euros	Loan from central bank :+100,000 euros	Loan to bank A: +100,000 euros	Reserves: +100,000 euros

Table 4.7 Interbank clearing

Bank A		Bank B	
Assets	Liabilities	Assets	Liabilities
Reserves : – 100,000 euros	Loan from central bank: 100,000 euros Deposit: –100,000 euros Net assets: –100,000 euros	Reserves: 100,000 euros	Deposit: +100,000 euros

Bank A now has the necessary reserves to repay its debt to Bank B. The balance sheets of the two banks change as follows (Table 4.7):

In this example, Bank A's net worth is decreasing, as it has had to borrow the full amount of reserves required from the Central Bank. However, the transaction remains profitable for Bank A as long as the interest rate it charges on loans exceeds the interest rate which it has to pay to the Central Bank[5]. Nowadays, all the above accounting entries are made almost simultaneously, via lines of computer code.

The functioning of the modern payment system is therefore based on the lender-of-last-resort status of the Central Bank, an institution located at the top of the monetary pyramid (see Fig. 4.1) which, as part of its mandate, has the monopolistic and unlimited power to create reserve money. This arrangement gives banking institutions continuous access to reserve money, and ensures that the preexisting supply of reserves in no way limits banks' lending capacity.

[5] It's easy to see why the interest rate charged by the central bank on new reserve loans (such as the Fed rate in the US) is so often commented on and analyzed in the financial press. For example, an increase in this rate can lead banks to raise the rate charged to borrowers, thereby reducing demand for credit, the issuance of credit money, and therefore spending (and income) circulating in the economy.

4.2 Monetary Initiatives and Sustainable Development

Local Complementary Currencies

In recent years, increasing awareness of sustainability issues has been a catalyst for the creation of *local complementary currencies*. These currencies are diverse in nature, but in some ways, they resemble E. F. Schumacher's (1973) slogan "*small is beautiful*", according to which the community is the relevant level of decision and action. Their main objective is to re-appropriate money as a common good (Chapter 3), which is why they have set up a charter of values and a system of governance that allows each member to express his or her views freely. By relying on strong values (reciprocity, redistribution, solidarity, sharing, etc.) that go beyond simple market relations, the community of local currency users becomes a tightly-knit *local monetary community*. For example, the founders of Eusko, France's largest local currency (as measured by the circulating volume expressed in euros), chose to draw up a concise charter of values. The values defended by the users of this local currency are directly linked to the sustainable development goals: sustainable cities and communities (SDG11), responsible consumption and production (SDG12), the fight against climate change (SDG13), and partnerships to achieve the goals (SDG17).

These monetary initiatives do not aim to compete with legal tender and are part of the payment system; nevertheless, they seek to change consumption patterns by promoting local and ethical consumption, and can in some cases be a substitute for legal tender. In fact, this is what can be seen from observing the local currencies that have developed in South America, some of which have several thousand users (e.g. *Palmas* in Brazil). In any case, a local currency socially appropriates the territory in which it circulates, transforms it and in return adapts to it. This territory is also generally referred to as a 'living area', to make it clear that it is a social and political construct that does not necessarily correspond to an administrative or geographical division.[6]

The most common operating principle is as follows: anyone who has paid a membership fee to the association managing the local currency—and ratified its charter of values—can exchange the desired amount of legal tender (the euro) for local currency, at a fixed exchange rate. The amount of legal tender obtained in this way, known as the 'reserve fund', provides cover for the local currency issue. It is usually placed in a solidarity-based financial institution—such as *La Nef* in France—so that it can be used to finance other projects in line with the association's charter of values.

On the other hand, the reverse conversion of local currencies into euros is generally forbidden for individuals, but possible for professional members, subject to a penalty representing a certain percentage of the amount converted (typically between 2 and 5%). These local currencies can very easily set themselves economic and social objectives in the territory where they are to circulate, in a *bottom-up* approach. Finally, it's worth noting that various mechanisms, such as 'demurrage', tend to discourage savings in local currency. The face value of bills of a demurrage currency depreciates periodically to encourage holders to spend them, although the initial face value can be restored by purchasing a stamp from the issuing organization. The Bristol pound in the UK is a famous example of a local complementary currency (see Box 4.2).

Box 4.2: The Bristol pound

Bristol Pound was founded in 2012 by a group of financial activists and campaigners, based on the slogan *"Our city, our money"*.

After circulating as paper coupons and then in digital form (with over a million pounds of transactions a year), the Bristol Pound has been associated since 2020 to a not-for-profit payment platform, with all earnings reinvested in social and environmental projects, with the aim of making Bristol a zero-carbon city by 2030.

Source https://bristolpound.org

Clearly, a local complementary currency fulfills functions that the official currency is unwilling—or unable—to fulfill: solidarity, belonging to a territory, sharing, reciprocity, etc. This explains the sometimes ambiguous relationship with public authorities, as the development of local complementary currencies can, in some cases, be perceived as a threat to monetary sovereignty (see Box 4.3).

[6] One example is the *Transition Towns* network: https://transitionnetwork.org/about-the-movement/what-is-transition. The movement created by Rob Hopkins gained visibility in France by appearing in the documentary film *Demain* directed by Cyril Dion and Mélanie Laurent, released in 2015.

Box 4.3: The Wörgl experiment

By 1931, the small Austrian town of Wörgl (population 4,300) had been so badly hit by the Great Depression that it had almost 1,500 unemployed. The town's mayor decided to launch a number of public development projects to employ the idle residents and boost the local economy. As tax revenues were too low to pay municipal employees, he created democratically-issued municipal 'work certificates' in the form of vouchers of 1, 5 and 10 shillings, whose value decreased by 1% per month (through a demurrage mechanism). The value of the voucher could be recovered at the end of each month by stamping the ticket issued by the town hall, in return for payment of this 1% value. And to instil confidence, municipal employees, including the mayor, received half their salary in this local currency. This experiment became a textbook case: not only did the city successfully complete its development projects, it also managed to pay off its arrears. Observers from all over the world came to Wörgl to witness the 'economic miracle', and other towns tried to emulate the experience. Unfortunately, questions of monetary sovereignty resurfaced when the Central Bank of Vienna took the mayor of Wörgl to the Supreme Court for violation of its currency-issuing privilege. The local currency was banned at the end of 1933.

Blockchain and Complementary Currencies

In recent years, more and more local complementary currency movements have shown an interest in the blockchain technology, and some have taken the plunge, such as *moneda PAR* in Argentina or *Léman* in the Lake Geneva region (see Box 4.4). Other local complementary currencies are being transformed by technology; for example, the *Sou*, a complementary local currency developed by a collective in the French Mayenne region, has been transformed into a digital currency, the 'G1', based on the *Duniter* software and the associated blockchain. Admittedly, this currency does not fall within the official scope of local complementary currency schemes (as defined by the French law of July 31, 2014, on the social and solidarity economy), but it shows that blockchain technology can also be used to defend objectives linked to sustainable development.

Box 4.4: The case of *Lake Geneva*

Léman is the local currency used since 2015 in the Lake Geneva basin (canton of Geneva, part of the cantons of Vaud and Valais, part of Haute-Savoie). It exists in the form of banknotes and in electronic form, via a payment app (*Biletujo*) enabling access to the blockchain (*Com'Chain*) (the latter does not remunerate mining, hence a lower energy consumption, as compared to the Bitcoin blockchain).

Léman has two notable features. Firstly, the value of each banknote is recorded on the blockchain, enabling the managing association to activate the banknotes when they are put into circulation and deactivate them in the event of theft, for example. The association also offers a complementary local currency, as well as a mutual credit system aimed primarily at businesses, where the account of the person providing a service is credited and the account of the member receiving the service is simultaneously debited. So there's no longer any need to sell Swiss francs to obtain Lemans.

Source https://monnaie-leman.org

4.3 Conclusion

- Money is endogenous: in the modern economy, money creation depends for the most part on loans granted by banks. Repaying debts and paying taxes destroys the money in circulation.
- The central bank, which issues reserve money, is the guarantor of the payment system in its capacity as lender of last resort. Its liabilities lie at the top of the pyramid-shaped payment hierarchy.
- Local complementary currencies aim to give new functions to money: solidarity, belonging to a territory, sharing, reciprocity, and so on. Although these initiatives are generally connected to the monetary system, they nonetheless also constitute a form of monetary contestation.

Activities

Questions for Discussion

1. Does the assertion that banks lend out their depositors' savings seem correct to you?
2. You pay for your soccer club membership by bank transfer. Using double-entry bookkeeping, analyze the impact of this transaction on banks' balance sheets. Assume that the soccer club's bank is different from yours and that your bank needs to borrow reserves from the Central Bank to settle the transaction.
3. You withdraw ten euros from an ATM. Using the payment pyramid, explain how this operation involves the transformation of a bank liability. You then pay for your meal with these ten euros. Explain to what extent you have paid for your meal using the Central Bank's debt.

Mini-case: Local Authorities and Payments in Local Currency

Research the local currency of your choice on the Schumacher Center for a New Economics website (https://centerforneweconomics.org/apply/local-currencies-program/localcurrencies-directory/). Then answer the following questions in a few lines:

1. Present the history, mission, governance and operation of the selected local currency.
2. Does the latter challenge the monetary sovereignty of the State?
3. What benefits could companies or individuals expect to derive from its use?
4. To what extent can this local currency contribute to the sustainable development goals?

5 Interest Rates and Monetary Policy

Thomas Lagoarde-Ségot

Putting Things into Perspective

One of the first central banks, the Bank of England was established in 1694 and remains one of the world's most respected monetary institutions. For several centuries, the Bank of England has used the *Bank Rate* as a monetary policy tool. This is a single rate at which it charges commercial banks that borrow reserves from it and remunerates the reserves that banks accumulate at its deposit facility. The figure below shows the evolution of the *Bank Rate* since 1694.

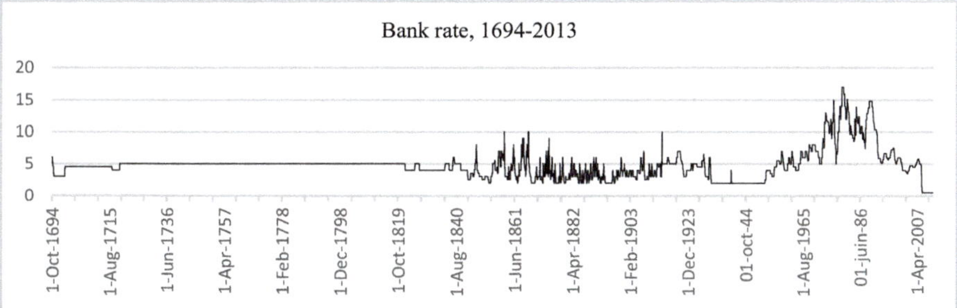

Since the 17th century, the British economy has been through a number of upheavals: industrial revolutions, wars, financial crises, recessions, inflation, climate change… Does the evolution of the *Bank Rate* reflect changes in economic conditions, or is it rather the opposite? How is this interest rate transmitted to the financial markets and the economy? What impact does it have on the money supply? How does a central bank operate? These are just some of the questions addressed in this chapter.

T. Lagoarde-Ségot (✉)
KEDGE BS & SDSN France, Talence, France
e-mail: thomas.lagoardesegot@kedgebs.com

T. Lagoarde-Ségot (ed.), *Ecological Economics and Finance*, https://doi.org/10.1007/978-3-031-71249-4_5

Learning Objectives

- Understanding the preference for liquidity
- Discovering how a central bank works
- Linking interest rates and monetary policy

5.1 Preference for Liquidity

In the modern economy, money is an entirely separate financial asset. Unlike any other asset that can be used as a store of value, money commands immediate purchasing power. At any time, we can exchange it for goods, or for other assets (real and financial). On the other hand, all other financial assets must first be converted into money in order to command purchasing power. *Liquidity* refers to the speed with which an asset can be converted into purchasing power. The monetary aggregate M0 naturally represents the liquid asset par excellence.

For an equivalent return, a rational investor will always prefer to hold a more liquid asset. The *preference for liquidity* therefore explains the existence of interest rates: giving up money represents a cost, which must be offset by an expectation of future gain.

The level of liquidity preference depends on agents' expectations. For example, the imminence of a recession may lead entrepreneurs to increase their liquid assets (to be able to meet unforeseen expenses) rather than invest in less liquid assets (such as buildings). Similarly, if financial markets fall, banks and households will tend to reallocate their portfolios towards more liquid assets (for example, by selling their stocks and bonds before they lose value). On the other hand, galloping inflation may lead savers to flee from money, i.e. to forego liquidity in order to preserve the real value of their assets (e.g. by acquiring land, or a more stable currency).

In economic and financial terms, money is not neutral. Indeed, economic agents faced with *radical uncertainty* (see Box 5.1) are particularly sensitive to liquidity. When fear of the future increases, they divert their income from the purchase of goods and financial assets to demand additional liquidity—which generally leads to a rise in interest rates.

Box 5.1: Radical Uncertainty

Post-Keynesian economist Marc Lavoie (2022) draws a useful distinction between certainty, risk and uncertainty. *Certainty* describes a situation where a given action produces an invariable result (for example, a ball always bounces against a wall). *Risk* describes a situation where a given action can produce several known, probabilistic outcomes (for example, I have a one-in-six chance of rolling a six). *Radical uncertainty* describes a situation where the possible outcomes of an action, as well as their probability of occurrence, are unknown. We make our financial decisions in an environment of radical uncertainty. For example, should I stay a tenant or try to become a homeowner? The answer to this question will only become clear to me *after the fact*, depending on factors that are unknown today: the future evolution of the property market, interest rates, my income, the cost of foregoing other investments that may arise tomorrow, the number of years I will live in this home, etc. Holding money enables us to protect ourselves from a radically uncertain future.

Source: Lavoie, M. (2022). *Post-Keynesian Economics*. Cheltenham, UK: Edward Elgar Publishing.

5.2 Illustration: The Term Structure of Interest Rates

The term *structure* of interest rates refers to the empirical relationship between interest rates and the maturities of different financial instruments. As shown in Fig. 5.1 (for the USA in the early 2010s), Treasury bond yields are typically highly correlated, and short-term rates are lower than longer-term rates.

Short-term bonds are therefore the *preferred habitat* of investors. This is because investors are reluctant to forego liquidity and will only buy long-term bonds if they offer a higher yield.

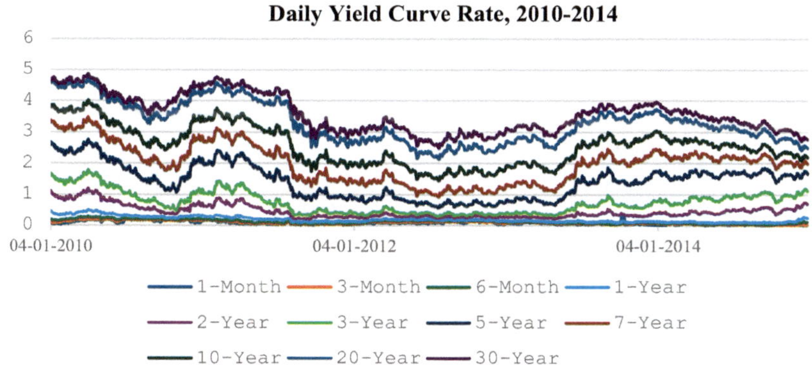

Fig. 5.1 Yield curve for US Treasury bonds, 2010–2014 (*Source*: https://www.quandl.com/data/USTREASURY/YIELD-Treasury-Yield-Curve-Rates)

It follows that, to ensure financial market equilibrium, asset yields, adjusted for risk, must be equal. Otherwise, some assets would remain unsold, as no investor would be willing to hold them. Assuming σ to be the liquidity premium associated with each asset, the following equality holds at all times on the markets:

$$i_{CB} = i_{ST} - \sigma_{ST} = i_{LT} - \sigma_{LT} \quad (5.1)$$

In Eq. (5.1), i_{CB} represents the prime rate. This is the rate at which banks can borrow the most liquid asset (the monetary aggregate M0). i_{ST} and σ_{ST} respectively represent the interest rate and the risk premium on short-term securities, and i_{LT} and σ_{LT} respectively represent the interest rate and risk premium on long-term securities. This reasoning is described in Fig. 5.2, which

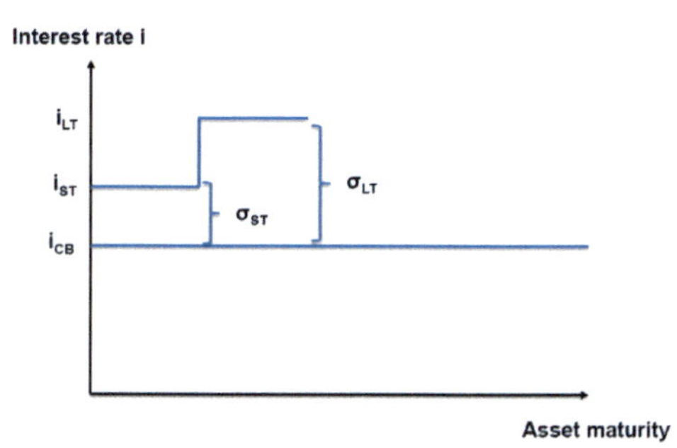

Fig. 5.2 Interest rates and liquidity premium (*Source* Lavoie [2022])

expresses the term structure of interest rates as a function of the liquidity premium (σ).

For example, in March 2020, during the COVID-19 epidemic, the US Federal Reserve brought the prime rate i_{CB} to near-zero levels. As Fig. 5.3 shows, this cut prevented a surge in long-term bond yields and the ensuing financial crisis (despite the increase in the liquidity premium linked to the health context).

The prime rate (i_{CB}) is an off-market rate set by the central bank as part of its monetary policy. It follows, as this chart shows, that "the monetary authorities set the short-term rate, and the preference for liquidity (as well as other considerations) determines the increase in long-term rates" (Dow & Dow, 1989).

Nevertheless, the relationship between the prime rate and long-term rates is unstable. For example, long-term interest rates may remain high despite a cut in the prime rate if investors consider the cut to be only temporary. Furthermore, a reduction in the prime rate i_{CB} may prove insufficient to stem the rise in long-term rates, if at the same time the preference for liquidity (σ) increases more than proportionally. This can happen, for example, when investors anticipate a recession. Good communication and timing are therefore essential to the success of central bank interventions.

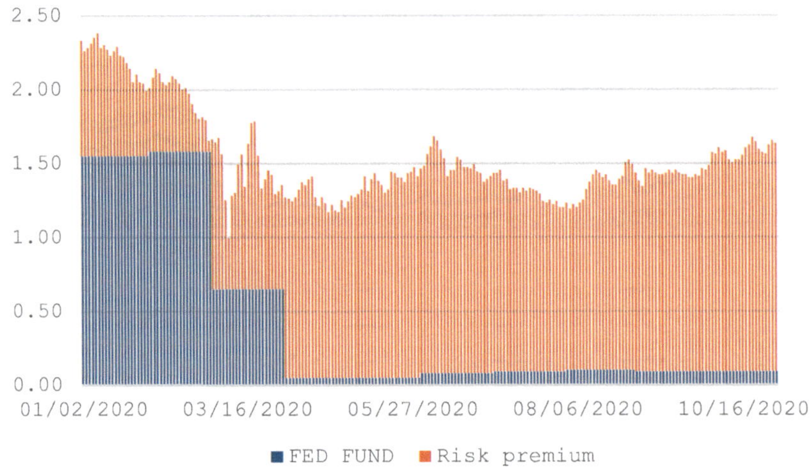

Fig. 5.3 Evolution of the US risk premium during the first COVID-19 epidemic (*Note* Author's calculations based on data from *Federal Reserve Economic Data* [FRED]. The Fed's key interest rate is shown in blue. The risk premium on 30-year Treasuries is in orange)

5.3 The Role of the Central Bank

Key Interest Rates

Modern monetary systems guarantee banks continuous access to the ultimate liquidity represented by M0. This monetary aggregate is recorded as a liability of the central bank, which is its sole issuer (Chapter 4). In addition, prudential regulations require banks to hold reserve deposits with the Central Bank, in fixed proportion to their total liabilities. In the eurozone, bank reserve requirements are set at 1% of the value of public deposits. Any bank can then access the required reserves through three channels: (i) by borrowing them from the Central Bank; (ii) by borrowing them from other banks on the interbank market; (iii) by selling financial assets directly to the Central Bank on the *open market*. To establish the prime rate (i_{CB}) in the eurozone, the European Central Bank (ECB) sets three key rates:

- the *marginal lending* rate, at which banks borrow reserves overnight;
- the *main refinancing* operations rate, at which banks borrow longer-term reserves (usually seven days);
- the *deposit facility* rate at which the ECB remunerates excess reserves deposited by banks.

Figure 5.4 shows the evolution of these three rates between 1999 and 2024. The lowest of the three rates is the deposit facility rate. The ECB moved this rate into negative territory between 2013 and 2022 to encourage banks to hold riskier long-term assets (such as long-term corporate bonds), before raising it again in the summer of 2022 to curb the return of inflation. The marginal lending facility rate and the main refinancing operations rate are higher—the main refinancing operations rate generally being the highest. By setting these three rates, the ECB influences the rate at which banks are willing to lend on the interbank market, as well as overall financial conditions in the economy. This has extra-financial consequences, particularly in terms of income distribution (see Box 5.2).

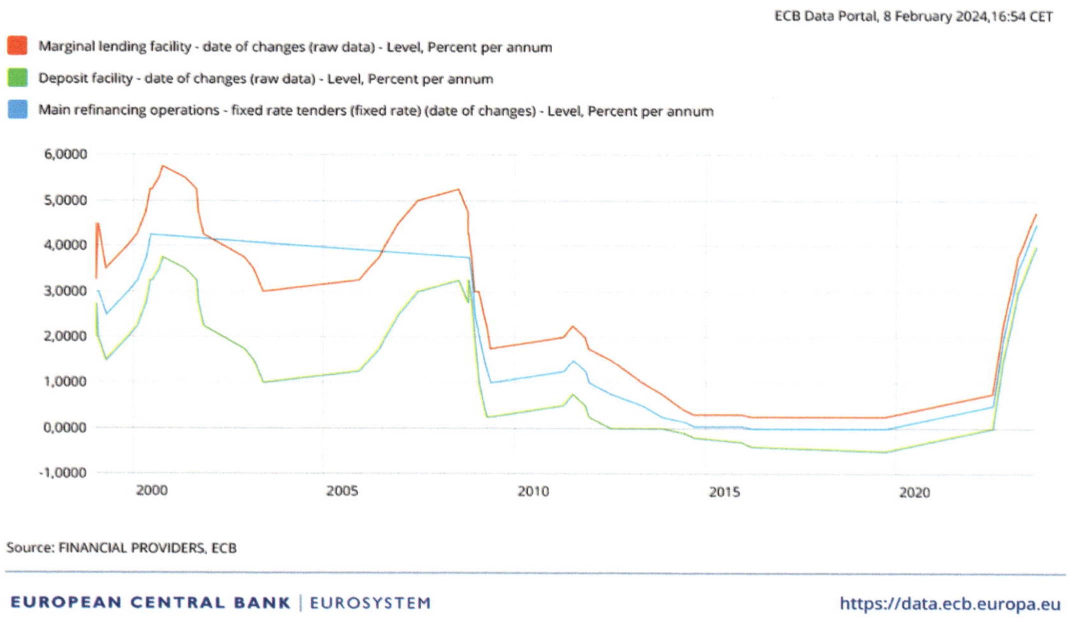

Fig. 5.4 Eurozone key rates, 1999–2024 (*Source* https://sdw.ecb.europa.eu/)

Box 5.2: The Fair Interest Rate

Interest payments are an income for creditors, but also an expense for borrowers. To achieve the social component of sustainable development goals (SDG), it may therefore be necessary to define a fair interest rate at the macroeconomic level. For post-Keynesian economists, such an interest rate should enable borrowers and lenders to ensure that "the purchasing power temporarily exchanged between borrower and lender remains constant over time" (Lavoie, 2022). This reasoning can be written as follows:

$$i_{fair} = \widehat{y} + \widehat{p}$$

where i_{fair} is the equitable interest rate, $\widehat{y}$ is the growth rate of labour productivity and $\widehat{p}$ is the inflation rate. Thus, in a world without technical progress and inflation, the equitable interest rate is zero. This reasoning could serve as a basis for formulating new financial and monetary policies in line with the SDGs.

Source Lavoie, M. (2022). *Post-Keynesian Economics*. Cheltenham, UK: Edward Elgar Publishing

Refinancing Operations

In the eurozone, commercial banks borrow reserves from the European Central Bank (ECB) as part of their *main refinancing operations*. Table 5.1 shows the simplified balance sheets of a commercial bank and the ECB during this transaction, which takes the form of a repurchase agreement (*repo*).

The borrowing bank provides the Central Bank with a low-risk collateral asset (e.g. a Treasury bill) and undertakes to buy it back at a given price. After assessing the quality of the collateral, the Central Bank applies a *haircut* to calculate the maximum amount of the reserve loan granted. For collateral of 100 and a 5% haircut, the reserve loan is equal to 100/

Table 5.1 The main refinancing instruments

Central bank		Bank A	
Assets	Liabilities	Assets	Liabilities
Loan	Reserves	Reserves (collateral)	Loan

(1 + 5%) = 95.23 euros. This loan, covered by the collateral, is carried as an asset on the central bank's balance sheet. If the bank repurchases the collateral for 104.76 euros, the interest rate on the reserve loan (the *repo* rate) is 10% (since 95.23 (1 + 10%) = 104.76).

Finally, it should be noted that in many countries, accounting rules allow banks to keep collateral on their balance sheet throughout the transaction. This is why it is shown on the assets side of bank A's balance sheet in Table 5.1.

In the euro zone, transactions of this type are organized every week (on Tuesdays), and the maturity of the loans granted is generally one week. If a bank has an urgent need for reserves (for example, to settle an interbank balance), it can also obtain them through the *marginal lending facility.*

The reserves issued by the Central Bank are created *ex-nihilo* (out of nothing). This is because the central bank has unlimited power to create reserve money, within the framework of its mandate conferred by the state. For a growing number of observers, this public mandate calls on Central Banks to modify these refinancing mechanisms in order to contribute to the Sustainable Development Goals (SDGs).

The Interbank Market

Commercial banks can borrow short-term reserves from other banks on the interbank market. Such loans are recorded on the liabilities side of the Central Bank's balance sheet, which transfers the reserves from the creditor bank to the debtor bank, and then reverses the operation when the loan matures (usually on the same day).

The rates on the European interbank market are the *Euro Interbank Offered Rate* (EURIBOR) and the *European Short-Term Rate* (ESTER). EURIBOR is collected by telephone surveys of several major banks during daily conference calls between representatives of these banks. The more reliable ESTER is the ECB's official rate, calculated from interbank transaction data. ESTER has replaced the former rate known as EONIA (*Euro Over Night Index Average*) since 2019. Since banks can also borrow reserves urgently from the central bank, the interbank market rate is generally lower than the marginal lending rate, but not too far from it (see Fig. 5.4).

Table 5.2 Open market reserve issues

Central bank	
Δ Assets	Δ Liabilities
Treasury bond = 100	Reserves = 100
Bank A	
Δ Assets	Δ Liabilities
~~Treasury bond = 100~~ Reserves = 100	

Open Market Transactions

Finally, banks can obtain reserves from the Central Bank by exchanging them for financial assets on the *open market*. In Table 5.2, which schematically represents such a transaction, new reserves are entered on the assets side of the bank's balance sheet and on the liabilities side of the Central Bank's balance sheet. These reserves are offset by the transfer of an equivalent asset (in this case, a Treasury bond) from the bank's balance sheet to the Central Bank's balance sheet.

These operations are generally initiated by the central bank. They enable it to achieve its rate target when external shocks affect the supply of or demand for available reserves (such as fluctuations in the Treasury balance, or foreign exchange transactions). *Open market* operations also enable the central bank to steer market expectations. The gradual drying-up of the Central Bank's securities purchases in the eurozone between 2019 and 2024 visible on the chart has given the market a clear signal of a sustained rise in the target rate (Box 5.3).

Box 5.3: ECB Open Market Purchases

Throughout the 2010 decade, and even more so during the COVID-19 crisis, the European Central Bank used the open market to provide banks with liquidity. The ECB deployed the Private Sector Purchase Program (CSPP), the Public Sector Purchase Program (PSPP), the Asset-Backed Securities Purchase Program (ABSPP) and the third Covered Bond Purchase Program (CBPP3). The *ex-nihilo* creation of reserves, as a counterpart to these purchases, enabled the interbank rate to converge towards the floor rate of the deposit facility, and facilitated direct steering of the interbank rate. In addition, the accumulation of reserves enabled bank balance sheets to be cleaned up, and supported the value of bond prices, thereby averting the spectre of a financial crisis.

Cumulative net asset purchases by the ECB, 2015–2024

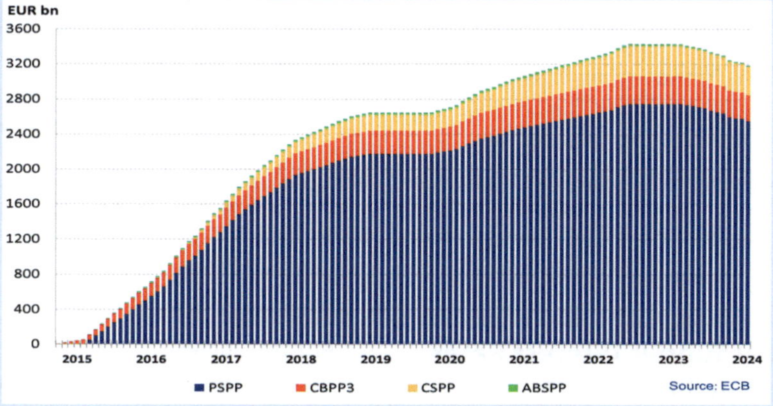

But given the scale and duration of these interventions, many observers, such as Jacques Ninet (2020), claim that the European financial system is being kept in a state of coma, on a drip-feed of ECB reserves. And while such interventions could be justified in a world of negative interest rates, the gradual rise in the deposit facility rate from 2019 onwards entrenches the payment of a central bank subsidy to commercial banks (through interest payments on deposit facility accounts)—without the banks being required to provide any economic, social or ecological counterpart. Finally, insofar as the ECB does not take into account the social and environmental impact of the issuers of the securities it carries on its balance sheet, the latter is far from exemplary… On a more positive note, such experiments have enabled some economists to imagine new monetary policy tools aligned with sustainable development objectives, such as "voluntary money" schemes or innovative monetary treatments of public debt (Dufrêne, 2023; Couppey-Soubeyran, Delandre & Sersiron, 2024) Sources:

Couppey-Soubeyran, J., Delandre, P., and Sersiron, A. (2024). *Le Pouvoir de la monnaie. Transformons la monnaie pour transformer la société*. Les Liens qui Libèrent, 400 p. (untranslated)

Dufrêne, N. (2023). *La Dette au xxie siècle. Comment s'en libérer*. Odile Jacob, 336 p. (untranslated)

Ninet, J. (2020). *Taux d'intérêt négatifs. Le trou noir du capitalisme financier.* Garnier, 272 p. (untranslated)

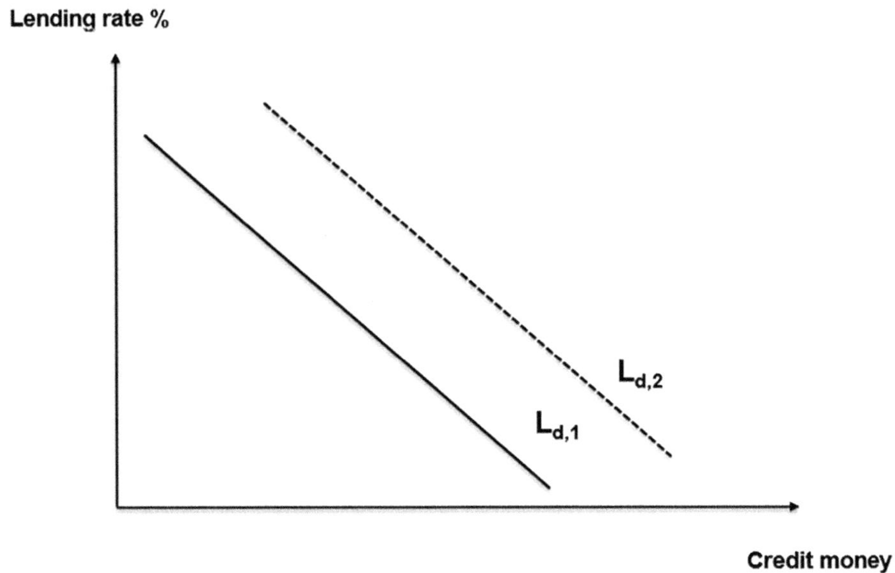

Fig. 5.5 The demand for credit money (*Note* it is important to differentiate between a variation in credit demand induced by a variation in the interest rate [movement along the line L_d] from a variation induced at a constant rate by a shock to expectations [displacement of the line L_d itself])

5.4 Money Supply, Interest Rates and Monetary Policy

In this section, we analyse the relationship between money supply, interest rates and monetary policy, using the famous *horizontal* model[1] developed by Canadian economist Basil Moore (1933–2018).

Applying for a Bank Loan

At the macroeconomic level, the demand for bank credit money (L_d) is a decreasing function of lending rates (r_L) A rise in interest rates increases the cost of borrowing (Fig. 5.5). For a given interest rate, however, demand for credit money evolves as a function of two other factors:

- Agents' expectations, linked to the rate of economic growth (ΔY): robust economic growth augurs future profits, stimulates the *animal spirits* of entrepreneurs, and increases demand for credit money;
- Expected inflation (π): if the general price level rises, the demand for credit money, which is expressed in nominal terms, will also increase, since more money will be needed to carry out planned investments (which are measured in real terms).

The demand for credit money can therefore be expressed by Eq. (5.2) (see Fig. 5.5):

$$L_d = L(i_L, \Delta Y, \pi\ ) \qquad (5.2)$$

Bank's Credit Money Supply

The supply of credit money is based on the interest rate (i_L). To determine this rate, banks add a mark-up to the rate at which they borrow reserves (i_{CB}). This is shown in Eq. (5.3):

$$i_L = [1 + \sigma + m(L)]i_{CB};\ m(L) > 0 \qquad (5.3)$$

[1] In fact, this model contains a horizontal line representing the evolution of the central bank's prime rate.

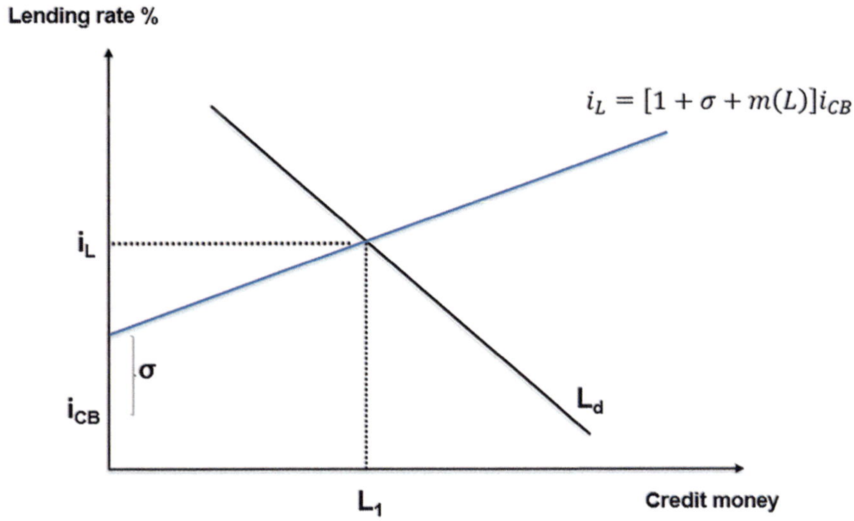

Fig. 5.6 Lending rate and credit money

The bank mark-up has two main components:

- the risk premium (σ): for a bank, holding a loan portfolio is riskier than holding reserves with the Central Bank. This risk premium fluctuates with the evolution of banks' liquidity preference;
- target margin rate $m(L)$: depending on its market power, each bank targets a unit profit (m) per loan granted. Moreover, this target rate tends to increase with the stock of loans (L) issued beforehand. This is because the quality of new borrowers tends to decline (as the macroeconomic debt-to-equity ratio increases). Banks hedge against this risk by increasing the target margin for each additional loan.

The flow of bank credit (L_1) is therefore located at the intersection of credit demand (L_d) and the lending rate (i_L)

The supply of credit money is therefore endogenous: it depends on the complex interactions between credit demand, bank behaviour and central bank decisions, which can modify the slope and intercept of the two curves shown in Fig. 5.6.

Prudential Regulation and the Central Bank

To describe the role of the Central Bank, it is necessary to incorporate several variables into the model. The complete list of equations is as follows:

$$L_d = L(i_L, Y, \pi) \tag{5.4}$$

$$i_L = [1 + \sigma + m(L)]i_{CB} \tag{5.5}$$

$$L_s = L_d \tag{5.6}$$

$$L_s + R = M \tag{5.7}$$

$$R = kM \tag{5.8}$$

$$H = R \tag{5.9}$$

We have already discussed Eqs. (5.4) and (5.5) in the previous section. Equation (5.6) is an equilibrium condition for the credit money market: the credit supply L_s is equal to the demand for credit L_d. Equation (5.7) breaks down the money supply M into two aggregates: bank deposits (L_s) and reserves (R).

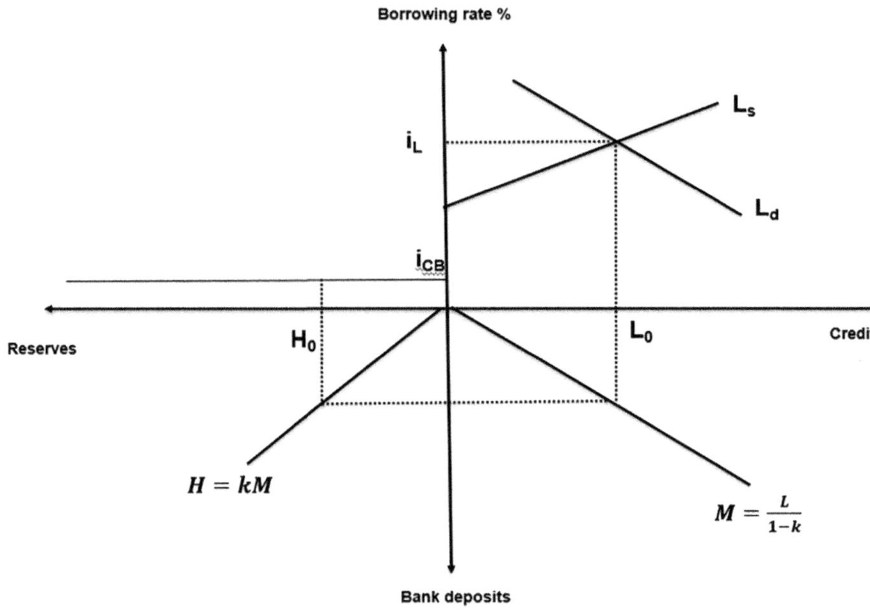

Fig. 5.7 The complete model

Equation (5.8) determines the demand for reserves R as the money supply (M) weighted by a parameter (k). The latter is a function of the reserve requirement ratio and the liquidity preference of the economy. Finally, Eq. (5.9) is the market equilibrium condition for bank reserves: the central bank's supply of reserve money (H) adjusts to the level required by the banks. It is then possible to determine the volume of credit money (L_s), total money supply (M), and reserve money (H), as shown in Eqs. (5.10) to (5.12):

$$L_s = L_d[[1 + \sigma + m(L)]r_F; Y; \pi] \quad (5.10)$$

$$M = \frac{L_s}{1-k} \quad (5.11)$$

$$H = kM = k\frac{L}{(1-k)} \quad (5.12)$$

The complete model is shown in Fig. 5.7.

Let us take a look at this model. The key rate (i_{CB}) set by the Central Bank is the anchor of the system. From Eq. (5.3), we can then determine the interest rate that banks charge their borrowers. This rate, interacting with the demand for credit (Eq. 5.2), determines the volume of bank credit and the total money supply (M), given the level of liquidity preference (k). During this process, the central bank accommodates the banks' demand for reserves (R) with a corresponding supply (H). In this model, the prime rate (i_{CB}) does not depend on the quantity of reserves in circulation, but on the Central Bank's discretionary choice (based on its mandate and economic conditions). This is why the line in the northwest quadrant is horizontal.

5.5 Conclusion

- Investors operate in an environment of *radical uncertainty*, with heterogeneous levels of *liquidity preference* that vary over time.
- The Central Bank oversees the interbank market and influences the structure of interest rates in line with its mandate. To this end, it has dedicated instruments at its disposal, including several interest rates and a collateral system.
- Interest rates depend on monetary policy, agents' expectations and banks' mark-up behaviour.

Activities

Questions for Discussion

Use the model presented in Sect. 4 to answer the following questions (all else being equal):

1. What is the impact of an increase in liquidity preference on the borrowing rate?
2. What impact does an increase in the economic growth rate have on the borrowing rate?
3. The central bank raises its prime rate. What impact should this policy have on interest rates and the money supply?
4. The central bank raises its prime rate, but the bank risk premium increases more than proportionally.
   a. How do interest rates react?
   b. How do monetary aggregates react?
5. Entrepreneurs anticipate strong growth due to rising property prices.
   a. How does the demand for money react?
   b. How do banks react?
   c. What do you think the central bank's reaction should be?
6. Discuss the following statement: "The Central Bank is the dominant player in the financial system."

Mini-Case: The ECB's Monetary Policy and the Sustainable Development Goals

Go to the European Central Bank's statistics site and construct a graph showing the daily evolution of its three key rates, as well as interbank rates. Interpret your results in the light of recent economic history.

Show the evolution of the volume of excess reserves held by banks on a diagram. Explain the relationship between excess reserves, the deposit facility rate and the interbank market rate.

Search and inspect the list of bonds held by the ECB as part of its *open market* operations. How could the ECB improve its contribution to the sustainable development goals?

Reference

Dow, A. C., & Dow, S. C. (1989). Endogenous monetary creation and idle balances. In J. Pheby (Ed.), *New directions inpost-keynesian economics* (pp. 147–164). Edward Elgar

Money, Debt, and the Public Deficit

6

Thomas Lagoarde-Ségot

Putting Things into Perspective

Achieving the sustainable development goals would require massive investment in excess of 100% of global GDP (Cingolani, 2022). However, more than half of these investments concern unprofitable public goods that cannot be produced by the private sector. This raises questions about the ability of national budgets to meet the necessary expenditure. Indeed, since 1980, the G7 countries have posted significant public deficits almost every year. Can a state perpetually accumulate debt? Can it go bankrupt? Does the current year's deficit add to the existing stock of public debt? How can the evolution of public debt be controlled? Such questions regularly surface in public debate, as they did during the eurozone sovereign debt crisis of the 2010s, or during the COVID-19 pandemic. The aim of this chapter is therefore to analyze the workings of public deficit and public debt.

Public budget balance as % of GDP in G7 countries, 1980–2019

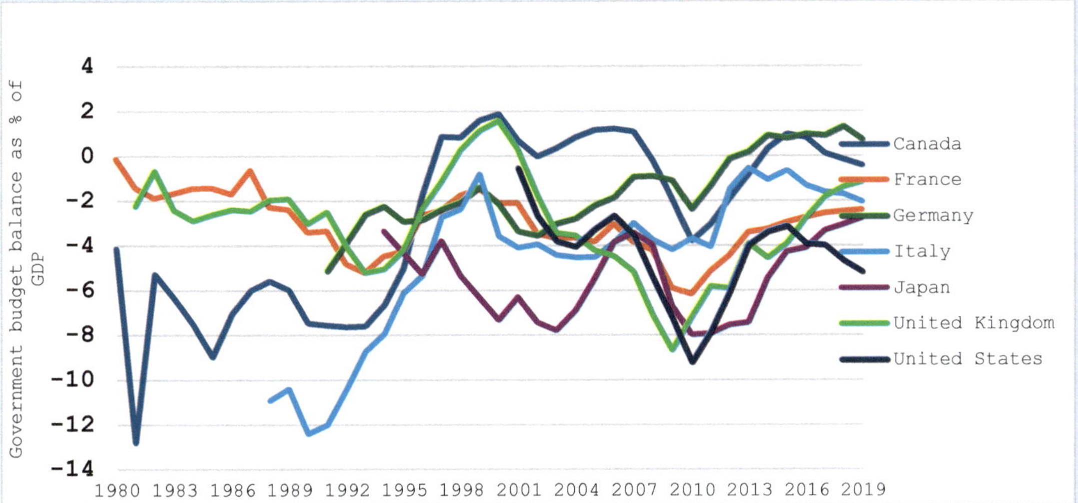

T. Lagoarde-Ségot (✉)
KEDGE BS & SDSN France, Talence, France
e-mail: thomas.lagoardesegot@kedgebs.com

T. Lagoarde-Ségot (ed.), *Ecological Economics and Finance*, https://doi.org/10.1007/978-3-031-71249-4_6

Source: https://www.imf.org/en/Data
Reference: Cingolani, M. (2022) Public and Private Financing of Sustainable Development Goals (SDGs), *Review of Political Economy*, https://doi.org/10.1080/09538259.2022.2063513.

Table 6.1 Two interconnected balance sheets

Household balance sheet at time *t*	
Assets	Liabilities
Tangible capital *Corporate bonds* Bank deposits	Bank loan Net wealth

Company balance sheet at time *t*	
Assets	Liabilities
Tangible assets Intangible assets Bank deposits	Bank loans *Corporate bonds* Shares Net wealth

Learning Objectives

- Situating the public deficit in a social accounting matrix
- Understanding the monetary dimension of sovereign bond issues
- Analyzing the dynamics of public debt

6.1 The Public Deficit Paradox

In the economy, the balance sheets of economic agents are interconnected: the revenues of some are the expenses of others, and the financial assets of some are the liabilities of others. These transactions are recorded in a single unit of account: money. For example, a corporate bond necessarily appears on the liabilities side of the balance sheet of the issuing company, and on the assets side of the balance sheet of its holder (see Table 6.1).

The principle of double-entry accounting enables national economic institutions to represent the macroeconomic situation in a system of national accounts, coordinated by the United Nations. Thus, social accounting matrices represent in a single table all the transactions carried out between the various economic agents grouped into institutional sectors (see Table 6.2).

Let us take a look at this table. The second column shows household incomes and payments. Income includes wages and salaries (*WB*), dividends (*Div*), interest earned on financial securities (INT_h). Expenditure includes consumption (*C*) and taxes (*T*). The difference between income and expenditure is household savings (SAV_h).

The third column shows revenues and payments of the corporate sector (including banks). Revenues from this sector include household consumption (*C*), government spending (*G*), and investment spending (*I*). Expenditure includes wages and salaries (*WB*), taxes (*T*), and interest

Table 6.2 A social accounting matrix

	Households	Financial and non-financial companies		Government	SUM
		Current account	Capital account		
Consumption (C)	$-C$	$+C$			0
Public expenditure (G)		$+G$		$-G$	0
Investment (I)		$+I$	$-I$		0
GDP (Y)		$[Y]$			
Wages (WB)	$+WB$	$-WB$			0
Profits (P)	$+Div$	$-P$	$+SAV_f$		0
Taxes (T)	$-T_h$	$-T_f$		$+T$	0
Interest payments (INT)	$+INT_h$	$-INT_f$		$-INT_g$	0
SUM	SAV_h	0	$SAV_f - I$	SAV_g	0

Source Godley and Lavoie (2012, p. 33)

paid on bonds (INT_f). The difference between revenues and payments is corporate profit (P). This is broken down into shareholder remuneration (dividends (Div)) and retained earnings (corporate savings (SAV_f)). The fourth column shows the investment financing constraint. The difference between capital expenditure (I) and corporate savings (SAV_f)) corresponds to their external financing requirement ($SAV_f - I_f$). The fifth column shows the government accounts: public expenditure (G), debt servicing (INT_g), and revenues (taxes (T)). Government savings (SAV_g) correspond to the government surplus (or deficit) at the end of the fiscal year. The sixth column contains the sums of sectoral accounting entries for each type of transaction. These sums are equal to zero since the expenditure of some is the revenue of others. Finally, the last row of the matrix expresses the accounting relationship between the sectoral balances. It verifies the macroeconomic identity between savings (SAV) and investment (I) (Eqs. 6.1 and 6.2).

$$SAV_h + (SAV_f - I) + SAV_g = 0 \quad (6.1)$$

$$\rightarrow I = SAV_f + SAV_h + SAV_g = SAV \quad (6.2)$$

Equation (6.2) can also be rewritten as follows:

$$\rightarrow (SAV_f - I) + SAV_h = -SAV_g = DEF \quad (6.3)$$

The public deficit ($-SAV_g = DEF$) is therefore the accounting counterpart of the sum of net household (SAV_h) and corporate savings ($SAV_f - I$). Equation (6.3) thus highlights the monetary dimension of fiscal policy:

- When the public balance shows a deficit ($DEF > 0$), the financial wealth of the private sector increases by the same amount. (($SAV_f - I) + SAV_h > 0$). The government puts money into circulation, as well as the full range of sovereign securities (short-term Treasury bills, term bonds), which are credited to the assets of the private sector. The money supply then tends to increase.
- When the public balance shows a surplus ($DEF < 0$), private financial wealth falls by the same amount (($SAV_f - I) + SAV_h < 0$). Bank deposits and reserves are withdrawn from circulation, and sovereign securities (short-term Treasury bills, term bonds) are destroyed. The money supply tends to contract.
- When the public balance is balanced ($DEF = 0$), private sector net wealth is unchanged (($SAV_f - I) + SAV_h = 0$). Households and companies cannot simultaneously grow richer, since every new asset must have an accounting counterpart in the private sector: (($SAV_f - I) = -SAV_h$ (see Box 6.1).

Box 6.1: Assets Internal to the Private Sector

In most developed economies, households are net creditors and accumulate financial assets corresponding to the liabilities issued by companies. While this observation is true at the macroeconomic level, it can mask significant disparities. In France, for example, 55% of financial and real estate assets are held by the richest 10%. As shown by Thomas Piketty's *World Inequality database*, the rate of return on capital tends to settle naturally at much higher levels than the rate of increase in wages. In the U.S., a significant proportion of households are thus forced to take on debt to make ends meet, or to finance their children"s education, potentially generating major risks for banking stability (as demonstrated by the 2008 crisis).

Source https://wid.world/world/

The recurrent tendency of governments to run public deficits can therefore be partly explained by their monetary function. If we disregard international trade (see Chapter 9), the net wealth of the private sector can have only one counterpart liability: that of the State. By creating a situation of relative monetary abundance, the public deficit therefore enables the constitution of net private savings, and thus helps maintain economic and financial stability (see Box 6.2).

Box 6.2: Budget Rules: The MMT Perspective

Based on this observation, *Modern Money Theory* (MMT) economists, such as German economist Dirk Ehnts (b. 1977), recommend the complete abandonment of budgetary rules, such as the one requiring eurozone member states to keep their deficits below 3% of GDP. Indeed, these budget targets are rarely reached, given the random nature of tax revenues and public spending (which depend on economic activity that the government cannot control). For these economists, it would be wiser to consider the public balance as a simple statistical residual, measuring the annual evolution of the private sector's net financial wealth. This change of perspective would give an additional degree of freedom to fiscal policies, which could target variables that are far more fundamental to the economy (inflation rate, unemployment, external balance, etc.).

Source Ehnts, D., 2017. *Modern Monetary Theory and European Macroeconomics.* Routledge International Studies in Money and Banking, Oxon, UK.

Table 6.3 Issuing of a green sovereign bond, stage 1

Banque de France	
Δ Assets	Δ Liabilities
Reserve loan: + 100	Banking sector reserves: + 100
Banking sector	
Δ Assets	Δ Liabilities
Reserves: + 100	Central bank loan: + 100

Table 6.4 Issuing of a green sovereign bond, stage 2

Banque de France	
Δ Assets	Δ Liabilities
Reserve loan: + 100	~~Banking sector reserves: + 100~~ Treasury reserves + 100
Banking sector	
Δ Assets	Δ Liabilities
~~Reserves: + 100~~ Green sovereign bond: + 101	Central bank loan: + 100 *Net wealth: + 1*
Treasury	
Δ Assets	Δ Liabilities
Reserves: + 100	Green sovereign bond: + 101 *Net wealth: −1*

These mechanisms may seem disconcerting because they contradict our microeconomic intuition. Yet macroeconomic analysis does not consist of a set of microeconomic relationships that can simply be extrapolated to a more aggregate level. In economics, as in nature, the whole is more than the sum of its parts.

6.2 Public Deficit and Monetary Operations

Let us take a closer look at how the public deficit affects monetary and financial transactions. Let us consider the issue of a green sovereign bond (*OAT verte*) by the French government to finance the development of organic farming within the framework of the Paris Agreements. We will also assume that the value of this green sovereign bond at issue is equal to 100, and that its interest rate is 1%.

Article 123 of the Lisbon Treaty prohibits eurozone central banks from directly financing public investments.[1] The French Treasury therefore contacts—via the *Agence France Trésor* in charge of public debt management—the network of primary dealers (*spécialistes en valeur du Trésor*). This network brings together French and foreign institutions selected by the Minister of the Economy to participate in primary issues of French government bonds.[2] The operation may take the following form: a bank first borrows from the Banque de France the reserves needed to purchase the green sovereign bond at a rate of 0% (see Table 6.3).

[1] In other monetary systems (USA, Canada, Japan, Sweden, UK), such a transaction would be possible, without affecting our conclusions.

[2] See https://www.aft.gouv.fr/fr/presentation-svt.

Table 6.5 Issuing of a green sovereign bond, stage 3

Banque de France	
Δ Assets	Δ Liabilities
~~Reserve loan: + 100~~	~~Treasury reserves + 100~~ ~~Banking sector reserves: + 100~~
Treasury	
Δ Assets	Δ Liabilities
~~Reserves: + 100~~	Green sovereign bond: + 101 *Net wealth: −101*
Banking sector	
Δ Assets	Δ Liabilities
~~Reserves: + 100~~ Green sovereign bond: + 101	~~Central bank loan: + 100~~ Deposit: 100 *Net wealth: + 1*
Non-banking private sector	
Δ Assets	Δ Liabilities
Bank deposit: + 100	*Net wealth: + 100*

The bank then transfers these reserves to the Treasury's account at the Banque de France. In return, the Treasury recognizes a debt owed to the bank, equal in value to the principal and interest on the green sovereign bond. The interest receivable on the green sovereign bond increases the net wealth of the banking sector, and correspondingly reduces that of the Treasury (see Table 6.4).

The Treasury then uses these reserves to acquire new bank deposits. During this transaction, the banking sector records reserves on the assets side of its balance sheet, and credits the Treasury with new deposits. The latter then immediately transfers these deposits via a special vehicle (e.g., the "Fonds Avenir Bio") to the bank account of an organic farm meeting the specifications of the green sovereign bond. This is why the deposits appear as assets of the non-banking private sector (and not the Treasury) in Table 6.5. The banking sector is then in a position to repay its loan to the Banque de France. The reserves issued during the first stage (see Table 6.3) thus flow back into the central bank's balance sheet, and are destroyed.

The net wealth of the non-banking private sector increases by an amount equal to the value of newly created bank deposits (100 euros). The net wealth of the banking sector is increased by the value of interest at maturity on the green sovereign bond (1 euro). This net wealth finds its counterpart in the Treasury balance sheet, which shows a deficit (equal to 101 euros) (see Table 6.5).

An examination of the consolidated balance sheets of the private and public sectors confirms this result (see Table 6.6). The increase in the private sector's net financial wealth, broken down into the non-banking and banking sectors, is the exact accounting counterpart of the public deficit, as Eq. (6.3) shows.

Let us summarize the various steps in this transaction chain:

- The banking sector borrows new reserves issued by the Central Bank (see Table 6.3).
- The banking sector exchanges these reserves for a new green sovereign bond issued by the Treasury (see Table 6.4).
- The Treasury exchanges the reserves for new bank deposits (see Table 6.5).
- The Treasury passes on these bank deposits to the non-bank private sector (see Table 6.5).
- The banking sector returns the reserves to the Central Bank, which then destroys them (see Table 6.5).

Issuing this green sovereign bond involves a series of monetary operations in which the State,

Table 6.6 Consolidated balance sheets for the private and public sectors

Private sector balance sheet		Public sector balance sheet	
Δ Assets	Δ Liabilities	Δ Assets	Δ Liabilities
Deposit: + 100 (organic farm) Green sovereign bond: + 101 (banking sector)	Deposit: + 100 (bank) **Net wealth: + 101**		Green sovereign bond: + 101 (Treasury) **Net wealth: − 101**

in its capacity as issuer of money, increases the net financial wealth of the private sector.

A public deficit therefore constitutes an injection of monetary wealth, enabling the *creation* of new bank deposits, held by the non-banking private sector as a new net asset.[3] These deposits are backed by a new liquid financial instrument (the green sovereign bond) held by the banking sector, whose anticipated interest increases its net wealth.

Sovereign bonds outstanding on the markets constitute public debt. Regular payments to the financial institutions holding these securities (whose maturity rarely exceeds 30 years) involve a transfer of wealth, via the government budget, from taxpayers to the financial sector. Tax policy can therefore have indirect effects on income distribution. The currency in which the debt is denominated, the central bank's interest rate policy and the markets' perception of the quality of the government's credit rating influence these distributional effects, among others.

Finally, until the 1970s, governments frequently printed money to finance their net expenditures (see Box 6.3). The central bank credited the Treasury with new reserves, which the latter exchanged for new bank deposits. The increase in the monetary base (M0) then frequently pushed down interbank market rates, limiting the central bank's autonomy. The development of sovereign securities markets in the 1980s made it possible to back up public deficits with a mechanism for refluxing reserves into the central bank's balance sheet (see Table 6.5). This sterilization of the monetary base now makes it easier for the central bank to conduct an autonomous monetary policy.

Box 6.3: American Financing of the "Arsenal for Democracy," 1942–1945

Whereas the European belligerents had financed the First World War mainly by raising taxes and borrowing abroad (leading to the monetary disorder of the 1920s), the United States financed the Second World War's Arsenal for Democracy via an innovative collaboration between the US Treasury and the Federal Reserve. The Treasury issued as many war bonds as were needed to finance military spending. For its part, the Federal Reserve credited the banks with the reserves needed to acquire these bonds (large quantities of which it bought itself). This cooperation kept the cost of financing the American military effort very low, by fixing the interest rate on short- and long-term Treasury bonds at 0.375% and 2.5% respectively. These war bond issues led to a rapid increase in US military spending, which rose from a few hundred million dollars a year before the war, to $85 billion in 1943, then $91 billion in 1944, or 45% of US GDP. Since most of this spending was in dollars, the American economy recovered rapidly after the war, unhampered by the burden of foreign debt

[3] The widespread idea that the public deficit is a borrowing from the private sector's existing stock of savings—preventing the latter from making its own investments through a crowding-out effect—is therefore erroneous.

Understanding the Dynamics of Public Debt

The evolution of public debt is one of the economic ratios most commented on in the financial press, with fears of government bankruptcy regularly recurring in public debate (see Box 6.4). On a scientific level, however, the American economist James Galbraith (b. 1952) has made a major contribution to our understanding of the dynamics of public debt. As Eq. (6.4) shows, the volume of public debt D for the current fiscal year (t) is equal to the principal of the debt inherited from previous periods, plus the interest due on this stock of debt (r), and minus the value of the public budget balance (P) (i.e., the difference between tax revenues and public spending).

$$D_t = (1 + r)D_{t-1} - P_t \quad (6.4)$$

Public debt is expressed as a proportion of GDP. If we denote GDP by the letter Y, we obtain Eq. (6.5):

$$\frac{D_t}{Y_t} = (1 + r)\frac{D_{t-1}}{Y_t} - \frac{P_t}{Y_t} \quad (6.5)$$

We now denote the annual growth rate of GDP, expressed as a percentage (from year t—1 to year t) by the letter g. The value of GDP in year (t) is therefore equal to that of the previous year, multiplied by $(1+g)$:

$$Y_t = (1 + g)Y_{t-1} \quad (6.6)$$

By inserting Eq. (6.6) into Eq. (6.5), we obtain Eq. (6.7). To simplify writing, we denote each variable expressed as a proportion of GDP by a lower-case letter. This gives us Eq. (6.8).

$$\frac{D_t}{Y_t} = \frac{(1 + r)}{(1 + g)}\frac{D_{t-1}}{Y_{t-1}} - \frac{P_t}{Y_t} \quad (6.7)$$

$$d_t = \frac{(1 + r)}{(1 + g)}d_{t-1} - p_t \quad (6.8)$$

By moving (p_t) to the left of Eq. (6.8), we can then express the annual budget balance as follows:

$$p_t = \frac{(1 + r)}{(1 + g)}d_{t-1} - d_t \quad (6.9)$$

Equation (6.9) shows that the value of the public budget balance (p_t) depends on the average interest rate on the stock of debt (r) the economic growth rate (g) and the stock of public debt observed in the current year (d_{t-1}) and in the previous year (d_{t-1}). It thus appears that fiscal policy alone is unable to control the value of this balance, which depends on other exogenous variables.

By letting $d_{t-1} = d_t$ in Eq. (6.9), it is now possible to calculate the value of the public balance (p_t^*) compatible with stabilizing the stock of public debt:

$$p_t^* = \frac{(1 + r)}{(1 + g)}d_{t-1} - d_{t-1} \quad (6.10)$$

$$p_t^* = \frac{(1 + r)}{(1 + g)}d_{t-1} - \frac{(1 + g)}{(1 + g)}d_{t-1} \quad (6.11)$$

$$p_t^* = \frac{(r - g)}{(1 + g)}d_{t-1} \quad (6.12)$$

Since the economic growth rate (g) rarely exceeds 5%, the latter equation can be approximated by:

$$p_t^* = (r - g)d_{t-1} \quad (6.13)$$

Equation (6.13) shows the approximate value of the public balance (p_t^*) required to stabilize public debt. Thus:

- A public deficit ($p_t<0$) can stabilize public debt if the interest rate (r) is lower than the economic growth rate (g). In this case $(r - g) < 0$ and $p_t^*<0$.
- A public budget surplus ($p_t>0$) is necessary to stabilize public debt if the interest rate (r) exceeds the economic growth rate (g). Indeed, in this case, $(r - g) > 0$ and $p_t^*>0$. However, if the budget balance settles at p_t such that $0<p_t<p_t^*$, public debt increases despite the presence of a budget surplus.

The evolution of public debt therefore depends on fiscal policy, but also on exogenous macroeconomic conditions (the interest rate and the rate of economic growth).

If the rate of economic growth exceeds the interest rate, the level of public debt tends to stabilize automatically, without the need to adjust taxes or public spending. When the public deficit stimulates private consumption and investment, GDP (g) increases, as do tax revenues. The resulting rise in private financial wealth fuels demand for sovereign bonds, pushing down the interest rate (r). Taken together, these factors can mechanically stabilize debt levels. This favorable context was observed in most Western countries between 1945 and 1970.

If, on the other hand, banks are reluctant to acquire new sovereign bonds, the Treasury may be forced to raise the interest rate (r). To please financial markets, the government can certainly cut public spending and raise taxes. However, if such a policy of fiscal austerity reduces the rate of economic growth (g), the debt ratio tends to rise (if $(r - g) > 0$). This can set off a spiral of austerity, recession, and debt. Greece had bitter experience of this during the decade 2010–2020.

Box 6.4: Can a State go Bankrupt?

Historical examples of public debt defaults are usually the manifestation of deeper political and institutional crises (e.g., the Russian Revolution of 1917). Indeed, markets readily acknowledge that under a floating exchange rate regime, a government that finances itself in its own currency is not exposed to the risk of insolvency or illiquidity. This is because the State can roll over its debt by issuing new securities to repay—and destroy—the old ones. With a public debt/GDP ratio of 261%, Japan could issue long-dated sovereign bonds (40 years) at the very low rate of 1.8% in 2023. However, the situation is quite different when a government borrows in a foreign currency, or when it guarantees the convertibility of its currency into a foreign currency. Such a state loses its privilege of issuing currency. This was the case, for example, with Argentina in 2001. This country had "irrevocably" fixed the value of the peso in U.S. dollars in 1991, and defaulted ten years later with a moderate public debt-to-GDP ratio (48%). Historical studies have shown that foreign currency loans increase the risk of sovereign default. We can also classify monetary regimes in ascending order according to the degree of fiscal freedom they grant the government: dollarization, currency board, fixed exchange rate regime, and finally floating exchange rate regime.

Source Reinart, C. and Rogoff, K., 2009. *This time is different. Eight centuries of financial folly*. Princeton University Press, 463 pp.

6.3 Conclusion

- Without taking foreign trade into account, the net financial wealth of the private sector mirrors the public deficit.
- Sovereign bond issues involve a series of monetary and financial operations involving the Treasury, the private banking sector, the private non-banking sector, and the Central Bank.
- The evolution of the public debt ratio depends on four main factors: public spending, tax revenues, interest rates, and the rate of economic growth.

Activities

Questions for discussion

1. Over the course of a calendar year, implementing a public investment plan approved by Parliament requires spending in excess of tax revenues.

a. How can a country like France finance this deficit?
b. Break down the impact of a sovereign bond issue on the balance sheets of the parties involved.
c. What is the impact on private sector savings?
d. What is the impact on the monetary base?
e. What financial risks would such a transaction entail?

2. Go to the Bank of Japan website. Download historical data on the evolution of public debt and interest rates between 2000 and 2020, and show them on a graph. How can you explain the dynamics observed?
3. The famous concept of the 'crowding-out effect' (or 'Ricardian equivalence') postulates that public deficit financing diverts the allocation of savings from private investment to the public sector. Do you think this mechanism accurately describes the workings of a modern monetary system?
4. Download from the Internet the most recent value of the debt ratio (public debt/GDP) for the country of your choice. Then calculate the value of the public balance (as a percentage of GDP) compatible with stabilizing the debt ratio in the following scenarios:
   i. The economic growth rate is 5% and the interest rate on Treasury bonds is 1%.
   ii. The economic growth rate is 1% and the interest rate on Treasury bonds is 5%.
   iii. Do you think that tax policy can help target the public debt ratio? Why or why not?
5. Visit the *Agence France Trésor* website and analyze the French public debt market by answering these three questions:
   a. Present the latest trends in public debt markets: new issues, yields, average maturities, types of holders, market liquidity…
   b. What are the main issuance methods used by *Agence France Trésor*? What role do primary dealers play in this process?
   c. Describe the process for issuing a green sovereign bond. Compare its interest rate with that of a corporate bond of equivalent maturity. Which of these two financial instruments seems to be considered riskier by the financial markets? Why or why not?
6. Study the article Historical Patterns and Dynamics of Public Debt-Evidence From a New Database published in the *International Monetary Fund* (IMF) *Economic Review* in 2011. Then answer the following questions:
   a. Focus on lines 5, 6, 7, and 8 of Table 6.1 (p. 734). For each line, calculate the percentage of the observed reduction in public debt due to an increase in the budget surplus and the percentage due to a change in the growth-interest rate differential, respectively. Present your results in a table.
   b. What can we learn from the previous question about macroeconomic levers for stabilizing public debt? What are the implications for contemporary debates on the evolution of public debt?

References

Cingolani, M. (2022). Public and private financing of sustainable development goals (SDGs). *Review of Political Economy*.https://doi.org/10.1080/09538259.2022.2063513

Godley, W., & Lavoie, M. (2012). *Monetary economics: An integrated approach to credit, money, income, production and wealth* (2nd ed., p. 530). Palgrave-Macmillan.

Introduction to Ecological Macroeconomic Modeling

7

Thomas Lagoarde-Ségot

Putting Things into Perspective

Shortly after the 2008 financial crisis, Greece fell victim to speculative attacks on its sovereign debt. Faced with the risk of the eurozone breaking up, some economists (such as Nobel Prize winner Paul Krugman and Greek Economy Minister Yanis Varoufakis) recommended protecting economic growth, and sharing the burden of relief between creditors and debtors. Others—mainly representatives of the *Troika* (the European Commission, the International Monetary Fund, and the European Central Bank) and the banking sector—instead demanded fiscal austerity (tax hikes, spending cuts) to restore the confidence of financial markets. At the time, the International Monetary Fund's macroeconomic model predicted that fiscal austerity would be painless in macroeconomic terms. This strategy therefore prevailed. The unfortunate result was an unprecedented rise in unemployment (particularly among young people), and a lost economic decade for Greece.

Sometime later, Olivier Blanchard, the IMF's chief economist, recognized that the institution's macroeconomic model was based on obsolete data, and had largely underestimated the impact of fiscal policy on economic growth. Indeed, in this model the value of multipliers was "too low by about one point" (Blanchard and Leight, 2013, p. 4).

In this way, modeling helped to justify decisions that turned out to be disastrous in retrospect. This example reminds us that, while models can help set the parameters for democratic debate, they should not replace it.

Source Blanchard, O.J., Leight, D., 2013. "Growth forecast errors and fiscal multipliers". *International Monetary Fund Working Paper* No. 2013/001.

Learning Objectives

- Understand the importance of modeling in economics
- Building a miniature ecological macroeconomic model
- Simulating the economic and climatic effects of monetary dynamics

7.1 The Challenges of Economic Modeling

In economics, as in the sciences, modeling simplifies a complex reality and enables us to reach deductive conclusions that are not obvious from

T. Lagoarde-Ségot (✉)
KEDGE BS & SDSN France, Talence, France
e-mail: thomas.lagoardesegot@kedgebs.com

T. Lagoarde-Ségot (ed.), *Ecological Economics and Finance*, https://doi.org/10.1007/978-3-031-71249-4_7

observation. Admittedly, the map is not the territory, but if the map is clear enough and we know how to interpret it, it can help us get our bearings. Economists use mainly mathematical models, econometric models, or macroeconometric models that combine these two approaches (such as the forecasting models used by central banks or government ministries).

Of course, modelers try to approximate reality. But the more complex the model, the less reliable the estimate, and the more difficult it is to interpret. And beyond a certain threshold of complexity, modeling loses its interest (see Box 7.1). What's more, a model is built on assumptions that affect its conclusions. One such assumption is that the economic world is governed by stable laws of causality. However, some economists (such as the Austrian Friedrich Von Hayek, 1899–1992) assert that, in reality, the parameters defining the relationships between economic variables, as well as the structure of these relationships, are highly unstable. While modeling is an indispensable tool, it must be used with caution—and humility.

Box 7.1: The Paradox of the Perfect Map

A model can be compared to a map of the economy. Every geographer knows that drawing a perfect map (on a scale of 1:1) would be both impossible and pointless. Indeed, such a map would cover the territory it is supposed to represent.

In this empire, the art of cartography was pushed to such perfection that the map of a single province occupied an entire city, and the map of the Empire an entire province. In time, these excessive maps ceased to give satisfaction, and the colleges of cartographers produced a map of the Empire, which had the format of the Empire and coincided with it, point by point. Subsequent generations, less keen on the study of cartography, found this dilated map useless and, not without impiety, abandoned it to the inclemency of sun and winter. In the deserts of the west, ruins of the map remain. Animals and beggars inhabit them. Throughout the country, there is no longer any trace of geographical disciplines.

Source On the rigor of science (Del rigor en la ciencia), Jorge Luis Borges, 1946.

7.2 SIM-E: Principles and Assumptions

In this chapter, we present the SIM-E model (the *SIMplest Ecological model*). In line with the principles of Chapter 1, SIM-E describes the joint evolution of the economy and the Earth system in a simplified framework (see Fig. 7.1).

SIM-E is a *theoretical* model that borrows from two other models well known to economists:

- the SIM model (*SIMplest model*) developed by Marc Lavoie (b. 1954) and Wynne Godley (1926–2010) in 2012;
- the DEFINE-CLIMATE model, one of the first ecological macroeconomic models developed by Yanis Dafermos, Giorgos Galanis, and Maria Nikolaidi in 2018.

In addition, SIM-E belongs to the category of stock-flow consistent (SFC) models. This category of model employs a consistent accounting architecture, in which each macroeconomic flow (e.g. a purchase) gives rise to an opposite entry (e.g. a sale) in another sector. Then, at the end of each period, the financial result obtained by

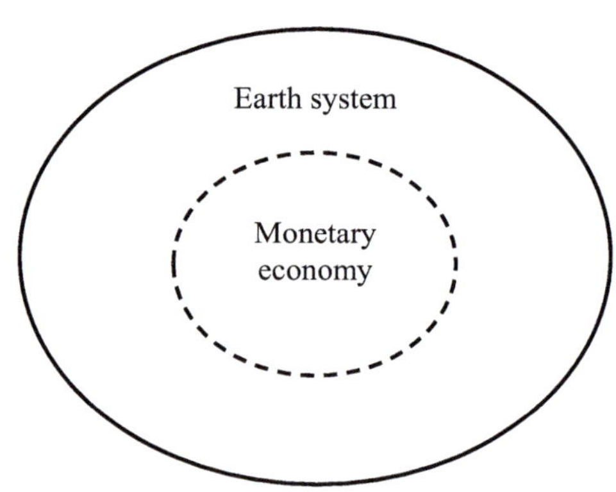

Fig. 7.1 An ecological macroeconomic model

each sector induces an equivalent variation in its financial wealth, with an opposite counterpart on the balance sheet of another sector. This approach allows for the complete integration of the real and financial spheres in macroeconomic analysis (see Box 7.2).

Box 7.2: SFC Modeling and Monetary "Piping"

In an SFC model, each sector can be compared to a piece of plumbing through which money, not water, flows. If someone turns on the spending tap, money flows into the sink (the balance sheet). If this flow is too great, a stock of money (savings) will accumulate in the sink. If the tap closes, the sink empties and the money moves to another sector (the siphon under the sink). Finally, for a certain ratio between the flow of money and the diameter of the sink, money circulates, but the accumulated stock in each sector is stable (the economy is in a stationary state).

SIM-E is not intended to be used for forecasting purposes. It is a tool for refining our understanding of the dynamic mechanisms of money creation, in relation to the earth system. SIM-E therefore locks in (without ignoring) several aspects of reality. The model's simplifying assumptions are as follows:

1. The model represents the world's economy.
2. Production is handled by individual agents.
3. Producers don't build up inventories.
4. There is no banking sector or financial markets.
5. The government's budget constraint fully modulates the money supply.
6. Supply adjusts immediately to demand.
7. Climate-related destruction only affects household consumption.

7.3 The Economic Side

SFC models represent the balance sheets of the various sectors of the economy in matrix form. Each financial asset held by a sector has a counterpart—a liability—on the balance sheet of one (or more) other sector(s). The balance sheet matrix of the SIM-E model is very simple, since it includes only one financial asset: money, designated by the letter (H). Money takes the form of coins and banknotes issued by the State, and due in payment of taxes.

Table 7.1 End-of-year balance sheets

	1. Households	2. Companies	3. Government	SUM
Money supply	H^{ASSET}	0	$-H^{LIABILITY}$	0

Table 7.2 Social accounting matrix

		1. Households	2. Companies	3. Government	4. SUM
Real sector	1. Consumption	− C	+ C		0
	2. Public expenditure		$+G$	$-G$	0
	3. GDP		$[Y]$		
	4. Wages	+ W.*N*	− W.*N*		0
	5. Taxes	$-T$		$+T$	0
Financial sector	6. Change in money stock	$-\Delta H^{ASSET}$		$+\Delta H^{LIABILITY}$	0
	7. SUM	0	0	0	0

Note (+) indicates a source of wealth, (-) a use of wealth. The symbol (Δ) describes a change between the beginning and end of the period under consideration, i.e. a flow: $\Delta H = H - H_{-1}$

Source Godley, W., Lavoie, M., 2012. *Monetary Economics. An integrated Approach to Credit, Money, Income, Production, and Wealth.* Second Edition. Palgrave Macmillan, UK

Money supply (H)—the only financial asset in the model—is recorded on the assets side of the private sector balance sheet. It represents the stock of savings accumulated over time. Since households are, by assumption, the owners of companies, money supply does not appear on the latter's balance sheet. Instead, it is recorded on the liabilities side of the government balance sheet (see Chapter 6) (see Table 7.1).

To understand how balance sheets are drawn up at the end of the year, it is necessary to reconstruct all the annual flows of expenditure and income. These flows are described in Table 7.2, which presents a social accounting matrix inspired by national accounting.

Lines 1 to 5 of Table 7.2 represent all transactions between sectors in a given year. For the sake of consistency, each accounting entry in one sector is matched by a corresponding entry in another sector. This is why the sum of each line is zero (column 4). Households therefore receive wages (+ $W.N$) paid by companies ($-W.N$). W represents the hourly wage and N the number of hours worked. Households spend part of their wages on goods and services ($-C$), which corresponds to income for companies (+ C). The State acquires goods and services from the private sector through public spending ($-G$). This expenditure is a source of income for companies (+ G). The State levies taxes (+ T) paid by households ($-T$). Line 6, shaded in gray, describes the variation in each sector's balance sheet at the end of the year. The symbol (Δ) describes the change in the stock of money between the beginning and end of the period under consideration, i.e. $\Delta H = H - H_{-1}$.

Since each transaction appears on the balance sheets of both sectors (with an opposite sign), the variation in the balance sheet of a given sector, at the end of the year, has as its counterpart an opposite variation in the balance sheet of the rest of the economy. If, for example, households don't spend all their wages, they accumulate savings (in the form of money). $\left(\Delta H^{ASSET}\right)$. The counterpart of this new savings is a public deficit $\left(\Delta H^{LIABILITY}\right)$. This brings us back to the public deficit paradox discussed in Chapter 6. Equation (7.1) (corresponding to line 6) shows that private sector savings $\left(\Delta S = \Delta H^{ASSET}\right)$ is the accounting counterpart of the public deficit:

$$\Delta S + \Delta H^{LIABILITY} = 0 \tag{7.1}$$

Row 3 of the matrix contains the gross domestic product (Y). In national accounting, GDP is equal to the final expenditure and total income distributed in the economy. Thus, column 2 verifies that $Y = C + G = W.N$. Table 7.2 forms the accounting backbone of the model. It contains accounting identities that will be verified in all simulations.

We now write the model by defining its accounting and behavioral equations. Each variable has a suffix to interpret the transaction: d (demand) or s (supply). The first four equations represent equilibrium conditions:

$$C_s = C_d \tag{7.2}$$

$$G_s = G_d \tag{7.3}$$

$$T_s = T_d \tag{7.4}$$

$$N_s = N_d \tag{7.5}$$

These equations imply that, over a given period, the supply of goods and services (Eqs. 7.2 and 7.3), taxes (Eq. 7.4), and labor (Eq. 7.5) adjust to the level of demand. Equation (7.4) represents the labor market, in which firms obtain the quantity of labor demanded regardless of the wage offered. These equations reflect a demand-driven economy. The other equations are as follows:

$$Y_D = W.N_s - T_S \tag{7.6}$$

$$T_D = \theta.W.N_s; 0 < \theta < 1 \tag{7.7}$$

$$C_D = \alpha_1.Y_D + \alpha_2.H_{d-1} - d_t (0 < \alpha_2 < \alpha_1 < 1) \tag{7.8}$$

$$\Delta H_s = H_s - H_{s-1} = G_D - T_D \tag{7.9}$$

$$\Delta H_d = H_d - H_{d-1} = YD - C_D \tag{7.10}$$

$$Y = C_s + G_s \tag{7.11}$$

$$Y = W.N_d \leftrightarrow N_d = \frac{Y}{W} \tag{7.12}$$

Equation (7.6) indicates that disposable income (YD) is equal to payroll, net of taxes. Equation (7.7) indicates that taxes are (T) are proportional to household income (θ) . The tax rate ($0 < \theta < 1$) is an exogenous parameter (chosen by the government). Equation (7.8) indicates that the level of household consumption (C_D) depends on their disposable income (YD) (through the parameter α_1) and the stock of available savings (H_{d-1}) (through parameter α_2). The total level of consumption, however, decreases with climate-related destruction (d_t).

Equations (7.9) and (7.10) are taken from Table 7.2. Equation (7.9) shows that the change in money supply (ΔH_s) is equal to the difference between public spending (G_d) and taxes (T_d). Equation (7.10) shows that the variation in annual household savings (ΔH_d) is equal to the difference between disposable income (YD) and consumption (C_D).

Equation (7.11) defines GDP (Y) as the sum of spending in the economy. Finally, Eq. (7.12) deduces the demand for hours worked (N_d) from the ratio of GDP and hourly wages.

The economic block thus takes the form of a system of 11 equations with 11 unknowns: $Y, YD, T_d, T_s, H_s, H_h, G_s, C_s, C_d, N_s, N_d$. This system produces a unique solution for each possible combination of values.

The model also includes three exogenous variables: public spending (G_d), the tax rate (θ) and hourly wages (W). The consumption function depends on two parameters: α_1, and α_2 which relate the level of macroeconomic consumption to disposable income and accumulated wealth, respectively.

Given the accounting consistency of the model, the equality between public deficit and annual private sector savings, $\Delta H_d = \Delta H_s$ (shown in row 6 of Table 7.2) can be verified without the need for an explicit equation. The public deficit paradox (Eq. 7.1) thus results from the model's accounting structure.

7.4 The ecosystem

This economic system is linked to the earth system by Eqs. (7.13) to (7.18). Equation (7.13) expresses the annual energy required for production E (measured in exajoules) as a function of annual GDP (via a parameter ε).

Equations (7.14) and (7.15) break down energy consumption into (E) into fossil energy (E_f) and renewable energy (E_r) through a parameter (μ) measuring the share of renewables in the energy mix. Equation (7.16) indexes industrial CO_2 emissions to fossil energy consumption using a parameter (ω). This parameter measures the carbon intensity of the economy, i.e. the quantity of industrial emissions produced by the consumption of an exajoule of non-renewable energy. Equation (7.17) calculates the stock of industrial CO_2 emissions accumulated in the atmosphere. Equation (7.18) relates atmospheric temperature to carbon emissions as a function of a parameter (τ). Finally, Eq. (7.19) defines climatic destruction (d_t) as an exponential function of climate disruption, measured by the difference between observed temperatures in the current year ($T_{at,t}$) and the temperatures that would have been observed in the absence of industrial carbon emissions since the simulation began ($T_{at,0}$).

$$E = \varepsilon Y \tag{7.13}$$

$$E_f = (1 - \mu)E \tag{7.14}$$

$$E_r = \mu E \tag{7.15}$$

$$EMIS = \omega E_f \tag{7.16}$$

$$CO2_{cum} = CO2_{cum,-1} + EMIS \tag{7.17}$$

$$T_{at} = T_{at,-1} + \tau.EMIS \tag{7.18}$$

$$d_t = e^{T_{at,t} - T_{at,0}} \tag{7.19}$$

7.5 Simulations

The model is so simple that it can easily be implemented in Excel. We will describe two simulations. In a first reference scenario, we will analyze economic and monetary dynamics without taking the ecosystem into account. In a second scenario, we will activate the ecosystem block to observe interactions between the economy and the Earth system. In both cases, we'll start from an economy where nothing has been produced (Y = 0), and we'll launch the simulation with a net public expenditure.

Macroeconomic Dynamics

By setting the tax rate (Eq. 7.7) at 20% and the value of the consumption function parameters (Eq. 7.8) α_1 and α_2 at 60% and 40% respectively, macroeconomic dynamics can be described as follows.

Let's assume that the government spends 20 by issuing cash recorded as a liability on its balance sheet, and recorded as income on that of the private sector. Households pay a tax of 20% on this income, i.e. 20*0.2 = 4. This amount is then withdrawn from circulation (destroyed). Then, according to Eq. (7.8), households will buy goods and services worth 60% of their disposable income, i.e. 60%*(20–4) = 9.6. The residual income (i.e. 40%*(20–4) = 6.4) is then added to their savings. This consumption expenditure of 9.6 is additional income for producers. Households pay a 20% tax on this income, i.e. 9.6*0.2 = 1.92. This sum is withdrawn from circulation.

According to Eq. (7.8), the additional disposable income breaks down into consumption expenditure (60%*(9.6–1.92) = 4.608) and savings (40%*(9.6–1.92) = 3.072). This consumption of 4.608 induces new payments of income, taxes, savings... The cycle continues until the flows are completely extinguished.

Within this framework, it is possible to arithmetically determine the value of GDP at the end of the year. Since, at the start of the simulation, households have no savings, the consumption function (Eq. 7.8) is therefore equal to $C_D = \alpha_1.Y_D$. Now, $Y_D = Y - T = Y - \theta$Y. GDP (Eq. 7.11) can therefore be written as:

$$Y = C + G = \alpha_1[Y(1 - \theta)] + G \tag{7.20}$$

Placing Y in the left-hand term of Eq. (7.20), we obtain:

$$Y^* = G/[1 - \alpha_1(1 - \theta)] \tag{7.21}$$

Since $G = 20$, $\alpha_1 = 0.6$ and $\theta = 0.2$, GDP is:

$$Y^* = 20/[1 - 0.6(1 - 0,2)] = 38.5 \quad (7.22)$$

For an initial money creation of 20, GDP reaches 38.5 at the end of the year. By normalizing this ratio by one, we obtain the value of the *fiscal multiplier*:

$$Y^* = 1/[1 - 0.6(1 - 0.2)] = 1.92 \quad (7.23)$$

For every euro generated by net public spending, GDP increases by 1.92 euros at the end of the year. Conversely, for each euro destroyed by a surplus in the public accounts, GDP falls by 1.92 euros. Having established the level of GDP, we can now calculate the value of financial balance sheets. At the end of the year, households will have accumulated new savings (12.3) (line 7), the accounting counterpart of which is the public deficit observed at the end of the year (line 6). This stock of savings will then, via the consumption function (Eq. 7.8), generate expenditure and income in year 1 and subsequent years. Table 7.3 (built with Excel) shows the evolution of the model's macroeconomic variables over time.

A net public expenditure of 20 euros at the start of year 0 leads to a GDP of 38.5 at the end of the year (lines 1 and 2). The public deficit and corresponding private savings are both 12.3. It should be noted that the public debt (12.3) is lower than the initial deficit (20) due to the payment of taxes on the various waves of infra-annual income.

In year 1, households allocate 40% of the savings inherited from the previous year to consumption expenditure, according to Eq. (7.8). As a result, GDP increases in year 1 and beyond. This is because households spend part of their disposable income, drawing on savings accumulated in previous periods and fed by the annual public deficit.

With public spending fixed at 20 throughout the simulation, the rise in GDP, which gradually increases tax payments indexed to it (Eq. 7.7), eventually balances the government budget. When this happens, households stop accumulating savings, which stabilizes their consumption, and therefore also GDP. The economy thus reaches a stationary state, in which transaction flows and wealth stocks reach stable values. Figure 7.2 shows the economy's trajectory toward this steady state.

Compared to initial values, GDP, household disposable income, consumption, and savings have all increased. What's more, with the exception of money creation, which in the model is the sole responsibility of the State, the entire economic dynamic has been driven by the private sector.

Interactions with the Ecosystem

Let's now show the simulations of a second scenario in which we activate the ecosystem block of the model. As shown in Fig. 7.3, economic dynamics have an impact on the earth system. The graph on the left shows the increase in energy consumption, which is indexed to GDP. Energy consumption is broken down into fossil fuels (95%) and renewable energies (5%). The graph on the right shows that the increase in industrial CO_2 emissions leads to a global temperature rise of 3.5 degrees Celsius at the end of the simulation (compared with the reference scenario). This climate disruption then causes

Table 7.3 Trends in macroeconomic variables

Variables/Time	*Symbols*		*0*	*1*	*(…)*	∞
Public expenditure	G	–	20.0	20.0		20.0
GDP	Y=C+G	–	38.5	47.9		100.0
Taxes	T=θY	–	7.7	9.6		20.0
Disposable income	YD=Y-T	–	30.8	38.3		80.0
Consumption	C=(α1.YD)+(α2 H-1)	–	18.5	27.9		80.0
Public deficit	ΔH_s=G-T	–	12.3	10.4		0.0
Savings	ΔH_{hd}=YD-C	–	12.3	10.4		0.0
Money supply	H=ΔH_s+H-1	–	12.3	22.7		80

Source Godley, W., Lavoie, M., 2012. *Monetary Economics. An integrated Approach to Credit, Money, Income, Production, and Wealth*. Second edition. Palgrave Macmillan, UK

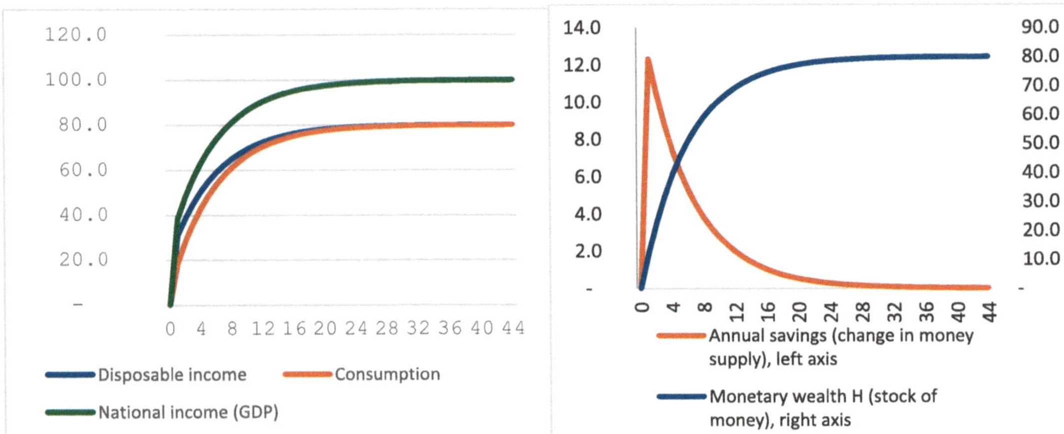

Fig. 7.2 Macroeconomic trajectory

destruction, reducing household consumption and generating GDP losses. As a result, tax revenues fall and the public deficit rises, even though public spending remains constant. In this model, therefore, climate change reduces the value of the multiplier and the effectiveness of fiscal policies. Finally, it should be noted that the observed fall in GDP reduces energy consumption, but not enough to prevent temperatures from rising.

7.6 Conclusion

- Modeling is a useful fiction for analyzing the causal mechanisms at work in the economy.
- The SIM-E model focuses on the effects of fiscal policy within a coherent accounting framework, linked to the ecosystem.
- In SIM-E, net public spending increases GDP, household disposable income, consumption, and savings. In the long term, public spending tends to be self-financing via the increase in tax revenues generated by growth.
- In SIM-E, economic growth increases fossil fuel consumption (assuming a constant energy mix). This generates industrial CO_2 emissions and rising temperatures.
- In SIM-E, the destruction caused by climate change has a knock-on effect on the economy, reducing household consumption, GDP and the value of the fiscal multiplier, and increasing the public deficit.

Activities

Questions for Discussion

1. The coefficients linking the different variables in the real economy fluctuate over time. Explain why, giving a few concrete examples. What implications do you draw from this for the use of economic models?
2. To what extent can we study economics using methods imported from the 'hard sciences', such as modeling?
3. Can an economic model be totally objective?

Mini-Case: Using the SIM-E Model

1. Examine the transaction matrix of the SIM-E model. Why are the sums of each row and column all zero?
2. Explain why an increase in the public deficit constitutes net money creation? What is the accounting counterpart of the public deficit in the private sector balance sheet?
3. Examine the equations in the model. Classify them in a table into three categories: accounting equations, equations that reflect economic behavior, and equations that represent the

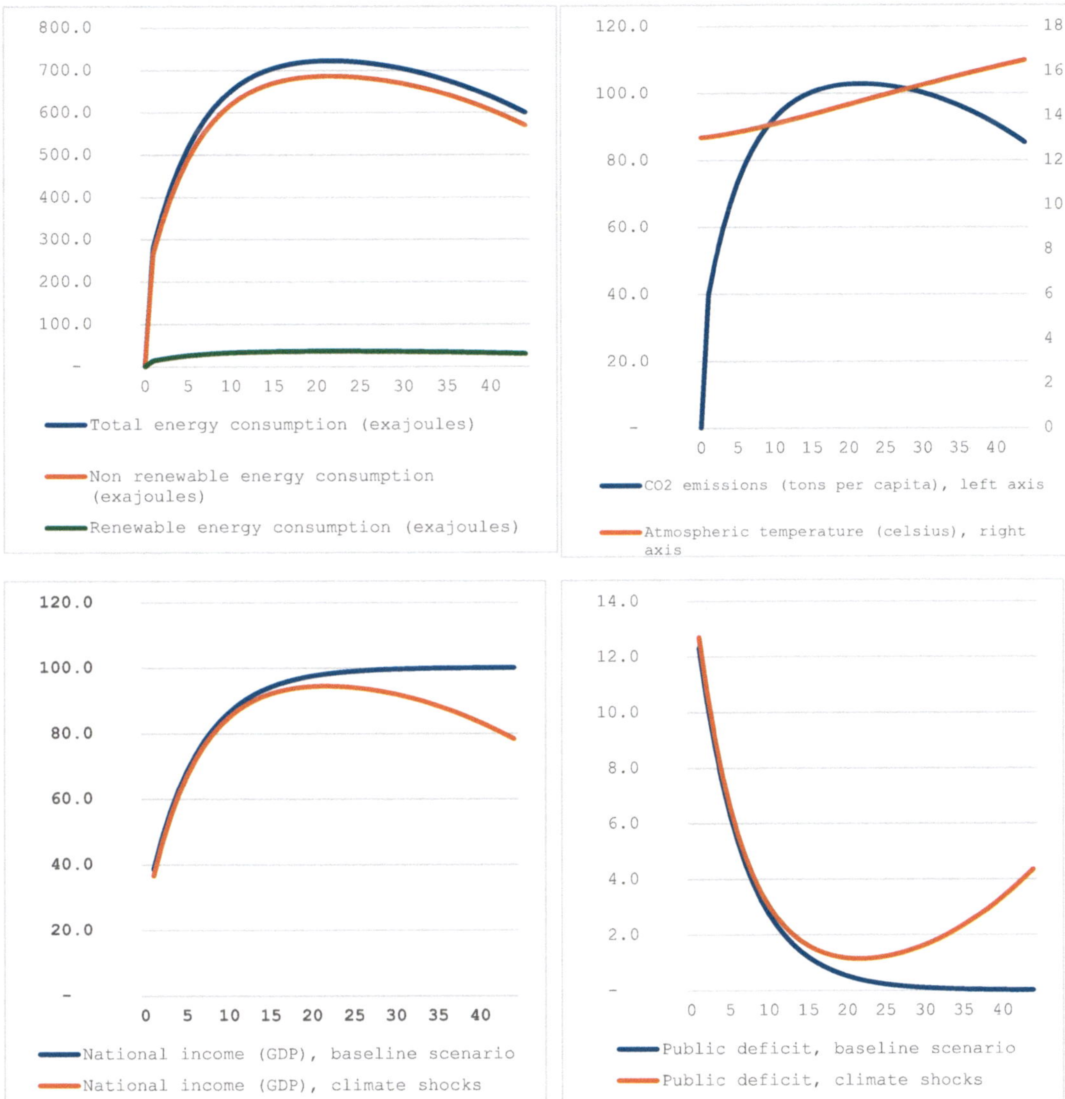

Fig. 7.3 Impact on the earth system

ecosystem. Explain the meaning of each equation in the second column of the table.

4. Examine the model's variables. Classify them in a table into two categories: endogenous variables (calculated by the model) and parameters (fixed). Explain the meaning of each variable in the second column of the table.
5. Download the Excel spreadsheet containing the SIM-E model onto your computer. Then answer the following questions:
   a. Construct a diagram explaining how SIM-E models the impact of public spending on consumption, disposable income, GDP, savings, and the public deficit over time.
   b. Draw a diagram explaining how SIM-E models the interactions between the economy and climate.

c. Keeping all other model parameters constant, run the three simulations below separately:

   - Simulation 1: tax rate (T) increases by five points.
   - Simulation 2: public spending (G) increases by five points.
   - Simulation 3: public spending (G) increases by five points and the share of renewable energy in the energy mix (μ) increases from 5% to 30%.

   For each simulation, describe the evolution of consumption, disposable income, national income, savings, and the ecosystem.

d. What can you learn from these simulations about the macroeconomic implications of sustainable development objectives?
e. If you were to work on an improved version of SIM-E, what changes would you make and why?

8 Interpreting the Balance of Payments

Thomas Lagoarde-Ségot

Putting Things into Perspective
Today, oligopolistic multinational companies (such as IBM, Microsoft, Sony, Coca-Cola, Accenture, Axa…) control around two-thirds of the world's trade flows. These multinationals and their foreign subsidiaries, which together account for a third of global GDP, exchange a variety of goods and services with their affiliates and/or international suppliers. Their subcontractors are then integrated into fragmented production processes, controlled by a standard of financial profitability imposed by shareholders. This global production chain tends to lock in the terms of trade: advanced, high-wage economies, which supply consumer markets, generally specialize in the design and development of high value-added products, while the bulk of production and polluting extractive activities take place in emerging or developing countries, where environmental standards are less stringent and wages much lower.

How can we measure the effects of international trade on a country's macroeconomic equilibrium? In what way are the imbalances observed also a vector of systemic financial risk? What are the main social and environmental controversies linked to international trade? These are just some of the issues addressed in this chapter.

Learning Objectives

- Interpreting a country's balance of payments
- Using it for macroeconomic analysis
- Understanding the factors behind external debt trends
- Understanding the limits of the balance of payments system

8.1 Anatomy of a Balance of Payments

In an open economy, the accounting equilibrium comprises three macroeconomic sectors: a private sector (resident companies and households); a public sector (the various branches of government); and the rest of the world (foreign companies, households, and governments). Economic relations with the rest of the world are recorded in a key document: the balance of payments. The method of calculating this document is the responsibility of the International Monetary Fund, which applies it to all its member countries. The balance of payments records

T. Lagoarde-Ségot (✉)
Kedge Business School, Talence, France
e-mail: thomas.lagoardesegot@kedgebs.com

T. Lagoarde-Ségot (ed.), *Ecological Economics and Finance*, https://doi.org/10.1007/978-3-031-71249-4_8

Table 8.1 Main Balance of Payments Financial Account Items

(-) Sign	(+) Sign
Acquisition of financial assets (capital outflows) of which:	*Issuance of financial liabilities (capital inflows) of which:*
Foreign direct investment	Non-resident direct investment
Outward portfolio investments	Non-resident portfolio investment
Increase in official reserves	Decline in official reserves
Other foreign investments (bank loans to non-residents or increase in foreign deposits)	Other investments by non-residents in the domestic economy (loans from foreign banks or increase in deposits held by non-residents)

all payment flows exchanged between a country and the rest of the world over the course of a calendar year. It breaks down into four balances corresponding to the major categories of international payments:

- the balance of goods and services, calculated as the difference between exports (X) and imports of goods and services (IM). Excluding services from this calculation gives the trade balance;
- the balance of current income and transfers (Tr_f), calculated as the difference between incoming and outgoing flows of official development assistance, humanitarian aid from NGOs, and income transfers from immigrant workers to their countries of origin;
- the balance of financial income (r_f) calculated as the difference between incoming and outgoing interest and dividend payments;
- the balance of the financial account (S_f) calculated as the difference between financial asset acquisition flows. These include foreign direct investment, portfolio investment, and official central bank transactions. This balance therefore measures net capital inflows (see Table 8.1).

The balance of payments uses a double-entry method of accounting. Each payment gives rise to two accounting entries: a credit (+) and a debit (-). Thus, to record an export, the current account balance is credited, and the financial account balance is debited. By virtue of this accounting principle, the balance of payments respects the following equality (Eq. 8.1):

$$(X - IM) + Tr_f + r_f + S_f = 0 \qquad (8.1)$$

Defining the current account balance (CAB) as the sum of the balances of goods and services, current income and transfers, and financial income ($CAB = (X - IM) + Tr_f + r_f$) results in equality (8.2):

$$CAB = -S_f \qquad (8.2)$$

A current account surplus is therefore always the accounting counterpart of net capital outflows, and vice versa. Thus, countries with a trade surplus—such as China—necessarily accumulate foreign financial assets. These financial transactions are recorded as net capital inflows in deficit countries—such as the USA. The increase in net capital flows in the global economy since the 1980s is therefore one of the manifestations of growing imbalances in international trade.

Conversely, current account deficits and surpluses in different countries can be influenced by the investment strategies of major banks and investment funds. Massive inflows of (highly volatile) portfolio flows or FDI can then widen trade deficits and external debt. This is why many emerging countries are reluctant to lift all restrictions on international capital flows.

8.2 An Economic Analysis Tool

Newspapers often comment on a country's current account as if it were a company's income statement. However, commenting on such a balance in isolation, without taking into account its accounting counterparts, is not very relevant. Instead, the data provided by the balance of

Table 8.2 Historical examples of balance of payment positions

Balance of goods, services, income, and current transfers ($X - IM + Tr_f$)	Balance of financial income (r_f)	Current account balance ($X - IM + Tr_f + r_f$)	Financial account balance (S_f)	Example
–	–	–	+	Heavily indebted poor countries (HIPC)
–	+	–	+	United States
+	+	+	–	China, Germany
+	–	+	–	France (before 1914) Emerging countries
–	+	+	–	Great Britain (before 1914)

payments should be analyzed in their entirety to understand how an economy fits into international trade (see Table 8.2).

The current account balances of Heavily Indebted Poor Countries (HIPC) economies are frequently negative, reflecting a double deficit in the trade and financial income balances. On the other hand, these economies record net capital inflows, in the form of direct or portfolio investments, or multilateral loans. These capital inflows nevertheless have the effect of increasing the volume of external debt and interest payments abroad. The structure of the balance of payments therefore tends to keep these economies under the thumb of their international creditors.

Since the mid-1980s, the US balance of payments has shown a negative current account balance. In return for this deficit, the US economy receives capital inflows, which are recorded in the financial account. Despite its growing external indebtedness, the US investment income balance is nevertheless positive. The asymmetry of the international monetary regime, which sharply reduces the interest paid by the United States on its external debt—which is denominated in dollars—helps to explain this paradox (see Chapters 9 and 10).

Some countries, such as China and Germany, regularly run current account surpluses. Their resident financial institutions must therefore accumulate foreign assets (for example, US sovereign bonds in the case of China). As a result, their financial systems are increasingly exposed to a potential international debt crisis.

Another configuration—observed, for example, in France during the *Belle Époque*, or in many emerging countries—combines a current account surplus, a financial account deficit, and a financial income deficit. In this case, the current account surplus enables the accumulation of international claims, but the income generated by these claims is insufficient to cover the servicing of the international debt contracted in the past. In the case of emerging countries, this debt stems from investments required in the early stages of economic development. It can also stem from political events, such as the reparations owed to Germany by France after its defeat in the Franco-Prussian War of 1871.

Finally, the balance of payments of Victorian Britain, the hegemonic power of the XIXth century, combined a trade deficit with net capital outflows. This position, characteristic of a rentier economy, was due to a very high balance of investment income. Indeed, British investments in the Empire generated sufficient interest income to maintain a current account deficit and make additional investments abroad.

Knowing how to analyze the balance of payments is therefore essential to deciphering the major controversies in international economics—such as those surrounding trade imbalances (see Box 8.1).

Box 8.1: The Dark Side of Current Account Surpluses

In the film *Adults in the Room* (Costa Gavras, 2019), Greek Economy Minister Yannis Varoufakis shocks guests at a diplomatic dinner by claiming that "*the only purpose of the debt treatment plan imposed on Greece is to save German banks!*".

This reasoning can be justified by the balance of payments analysis. The success of Germany's strategy of growth driven by current account surpluses required its banks to acquire financial instruments issued by Greek companies and public organizations. For Yannis Varoufakis, the prevailing discourse attributed the deficits to Greece's alleged macroeconomic irresponsibility… without seeing that this was also the accounting counterpart of the German surpluses.

Some observers still present economies with current account surpluses (such as China or Germany) as virtuous examples that deficit countries should emulate. From an accounting point of view, however, this analysis is an aberration. Since, in accounting terms, the current account surpluses of some countries are the deficits of others, it is impossible for all countries to simultaneously post a current account surplus. What's more, the responsibility for global imbalances is also attributable to surplus countries: econometric models have shown that the fiscal austerity policies of countries in the center of the eurozone lead to rising public and trade deficits in countries on the eurozone periphery and in the southern Mediterranean neighborhood (Gaysset et al., 2019).

Macroeconomic strategies based on the pursuit of trade surpluses can therefore be interpreted as a form of economic aggression. They are also an important vector of systemic financial risk: by pushing certain countries into debt, current account surpluses swell the volume of international debt, exposing the entire financial sector to an increased risk of default.

This is why, as part of the 'macroeconomic imbalance procedure'[1], the European Union "monitors, prevents and corrects problematic developments that could have a negative effect on other EU countries". Germany was asked to take corrective action between 2014 and 2017 to reduce its trade surpluses, which were deemed excessive and a long-term threat to the integrity of the eurozone.

Source Gaysset, I., Lagoarde-Ségot, T., Neaime, S., 2019. Twin deficits in the eurozone periphery. A Keynesian perspective. *Economic Modelling* 76, pp. 101–116.

8.3 Terms of Trade and Inequalities

The value of the various balance of payments balances depends not only on the volumes of goods imported or exported, but also on their relative prices. The latter can be captured by the terms of trade ratio[2], which is obtained by dividing the average price of domestic exports (P_X) by the average price of domestic imports (P_M) (Eq. 8.3):

$$ToT = \frac{P_X}{P_M} \tag{8.3}$$

When the terms of trade are less than 1, balancing the current account requires a volume of exports greater than the volume of imports—and vice versa. Noting (Q_X) and (Q_M) respectively the volume of goods exported and imported, balancing the balance of goods and services implies the following equality (Eq. 8.4):

$$P_X Q_X = P_M Q_M \tag{8.4}$$

[1] See https://economy-finance.ec.europa.eu/economic-and-fiscal-governance/macroeconomic-imbalance-procedure_en.

[2] International data on terms of trade are available at: https://data.worldbank.org/indicator/TT.PRI.MRCH.XD.WD.

If the terms of trade are, for example, 0.5, then $P_X = 0.5P_M$ and $Q_X = 2Q_M$. The national economy will therefore have to export twice as many goods to finance its imports without increasing its foreign debt. It is therefore preferable to enter international trade by exporting high value-added goods for which international demand is stable (automobiles, industrial equipment parts) than raw materials (coffee, cocoa, rubber, etc.) or services (tourism, call centers, etc.) whose price are highly volatile (see Box 8.2).

Box 8.2: Commodity Price Volatility and Unequal Trade

The price of commodities such as coffee or cocoa depends not only on supply and demand conditions, but also on developments in the derivatives market, i.e. speculative financial bets on their future price. As the following graph shows, this results in highly volatile prices for these raw materials. This volatility destabilizes not only farmers' incomes, but also the balance of payments of producing countries.

World Coffee and Cocoa Prices, 1990–2024

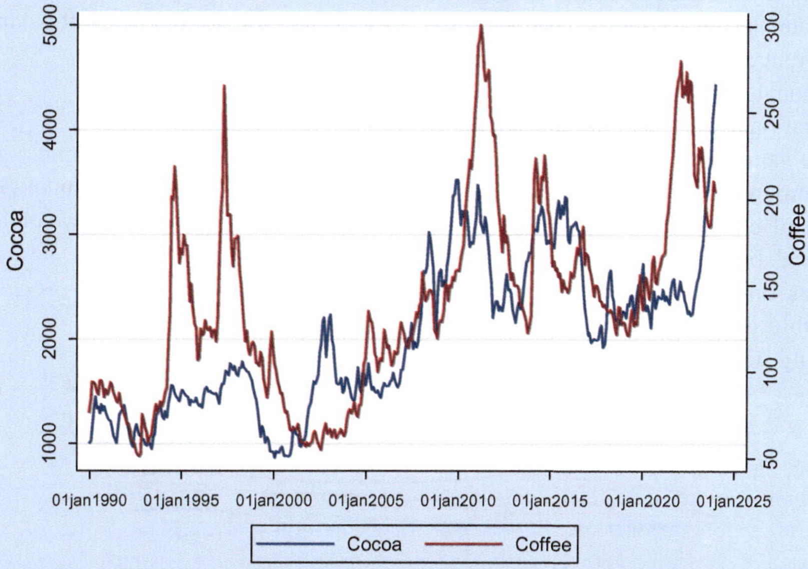

Source https://www.imf.org/en/Research/commodity-prices

Note in this graph, the price of cocoa is expressed in dollars per ton and the price of coffee in cents per pound.

The vulnerability of countries in the global South has been theorized by structuralist economists such as Samir Amin (1931–2018), Immanuel Wallerstein (1930–2019), and Raul Prebisch (1901–1986). This approach emphasizes that countries exporting primary products (such as agricultural produce) are subject to erratic market fluctuations and intense price competition. When their domestic companies lose international markets, domestic unemployment rises, driving down wages and prices. The result is a further deterioration in the terms of trade, a current account deficit, and an increase in external debt (often denominated in dollars), which helps to maintain their dependence on the North.

For several decades, many economists have been recommending the creation of international mechanisms to stabilize the terms of trade (for example, by taxing or banning speculative transactions in food derivatives). Others call for the implementation of industrial policies that would enable countries in the South to diversify their economies and reduce their dependence on raw material exports. Such proposals are often put forward by the United Nations Commission on Trade and Development (UNCTAD). The various fair trade initiatives (e.g. the *Max Havelaar* label), which offer a guaranteed price to producers in the global South, are efforts in the same direction.

8.4 International Financial Position

In a globally integrated economy, where current account imbalances are the counterpart of capital allocation, there is no reason why the current account should be in balance every period. As a result, net stocks of financial assets and liabilities accumulate on the balance sheets of countries with current account surpluses (or deficits). The International Financial Position published by the International Monetary Fund enables us to analyze the value of these stocks.

This document establishes the net financial position of each economy by calculating the difference between international assets and liabilities on its balance sheet. Analysis of the available data reveals that the increase in outstanding international financial assets is largely attributable to the financial position of the United States (see Fig. 8.1) (see Chapter 9).

To understand how the international financial position is established in a given year t, we need to define external debt as the sum of debt service accumulated over previous periods (at interest rate r) and the current account balance D_t (CAB_t) (Eq. 8.5):

$$D_t = (1 + r)D_{t-1} - CAB_t \tag{8.5}$$

Let g denote the economic growth rate, $Y_t = Y_t = (1 + g)Y_{t-1}$ the annual GDP, and posing $d_t = \frac{D_t}{Y_t}$ and $cab_t = \frac{CAB_t}{Y_t}$ we obtain:

$$d_t = (1 + r)\frac{D_{t-1}}{Y_t} - cab_t \tag{8.6}$$

$$\rightarrow d_t = \frac{1 + r}{1 + g} \times \frac{D_{t-1}}{Y_{t-1}} - cab_t \tag{8.7}$$

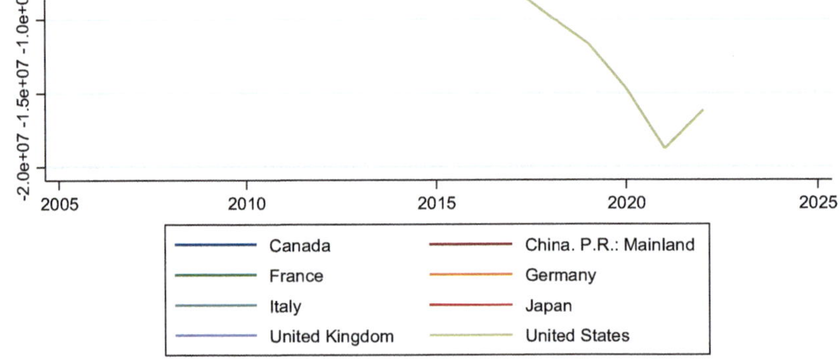

Fig. 8.1 Net International Financial Position of G7 Countries+China, 2005–2022 (in US Dollars) (*Source* https://data.imf.org/)

$$\rightarrow d_t = \frac{1+r}{1+g} \times d_{t-1} - cab_t \tag{8.8}$$

The external debt stabilization condition is written as $d_t = d_{t-1}$. If this condition is met, then:

$$d_t - d_t \times \frac{1+r}{1+g} = -cab_t \tag{8.9}$$

By transferring the current account balance (cab_t) into the left-hand term of Eq. (8.9), we obtain:

$$cab_t = d_t \times \frac{1+r}{1+g} - d_t = d_t \times \frac{1+r}{1+g} - \frac{1+g}{1+g} d_t \tag{8.10}$$

$$\rightarrow cab_t = d_t \times \frac{r-g}{1+g} \tag{8.11}$$

Since the annual economic growth rate g rarely exceeds 10%, the following approximation is acceptable:

$$cab_t = d_t(r-g) \tag{8.12}$$

Consider an economy with an external debt ratio (d_t) is 35%. Assuming an economic growth rate (g) of 5% and an international interest rate (r) of 3%, it is possible to reconcile a current account deficit with a stabilization of external debt. Indeed, the latter decreases as soon as the current account balance exceeds 35% * (3% – 5%) = –0.7% of GDP. However, if foreign investors suddenly demand a 7% risk premium due to a change in sentiment, the economy will have to aim for an annual current account surplus equal to 35% * ((3% + 7%) – 5%) = 1.75% of GDP to stabilize its external debt. In this way, changes in the international financial position simultaneously reflect variations in international interest rates, economic growth, and the dynamics of the current account balance.

8.5 Limitations of the Balance of Payments

Although indispensable, the data provided by the balance of payments are biased by the incompleteness of official data. This is borne out by the figures entered in the 'net errors and omissions' reconciliation account, which ensures the accounting balance of the balance of payments, but reveals a black hole in international trade (see Fig. 8.2).

Apart from the inevitable time lags (if, for example, a credit is recorded in December and the corresponding debit in January of the following year), three factors may explain this black hole.

The first, on the goods and services account, concerns fraud and the illegal trafficking of goods. In the sea freight sector, some unscrupulous shipowners use flags of convenience (i.e. ships flying the flag of a country other than their own). This fraud enables them to evade their country's maritime laws and employ cheaper

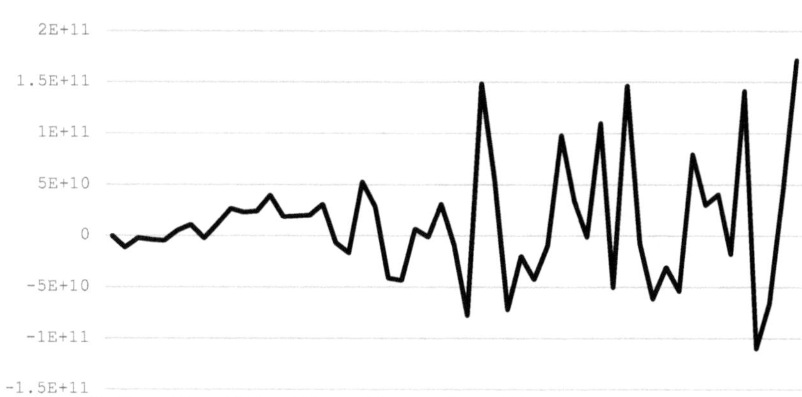

Fig. 8.2 Net Errors and Omissions, US Balance of Payments, 1970–2022 (Current Dollars) (*Source* https://data.imf.org/)

labor. Fictitious payments are then declared to countries such as Barbados or Bolivia, distorting the balance of payments.

The second factor, which concerns the financial account, is linked to the increasing financialization of the global economy since the 2000s. This financialization is reflected in a threefold increase in the speed of international capital flows, the complexity of financial instruments, and price volatility. The result is a growing opacity of international financial transactions, inevitably leading to inconsistencies in the data used to construct the balance of payments.

In an influential article, economists Philip Lane and Gian Maria Milesi-Feretti (2007)[3] have also pointed out that these inconsistencies are largely attributable to the under-reporting of assets held abroad, and the income associated with them (dividends, interest, capital gains of all kinds, etc.). Tax evasion in tax havens obviously plays a major role here (see Box 8.3).

Box 8.3: Tax Evasion, the Scourge of Globalized Capitalism

Tax evasion refers to operations whereby high-income individuals or companies artificially relocate their income or profits to tax havens to reduce the amount of tax they pay. According to estimates by economist Gabriel Zucman[4] (2017), around 8% of the world's financial assets ($7.6 trillion) are domiciled in tax havens. More than half the international revenues of US multinationals are declared in tax havens, often through shell companies. Switzerland, home to around 30% of these assets, is the epicenter of this phenomenon.

In addition to reducing the reliability of the balance of payments, tax evasion represents a considerable social cost. In the case of France, the NGO Oxfam estimates its annual cost at nearly 80 billion euros—an amount greater than the public education budget (52 billion euros in 2020). Tax evasion also leads to a race to the bottom between countries as they compete to attract international savings. And despite the fact that all OECD countries are increasingly tax-efficient for high-income earners, tax evasion continues to rise, as the graph below shows.

Estimation of the Proportion of European Assets Held in Tax Havens (1910–2013)

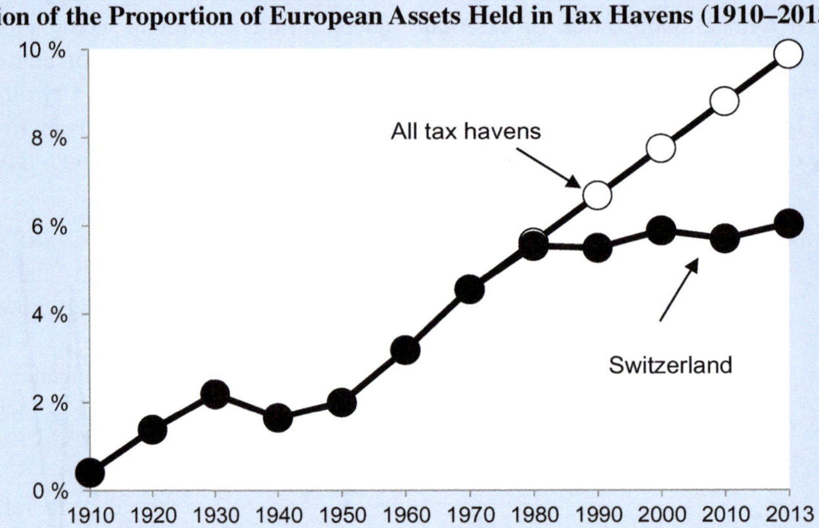

[3] Lane, P.R. and Milesi-Ferretti, G.M., 2007. The external wealth of nations mark II: Revised and extended estimates of foreign assets and liabilities, 1970–2004. *Journal of International Economics*, Elsevier, Vol. 73(2), pp. 223–250.

[4] See http://gabriel-zucman.eu/hidden-wealth/

Source Zucman, G (2015). *The Hidden Wealth of Nations. The Scourge of Tax Havens.* University of Chicago Press, 200 pp.

As a result, many are now calling for tax havens to be abolished and for an international financial registry to be set up, enabling national accountants to identify the real owners of financial assets.

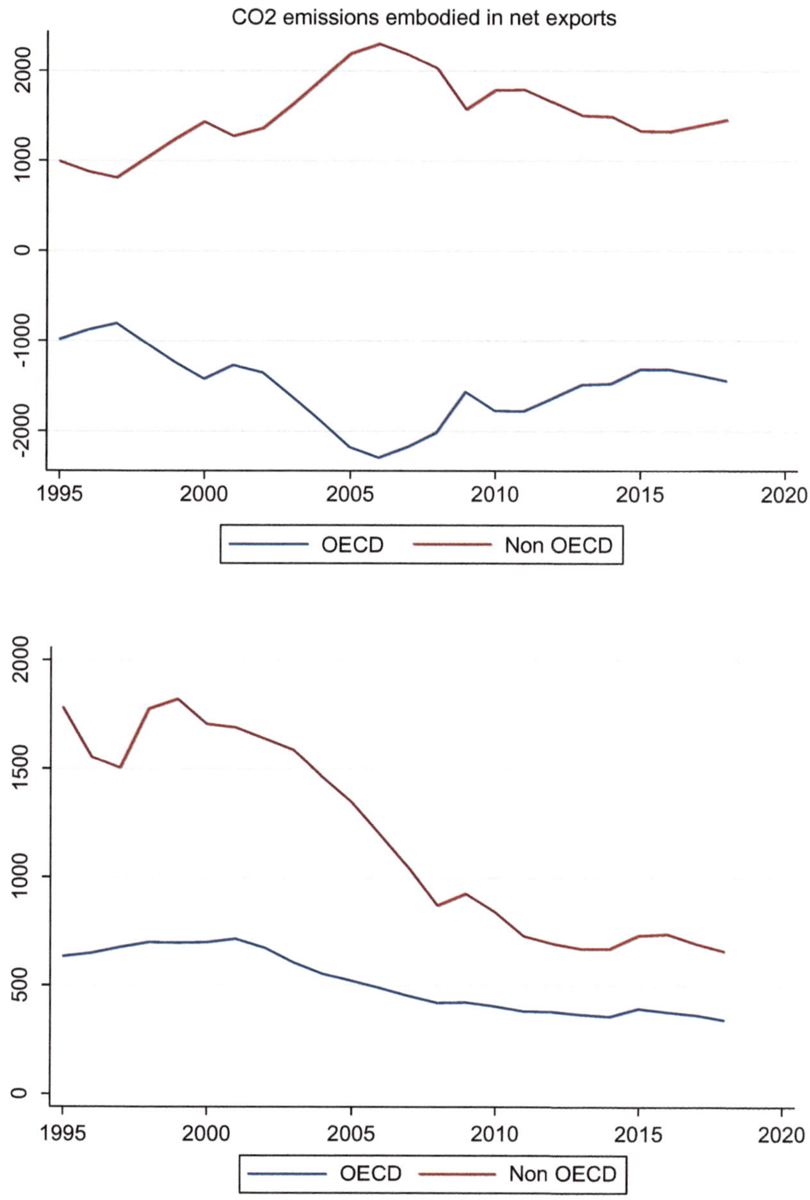

Fig. 8.3 CO_2 Emissions and World Trade, 1995–2018 (*Source* https://stats.oecd.org/. The vertical axis measures the tons of CO_2 emitted for each million dollars of export revenue)

Finally, and this is the third factor, the balance of payments does not provide an accurate picture of the stakes involved in climate justice. The few data available indicate that OECD countries are net importers of CO_2, while non-OECD countries are net exporters. The current organization of international trade therefore enables industrialized countries to relocate CO_2 emissions linked to their consumption needs to less developed countries, which suffer the immediate costs in terms of public health. As a result, most of the adjustments linked to the climate transition will have to be carried out by these same countries (see Fig. 8.3).

8.6 Conclusion

- The balance of payments records all payment flows exchanged between a country and the rest of the world over the course of a calendar year.
- The current account balance mirrors the financial account balance. Net international capital flows are therefore the counterpart to trade imbalances.
- Analyzing the relationship between balance of payments balances enables us to understand how an economy fits into international trade.
- The reliability of balance of payments data is limited by fraud, tax evasion, and the failure to take account of climate justice issues.

Activities

Questions for Discussion

1. To what extent is a country's international investment position determined by the dynamics of international trade?
2. Explain the meaning of the following equality: $(X - IM) + Tr_f + r_f = -S_f$. Define each of the terms in this equality and analyze their relationship.
3. How do trade imbalances pose a risk to international financial stability?
4. For some observers, the pursuit of current account surpluses by other countries represents a form of economic aggression. Does this point of view necessarily imply a protectionist stance hostile to free trade?

Mini-Case

1. Visit the Banque de France website and look for information on the carbon footprint of the French economy. In your opinion, which French balance of payments accounts would need to be modified to reduce France's share of global CO_2 emissions?
2. Identify the origin of the products you consume on a typical day. Then, using a map, link each product to its country of origin and calculate the distances traveled. Based on this information, estimate your annual carbon footprint. How could you align your consumption habits with the United Nations' Sustainable Development Goals?

9 Global Imbalances and the International Monetary System

Raphaël Didier and Thomas Lagoarde-Ségot

Putting Things into Perspective

In February 2012, at the height of the European sovereign debt crisis, German Finance Minister Wolfgang Schäuble exclaimed: "Greece must stop being a bottomless pit!". Indeed, as the graph on the left below shows, the Greek economy posted twin deficits (public deficit and trade deficit) every year between 1999 and 2012. But, at the same time - something Mr. Schäuble failed to note—an accounting counterpart to the Greek deficit was the accumulation of trade surpluses by the German economy over the same period, as shown in the graph on the right.

Greek and German Macroeconomic Balances, 1999–2018

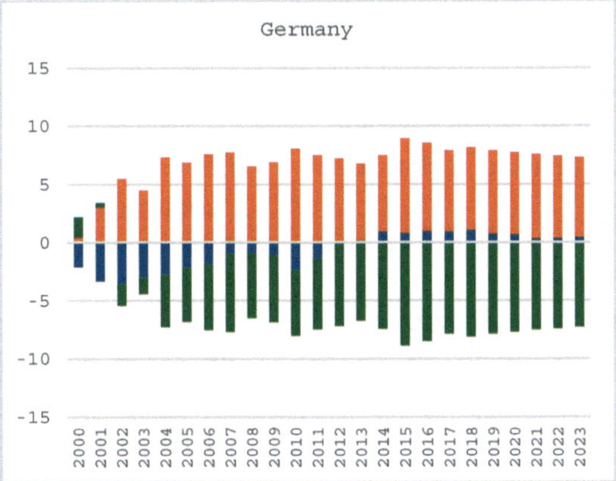

R. Didier
Université de Lorraine, Metz, France

T. Lagoarde-Ségot (✉)
KEDGE Business School, Talence, France
e-mail: thomas.lagoardesegot@kedgebs.com

T. Lagoarde-Ségot
Sustainable Development Solutions Network, Paris, France

T. Lagoarde-Ségot (ed.), *Ecological Economics and Finance*, https://doi.org/10.1007/978-3-031-71249-4_9

Source International Financial Statistics, IMF

The orange bar is the domestic private sector balance. The blue line is the domestic public sector balance. The green line is the foreign sector balance (which corresponds to the capital account of the balance of payments). All values are expressed in % of domestic GDP.

Learning Objectives

- Constructing and interpreting a country's macroeconomic equilibrium over time
- Analyzing the causes of international trade and financial imbalances
- Familiarizing yourself with recent developments in the international financial architecture

1 The International Macroeconomic Equilibrium Equation

In a closed economy, the private sector deficit (or surplus) is the accounting mirror of the public sector surplus (or deficit). But economic openness renders this equality partially obsolete. We now need to consider the accounting relationships between the national private and public sectors and the rest of the world. A third sector must therefore be included in the analysis, as shown by the macroeconomic equilibrium Eq. (9.1):

$$\begin{aligned}&\text{Private Sector Balance}\\&+\text{Public Sector Balance}\\&+\text{External Sector Balance}=0\end{aligned} \tag{9.1}$$

In Eq. (9.1), the balance of each sector corresponds to its savings, i.e. the share of its annual income that is not spent. Savings can be positive (if income exceeds expenditure) or negative. Thus, for a given year:

- the *private sector balance* corresponds to the difference between household and business income and expenditure; this balance is equal to national savings, net of the public sector balance;
- the *public sector balance* corresponds to the difference between tax revenues and public expenditure; this balance is equal to the annual public deficit (or surplus);
- the *balance of the external sector* corresponds to net capital inflows, which measure the net claims granted to the national economy by non-residents; this balance is equal to the value of the financial account of the balance of payments.

As the financial position of one macroeconomic sector is strictly equal to the sum of the net positions of the other two, it is impossible for all three sectors to simultaneously accumulate financial wealth (or to issue debt). For a macroeconomic sector to record a surplus, at least one of the other two must post a deficit.

2 Demonstration Using National Accounts

Equation (9.1) is an identity derived from national accounting. Post-keynesian economist Marc Lavoie (2016) shows how to achieve this equation with the following demonstration. Let's start by defining gross domestic product (GDP) as all spending in the economy over the course of a year. As shown in Eq. (9.2), GDP is the sum of consumption (*C*), private sector investment (*I*), government spending (*G*), and the balance of payments trade balance (exports, *X*, minus imports, *M*):

$$GDP = C + I + G + (X - M) \quad (9.2)$$

By adding to GDP the net income received from the rest of the world, i.e. transfers (Tr_f) and returns on foreign assets (r_f), we obtain gross national income (GNI) (Eq. 9.3):

$$GNI = C + I + G + (X - M) + Tr_f + r_f \quad (9.3)$$

In Eq. (3), the term $((X - M) + Tr_f + r_f)$ is equal to the current account balance of the balance of payments (S_c). This account is the accounting mirror of the balance of payments financial account balance (S_f). Posing $S_f = -S_c$ we obtain Eq. (9.4):

$$GNI = C + I + G - S_f \quad (9.4)$$

Gross national income is broken down into consumption expenditure (*C*), savings (*S*), and tax payments (*T*) (Eq. 9.5):

$$GNI = C + S + T \quad (9.5)$$

Combining Eqs. (9.4) and (9.5), we finally obtain Eq. (9.6):

$$\begin{aligned} &C + I + G - S_f = C + S + T \\ &\rightarrow (S - I) + (T - G) + S_f = 0 \end{aligned} \quad (9.6)$$

Equation (9.6) gives the international macroeconomic equilibrium (defined in Eq. 9.1). It indicates that the sum of the balances of the private sector (S-I), the public sector (T-G) and the rest of the world (S_f) is always equal to zero. This equation contains fundamental mechanisms in international macroeconomics. All other things being equal:

- A public deficit or trade surplus has the counterpart of enriching the domestic private sector. Indeed, if $(T - G) < 0$ and $S_f = -S_c < 0$, then $(S - I) > 0$.
- A public budget surplus or trade deficit has the counterpart of impoverishing the domestic private sector. Indeed, if $(T - G) > 0$ and $S_f = -S_c > 0$, then $(S - I) < 0$.
- A trade deficit or surplus in the domestic private sector has as its counterpart an increase in the public deficit. Indeed, if $S_f = -S_c > 0$ and $(S - I) > 0$, then $(T - G) < 0$.

The graph in Fig. 9.1 shows the French macroeconomic equilibrium between 1980 and 2024. Three main periods can be identified: between 1980 and 1992, the domestic private sector and the foreign sector posted a surplus, the counterpart of which was the public deficit. Between 1992 and 2008, the domestic private sector posted a surplus, offset by the public deficit and the trade surplus. Between 2008 and 2024, surpluses in the domestic private sector and in the foreign sector were again counterbalanced by the public deficit. The different amplitudes of these three balances over time reflect changes in national and international macroeconomic conditions. In France, during this period, macroeconomic equilibrium enabled the domestic private sector to accumulate net financial wealth every year, ruling out the possibility of a banking or financial crisis.

3 Trade and Financial Interdependencies

The external position of each economy depends on internal and external dynamics. To understand how macroeconomic equilibrium is established (see Fig. 9.1), it is necessary to define national savings (S^N) as the sum of annual

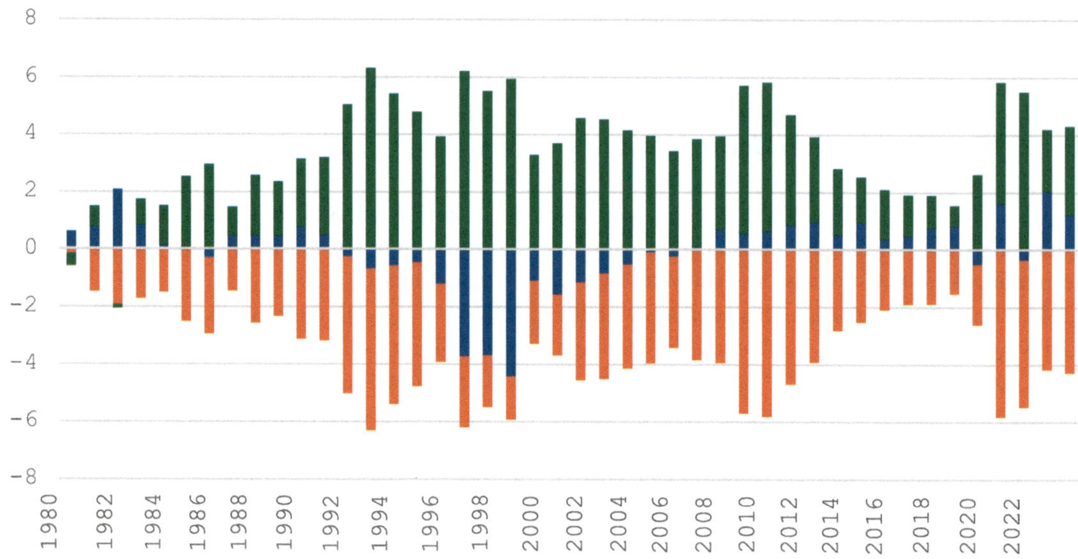

Fig. 9.1 France's Macroeconomic Balance, 1980–2024 (*Source* World Economic Outlook Database, International Monetary Fund. https://www.imf.org/en/Publications/WEO/weo-database/)

private-sector savings (S) and public-sector savings (tax revenues, T, net of public spending, G):

$$S^N = S + (T - G) \tag{9.7}$$

Inserting Eq. (9.7) into Eq. (9.6), we obtain:

$$\begin{aligned}&\left(S^N - I\right) + S_f = 0\\&\rightarrow \left(S^N - I\right) = -S_f = S_c\end{aligned} \tag{9.8}$$

Equation (9.8) shows that the trade position (S_c), which is the accounting mirror of net capital inflows (S_f), reflects a gap between national savings and domestic investment. Thus:

- when national savings exceed capital expenditure ($S^N > I$), the domestic economy generates financing capacity, which is invested abroad. In this case, net capital outflows($S_f < 0$) equal to the current account surplus of the balance of payments($S_c > 0$);
- when national savings do not cover capital expenditure ($S^N < I$), these are financed by the rest of the world. In this case, net capital inflows ($S_f > 0$) equal to the current account deficit of the balance of payments ($S_c < 0$).

External imbalances therefore mirror national imbalances between savings and investment. At first glance, it would seem possible for an economy to steer its trade balance by adjusting its domestic demand. For example, higher taxes combined with lower public spending could increase national savings, thereby generating a trade surplus (and net capital outflows). However, the external position of an economy also reflects the net savings of the rest of the world. For example, let's consider a world made up of the national economy (i) and the rest of the world (j). The interplay of trade and financial interdependencies is written as follows:

$$\left(S_i^N - I_i\right) = -S_{f,i} = S_{c,i} = -S_{c,j} = S_{f,j} = \left(I_j - S_j^N\right) \tag{9.9}$$

Equation (9.9) shows that the internal and external imbalances ($\left(S_i^N - I_i\right)$ and $(S_{c,i} = -S_{f,i})$, respectively) of the national economy mirror the internal and external imbalances ($\left(I_j - S_j^N\right)$ and $(S_{f,j} = -S_{c,j})$, respectively) of the rest of the world. For the domestic economy, a trade surplus ($S_{c,i} > 0$) is only possible if net investment in the rest of the world is positive

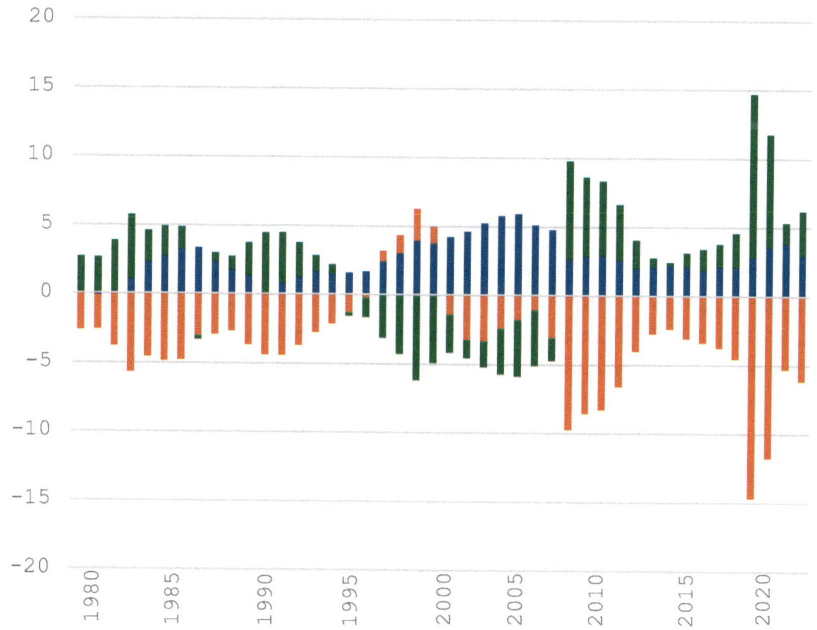

Fig. 9.2 US macroeconomic balance, 1980–2024 (*Note* The blue line represents the balance of the external sector. The green line represents the private sector balance. The orange line represents the public sector balance. *Source* World Economic Outlook Database, International Monetary Fund. https://www.imf.org/en/Publications/WEO/weo-database/ & Federal Reserve Bank of St. Louis . Authors' calculations)

$((I_j - S_j^N) > 0)$. However, national macroeconomic policy has no influence on the economies of the rest of the world, and vice versa. The two economies are therefore *interdependent*.

4 US Twin Deficits and the Global Economy

The principle of interdependence allows us to analyze the evolution of the global economic and financial system from the point of view of the country that has anchored it since 1945: the United States.

As the graph in Fig. 9.2 shows, the US macroeconomic position has been marked since the 1980s by recurrent *twin* public and trade deficits. Equation (9.8) shows that the American trade deficit $(S_c < 0)$ is the counterpart of excess investment in national savings $(S^N < I)$ financed by net capital inflows $(S_f > 0)$. The US economy is characterized by net imports, high public spending (notably on the military), and low taxes (especially for high-income earners). Given Eq. (9.1), macroeconomic balancing requires massive net international capital inflows.

Over time, the US authorities have pulled several levers to achieve this goal. Firstly, the Federal Reserve raised its key interest rate sharply in the early 1980s to attract foreign capital (the *Volcker shock,* named after the Fed governor). At the same time, the American Republicans implemented a major tax cut on capital income, backed by a program of financial deregulation. This gave Wall Street investment banks the opportunity to offer new financial products to foreign investors.

Yanis Varoufakis, former Greek Minister of the Economy, described this system as a "planetary minotaur" (2015). Like the Minotaur of Crete, who devoured the young men he claimed from Aegean[1], the United States was able to run a double public and trade deficit, by draining financial surpluses from the rest of the world. As Eq. (9.9) shows, these surpluses were the accounting counterpart of excess US domestic investment.

For many countries, these twin deficits would have led to a depreciation of the national currency. But, because of its status as an international currency (see Box 9.1), the US dollar remained remarkably stable.

Box 9.1: What is an International Currency?

To qualify as international, a currency must fulfill the three traditional functions of a currency, but at a global level: international unit of account, international medium of exchange, and international store of value. These functions can then be broken down according to whether the currency is used by the public sector—mainly central banks—or by the private sector (Bénassy-Quéré, 2023):

Currency function	Private sector	Public Sector (Central Banks)
Medium of exchange	Trade vehicle	Vehicle for foreign exchange market interventions
Unit of account	Currency used to denominate key assets (such as oil)	Anchor currency used to assess the value of the national currency
Store of value	Investment vehicle	Reserve currency

The graph below shows that the dollar's monetary supremacy in global transactions remains unchallenged for the time being.

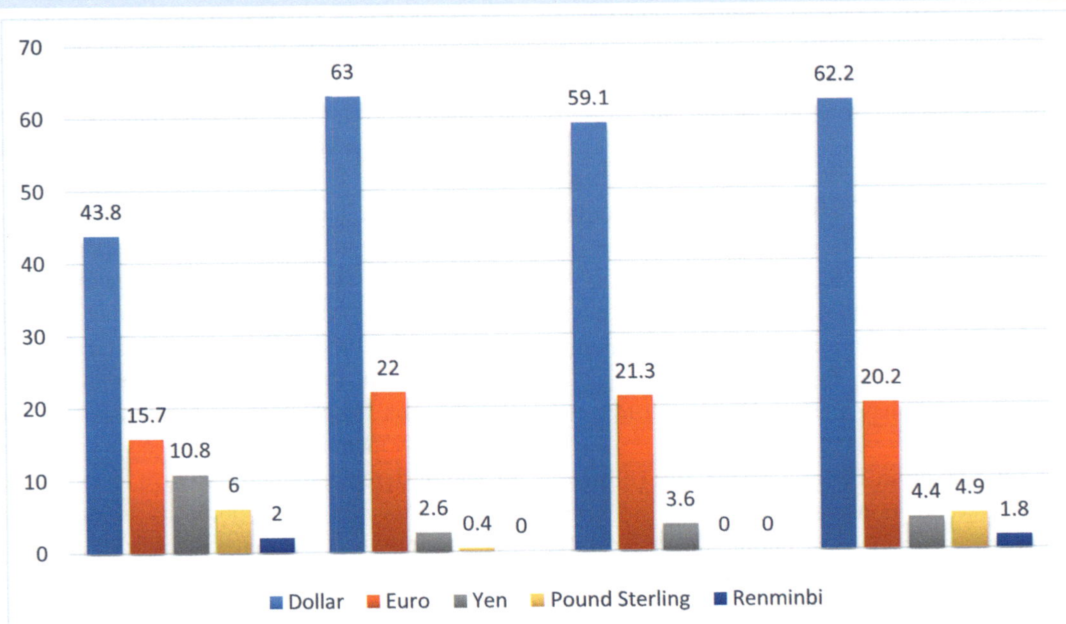

[1] In Greek mythology, the Minotaur was a fabulous half-man, half-bull monster who was imprisoned by Minos in the labyrinth built by Daedalus in central Crete. Every nine years, Aegeus, King of Athens, was forced to sacrifice seven boys and seven girls to the Minotaur. Aegeus' son Theseus finally succeeded in killing him.

[*Source* Eichengreen B. and Guangtao X., 2019, China and the SDR: Financial Liberalization through the Back Door. Quarterly Journal of Finance, vol. 9, n° 3]. These four sets of histograms show the value of forex operations, international debt, international loans, and official reserves (from left to right, respectively), per currency.

In his book, *Gold and the dollar crisis: the future of convertibility* (1960), Robert Triffin showed that the dollar must satisfy two irreconcilable objectives (Triffin's dilemma): to be a stable standard for trade and to be issued in abundance. Since, moreover, successive US governments have consistently abused the dollar's privileged status by allowing twin deficits to grow with very little national savings, this could eventually degrade the dollar's quality, and lead to the loss of its hegemony.

In his book *Exorbitant Privilege: the Rise and Fall of the US Dollar and the Future of the International Monetary System* (2011), economist Barry Eichengreen explains that the dollar ultimately enables American households to live structurally beyond their means, as investors around the world are fond of dollar-denominated debt. In particular, the United States provides the rest of the world with risk-free debt in the form of Treasury bills, which are used to finance the US public deficit.

Indeed, whenever there is turbulence in global finance, international investors flock to US debt securities (especially Treasury bonds and bills). During the late 20th century, Wall Street swallowed nearly three-quarters of international financial flows, a situation which lasted until the 2000s. Paradoxically, the US economy was then suffering from stagnating productivity gains, while serious competitors were emerging on a global scale: first Japan, then China.

As early as 2005, former US Fed Chairman Paul Volcker predicted: "I know of no country that has succeeded for any length of time in consuming and investing 6% more than it produces". The only way to perpetuate this system was to maintain Wall Street's position as the epicenter of global finance. This meant completing deregulation, and encouraging the unbridled development of financial engineering and derivatives. From then on, profits returned to investors were no longer generated in the real economy, but in the virtual mazes of Wall Street.

As Fig. 9.2 shows, by the end of the 1990s, the US public balance was in surplus for the first time. This was hailed by many experts as a sign of sound macroeconomic management, testifying to the robustness of the new finance-led US capitalism. But, coupled with the trade deficit, this surplus in the public balance could only be the mirror image of a dangerous accounting counterpart: the appearance of a negative balance in the private sector (Eq. 9.1). This toxic private debt was, of course, to be found in the financial maze of Wall Street. After an initial warning in 2001, with the collapse of the dotcom bubble, the inevitable crash occurred in 2008, following a—albeit minor—downturn in the US housing market (see Box 9.2).

Box 9.2: The *Subprime* Crisis

One of the most popular financial engineering techniques on Wall Street in the early 2000's was the securitization of mortgages in financial packages of staggering complexity. This technique involved combining credit derivatives with tranches of bank loan portfolios using sophisticated statistical and computer methods. The new derivatives (known as collateralized debt obligations, or CDOs) thus obtained were then re-securitized, i.e. combined with other securities to form new instruments whose collateral was linked to the tranches created in the previous securitization wave.

These financial arrangements were so complex that no expert was able to calculate the extent of the losses when the original borrowers defaulted on their mortgages. A wave of panic swept through the global economy, paralyzing bond and interbank markets, freezing credit to households and businesses, causing the US stock market index to plunge by 40% and international trade to contract by 12%. The scale of the losses was staggering: 54 million jobs and 4,000 billion in financial assets were destroyed worldwide. For many observers, this crisis marked the beginning of the new, uncertain economic world of the 21st century. To avert a widespread collapse, the US House of Representatives voted on September 29, 2008 for a $700 billion bank rescue plan. In Europe, the aid granted between October 2008 and December 2010 was even greater, amounting to $1,000 billion, or 10% of the eurozone's GDP.

5 Contagion to the European Sovereign Debt Market

While government interventions prevented the international financial system from collapsing, they were tantamount to transferring bank debt to taxpayers. In a way, the banks had externalized their debts by transferring them to the States, whose deficits rose sharply (see Fig. 9.2). In the eurozone, unlike in the US, the Central Bank could not finance governments directly under Article 123 of the Lisbon Treaty. States therefore had to finance themselves through bond issues underwritten by the private sector. This situation theoretically created the possibility of a default by European states on their public debt.

As for the banks, once reanimated by the public sector, they adopted a zombie behavior and unleashed coordinated speculative attacks against the bonds issued by the European states deemed most fragile: Portugal, Ireland, Italy, Spain, and Greece—a group of countries then dubbed by the financial markets with the inelegant acronym PIIGS. While interest rate spreads had been very low since the introduction of the euro—which had largely contributed to the creation of real estate bubbles in the countries concerned—they soared, allowing banks to reap substantial profits in several market segments (see Fig. 9.3).

Faced with the imminent risk of implosion of the eurozone, the European Union took two important decisions, which put an end to the rise in interest rates:

1. Curbing speculation on government debt rates by prohibiting naked credit default swaps (CDS) operations, and by strictly regulating short sales (November 16, 2011).
2. Allowing the European Central Bank (like the US Fed) to acquire sovereign bonds through direct monetary operations, making it impossible for a member state to default on its public debt (August 2, 2012).

Shortly after these two announcements, interest rate spreads within the eurozone narrowed once again. Thus institutionally armed, the eurozone was able to weather the 2020 Covid crisis without fear of speculative attacks on sovereign bonds. But the crisis of 2012, which left deep scars on the economies and societies of the countries affected by the crisis, severely undermined the political legitimacy—still under construction—of a true European monetary sovereignty.

6 Can the International Financial Architecture Be Reformed?

The trade and financial imbalances accumulated in the US since the 1980s culminated into the major crisis of 2008, which led to an economic lost decade for many countries. Deploring the persistence of global imbalances linked to the role of the dollar, many economists are calling for a concerted reform of the International Monetary System (IMS)—i.e. the set of rules and

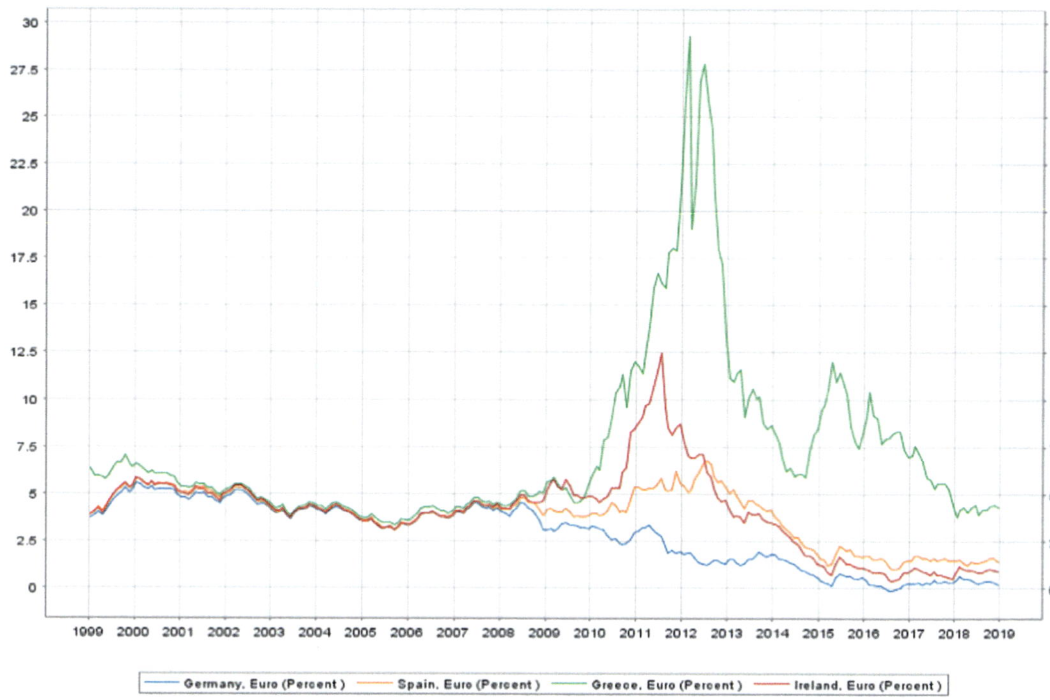

Fig. 9.3 Interest rate spreads within the Eurozone, 1999–2019 (*Source* https://sdw.ecb.europa.eu/)

institutions that determine exchange rates and the nature of international reserves (gold, foreign exchange, etc.). The aim would be to lay the foundations for international macroeconomic cooperation, making it possible to reduce trade and financial imbalances, in line with the Sustainable Development Goals (SDGs). The rules of the game of international trade and finance are geopolitical constructs reflecting economic doctrines, geopolitical power relations, and the needs of each era. One example is the creation of the Special Drawing Right (SDR) in 1969 (see Box 9.3). History shows that the IMS can be reformed to adapt to changing circumstances (see Fig. 9.4).

Box 9.3: Special Drawing Rights (SDR)

The SDR was created by the IMF in 1969 as a complementary international reserve asset under the Bretton Woods system of fixed exchange rates. Each country participating in the system was required to hold official reserves—gold held by the government or Central Bank and widely accepted foreign currencies—that could be used to buy back its national currency on the international foreign exchange markets, if necessary, to maintain its exchange rate.

But because of the shortage of international gold and dollars, the international community decided to create a new global reserve asset: the SDR. Strictly speaking, the SDR is neither a currency nor a claim on the IMF; it is a virtual claim on the currencies of IMF member countries. In addition to its role as a complementary reserve asset, the SDR serves as a unit of account for the IMF and several other international organizations. Its value was originally set at 0.888671 grams of fine gold, which then corresponded to one dollar. After the collapse of the Bretton Woods system in 1973, the value of the SDR was determined by reference to a

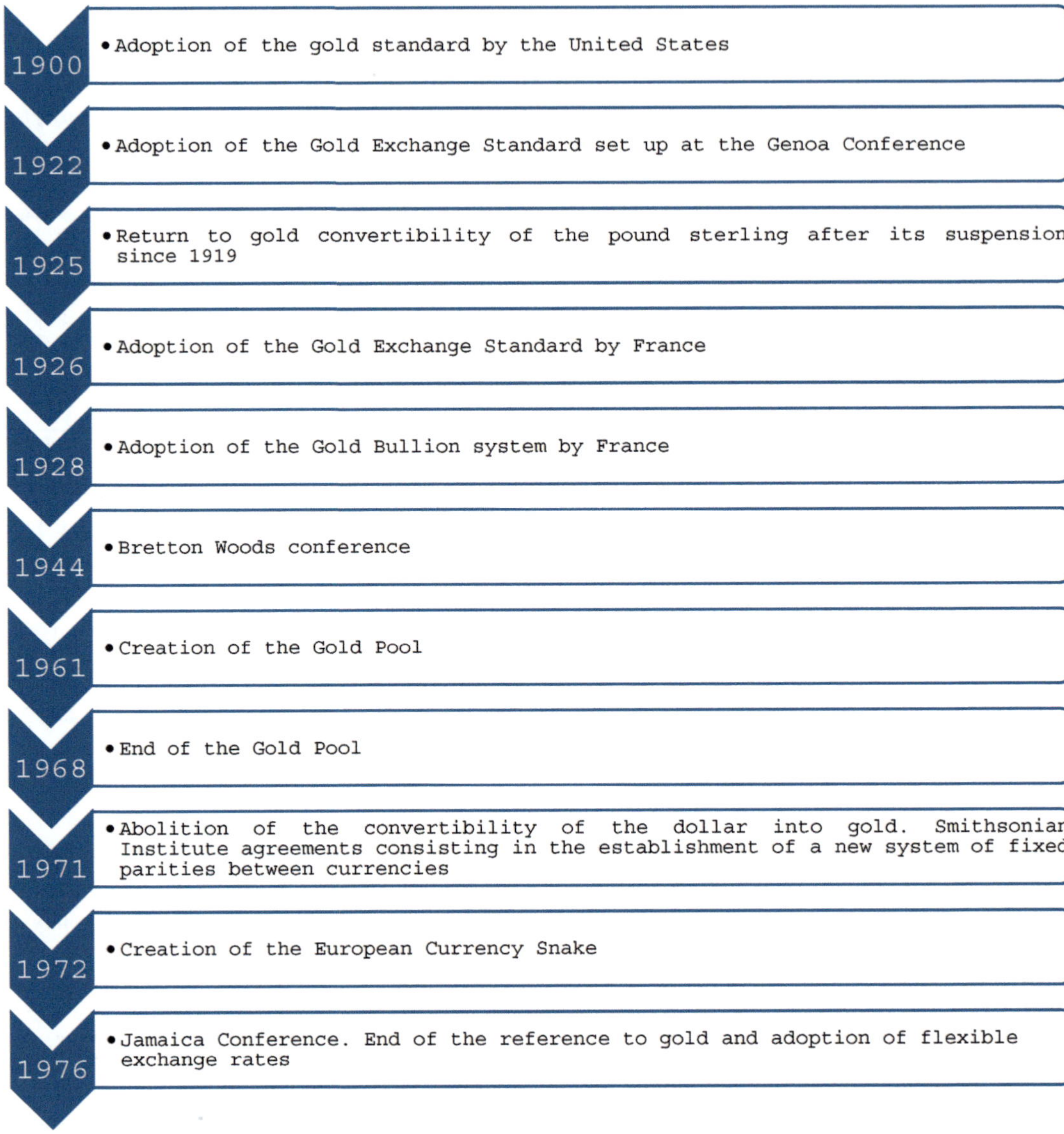

Fig. 9.4 The Evolution of the International Monetary System from 1900 to 1976

basket of currencies, the composition of which is reviewed at least every five years by the IMF Executive Board. Since 2021, the basket has been made up of the dollar, euro, pound sterling, yen and renminbi[2].

The value of the SDR in US dollars—calculated as the sum of the values in US dollars, based on market exchange rates, of the currencies in the basket—is determined daily and posted on the IMF website.

[2]The yuan is the unit of account of the renminbi (literally: 'the people's currency'), which is China's actual currency.

7 Conclusion

- The international macroeconomic equilibrium equation visualizes an economy's internal equilibrium and its position in relation to the rest of the world.
- Trade deficits lead to net capital inflows, reflecting the gap between national savings and domestic investment.
- The internal and external imbalances of the national economy reflect the inverse imbalances of partner economies.
- The twin US deficits led to a considerable rise in global systemic risk, culminating in the 2008 crisis and its contagion to the eurozone.
- The international monetary system is an evolving political construct.

Activities

Questions for Discussion

1. Explain the meaning of Eq. (6): $(S - I) + (T - G) + S_f = 0$. Define each of the terms and explain their relationships.
2. Why do national external imbalances reflect internal imbalances in the rest of the world?
3. From the following information, deduce the net financial position of the private sector:
   a. The current balance of payments shows a surplus of 1000 million euros, and the public budget is balanced.
   b. The public balance showed a surplus of 500 million euros, while the financial account of the balance of payments showed a deficit of 100 million euros.
   c. The current account balance showed a deficit of 50 million euros, and the public budget balance a deficit of 100 million euros.

Mini-Case: Building a Mirror Image of International Macroeconomic Equilibrium

The aim of this case study is to enable you to analyze the macroeconomic position of the country of your choice, taking the following steps.

1. Visit the World Economic Outlook database of the International Monetary Fund (IMF): https://www.imf.org/en/Publications/SPROLLs/world-economic-outlook-databases#sort=%40imfdate%20descending
2. Select the following variables:
   - *Total investment (as a percentage of GDP)*
   - *Gross national savings (as a percentage of GDP)*
   - *General government structural balance (as a percentage of GDP)*
   - *Current account balance (as a percentage of GDP)*
3. After importing these data into a spreadsheet, answer the following questions:
   a. Determine the annual value of the balance of payments' financial account (as a percentage of GDP).
   b. Calculate the economy's annual financial position (as a percentage of GDP), defined as the difference between gross national savings and total investment.
   c. Subtract the general government structural balance from the macroeconomic financial position calculated in the previous step, to obtain the annual financial position of the private sector (as a percentage of GDP).
   d. After selecting the required variables, represent the evolution of macroeconomic equilibrium in the form of a stacked histogram (as in Figs. 9.1 and 9.2).
   e. Comment on your results and illustrate your point by searching the Internet for additional information on the economy of the chosen country.

References

Bénassy-Quéré, A. (2023). *Economie Monétaire Internationale*. 3rd edition, Economica, France pp. 274 (untranslated).

10 Exchange Rates and the International Monetary Regime

Thomas Lagoarde-Ségot and Jean-François Ponsot

Putting Things into Perspective

Most international commercial or financial transactions require the purchase or sale of bank deposits in foreign currencies. The relative price of these currencies (the *exchange rate*) has a significant impact on balances of payments. For example, the value of the yuan in euros was used to invoice European imports of Chinese-made surgical masks during the Covid-19 pandemic.

As the graph below shows, the Chinese currency has fluctuated widely over the past 20 years. For example, one euro was worth between 7 and 8 yuan between 2000 and 2002. The euro then appreciated to over 10 yuan between 2003 and 2008, before depreciating continuously until 2015, and returning to a range between 7 and 8 yuan between 2016 and 2024.

T. Lagoarde-Ségot (✉)
KEDGE Business School (KEDGE BS), Talence, France
e-mail: thomas.lagoardesegot@kedgebs.com

J.-F. Ponsot
Université Grenoble Alpes, Grenoble, France
e-mail: jean-francois.ponsot@univ-grenoble-alpes.fr

T. Lagoarde-Ségot (ed.), *Ecological Economics and Finance*,
https://doi.org/10.1007/978-3-031-71249-4_10

Euro/Yuan Exchange Rate, 2000–2024

Source https://sdw.ecb.europa.eu/

Where and how are exchange rates formed? To what extent do they affect the external competitiveness of economies? How do central banks intervene? What are the main implications of the current monetary regime? These are the main themes addressed in this chapter.

Learning Objectives

- Discovering the structure of the foreign exchange market
- Differentiating between nominal and real exchange rates
- Analyzing central bank interventions

10.1 Structure of the Foreign Exchange Market

Unlike other financial assets (such as equities or bonds), the value of currencies is not determined on a centralized market. Instead, currencies are traded on a global network of traders known as the *forex*. On this over-the-counter market, foreign exchange dealers—specialized agents operating on behalf of a network of international corporations, pension funds, insurance companies, hedge funds, and other major investors—hold stocks of currencies which they are ready to buy and sell to anyone who comes to the counter (usually international banks and asset managers). Exchange rates on the *forex* are highly volatile on a day-to-day basis, with sustained bullish and bearish phases (see Fig. 10.1).

However, *forex* transactions are not limited to spot currency transactions. The Bank for International Settlements (BIS) groups foreign exchange transactions into five main categories:

- **spot transactions,** which consist of purchases of foreign currencies;
- **forward transactions**, which consist of contractual agreements entered into today to exchange currencies at a predetermined future date;

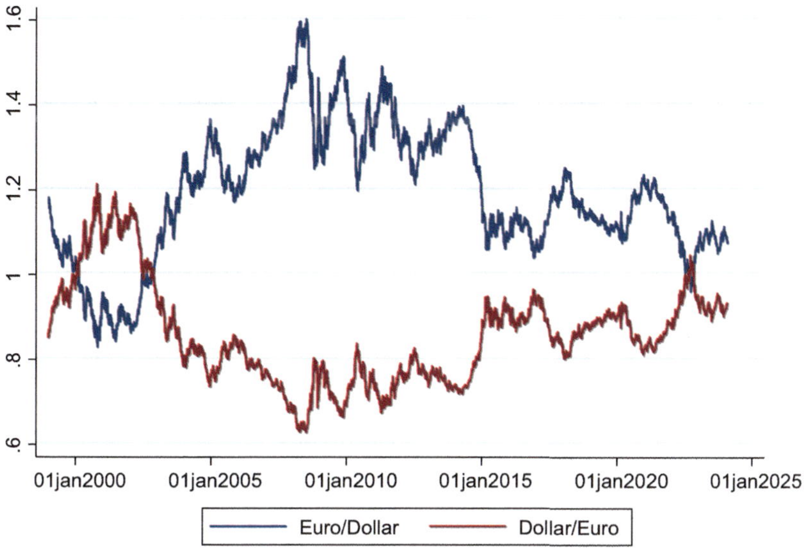

Fig. 10.1 Dollar/Euro overnight spot exchange Rate, 2000–2024 (*Source* https://data.ecb.europa.eu/. The blue line indicates the price of a euro in dollars, and the red line indicates the price of a dollar in euros. Generalizing to two countries i and j, the following relationship applies: $\lambda_{i,j} = \frac{1}{\lambda_{j,i}}$)

- **currency swaps**, in which one party buys (sells) deliverable currencies at a given date with a commitment to resell (repurchase) them at a later date;
- **currency swaps**, in which one party exchanges the repayment of a loan denominated in one currency for a loan of the same value denominated in another currency;
- **currency options**, in which one party acquires the contractual right to buy or sell a currency stock at a specific rate on a predetermined future date.

Figure 10.2 shows the trend in average *daily* turnover on the foreign exchange market between 2010 and 2022. In 2022, average daily turnover reached around $7,500 billion. By comparison, in that year, the *annual* value of world trade in exported goods was $25,000 billion. Three days of forex trading were roughly equivalent to a year's worth of world trade. With almost 90% of foreign exchange orders reversed in a single day, the forex is unequivocally one of the world's most speculative financial markets.

Furthermore, Table 10.1 shows that the overwhelming majority of spot foreign exchange transactions—around 90%—involve the US dollar. The other most-traded currencies are the euro (30.5% of transactions in 2022), the Japanese yen (16.7% of transactions) and sterling (12.9% of transactions).

One of the reasons for the US dollar's hegemony is that it serves as a vehicle for international transactions, particularly those involving little-traded currencies. For example, it is difficult to directly exchange Uruguayan pesos for Tunisian dinars. To carry out such a transaction, it may be necessary first to exchange pesos for dollars, then dollars for dinars. Holding US dollar-denominated assets thus offers greater *liquidity* to foreign exchange market participants. This, of course, reinforces the global currency hierarchy (see Box 10.1).

Box 10.1: The Global Currency Hierarchy

Since the dollar's convertibility was suspended in 1971, international monetary relations have no longer been governed by a system organized by international agreements. It is no longer rules adopted collectively and applied universally that regulate international monetary practices,

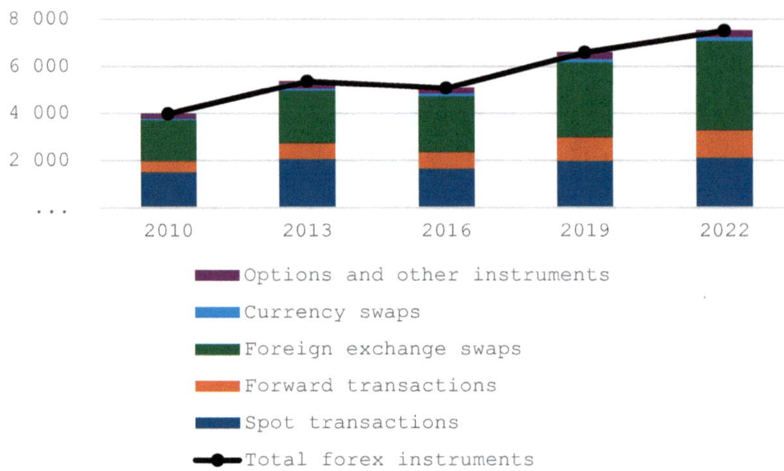

Fig. 10.2 Average daily sales in foreign currencies (millions of US dollars), 2010–2022 (*Source* https://www.bis.org/statistics/rpfx22.htm)

but conventions and power relations. This lack of a coherent architecture has established the hegemony of the US dollar and a hierarchical monetary system that is increasingly contested, as it generates negative externalities and asymmetries.

The *monetary hierarchy* (Fritz, De Paula, and Prates, 2018) that characterizes international relations is profoundly inequitable in the sense that it structures significant asymmetry effects. In economic terms, it confers an exorbitant privilege on the United States, allowing it to take on large, even almost unlimited, debts in its own currency. Unlike emerging and developing economies, the United States can pursue autonomous counter-cyclical policies without worrying about their consequences for the rest of the world, following the principle that "the dollar is our currency, but your problem" (as stated by US Treasury Secretary John Connally in 1971).

The situation is quite different in emerging and developing economies. For example, loans granted by major commercial banks to companies in developing countries are often denominated in US dollars. When the US dollar appreciates, the debt burden of issuers in developing countries increases. Since the global financial crisis, and especially since the war in Ukraine, emerging economies have stepped up their efforts to emancipate themselves from the dollar. While this challenge to the monetary hierarchy is perfectly legitimate, it does present a risk: that of monetary fragmentation, the costs of which could be high in the absence of international coordination.

Source Fritz, B., De Paula, L. and Prates, D. (2018), "Global currency hierarchy and national policy space: a framework for peripheral economies", *European Journal of Economics and Economic Policies: Intervention*, vol. 15(2), pp. 208–218.

10.2 Effective Exchange Rate

Of course, a national currency can depreciate against some currencies, and appreciate against others. To make parities easier to read, government agencies, banks, and international organizations construct a synthetic indicator: the *effective exchange rate* (EER). This corresponds

Table 10.1 Breakdown of spot foreign exchange transactions, 2010–2022

	2010		2013		2016		2019		2022	
	Amount	%	Amount	%	Amount	%	Amount	%	Amount	%
USD	3371	84,9	4662	87.0	4437	87.6	5811	88.3	6639	88.4
EUR	1551	39,0	1790	33.4	1590	31.4	2126	32.3	2292	30.5
JPY	754	19,0	1235	23.0	1096	21.6	1108	16.8	1253	16.7
GBP	512	12,9	633	11.8	649	12.8	843	12.8	968	12.9
CNY	34	0,9	120	2.2	202	4.0	285	4.3	526	7.0
AUD	301	7,6	463	8.6	349	6.9	446	6.8	479	6.4
CAD	210	5,3	244	4.6	260	5.1	332	5.0	466	6.2
CHF	250	6,3	276	5.2	243	4.8	326	4.9	390	5.2
HKD	94	2,4	77	1.4	88	1.7	233	3.5	194	2.6
SGD	56	1,4	75	1.4	91	1.8	119	1.8	182	2.4
SEK	87	2,2	94	1.8	112	2.2	134	2.0	168	2.2
KRW	60	1,5	64	1.2	84	1.7	132	2.0	142	1.9

Source https://www.bis.org/statistics/rpfx22.htm

to the weighted average of a currency's bilateral exchange rates. The weights used, which are regularly updated, reflect the share of each foreign currency in the international trade of the country concerned.

A second indicator, the *real effective exchange rate* (REER), captures an economy's external competitiveness. It corresponds to the effective exchange rate adjusted for inflation differentials. By noting $\lambda_{i,j}$ the nominal effective exchange rate of currency i, $\frac{P_i}{P_j}$ the ratio between the domestic price index (P_i) and the average price index of trading partners (P_j) Eq. (1) gives the *real* exchange rate $\widehat{\lambda_{i,j}}$:

$$\widehat{\lambda_{i,j}} = \lambda_{i,j} * \frac{P_i}{P_j} \tag{1}$$

If $\widehat{\lambda_{i,j}}$ increases, the price competitiveness of country i decreases, and vice versa. The cause of changes in the REER can be identified by transforming Eq. (1) into a first difference:

$$\Delta\widehat{\lambda_{i,j}} = \Delta\lambda_{i,j} * \frac{\Delta P_i}{\Delta P_j} \tag{2.1}$$

$$\rightarrow \log\left(\Delta\widehat{\lambda_{i,j}}\right) = \log(\Delta\lambda_{i,j}) + \left(\log(\Delta P_i) - \log(\Delta P_j)\right) \tag{2.2}$$

Equation (2.2) shows that changes in an economy's price competitiveness can come from a change in the nominal exchange rate (i.e. an increase in $\lambda_{i,j}$), in the domestic inflation ($log(\Delta P_i)$) or in the foreign inflation ($log(\Delta P_j)$).

Within the euro zone, the European Central Bank (ECB) calculates the nominal and real effective exchange rates of the single currency. These exchange rates take into account relative inflation rates and bilateral exchange rates between the euro zone and its 42 trading partners in the rest of the world. The ECB determines the weights required for this calculation on the basis of trade volumes in manufactured goods and services between the euro zone and its external partners.[1] For instance, the euro/dollar and euro/yuan exchange rates each represented about 15% of the euro's nominal effective exchange rate in 2021.

In nominal terms, the euro has steadily appreciated against other currencies since its creation. European citizens and companies can now exchange one euro for more units of the representative basket of foreign currencies than in the past. On the other hand, the real effective exchange rate has been stable over time. This implies that the inflation rate in the eurozone

[1] The weightings used are available at: https://www.ecb.europa.eu/stats/balance_of_payments_and_external/eer/html/index.en.html.

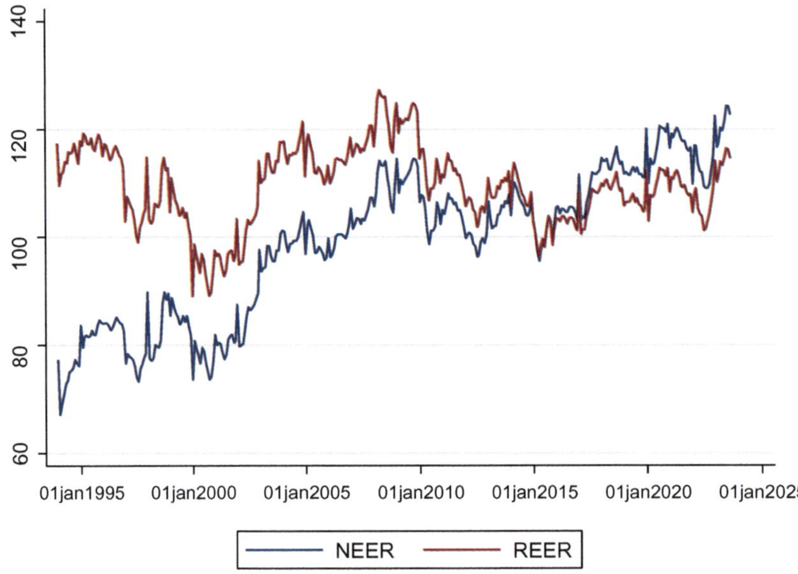

Fig. 10.3 Euro nominal and real effective exchange rates, 1994–2024 (*Source* https://sdw.ecb.europa.eu)

has remained lower overall than in the rest of the world (Eq. 2.2). Adjusted for price differentials, the evolution of the euro's nominal exchange rate therefore has no lasting impact on the purchasing power of European citizens. Nevertheless, these data, which are aggregated at euro zone level, mask significant internal disparities (see Box 10.2) (Fig. 10.3).

Box 10.2: Intra-European Divergences in the REER, 1995–2024

The following graph shows the evolution of the real effective exchange rate between 1995 and 2024 for four member countries of the European Union, then of the Eurozone: Germany, Spain, Greece, and Ireland.

Germany's real exchange rate fell steadily throughout this period, during which the country recorded gains in external competitiveness. The real exchange rates of Spain, Greece, and Ireland, on the other hand, were more chaotic. During the early years of the euro, between 1999 and the onset of the financial crisis in 2008, their real exchange rates rose sharply, implying a deterioration in the external competitiveness of these economies. The trend then reversed, first in Ireland with the bursting of the real estate bubble in 2009, then in Spain and Greece with the eruption of the sovereign debt crisis in 2013. Since these four countries use the same currency (the euro), the differences in real exchange rates observed stem exclusively from domestic price trends. Indeed, massive capital inflows into Ireland, Greece, and Spain led to high inflation in the 2000s, fuelled by bank credit and real estate speculation. Subsequently, the fiscal austerity programs implemented in these countries during the European sovereign debt crisis led to price cuts and restored their external competitiveness—at the cost of a severe recession. To describe this type of adjustment, in which real exchange rate depreciation is caused by domestic deflation, economists sometimes use the term *internal devaluation*.

Four European real effective exchange rates, 1995–2024

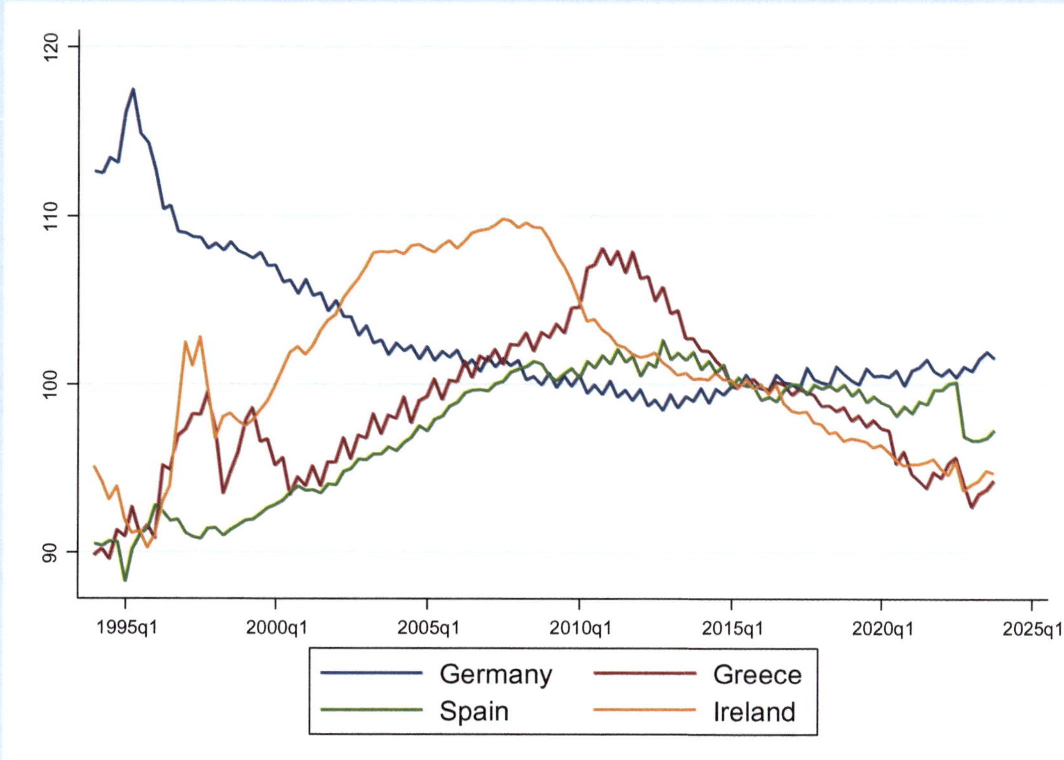

Source https://db.nomics.world/

10.3 Central Bank Interventions in the *Forex*

The *forex* is an uncertain environment dominated by self-referential rationality, intrinsic instability, and speculative calculations (see Chapter 11). In practice, however, central bank intervention moderates currency floating. These interventions—which may be isolated or coordinated, public or secret, planned or surprising—generally aim to align the real exchange rate with a target value. The Central Bank establishes the latter as part of its mandate, with reference to internal objectives (e.g. economic growth, employment, and inflation) or external objectives (if the country is a member of an exchange rate agreement).

An Example: The Bank of Algeria

To describe how these interventions work, we'll take the example of an emerging North African hydrocarbon-exporting country: Algeria. Since the early 1990s, this country has adopted a managed float regime for its currency (the Algerian dinar). The Bank of Algeria's interventions on the forex market are aimed at bringing the nominal value of the dinar down to an annual target. This target is expressed as a real effective exchange rate, and has three objectives: to support economic growth, maintain price stability, and generate a current account surplus.

Let's imagine that the euro depreciates sharply, and the Bank of Algeria wishes to avoid

Table 10.2 Impact of anti-appreciation intervention on the central bank's balance sheet

Δ Assets	Δ Liabilities
Foreign exchange reserves: + 100	Domestic reserves: + 100

Table 10.3 Impact of sterilization on the central bank's balance sheet

Δ Assets	Δ Liabilities
Treasury bills: - 100	Domestic reserves: - 100

an appreciation of the dinar. In this case, it can issue new domestic reserves, which it immediately exchanges on the foreign exchange market for sovereign securities of euro zone member states (German *Bunds*, for example). As shown in Table 10.2, this operation inflates its balance sheet, both on the assets side (the volume of foreign exchange reserves) and on the liabilities side (the monetary base).

This operation symmetrically increases the supply of dinars and the demand for euros on the forex market. All other things being equal, the value of the Algerian dinar should appreciate and converge toward the Bank of Algeria's target.

Nevertheless, the increase in the monetary base may cause the interbank interest rate to slip below its target (see Chapter 5). In response, the Bank of Algeria may sell a financial asset (e.g. an Algerian Treasury bond) against reserve money on the *open market.*

As shown in Table 10.3, this *sterilization* operation reduces the size of the central bank's balance sheet: its assets and liabilities will fall by 100. The reflux of reserves onto the central bank's balance sheet dries up the interbank market and limits the fall in the interbank interest rate. The central bank can thus hope to achieve its external and internal monetary policy objectives.

Now imagine the opposite situation: the euro appreciates sharply, leading to a sudden depreciation of the Algerian dinar. To maintain the dinar's value, the Banque d'Algérie must then draw on its foreign exchange reserves (e.g. German *Bunds*) to acquire dinars. This operation shrinks its balance sheet, leading to a contraction in the national money supply (see Table 10.4).

Table 10.4 Impact of anti-depreciation intervention on the central bank's balance sheet

Δ Assets	Δ Liabilities
Foreign exchange reserves: - 100 (euro zone sovereigns)	Domestic reserves: - 100

Table 10.5 Impact of sterilization on the central bank's balance sheet

Δ Assets	Δ Liabilities
Treasury bills: + 100	Domestic reserves: + 100

Nevertheless, the reflux of reserve money into the central bank's balance sheet could cause an unexpected rise in the interbank interest rate. The Bank of Algeria can then *sterilize* its anti-depreciation intervention by issuing new domestic reserves, which it immediately exchanges for domestic assets (e.g. Treasury bills) on the *open market* (see Table 10.5).

The Asymmetry of the International Monetary Regime

It can be deduced from the above that central banks have an interest in accumulating foreign exchange reserves to avoid unexpected depreciation of the national currency. Holding foreign currency is even more necessary in many developing countries, where commercial banks can only acquire the foreign currency needed for imports (e.g. medicines) by borrowing it from the central bank.

As official reserves are the accounting counterpart of trade surpluses (see Chapter 9), many economists point out that the current monetary regime encourages all economies—first and foremost those of the Global South—to compress domestic demand in order to lower the real exchange rate and increase external competitiveness. It therefore includes a *deflationary bias* unfavorable to growth and sustainable development.

Since the Covid-19 pandemic, rich-country central banks (such as the US Federal Reserve,

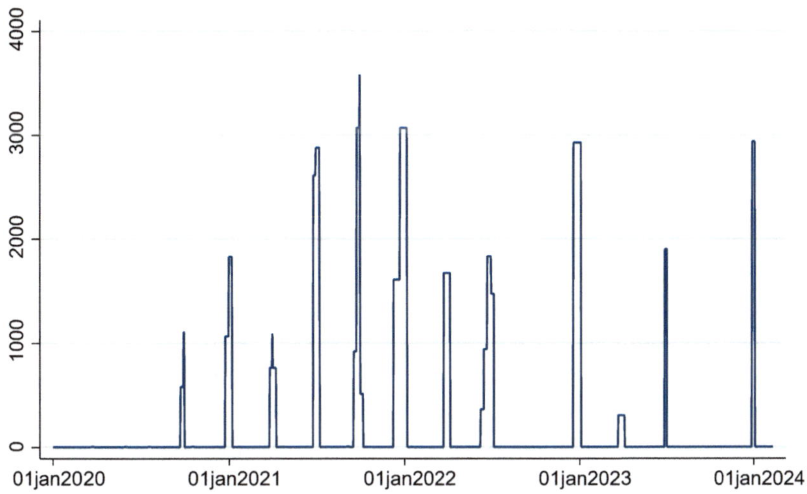

Fig. 10.4 Historical liquidity provided by the European Central Bank across all central bank liquidity lines, 2020–2024 (in millions of euros) (*Source* https://www.ecb.europa.eu/mopo/implement/liquidity_lines/html/index.en.html)

the ECB, the Bank of England, the Bank of Switzerland, the Bank of Canada, and the Bank of Japan) frequently lend official reserves to emerging-country central banks, within the framework of bilateral or regional memorandums of understanding (see Fig. 10.4). While such transactions are often essential to maintaining international financial stability, the rich countries derive a power of financial and geopolitical seigniorage from them. The situation of the countries of the Global South is quite different, as they are kept in a situation of triple commercial, financial, and monetary dependence. This is why many economists are now calling for a reform of the international monetary regime to make it a *global public good* (see Box 10.3).

Box 10.3: Understanding the Failings of the International Monetary Regime

According to Jean-François Ponsot (2016), the current international monetary regime contains four negative externalities corresponding to four "I"s:

The first "I" refers to monetary and financial instability. This not only concerns volatile exchange rates and capital movements, but also international foreign currency indebtedness.

The second "I" underlines the uncertainties ("*incertitude*" in French) arising from Triffin's dilemma: uncertainty about the supply of international liquidity when the United States has a surplus position relative to the rest of the world; and uncertainty about the future value of dollar assets when the United States are running large external deficits.

The third "I" refers to insufficient aggregate demand. Under the current international monetary regime, the burden of adjustment in the event of balance-of-payment imbalances is not shared equitably between surplus and deficit countries. The burden of adjustment generally falls on the deficit country, especially if it is a small one, and not on the surplus country. In order to adjust, the deficit country must activate austerity policies and boost price competitiveness by lowering unit labor costs, which penalizes aggregate demand and reduces the rate of economic growth. Another deflationary effect of the international monetary regime stems from the tendency toward excessive accumulation of foreign currency reserves: to protect themselves against financial instability, economies tend to stockpile large foreign currency reserves, which is costly and penalizes economic growth.

The fourth "I", inequity, stems from the first three. The inequitable nature of the international monetary regime, in both macroeconomic and political terms, is unsustainable in the long term. It considerably limits the room for maneuver of the most vulnerable economies to undertake ambitious economic development and ecological transition policies.

Source Ponsot, J.F. (2016), The 'four I's' of the International Monetary System and the International Role of the Euro. *Research in International Business and Finance* 37, pp. 299–308.

10.4 Conclusion

- The foreign exchange market is the largest, least regulated, and most speculative financial market in the world.
- One must distinguish between the nominal exchange rate, which expresses the relative value of a currency, and the real exchange rate, which measures an economy's external competitiveness.
- The current configuration of the international monetary regime is asymmetrical and contains several negative externalities.

Activities

Questions for Discussion

1. Go to the International Monetary Fund website and download the exchange rate and current account balance data for a country of your choice. Plot the data on a graph. Does the evolution of this country's nominal exchange rate seem correlated with its current account balance? Why or why not?
2. Go to the International Monetary Fund website and download the nominal exchange rate and real effective exchange rate data for a country of your choice. Plot the data on a graph. How do you explain the trends observed?
3. The euro appreciates by 1% against the US dollar. In the same year, inflation reached 0.75% in the euro zone and 2% in the United States. How has the euro zone's price competitiveness evolved?
4. The national currency is depreciating. How can the central bank try to reverse the trend? What are the conditions for successful intervention? What are the possible domestic effects? How can the central bank reconcile its exchange rate policy with its monetary policy?
5. Go to the European Central Bank website, and look for information on the liquidity lines that the ECB makes available to partner countries. Describe the different issuance mechanisms, distinguishing between swap and repo transactions. In your opinion, do these transactions make it possible to limit asymmetries in the monetary regime?

Mini-Case

After watching the BBC documentary *Black Wednesday* (1997), answer the following questions:

1. Describe how the European monetary system worked in 1992.
2. What vulnerabilities led to its collapse?
3. Who were the main protagonists in the currency crisis? What were their respective strategies?
4. Why has the Bank of England failed to defend the value of sterling?
5. Why was coordination between European central banks so difficult during the crisis?
6. Can the creation of the euro be seen as an appropriate response to the failure of the European monetary system?

Financial Markets: From Efficiency to Intrinsic Instability

11

David Bourghelle

Putting Things into Perspective
"Our times are characterized by a dangerous inversion in which the economic subsystem, driven by financial indicators, colonizes the bio-geo-physical super-system in which it is embedded." This is how Lagoarde-Segot and Martinez (2021) speak of the "transformation" brought about by financialized capitalism: finance disengaged from the economy, itself disengaged from the social and natural environment in which economic and financial players are immersed. What is finance? How do financial markets work? What role do they play? What risks do they pose for our societies? What accounts for financial instability and bubbles? Can finance be sustainable? These are the questions we'll be answering in this chapter.

Learning Objectives

- Acquire a sound knowledge of financial markets
- Learn to read quotes and calculate stock and bond prices
- Understanding the efficient market hypothesis and its limits
- Understanding financial bubbles
- Questioning sustainable finance

11.1 Financial Markets

Finance refers to all the means and instruments that enable economic agents to temporarily spend more than they earn. Households, companies, governments, and all organizations planning investments can thus finance the "advances" that their consumption and investment activities entail.

Financial markets are the place where financial securities are issued and traded. Their function is to:

- allocate financial resources to finance public or private productive investments;
- enhance the value of assets and facilitate the transfer of associated risks;
- ensure liquidity, i.e. the negotiability of securities.

New financial securities are issued on the primary market. These include IPOs, capital increases, and new bond issues. Secondary markets, on the other hand, enable investors to ensure, in principle, the reversibility of their investment. This is an important function, as the

D. Bourghelle (✉)
Université de Lille, Lille, France
e-mail: david.bourghelle@univ-lille.fr

T. Lagoarde-Ségot (ed.), *Ecological Economics and Finance*,
https://doi.org/10.1007/978-3-031-71249-4_11

liquidity of secondary markets reduces investors' anxiety about the risk of not being able to sell the securities they have acquired on the primary market.

Equity Markets

A share is a title to a company's capital. Its acquisition on the primary or secondary market confers a certain number of prerogatives on its holder: voting rights allowing a say in the company's management, a right to dividends (share of profits paid out each year), and rights over the company's net assets (shareholders' equity). Some shares have no voting rights, but are entitled to a priority dividend (preference shares).

Company shares are listed on the stock market. To illustrate this, let's take the case of Schneider Electric shares.[1] On a centralized electronic market (such as Euronext), bids and offers are matched directly in a computerized order book. Investors transmit buy (sell) orders, specifying the quantity and, where applicable, a price ceiling (floor) above (below) which they refuse to have their order executed.

During a trading session, the spread between buying and selling prices gives an indication of trading conditions at a given moment. If it is very wide, it means that the market for that stock is illiquid. Similarly, if the quantities of shares available for purchase and sale and/or the number of orders are low, the depth of the market for this stock is insufficient, which is also indicative of an illiquid market. Lastly, if the successive price levels observed in the queues are widely spaced, a large buy (sell) order will generate a cascade execution at increasingly higher (lower) prices, triggering significant price movements.

A stock that can be bought and sold instantly, cheaply and in large quantities is attractive to an investor because it can be released easily.

[1] https://www.boursorama.com/cours/1rPSU/.

Box 11.1: Determinants of a Stock's "Fundamental" Value

When an investor buys a financial security, the aim is to obtain a certain return. This comes from dividends (in the case of shares) and capital gains (on resale). Since this income is uncertain (there is no contractual obligation for the company to pay dividends), the purchase of a security is merely the acquisition of a promise of future income.

In this way, the value of a share at a given point in time is supposed to reflect expectations of future income (expected dividends and expected resale value VR) or all dividends D_1, D_2 … D_3 projected over an infinite horizon and discounted at the rate of return r expected by the investor:

$$V_0 = \frac{D_1}{1+r} + \frac{D_2}{(1+r)^2} + \ldots\ldots \frac{D_n}{(1+r)^n} + \frac{VR_n}{(1+r)^n}$$

When financial analysts seek to calculate the equity value of a mature company that offers its shareholders a constant rate of growth in future dividends, they use the Gordon-Shapiro (G-S) model:

$$V_0 = \frac{D_1}{r-g}$$

This ratio shows that share value is based on the future dividend (D_1), the expected dividend growth rate (g), and the rate of return expected by shareholders (r). As shown below, however, the results of this calculation are highly sensitive to changes in the value chosen for the parameters, particularly the growth rate (g):

Illustration

In August 2021, Schneider Electric's estimated dividend per share (DPS) was 2.75 euros, corresponding to a payout ratio of around 48% of earnings per share (EPS). Several assumptions can then be made concerning the expected dividend growth rate (g, assumed constant) and the expected rate of return (r).

Assumption 1: $D_1 = 2.75$ $g=5\%$ and $r = 6\%$ $V_0 = \frac{2.75}{6\%-5\%} = 275$ euros.

Assumption 2: $D_1 = 2.75$ $g=3\%$ and $r=6\%$. $V_0 = \frac{2.75}{6\%-3\%} = 91.66$ euros.

By varying g between 3 and 5%, the result obtained for the fundamental value of the share is tripled. Under these conditions, it is quite difficult to provide a precise value.

Bond Markets

A bond is a debt security issued by a company, bank, insurance company, or government. It is in fact a debt for the issuer (who is the seller of the securities and therefore the borrower) and a claim for the buyer (who is the lender). The purchase of bonds on the primary or secondary market gives entitlement to the payment of (often fixed) coupons. Unlike a bank loan, whose total amount is granted by a single creditor (a bank), the overall value of a bond loan is divided into a multitude of shares (bonds), whose unit face value is fixed at the time of issue. The life of the bonds varies from two to over 100 years. The loan is repaid over time (constant amortization, constant annuities) or at maturity (bullet repayment).

Bond Listings

The bonds are listed on the secondary market. Let's take a French OAT (*Obligation Assimilable du Trésor*) issued on May 25, 2017 for a term of 31 years (maturity date May 25, 2048), with a face value of 1 euro at a fixed rate (facial rate or coupon rate) of 2%. The annual remuneration for a buyer (holding a security for at least one year) is 0.02 euros ($2\% \times 1$).

The bond was issued at a price slightly higher than its par value, i.e. 100.07% of 1 euro (prices are expressed as a percentage of par value). Based on November 2023 quotations, the bond price was 74.95% (0.7495 euro). An investor who buys the bond on May 25, 2017 at 1.0007 and holds it to maturity will receive a total of 0.62 euros in interest (31 coupons of 0.02 euros), and the bond will be redeemed at 1 euro, giving a gain of 0.6193 (0.62–0.0007). If this same investor resold the bond, for example, on November 23, 2023, he would have done so at a price of 74.95% (the price then available). In this case, he would have realized a capital loss of 0.2512 (0.7495–1.0007), partly offset by the coupons received since his purchase.

Bond Yields

Following several decades of declining interest rate trends, the resurgence of inflation and the tightening of conventional monetary policies have pushed bond yields to levels not seen for over 15 years (see Box 11.2). These significant rate hikes are not without consequences for bond valuations (see Box 11.3).

Box 11.2: Inflation and Bond Yields

Headline & Core Inflation US 2019-2025

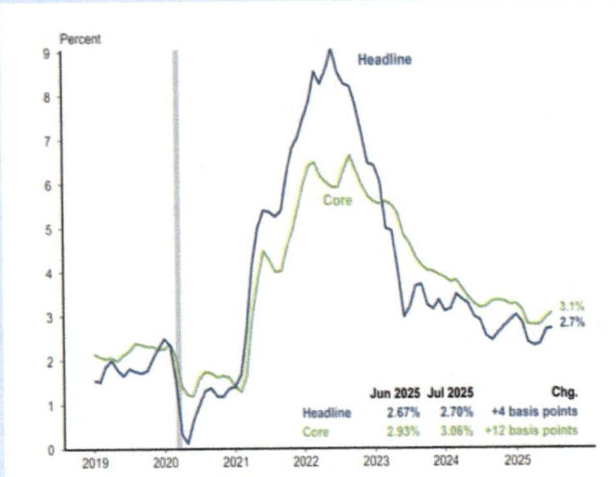

Source: Bureau of Labor Statistics via Haver Analytics. Gray shading indicates NBER recession dates.

Contributions to 12-month headline CPI inflation in the US zone

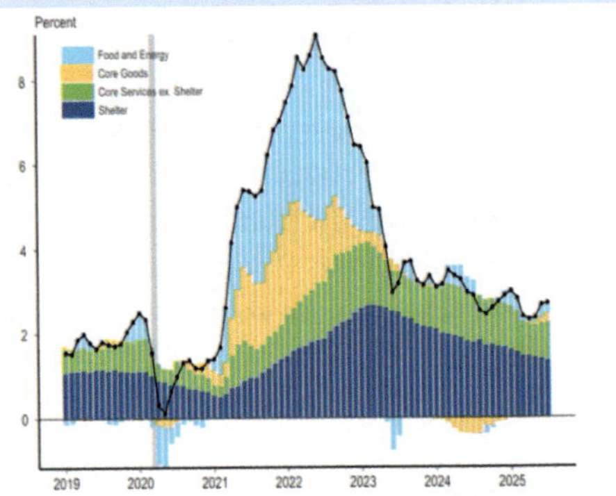

Source: Bureau of Labor Statistics via Haver Analytics and FRBSF staff calculations. Gray shading indicates NBER recession dates. Solid black line is the 12-month headline CPI inflation rate.

Headline & Core Inflation Eurozone 2019-2024

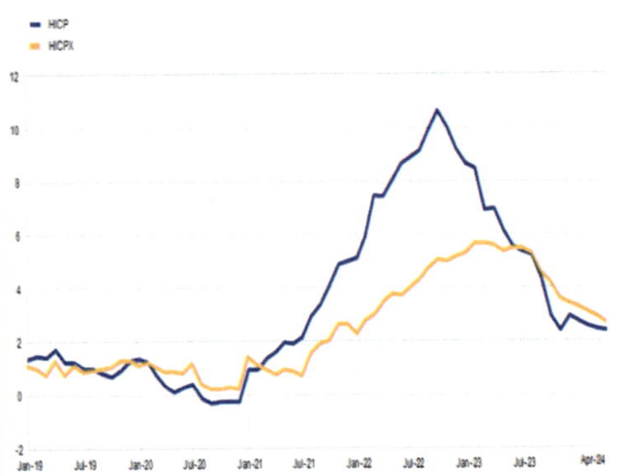

Sources: Eurostat.

Notes: HICP refers to headline inflation and HICPX to HICP excluding food and energy. The latest observation are for April 2024.

Contributions to headline HICP inflation in the Eurozone

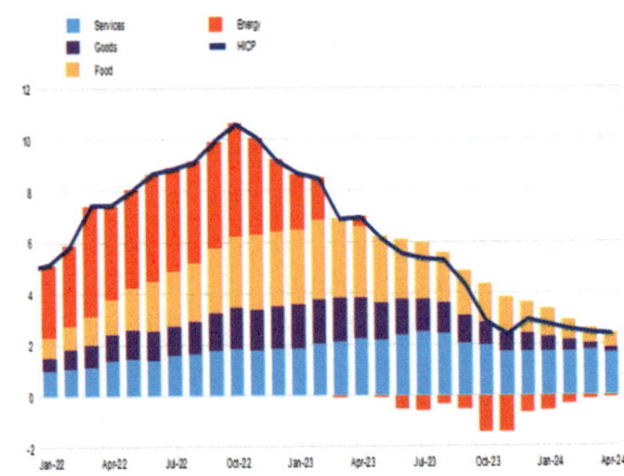

Sources: Eurostat and ECB staff calculations.

Notes: Goods refers to non-energy industrial goods. The latest observations are for April 2024.

US Long-term government bond yields -10 years (%)

Eurozone Long-term bond yields -10 years (%)

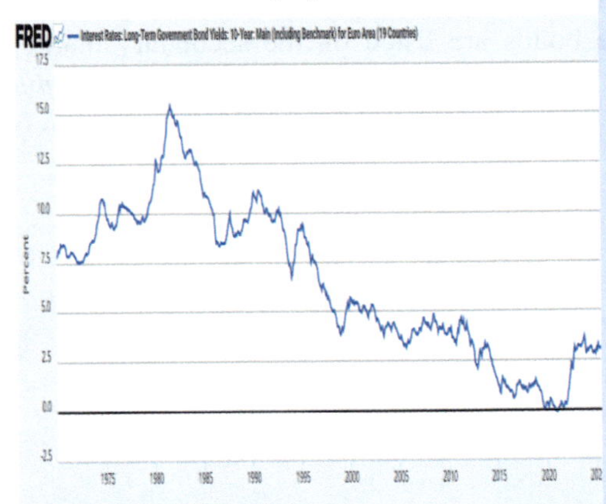

Source: Federal Reserve Bank of San Francisco (2024) CPI Inflation Contributions from Goods and Services. https://am.jpmorgan.com/content/dam/jpm-am-aem/emea/regional/fr/insights/market-insights/mi-guide-to-the-markets-fr.pdf

European Central Bank (2024). Inflation in the euro area. Speech by Philip R. Lane, Member of the Executive Board of the ECB, at the Institute of International and European Affairs, Dublin. https://www.ecb.europa.eu/press/key/date/2024/html/ecb.sp240527~13d86a7d66.en.html?utm_source=chatgpt.com

Box 11.3: Determinants of Bond Values

The value of a bond depends on a number of parameters: the expected rate of inflation, the level of interest rates, the risk of default (as perceived by investors on the basis of known information). The price of a bond paying a fixed coupon and redeemed in n years at par value VN is given by:

$$P_0 = \frac{C_1}{1+r} + \frac{C_2}{(1+r)^2} + \ldots\ldots \frac{C_n}{(1+r)^n} + \frac{V_n}{(1+r)^n} \cdots \leftrightarrow P_0$$

$$= \sum\nolimits_{t=1}^{n} \frac{C_1}{(1+r)^t} + \frac{V_n}{(1+r)^n} = c \times \left[\frac{1-(1+r)^{-n}}{r}\right] \frac{VN}{(1+r)^n}$$

From this formulation, it is possible to calculate the value of the bond from the sequence of flows and the expected rate of return r (*yield to maturity*). Thus, a five-year bond with a face value of 100 and an expected yield to maturity corresponding to the coupon rate of 2% will be quoted at issue:

$$P_0 = \sum_{t=1}^{5} \frac{2}{(1.02)^t} + \frac{100}{(1.02)^5} = 2 \times \left[\frac{1-(1+0.02)^{-5}}{0.02}\right] + \frac{100}{(1.02)^5} = 100 = 100\%$$

If, one year later, economic conditions have changed such that interest rates for the same maturity as the bond (four years in this case) have risen and/or the issuing company's default risk has increased, and the yield to maturity demanded by investors is no longer 2% but 3%, then the bond's market price adjusts downwards as follows:

$$P_1 = \sum\nolimits_{t=1}^{4} \frac{2}{(1.03)^t} + \frac{100}{(1.03)^4} = 2 \times \left[\frac{1-(1+0.03)^{-4}}{0.03}\right] + \frac{100}{(1.03)^4} = 96.2829\%$$

Conversely, if the yield to maturity demanded by investors is reduced to a level of 1%, the bond's market price will adjust upwards:

$$P_1 = \sum\nolimits_{t=1}^{4} \frac{2}{(1.01)^t} + \frac{100}{(1.01)^4} = 2 \times \left[\frac{1-(1+0.01)^{-4}}{0.01}\right] + \frac{100}{(1.01)^4} = 103.9019\%$$

11.2 From Market Efficiency to Intrinsic Instability

Standard financial theory is based on the risk-return trade-off. In essence, the riskier your investment, the higher the return you can expect. In other words, there is a hierarchy of risk-return pairs on the financial markets.

Historical returns can be calculated as the sum of a security's income and capital gains (on resale). Risk is most often associated with fluctuations in the price of financial assets over a given period, i.e. their volatility. Its most common measure is the standard deviation (square root of the variance, a statistical measure of the dispersion of fluctuations in the price of a security around its mean).

Using price series produced on financial markets, it is possible to estimate risk premiums, i.e. the additional remuneration (in relation to the risk-free rate) that an investor is entitled to expect, given the level of risk to which he is exposed.

The aim of investors, who do not all have the same level of risk aversion (some are more attracted to risk than others), is to position themselves in the asset class or classes whose risk/return ratios best match their expectations. It is possible to calculate the (break-even) return that an investor is able to demand, given the risk borne. The best-known model used by practitioners to calculate this 'equilibrium return' is the Capital Asset Pricing Model (CAPM). In practice, only those shares whose expected return (taking into account future income) is higher than the equilibrium return will find a buyer on the market. The self-regulating mechanisms prevailing on financial markets would then produce efficient prices that constitute a relevant estimate of the intrinsic value of assets.

The Theory of Efficient Markets

As the founding framework of modern financial theory,[2] the efficient market hypothesis supports the idea that competition produces fair prices, which are likely to constitute reliable signals for investors. In a context of competition, investors are able to identify and use the true law of probability governing economic dynamics (rational expectations hypothesis), thus converging prices toward objective and calculable intrinsic values (informational efficiency), and guaranteeing an optimal allocation of savings (allocative efficiency).

Figure 11.1 gives a schematic representation of how the market value of a share is determined, assuming an efficient market.

However, if we replace the probabilistic risk hypothesis with the alternative hypothesis of radical uncertainty about the future,[3] the principle of the existence of a fundamental value, identifiable *ex ante*, and whose price is a good estimator, is no longer tenable. Financial valuation is reduced to a mere judgment, a subjective bet on the future. In this alternative conceptual framework, the stock market price does not reveal a pre-existing fundamental value of an asset, but merely reflects a conjecture about the future, one scenario among others, unstable by nature because it is based on a volatile collective belief. Such is the conception of market functioning developed by the theory of financial conventions.

The Theory of Financial Conventions

Leaving behind the hypothetical world of probabilistic risk in standard financial theory, and entering a more realistic world of radical

[2] Fama, E. (1965). The behavior of stock market prices. *The Journal of Business*, Vol. 38, No. 1 (Jan., 1965), pp. 34–105

[3] We are referring here to radical uncertainty in the sense of Knight (1921) and Keynes, i.e. that the future cannot be objectively given in a probabilistically stationary and common knowledge form.

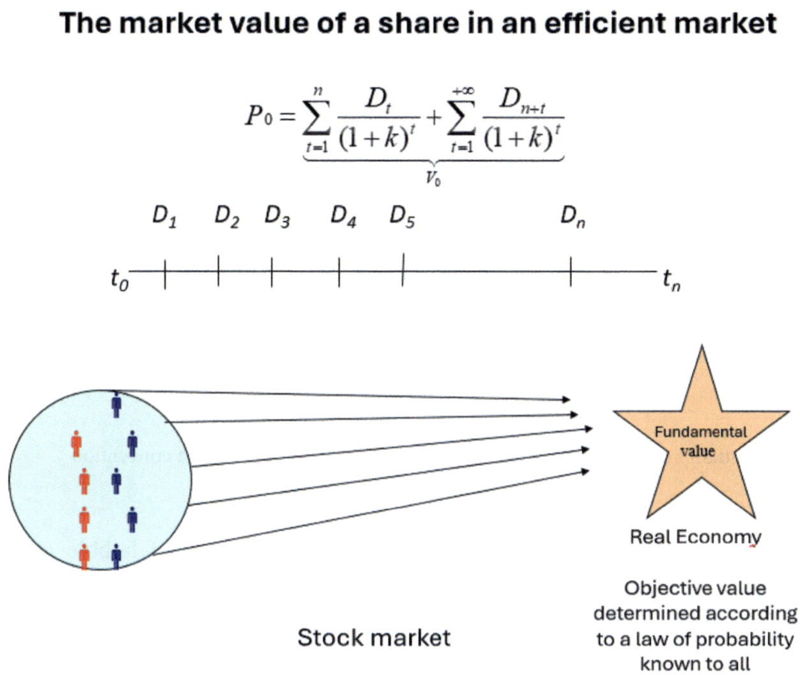

Fig. 11.1 Stock market value in an efficient market

uncertainty about the future, means giving stock prices a completely different meaning from that attributed to them by neoclassical financial theory. No actor, whatever his or her assessment of economic fundamentals, can escape the collective opinion that determines stock prices. Financial markets appear here as "cognitive structures that produce and select conjectures about the future of the economy and companies.[4]"

Price Production on Financial Markets: A Self-Referential Process

According to Keynes (1936), financial valuation is an unstable speculative process "*consisting in predicting the psychology of the market*" (*i.e.*, the majority opinion that determines the evolution of stock prices). It gives rise to short-term mimetic polarizations, to the detriment of forecasting long-term returns (the fundamental value of securities), which is the only way to allocate financial resources to productive investments.

In times of radical uncertainty, markets are characterized by phases of cognitive disarray, marked by high volatility. According to philosopher Jean-Pierre Dupuy (1989): "The most absurd rumors can (then) polarize a unanimous crowd on the most unexpected object, each finding proof of his value in the gaze or action of all the others.[5]" In this context, the identification of a point of equilibrium may prove permanently out of reach, and the intervention of a public actor may become an imperative necessity.

The volatility of market values finds a rational explanation here. It should no longer be perceived as an anomaly. It is the result of an unstable self-referential process, centered on the

[4] Orléan (2005).

[5] Dupuy, J.P., 1989. Convention et Common knowledge, *Revue économique*, Vol. 40, N° 2, L'économie des conventions (March 1989), pp. 361–400 (untranslated).

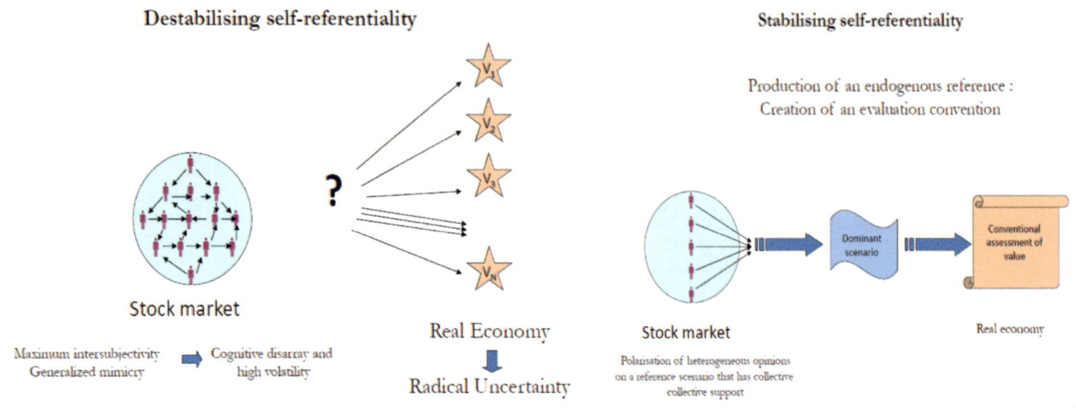

Fig. 11.2 Self-referentiality of financial markets and the emergence of a valuation convention

market price itself. Under these conditions, only the emergence of a valuation convention will enable markets to extricate themselves from this indeterminacy of values and stabilize, temporarily (see Fig. 11.2).

The Question of Financial Bubbles

In standard economic theory, the substantial value hypothesis prevails. The fundamental values of securities are calculable, but market prices can deviate from them more or less durably, due in particular to irrational behavior. In this theoretical framework, a bubble is therefore the progressive widening of a gap between market valuations and the fundamental economic values of assets. The bursting of a bubble is, in this case, a salutary return to "true value" (i.e. equilibrium).

In contrast, the self-referential approach is based on the idea of value as a social construct. Prices are the result of opinions and beliefs. In this context, a bubble is a collective dynamic supported by a certain hermeneutic of fundamentals. The bursting of a bubble then corresponds to a reversal of the dominant interpretation of the future (the convention that has supported and sustained the bullish dynamic). This is a bifurcation in the regime of collective affects in finance.

The recurrence of bubble episodes indicates that the predominance of speculation is not simply the result of irrationality. Rather, it is "the appropriate response of agents to the social constraints imposed on them by the development of liquidity" (Orléan, 1988).

Can promoting sustainable finance help remedy this situation?

11.3 Sustainable Finance Won't Save the World...

"Greening the economy," "sustainable finance," "finance at the service of the SDGs," "extra-financial analysis," "socially responsible investment (SRI)"... There are countless publications, communications, professional meetings, academic conferences, tools, financial products, institutional press releases, and other statements of principles referring to sustainable and responsible finance.

Clearly, the widespread inclusion of environmental, social and governance (ESG) criteria in investment processes, collective investment products, and corporate financing suggests that the investment community has (finally) woken up to the urgent need to reorient business models. And yet...

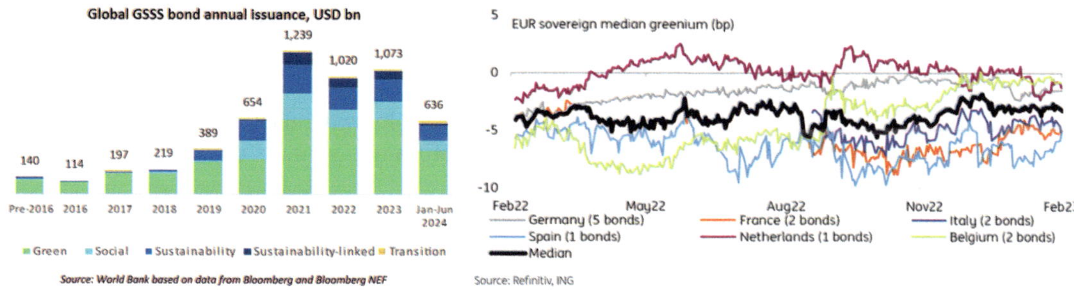

Fig. 11.3 Global issuance of green, social, sustainability, sustainability-linked Bonds and the *greenium* (*Source* https://am.jpmorgan.com/content/dam/jpm-am-aem/emea/regional/fr/insights/market-insights/mi-guide-to-the-markets-fr.pdf)

Green, Social or Sustainable? Her Name Is Bond!

Green and sustainable financing has developed rapidly since the first green bond was issued by the European Investment Bank (EIB) in 2007. A green bond is "a loan issued on the market by a company or public entity to investors to enable it to finance its projects contributing to the ecological transition".[6] Green bonds are enjoying considerable success, even though they still represent only a small percentage of global bond issues (around 5%). Companies (e.g. Neoen, EDF, Engie, Toyota, SNCF) and numerous governments have issued or are planning to issue green bonds. Problem: the actuarial rates of return demanded by investors are virtually the same for *green bonds* as for conventional bonds. The *spread* (*greenium*) remains marginal (see Fig. 11.3).

As for social or sustainability bonds, even if their cost (interest rate) increases if the issuer fails to meet the ESG objectives it has set itself and which are included in the issue contract, we remain skeptical about their ability to generate real transformations.

The Challenge of Integrating Extra-Financial Criteria into Valuation Models

Another major challenge facing finance is the integration of ESG criteria into valuation models. Even though numerous teams of SRI analysts have been set up and sometimes cooperate with traditional analysts, the standard models for calculating fundamental values based on discounted future cash flows do not lend themselves well to taking extra-financial information into account.

Nevertheless, attempts to do so are multiplying. Numerous academic and professional works have attempted to demonstrate the materiality of extra-financial criteria. (Simple) materiality refers to a quantitative assessment of the impact of ESG criteria on a security's risk/return ratio, or on a company's financial performance. From the development of the first metrics by SRI analysis to more recent indicators designed to internalize environmental costs, there is no shortage of examples of the efforts made by companies and the financial community to embody this materiality.

However, according to Van Weeren (2021), at this stage: "(…) The result is a financialization of ESG performance: it is no longer measured for its own sake, but for what it contributes to financial performance (…) extra-financial analysis is gradually being integrated into traditional financial analysis (…) If extra-financial analysts are trying to put finance at the service of extra-financial analysis, financial analysts are trying to put extra-financial analysis at the service of finance."

[6] https://www.ecologie.gouv.fr/obligations-vertes.

If finance is to play its part in transforming economic models, it will be necessary not only to consider the impact of environmental or climate degradation on financial risks (financial materiality), but above all to account for and limit its environmental and societal materiality, *i.e.* its impact on the natural environment and human societies.

11.4 Conclusion

According to Robert Boyer, "In a financialized economy, it is the monetary and financial regime that occupies the hierarchical place that the wage relationship had in the post-war growth model. Previous work has shown that this pre-eminence is the result of a de facto alliance between the managers of large listed companies and financial institutions, particularly investment banks. The consequence of this change in the basic compromise is an alteration of almost all other institutional forms under the impact of the financial regime.[7]"

If finance is ever to serve sustainable development and be truly integrated with the economy, society, and the bio-geo-physical super-system in which they are embedded, it will undoubtedly require the emergence of new institutional forms yet to be invented, and a radical transformation of its structures—in other words, a process of *sustainable de-financialization.*

Activities

Questions for Discussion

1. What determines the price of stocks and bonds?
2. To what extent is the theory of financial conventions a conceptual alternative to the efficient market hypothesis?
3. What are the main episodes of financial bubbles that have marked the economic history of the last three centuries? Identify and discuss the recurring mechanisms of bubbles and crashes.
4. What role can sustainable finance play in transforming business models?

Mini-Case: Regulating Markets Through Financial Transaction Taxes (FTT)?

The original idea for an FTT came from economist James Tobin. In the 1970s, this disciple of Keynes proposed applying it to the foreign exchange market in order to reduce currency volatility. Never actually implemented, this tax, of the order of 0.2% per round trip, would have had to be applied not only to the spot market, but also to the futures and *swaps* segments of the foreign exchange market, in order to be effective. Since then, other types of FTT have been introduced in certain countries (they already exist in nine of the G20 countries: Argentina, Brazil, China, France, India, Italy, South Africa, the United Kingdom, and the United States).

However, these FTTs do not generally apply to bond markets, derivatives markets (futures, swaps, options), or foreign exchange markets, where trading volumes are much higher than for securities. What's more, these taxes generally apply to transactions generating a transfer of ownership, and do not cover what is now the major feature of daily trading: intraday trading and high-frequency trading (HFT). For many economists, the introduction of even a small but automated tax on all order entries (and/or cancelations) in HFT would undoubtedly represent considerable progress in controlling speculative financial flows.

Take a look at existing FTT schemes around the world. Describe their characteristics, the amounts collected, their strengths, and limitations.

Search the academic literature for articles that have studied the feasibility of certain FTTs or the impact of such taxes on liquidity and asset price volatility. Summarize and discuss the main findings.

---

[7] Boyer, R., 2009. Feu le régime d'accumulation tiré par la finance, *Revue de la régulation* [En ligne], 5 | 1er semestre / Spring 2009, online since April 10, 2009, accessed October 31, 2021: http://journals.openedition.org/regulation/7367 (untranslated).

12 The Finance-Climate Nexus

Laurence Scialom

Putting Things into Perspective

2015 will go down in history as a pivotal year in terms of awareness of the role of finance in the fight against global warming, and the major risks this poses for the financial industry. The signatory countries of the Paris Climate Agreement committed to making financial flows "compatible with a pathway to low greenhouse gas emissions and climate-resilient development" (article 2.1(c)). This agreement confirmed the awareness of governments of the need to align financial flows with their climate commitments. Despite numerous declarations by financial intermediaries affirming their pro-climate commitments, no drastic changes have been observed in their practices.

Achieving carbon neutrality will require a profound transformation of finance, and a commitment from central banks and regulators.

Learning Objectives

- Uncovering the finance-climate vicious circle
- Understanding how the SDGs require a profound transformation of the financial system
- Understand how central banks and regulators can help achieve this goal

12.1 The Financial System and the Climate Challenge

Finance and Climate: A Vicious Circle

The interrelationships between finance and climate can be presented in terms of two questions that are often treated separately:

1. Questions of **financing the ecological transition** and realigning financial flows with the Paris Agreements. The massive redirection of funding from highly carbon-intensive (brown) activities and projects to investments supporting the ecological transition (green) is essential if we are to collectively meet our commitment made at COP 21.
2. The second question concerns the **systemic financial risks** generated by global warming.

In reality, these two issues are not separate, but intertwined and interdependent. A vicious circle links the activities of financial institutions and

L. Scialom (✉)
Université Paris Nanterre, EconomiX UMR, Nanterre, France
e-mail: laurence.scialom@parisnanterre.fr

T. Lagoarde-Ségot (ed.), *Ecological Economics and Finance*,
https://doi.org/10.1007/978-3-031-71249-4_12

climate change. By providing cheap and plentiful financing, whose risks are poorly priced, to companies involved in the research, exploration, and production of fossil fuels, financial institutions make climate change possible and even accelerate it. In turn, climate change is a major factor in financial instability. In a way, finance is warming the planet, and in turn, the climate is becoming an existential threat to finance.

Reallocation of Financial Flows

The financing needed to make a success of the ecological and social transition is considerable, but it must above all involve a reallocation of financial flows from brown to green. An independent global commission on the economy and climate established in 2013 and chaired by former Mexican President Felipe *Calderón* and economist Nicholas Stern issued its conclusions in 2015 in a report: "Better growth better climate?" These were updated in a fourth report in 2018.[1] It states that $90 trillion should be invested in infrastructure by 2030. These new investments in more sustainable infrastructures (land reclamation, access to drinking water and sanitation, combating deforestation, etc.) should, for the most part, be made possible by redirecting existing subsidies or financing.

According to the IPCC,[2] fossil fuels are responsible for 75% of greenhouse gas emissions. As Box 12.1 shows, banks bear a particular responsibility for carbon emissions.

> **Box 12.1: Banks Are Warming the Planet**
> Today, the banking system is the main source of financing for the oil and gas industry. In the five years since the Paris Agreement, the world's 60 biggest banks have granted over $3,800 billion to companies active in the gas, oil, and coal sectors. While US banks (JP Morgan Chase, Citi, Wells Fargo, and Bank of America) remain the biggest financiers of fossil fuels between 2016 and 2020, French banks are also heavily involved. Over the period, they financed fossil fuels to the tune of $296 billion. Far from reducing this financing, they actually increased it by an average of 19% per year. The policies of Chinese and Japanese banks with regard to financing the oil, gas, and coal sectors are highly problematic, with MIFG and Bank of China topping the rankings of polluting banks in these two countries.
>
> In this sense, it is legitimate to claim that banks are warming the planet. This is what a number of NGOs specializing in the collection, processing, and disclosure of information on the fossil fuel policies of the various players in the financial system are trying to show.
>
> *Source* NGO Reclaim Finance, https://reclaimfinance.org/site/wp-content/uploads/2021/03/BOCC__2021_vF.pdf.

Making a financial success of the ecological and social transition is therefore not just a matter of investing massively in activities and sectors in line with the Paris Agreements. Financing for sectors and activities that are unsustainable from a climate point of view must be dried up and made more expensive. This reallocation cannot be achieved by internal financial mechanisms, but requires the intervention of central banks and regulators.

The Four Financial Climate Risks

Systemic financial risks of climate origin have been recognized since Mark Carney's famous speech, "Breaking the Tragedy of Horizons", on September 29, 2015. He pointed to three types of climate risk that could be transmitted to the financial sphere: physical risk, transition risk, and liability risk, to which must be added the risk of major economic disruption.

[1] See https://newclimateeconomy.report/.

[2] See https://www.ipcc.ch/languages-2/francais/.

Physical Risk

Global warming is generating "extreme" meteorological events, i.e. those that statistically significantly exceed historically observed reference levels. The frequency, intensity, extent, duration, and timing of these events (cyclones, heatwaves, intense rainfall events, etc.) are unprecedented. Physical risks involve the destruction of asset stocks (forest fires, floods, cyclones, rising oceans, etc.), the reduced profitability of exposed businesses, and/or the deterioration of income streams (impact on tourism, fishing, harvests, or the incomes of workers in the areas concerned, etc.). This physical damage directly affects the longevity of capital by accelerating its depreciation.

The direct impact on financial stability comes via the often cumulative and highly correlated losses of insurers and reinsurers, but also via other transmission belts, sometimes just as direct, such as the rise in bad debts or the depreciation of assets on banks' balance sheets. These physical risks will generate contagion effects between sectors and regions that are very difficult to quantify, particularly in the event of tipping points in the climate system causing irreversible climate bifurcations.

By way of illustration and simplification, the melting of the ice caps would have a chain of effects, including a reduction in their solar heat-reflecting effect, rising sea levels, and effects on ocean circulation generated by differences in density due to differences in temperature and salinity of water masses, with melting ice causing a considerable influx of fresh water into salty oceans. The melting of permafrost (permanently frozen ground) would release massive quantities of greenhouse gases previously trapped in frozen soils, as well as extinct or unknown viruses that could cause pandemics.

Transition Risk

Transition risk in its financial dimension is defined as the risk of a sudden collapse in the prices of certain assets due to:

- the implementation or mere announcement of low-carbon policies (carbon tax, binding regulations on vehicle weight, etc.);
- a technological breakthrough enabling a rapid transition (such as a technological leap in hydrogen engines);
- a shift in individual preferences and social norms (less meat-based diets, massive reduction in air traffic, etc.).

Faced with such shifts in climate policy, technology, or behavior, the convergence of expectations on financial markets can lead to a sharp depreciation of assets backed by high-carbon activities before they have been made profitable. The fourth report of the Commission for the Economy and Climate (2018)[3] estimates that $12,000 billion worth of fossil-backed assets could be wiped out by 2035.

For example, the shares of companies heavily dependent on fossil fuels would plummet due to the sharp deterioration in the profit outlook for these sectors, while their debt securities (bonds) would become very risky as their businesses would contract sharply, with major risks of bankruptcy. These assets are referred to as *stranded assets*. Fossil fuel extraction and transportation infrastructures would be the first to be affected, but many industrial facilities upstream and downstream of fossil fuel combustion would also be heavily impacted (automotive, aeronautics, plastics industries, etc.). The longer policy and technology adjustments are delayed, the greater the transition risks.[4] Public policies in favor of the climate are subject to the famous tragedy of horizons, which designates the misalignment of temporality between the costs and benefits of climate policies. The costs are borne by current generations, who are the voters of our policy-makers, while the benefits will be

[3] See https://unfccc.int/fr/news/une-croissance-economique-respectueuse-du-climat-pourrait-rapporter-26-000-milliards-de-dollars-d.

[4] Carney, M. "A New Horizon," speech, March 21, 2019, https://www.bankofengland.co.uk/-/media/boe/files/speech/2019/a-new-horizon-speech-by-mark-carney.pdf?la=en&hash=F63F8064E0408F038CABB1F29C58FB1A0CD0FE25.

enjoyed by future generations. It's easy to see why the bias towards inaction is so strong.[5]

Liability Risk

Liability risk (also known as legal risk) refers to the consequences of legal proceedings brought by victims of disasters attributable to climate change against those who are sued as having actively contributed to global warming, despite scientific knowledge of what causes it. Lawsuits could be brought against the coal and oil extractive industries, or against major greenhouse gas emitters, as in the case of the tobacco and pesticide industries. But liability may also be imposed on companies that fail to take the necessary protective measures against the proven effects of global warming, thereby endangering populations through negligence. Such proceedings could hit hard not only the offending sectors but also their insurers when they benefit from liability insurance. In reality, this risk has already materialized.

Box 12.2: Pacific Gas and Electric or How Global Warming Can Bankrupt a Company

The case of Pacific Gas and Electric illustrates the risk of liability. PG&E is an energy giant, a stock company overseen by California state regulators, supplying gas and electricity to 16 million people. For the *Wall Street Journal*, this would be the first climate change-related bankruptcy [WSJ, January 18, 2019]. PG&E is accused of negligently causing deadly fires (*Camp Fire*) and extensive damage, killing 86 people and destroying 14,000 homes between November 8 and 26, 2018. More than 750 complaints representing 5600 plaintiffs have been filed against PG&E. The fire is believed to have been caused by sparks from high-voltage power lines, which ignited a forest that was abnormally dry due to global warming. It is therefore a failure to maintain PG&E's network that is incriminated, even though the company was aware of the increased risk of fire due to climate change. The company has estimated the amount of compensation claimed at $30 billion. In this case, the risk of liability came into full play. The company's share price plummeted and it finally filed for bankruptcy on January 19, filing for protection under Section 11 of the U.S. Bankruptcy Code. The main reason for the bankruptcy is the damages that PG&E will have to pay to victims of its network maintenance failures. The bankruptcy has had a cascading effect, particularly on the financial industry, with fund manager *Vanguard*, whose customers are virtually all US households, holding around half of the group's bond debt.

Source https://www.wsj.com/articles/pg-e-wildfires-and-the-first-climate-change-bankruptcy-11547820006

The Risk of Major Economic Disruption

The risk of major economic disruption arises when human activity comes to a halt or slows down sharply in the event of a major disruption (war, health crisis, extreme and widespread physical events, etc.). This risk is largely underestimated by public decision-makers and regulators. And yet, our economies experienced a manifestation of it with the Covid-19 pandemic crisis. The uninsurable nature of entire regions of the world in a +4 °C warming scenario is another way of looking at this risk. Under the *business-as-usual*

[5] Note that the tragedy of horizons can be described as a trade-off between transition risk and physical risk. Indeed, rapid decarbonization of the economy means short-term materialization of the transition risk, i.e. a climate-related financial crisis, but long-term mitigation of the physical risk. The time lag between the materialization of the economic, financial and social costs and the gains to society is a major obstacle to the implementation of ambitious climate policies.

scenario, we are on a global warming trajectory of between 3.7 °C and 4.8 °C by 2100.[6]

How the Climate Crisis Reveals the Limits of Conventional Finance

Finance is neither equipped to reallocate financial flows from "brown" to "green" nor to properly assess and price the financial risks associated with climate change. Finance allocates financial flows according to the anticipated risk/return trade-off, i.e. for a given risk, investors opt for the highest return, and for a given return, they opt for the lowest risk. All financial market players seek to maximize the return on savings, given the level of risk assumed. As Box 12.3 shows, pure financial analysis leads to investment projects being judged and arbitrated on the basis of short-term criteria that are totally indifferent to global warming.

Box 12.3: Financial Techniques, Short-Termism, and Unsustainability
Net present value (NPV) is a central tool in the financial management of a company. It is a decreasing function of the company's preference for the present (r) and its time horizon (n):

$$NPV = \sum_{i=1}^{N} \frac{net flows}{(1+r)^n}$$

Financial theory equates the price of time with the required rate of return, i.e. the average return on investment demanded by creditors and shareholders in return for their investment in the company's equity.

This discounting tends to place more value on short-term profits, which can lead investors to select polluting projects.

The only way to bring about a reallocation of financial flows in favor of sustainable and ecologically sustainable investments is to make this anticipated risk/return ratio relatively more attractive for green than for brown. Market mechanisms cannot achieve this, and the most profitable projects have no a priori reason to be compatible with the reduction trajectory adopted by COP 21.

The Thorny Question of Yields

Financial valuations assume that returns are fully monetarily captured by those who finance and take the risks associated with financial investment. In the case of ecologically sustainable investments, the return is not only financial but also has beneficial effects for society as a whole. These are the positive externalities linked, for example, to the non-emission of CO_2 enabled by ecologically responsible investments. These are not "priced" by the financial markets because those who finance them cannot appropriate the benefits.

So, structurally, there is under-investment in the ecological transition relative to what would be collectively optimal. Symmetrically, there is over-investment in sectors with high greenhouse gas emissions, because negative externalities do not weigh on financial profitability. This gap between social and environmental returns and private returns is symptomatic of the existence of a market failure that requires public intervention.

The Free Rider Problem

Climate and biodiversity are *global public goods*. Public goods are distinguished from private goods by two properties (see Chapter 2).

- **Non-rivalry** means that, unlike market goods, increasing the availability of a public good to one person or group does not reduce

[6] Some players in the insurance world, such as Henri de Castries when he was CEO of Axa (a French insurance company), warn of the difficulty of insuring a world at +4 °C. Indeed, certain economic activities cannot continue in the absence of insurance, or when insurance costs become prohibitive. See https://www.axa.com/fr/presse/evenements/cop-21-paris.

its availability to all others. Consumers are not rivals.

- **Non-exclusion** means that it's impossible to exclude anyone from using this public good, so it's impossible to charge for it (e.g., public lighting, air quality, or national defense).

Leaving the production of these public goods to the market is tantamount to under-producing them, since it is in everyone's interest for others to finance them. The generalization of this behavior leads to them not being produced at all. Yet these services or public goods are essential to the life of our societies. That's why the taxes that finance them are compulsory.

The problem of the free rider is even more acute in the case of *global public goods* (such as the fight against global warming or against the collapse of biodiversity), where non-rivalry and non-exclusion concern countries. States underfund the production of global public goods, waiting for other countries to do so, so they can benefit effortlessly.

Faced with the failure of markets and financial intermediaries to reallocate resources for the ecological transition, public authorities need to step in and steer agents' economic choices towards low-carbon investment and spending. How can we do this? Through public policies that reduce the risk of going green through state guarantees on part of losses, that improve the profitability of going green through subsidies and/or favorable taxation, that degrade the profitability of going brown through a carbon tax, and also by abolishing subsidies to fossil fuel industries. Direct public funding, restrictions on the financing of certain activities, and support for others, are legitimate.

Inadequate Risk Assessment

The risks of ecologically sustainable investments are perceived as high, due to the immaturity of the climate transition industries and the technologies supporting them. Conversely, the risks of carbon-intensive investments are structurally undervalued by financial markets.

The traditional approach to risk management in finance is based on historical data: measures of financial risk are extrapolative, based on the idea of continuity between past, present, and future. This presupposition is inoperative, and the statistical tool is powerless when it comes to financial climate risks. These are matters of radical uncertainty in the sense of F. Knight (1885–1972): certain events, contexts or socio-economic transformations are so unique that it is impossible to calculate their frequency. Consequently, if we continue to use our usual risk management methods, we seriously underestimate future events. This leads to economic policy errors that can be dramatic, given the irreversibilities inherent in climate dynamics. No market mechanism can guide collective action. Collective action must be shaped by an ethical principle that takes into account the well-being of future generations. Because of threshold and runaway effects, the transition must be ambitious and implemented rapidly. Making decisions in the face of radical uncertainty means breaking with the dogma of precise, systematic quantification, and accepting breakthrough methodologies that are more forward-looking, qualitative, and analytical, abandoning probabilistic approaches such as those based on scenario analysis. The difficulty of this break with the past creates a "bias towards inaction" in public policy, the effects of which are disastrous.

12.2 New Monetary and Prudential Policy Tools

Recognition of the threat to financial stability created by global warming was behind the creation of the network of central banks and supervisors for the greening of finance (NGFS) at the end of 2017. It aims to develop methodologies to better identify and measure the financial sector's exposure to climate risk, to draw up climate stress tests but also to promote financing for the transition to a low-carbon economy. While a consensus is beginning to form that central banks can no longer ignore climate change, there is no real agreement on the operational side of this consensus.

Towards a Greener Monetary Policy?

Central banking regimes vary considerably according to geographical zone and level of development.

Central Bank Mandates More or Less Open to Environmental Sustainability

Central banks in the most advanced countries often have price stability as their primary mandate, although they sometimes also have a broader secondary objective of supporting economic policies (ECB) or employment (Fed). Central banks in southern countries (China, Bangladesh, Brazil, etc.) tend to have a more global mandate, including development and sustainability issues. This makes active integration of climate priorities easier than for central banks in more developed areas.

What Are the Levers for a Green Monetary Policy?

Central banks can act on several levers and mobilize multiple instruments to green their monetary policy. For instance:

- Central banks could give preference to green collateral in their liquidity access policies, and penalize brown collateral. Collateral is a security that serves as collateral for a loan: a bank provides the central bank with an asset worth 100 on the market, for example, for a limited period; in exchange, the central bank will provide it with central bank money for the same period, but for less than 100—for example, 95. The difference between the value of the collateral and the amount of central bank money obtained by the bank, in our example 5, is the haircut. The riskier the asset, the higher the haircut, which is supposed to protect the central bank from a loss in the asset's value during the loan. The "greening" of collateral policy is a powerful tool, as access to central liquidity is crucial for banks that are highly vulnerable to liquidity risk. A deep discount on "brown" collateral can lead to a change in market conventions regarding the assessment of financial climate risks, and thus encourage the reallocation of financial flows.
- Other central bank liquidity facilities could be reformatted in line with climate objectives. For example, the maturities and refinancing rates of banks could be differentiated according to the degree of sustainability of the loans they grant. In this way, the central bank would direct banks' money creation towards climate-friendly activities such as thermal renovation of buildings, organic farming, and the circular economy.
- Central banks can also embark on a policy of purchase of assets issued by firms promoting the ecological transition (green QE).
- Monetizing public debt could give governments the leeway they need to address climate change. The mechanism would be as follows: the central bank credits the public treasury's account and records a non-refundable debt as an asset. The government can then allocate these sums to financing "green" projects and accompanying the stranding of "brown" sectors.

Towards a Macroprudential Climate Policy?

The aim of macroprudential policy is to ensure global financial stability and thus prevent systemic risk. It suffers from a bias towards inaction due to the non-directly observable nature of its successes (attenuation of the financial cycle and avoidance of financial crisis) and the time lag between its immediate costs and its more difficult-to-measure, time-delayed benefits. This "inaction bias" is exacerbated in the case of macroprudential climate policy. There is a strong temptation to wait until we have sufficiently improved the transparency, quality, and quantity of information on companies' exposure to climate risks, before implementing a macroprudential climate policy on the basis of this information.

The definition of a macroprudential climate policy must avoid the restrictive conception of quantifiable risk based on historical data that prevails in particular for the risk-weighted capital ratio promoted by the Basel accords, composed of bank capital (*K*) in the numerator and risk-weighted assets (*RWA) in the* denominator.

$$K/RWA$$

where $RWA = \sum_{i=0}^{n} (\alpha i . \omega i)$

αi being the weighting corresponding to the risk of the asset ωi calculated on the basis of historical data.

But financial climate risks are impossible to predict.

A variety of instruments can therefore be used[7]:

- The first option is to influence banks' regulatory capital ratios. There are two possible options: reduce capital requirements for "green" financing or increase them for brown financing. The first option would weaken banks' robustness by reducing their capacity to absorb unexpected losses. The second option, more consistent with the objective of sustainable finance, would make the financing of activities that are highly harmful to the climate more expensive in terms of capital, and thus encourage a reallocation of financial flows, while strengthening banks' resilience to the risks of stranding assets. In both cases, weightings can only be conventional and imposed by regulators to steer financial flows from dirty to sustainable.
- A second approach would be to impose sectoral leverage ratios, limiting excessive bank leverage in asset classes backed by carbon-intensive sectors with a high risk of stranding. Such a sectoral leverage ratio would take the following form:

$$\text{Capital Tier1/Exposures to brown sectors} > \gamma$$

The effect of sectoral leverage ratios would be quite similar to that of credit control policies but with the advantage of having an impact on the composition of the bank's liabilities (capital strengthening) and not just its assets, providing better protection against the risk of stranding. As information on these sectoral leverage ratios is public, they would help banks' counterparties assess their solidity in the face of financial climate risks.

12.3 Conclusion

Financial stability and climate stability are two interconnected public goods,[8] the preservation of which will require profound transformations in the governance of our socio-economic and financial systems. Central banks and regulators must be key players in these transformations. They will not be the *Deus Ex Machina* of the ecological transition, but the procrastination and/or lack of ambition of governments in the face of the climate challenge reinforces the need for their action, given the aggravation of financial climate risks resulting from the wait-and-see attitude of public authorities.

Activities

Questions for Discussion

1. So-called green finance focuses on investment in sustainable projects. Is this a sufficient conception of finance's contribution to the ecological transition?
2. How can we justify the fact that the control of climate-related financial risks is a matter of macroprudential policy rather than microprudential policy?

[7] See Schoenmakers, Dirk. [2021], "Greening Monetary Policy". *Climate policy*, Vol. 21, No. 4, 581–592.

[8] See https://www.banque-france.fr/intervention/green-swan-central-banking-and-financial-stability-age-climate-change-banque-des-reglements.

Mini-Case: Sustainability and Green Finance: Can We Count on Central Banks?

The extension of central banks' scope of action to climate finance is part of their ongoing adaptation to changes in the macroeconomic and institutional context in which they operate.

To explore this issue further, read the articles by S. Dikau and U. Volz (2021): "Central bank mandates, sustainability goals and the promotion of green finance", *Ecological Economics* 184, 107022 and by L. Scialom: Les Banques Centrales au défi de la transition écologique. Éloge de la plasticité", *Revue Économique*, March 2022 (untranslated).

Then answer the following questions:

1. Explain how the history of central banks provides arguments in favor of extending their policies to climate issues.
2. Identify the central banks whose mandate explicitly includes the promotion of sustainable development or growth, and explain why the fight against global warming and climate adaptation falls within their mandate.

Finance from a Social Science Perspective

13

Yamina Tadjeddine

Putting Things into Perspective

Although finance is omnipresent in contemporary society, paradoxically its nature is often misunderstood. Finance is a very real world, populated by workers and non-workers, organizations and the regulations that structure them. Finance is a social and political space before being a digital world. One branch of finance research, known as the *social studies of finance*, brings together researchers in the social sciences (economic sociology, political economy, anthropology, history, geography, political science and management) who observe and analyze financial spaces from the point of view of an abductive rather than deductive approach.

Learning Objectives

- Discover the social studies of finance
- Understanding the abductive approach and the role of observation
- Understanding financial markets as a social and political construct
- Reflect on how to act on finance so that it becomes consistent with the SDGs.

13.1 Deconstructing the Formal Vision of Finance

What distinguishes the social sciences of finance from classical financial theory? Their methodology (see Table 13.1).

The classical approach to financial theory starts from a set of normative postulates—isolated, perfectly rational individuals maximizing their utility expectation. It derives from two formal models: the theory of rational decision under risk and the theory of general equilibrium. A financial security is defined as a lottery based on probabilities or statistics. The financial market is then reduced to a space of vectors (securities) generally characterized by two dimensions: risk and return.

The social sciences of finance favor an abductive approach based on qualitative observations and interviews. This can involve immersions in trading rooms, interviews and questionnaires, as well as analysis of technical (algorithms, spreadsheets) and legal (laws, charters) devices. Based on rigorous analysis of these facts and their regularities, the researcher demonstrates and theorizes social regularities.

Social studies of finance (see Box 13.1) consider financiers as social beings rather than as optimizing agents and analyze the various forms of interaction between individuals and socio-technical devices.

Y. Tadjeddine (✉)
Université de Lorraine, CNRS, BETA, Nancy, France
e-mail: yamina.fourneyron@univ-lorraine.fr

T. Lagoarde-Ségot (ed.), *Ecological Economics and Finance*,
https://doi.org/10.1007/978-3-031-71249-4_13

Table 13.1 Comparison of formal economic and social science approaches

	Economics (microeconomic paradigm)	Social sciences
The scientific method	Hypothetico-deductive approach	Abduction
	Starting from behavioral assumptions (optimization) and a naturalized context (constraints, endowments, technology, population) to set up a formalized model.	Use observations of people's behavior in a social and historical context (qualitative data from the field or quantitative data from a survey) to establish stylized facts.
	The theoretical results obtained can then be compared with reality.	Taking observations into account within the framework of a theory.
Individual design	*Homo economicus*	*Homo sociologicus*
	No attachment to a society, to a history: free individual, like an atom.	A person is defined by his/her belonging to a society, a context, a history.
	Individual preferences are innate and specific to each individual.	Individual preferences are endogenous: they result from socialization.
Concept of human interaction	The only possible encounters take place at market equilibrium, through exchanges with anonymous individuals.	There are many forms of interaction and relationships between individuals.
	The market is a mathematical abstraction that enables the optimal allocation of resources.	The market is a social construct.

Source Author

Box 13.1: A Brief History of Social Studies on Finance

In the XIXth century, the development of banking and financial activities and the recurrence of crises made finance an essential subject of study for the social sciences. In 1857, Pierre-Joseph Proudhon (1809–1865) published *Manuel du spéculateur à la Bourse,* in which he described financial behavior. In 1894, Max Weber (1864–1920) wrote two now-famous texts, collected in the book *Die Börse* ("The Stock Exchange"). However, this literature did not continue much into the XXth century, with the exception of a few emblematic works.

The situation changed with the process of financialization that began in the 1980s: finance became an integral part of the economic world, but also of everyday household life. The seminal work *The Social Dynamics of Financial Markets,* coordinated by Adler and Adler and published in the USA in 1984, sparked a revival of interest in finance in the social sciences. But it was not until the 2000s, and especially after the 2008 financial crisis, that *social studies of finance* developed. In France, the SSFA association, founded in 1999, is at the forefront of this field. This trend is present in many countries, notably in the UK, with sociologist Donald MacKenzie in Edinburgh. The United States also boasts a number of renowned sociologists and anthropologists of finance, including Bill Maurer, Niel Fligstein and Viviana Zelizer.

Source Chambost I., M. Lenglet and Y. Tadjeddine, eds. 2018. *The making of finance: perspectives from the social sciences*. Routledge, 290 pp.

13.2 A Social and Political History of Finance

The long history of finance forces us to be humble and to distance ourselves from analyses that present it as a characteristic of contemporary capitalism.

Who Is Behind Financial Contracts: Merchants, Capitalists, States?

As we saw in Chapter 3, historians have been able to find financing (debt) and risk-hedging contracts in Mesopotamia. The first legal evidence of risk hedging can be found in Hammurabi's stele, dating from 1750 BC.

In Volume 2 of *Civilisation matérielle, Économie et Capitalisme*, historian Fernand Braudel (1992) highlights the role of finance in the development of trade. External financing through the sharing of assets—the limited partnership, forerunner of the joint-stock company—appeared as early as the XIIIth century to facilitate maritime trade. The original myth of finance developing as the response of daring bankers to entrepreneurial initiative legitimized the call for the independence of the financial sphere so that it could fully support innovation.

However, the vast majority of financial innovations have been the result of states seeking new sources of funding for their public deficits. American anthropologist David Graeber (1961–2020) reminds us in his book *Debt: The First 5000 Years* (2011) that the military conquests of Alexander the Great or the Roman Empire were as much motivated by reasons of power as by the search for new financing. French royal history under the *Ancien Régime* is also marked by the search for ways to make up the royal deficit. French king François Ist—a particularly expensive king, not only because of the many wars he waged but also because of the splendid castles he built—was very inventive in this respect: he created the lottery in 1539 and issued the first public bonds in 1522.

Adapting the Company to Financial Logic

American sociologist Bruce Carruthers (b. 1957) has opened up a field of study devoted to the social genesis of financial devices (see his *Economy/Society: Markets, Meanings, and Social Structure*, co-authored with Sarah Babb [2000]). His 1995 article[1] re-inscribes the history of financial innovations and the concomitant institutional transformations. Without the involvement of the state, education and, above all, the law, these new contracts could not have existed. This was the case, for example, with the creation of joint-stock companies at the end of the XIXth century and the beginning of the XXth century: the development of stock markets necessitated a profound transformation of property rights, with the empowerment of the shareholder (freed from penal or patrimonial obligations).

The adaptation of law to finance can also be approached through the theory of performativity. The notion of *performativity*, borrowed from the pragmatics of language, highlights the fact that the sciences do more than simply represent the world: they give it existence. Applied to finance, it highlights how theories shape behavior, algorithms, organizations and regulations. Sociologists Michel Callon (b. 1945), Fabian Muniesa (b. 1972) and Donald MacKenzie (b. 1950, see Box 13.2) are major figures in this movement.

Box 13.2: Further Study: The Performance of the Black and Scholes Formula According to MacKenzie (2006)

The central issue in option theory is the calculation of the premium. Practitioners had identified the factors influencing it: the current price of the underlying asset, the strike price, the time to maturity, the level of interest rates and volatility. However, it was not until the early 1970s that Fischer Black, Myron Scholes (1973) and Robert C. Merton (1973) developed a formal theory of options within a deductive framework based on ad hoc

[1] Carruthers, B. G. (2015). Financialization and the institutional foundations of the new capitalism. *Socio-Economic Review*, *13*(2), pp. 379-398.

assumptions. This formula was quickly adopted by the financial community and thus determined their behavior. Implied volatility began to follow exactly what was predicted by the theory. The Black-Scholes formula created the real world: financial reality became consistent with theory.

13.3 Opening the *Black Box of* XXIst Century Finance

The social sciences also play a part in revealing the social reality of finance.

The Social and Political Construction of Financial Markets

Max Weber: The Market as Community

While economists regard the market as a natural, spontaneous mechanism, socio-economists have set out to reveal its social and political nature. They propose to observe the market as it is, and to highlight the men/women, devices, rules and conflicts that underpin it. The first to open up this reflection and claim to be a socio-economist was the German Max Weber (1864–1920).

For Weber, the market is a society: the meeting of a supplier and a demander gives rise to a community, a "socialization". This community recognizes rules, such as peaceful struggle through competition, and adheres to common values. The path opened up by Max Weber has been followed by numerous works devoted to the concrete study of markets, particularly financial markets.

The Commoditization Process

In his book *L'Emprise des marchés: comprendre leur fonctionnement pour pouvoir les changer* (2017), Callon breaks down the process into five discrete phases or 'alignments': (1) passiva(c) tion; (2) qualculation; (3) organization of market encounters; (4) market engagement; and (5) price formulation (see Fig. 13.1).

1. The first stage, passiva(c)tion, aims to dissociate the good from all its social particularities. Anthropologists have pointed out that everything traded on the market today was

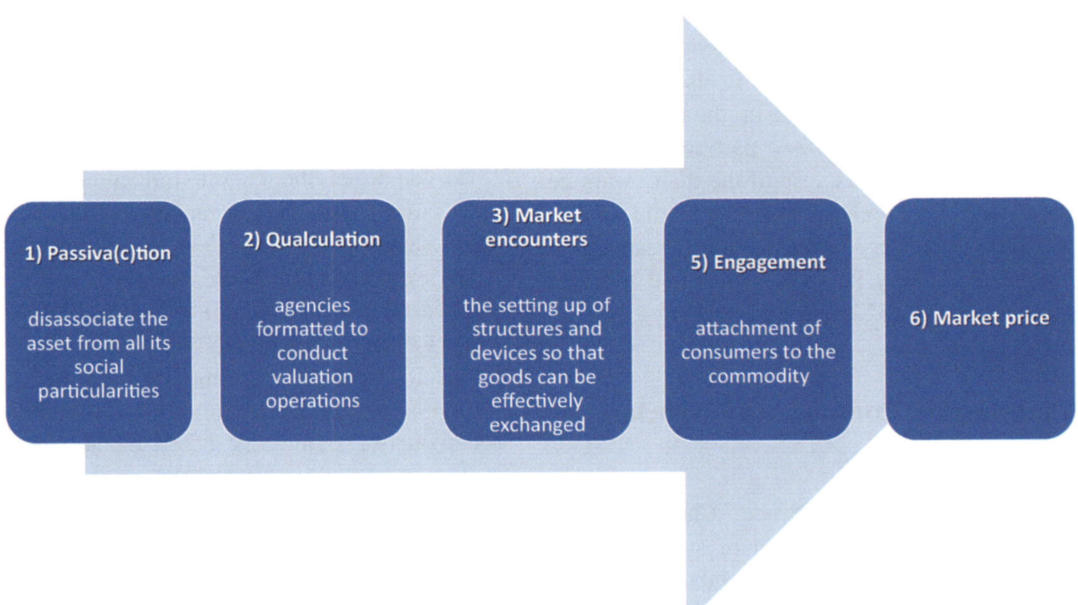

Fig. 13.1 The market making process (*Source* After Callon [2017])

originally made up of objects bearing symbols, cultures, sacred powers or social hierarchies. These objects have been progressively stripped of their links with nature and community, to become anonymous, standardized objects with property rights and monetary value. A society can, however, refuse to deprive an object of its symbolic attributes (see Box 13.3).

Box 13.3: Denial of life insurance in the U.S. on religious grounds

Economic anthropologist V. Zellizer (1978) studied the emergence and spread of the life insurance contract in the United States at the end of the XIXth century. This contract, first created in the UK, enjoyed great success in Europe, notably in France and Germany, but remained very marginal in the USA, despite its spread. According to V. Zellizer, the difficult spread of life insurance is due to the fact that Americans were more inclined to associate life and death with sacred events, linked to the divine. For them, any form of monetization and contractualization of death was inconceivable. In the United States, life insurance was still rooted in moral structures, making the "passiva(c)tion" stage impossible. V. Zellizer notes that the spread of life insurance was only possible after a transformation of social structures brought about by urbanization and industrialization at the beginning of the XXth century.

Source Based on Zelizer, Viviana A. "Human values and the market: The case of life insurance and death in 19th-century America". *American Journal of Sociology* 84.3 (1978): 591–610.

2. The second transformation, qualculation, sees the arrival of agencies (individuals and organizations) "formatted to carry out valuation operations". These valuations may be derived from a calculation giving a numerical value and/or from a judgment involving a more qualitative classification.

The example of the bond market illustrates this need for valuation agencies. Bonds were the main financial contract issued and traded in the XVIIIth and XIXth centuries. To keep operators informed, information structures were set up, such as specialized media, then rating agencies after the crash of 1929. Today, the American rating agencies—Moody's, Standard & Poors, Fitch—and the Chinese agency Dagong require all bond issues to be assigned a credit rating to assess the risk of default.

3. The third phase, market encounters, concerns the implementation of structures and devices enabling the effective exchange of goods, i.e. places and methods dedicated to the organization of encounters. In financial markets, centralization, with a limited number of authorized exchangers trading in a single place and visible to all, has become the norm. Nowadays, these meetings take place via competing algorithms.
4. The fourth stage, market attachment, enables us to understand the frameworks of addiction and consumer attachment to merchandise. A new commodity does not systematically find favor with the public. This is particularly true in the case of complex financial contracts. Contract sellers have to explain and translate these contracts to the layman, to make them intelligible.
5. The final stage is the creation of a digital prize. Prices do not arise naturally or spontaneously; they are the result of a multitude of socio-technical mechanisms that influence their nature, as well as individual and collective behavior. Practical observation of markets reveals the great diversity of price-setting methods: continuous quotation or fixing, for example.

The Structure of Financial Systems in the XXIst Century

In neoclassical microeconomics, capital markets bring together agents with financing capacity and agents with financing needs. It largely ignores the role of financial intermediaries. Without them, without their reputation, without the trust that the community places in them, securities would not circulate, since investors would not buy them.

These invisible players are characterized by their diversity. A financial organization is usually associated with a legal category such as an asset management company or a stock market intermediary. Sometimes, the intermediary has no legal personality; it's simply a tool or an algorithm.

Considering the organizations involved in the investment of savings and in the negotiation process means deconstructing the image of direct finance where only *homo economicus* exist and interact.

Financial Prices as Conventions

In the risky, even uncertain, context of finance, economic theory postulates that everyone uses their own independently formed expectations. As we saw in the previous chapter, reality contradicts theory: agents base their expectations on common frameworks called *conventions*.

Keynes's Contribution

The first person to use the term convention in finance was the economist John Maynard Keynes (1883–1946), who used the term in Chapters 12 and 17 of his *General Theory* (1936).

The speculative mechanism for constructing expectations and prices is described by Keynes in the famous allegory of the Beauty Contest:

> Professional investment [in stock trading] can be compared to those newspaper competitions in which contestants have to choose the six most beautiful faces from a hundred photographs, with the prize going to the contestant whose choice most closely matches the average preferences of all the contestants; so that each contestant has to choose, not the faces he himself finds most beautiful, but those he believes most likely to attract the attention of the other contestants, who are all looking at the problem from the same point of view. It's not a question of choosing those which, according to his judgement, are really the most beautiful, or even those which the average opinion really finds the most beautiful. We've reached the third stage, where we devote our intelligence to anticipating what the average opinion expects of the average opinion. And there are some, I believe, who practice the fourth, fifth and higher degrees. (Keynes, 1936, p. 156)

Each financial player seeks to determine the beliefs of the others, who in turn do the same (see Fig. 13.2). It is possible to distinguish three ways in which prices are formed, depending on whether exchangers seek information individually outside the market, by imitating each other or by following a convention.

Financial Convention in Social Studies of Finance

Financiers are socialized individuals. Thanks to this socialization, they can mobilize conventions to learn about, evaluate and choose financial securities. These conventions are not necessarily conscious or known to the actors who mobilize them. It's up to the social scientist to uncover them by observing the practices of the players in context.

From this perspective, financial analysts or rating agencies are seen as agencies that provide conventions for evaluating companies or states. These conventions are then used as the basis for decisions. However, the valuation carried out by analysts is not the result of an objective and true measurement; it is considered by the financial community to be the correct measurement.

As a result, financial instability can be understood on a social basis, rather than on the basis of individual misunderstandings. Financial investors base their decisions on consensus, without realizing that this signal is merely a convention.

By recognizing the social nature of value expressed on financial markets, it becomes possible once again to question metrics and propose alternative financial valuation conventions. In order to align finance with sustainability concerns (such as the UN's SDGs), institutions (law, education), organizations and conventions need to be transformed to promote new financial practices.

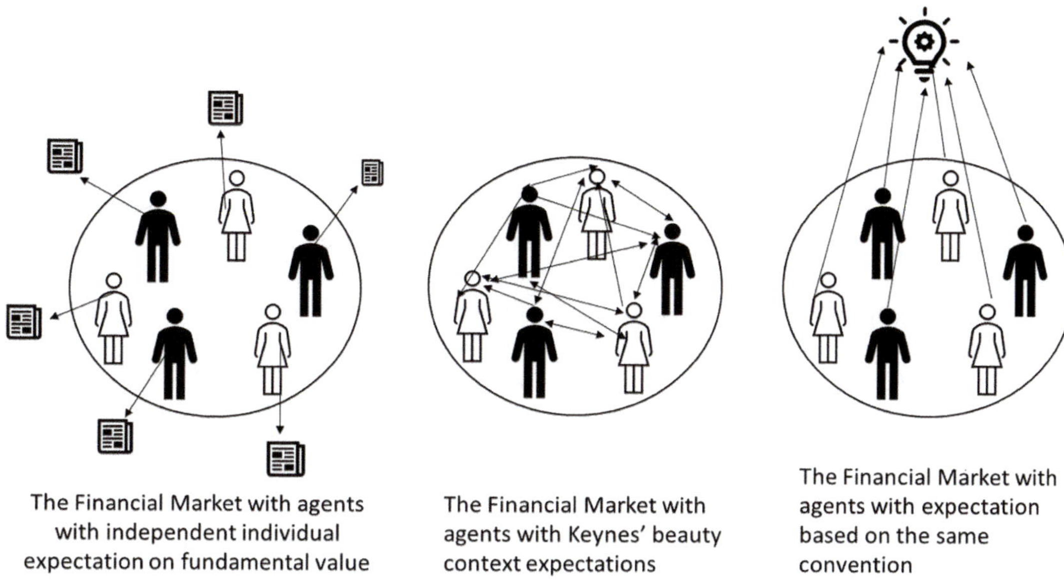

Fig. 13.2 The three modalities of price anticipation

13.4 Towards More Respectful Financial Innovation

The disciplinary pluralism of the social studies of finance is, in our view, relevant to examining how financial innovation can be put at the service of achieving the SDGs.

First of all, opening up the black box of finance is a necessary part of education (SDG 4). In a financialized world, it is essential for citizens to demystify finance so that they can act on it. Whether they like it or not, financial organizations play an eminently social role. It is therefore unacceptable for financial innovations to be conceived and designed exclusively for private use, in a legal and mathematical vocabulary inaccessible to lay people. Financial organizations must open themselves up to debate, so that direct and indirect stakeholders can discuss and understand the financial innovations that are likely to have an impact on their own future development.

Designing socially useful financial contracts makes it possible to respond to the need to finance activities linked to the achievement of the SDGs, such as the fight against poverty, the fight against inequality, or support for the ecological transition. Once we realize that a financial contract can take any form we wish, it is possible to imagine contracts dedicated to broader objectives than just short-term profit maximization. This approach is already at work in the field of alternative finance, which promotes financial organizations that are more supportive in their governance (associations, cooperatives) and in their objectives. While these more democratic organizations are not immune to social mission drift, they are proving particularly dynamic in proposing social and local innovations.

Digital transformations—first and foremost blockchain—are forms of democratization of technology and offer a new field for financial innovations produced by civil society to meet social aspirations. Crowdfunding, for example, enables savers to participate in the financing of selected projects. The spread of these innovations is facilitated by social networks and does not require the mobilization of the traditional financial system. Of course, these innovations do not reduce financial risk, the possibility of fraud or collective misconception. But they do democratize access to financing for production projects that are not commodities.

13.5 Conclusion

1. The social studies of finance propose an analysis of finance based on its observation.
2. Financial products are contracts.
3. The financial price is a convention, not a natural truth.
4. Market building is a process that follows five distinct phases: passiva(c)tion, qualculation, encounter, attachment and price formation.
5. Performativity in sociology highlights how theories can shape societies.
6. There is no such thing as direct financing; financial intermediaries perform a variety of functions.
7. Financial innovation can be democratized to achieve the SDGs.

Activities

Questions for Discussion

1. Why can financial education be a way of democratizing finance?
2. Why can social studies of finance be useful to the world of finance?

Mini-Case

The following is an excerpt from a scientific article by French financial sociologist Élise Penalva-Icher published in 2016, "La professionnalisation dans l'investissement responsable. Le cas des analystes extra-financiers". *Revue française de socio-économie*, (1), p. 147.

"The creation of French SRI took place in several stages. Before the arrival of Arese in 1996, there were a few ethical funds with a religious focus. The relatively small number of these investments and their specific objective made them a niche market.

It wasn't until the arrival of a proposed extra-financial rating agency in 1996 (Arese, since acquired by Vigeo) that SRI became a financial market for sustainable development. The success of Arese is clearly linked to that of the market. Indeed, Arese succeeded in convincing managers to use the extra-financial analysis it produced. This conversion was achieved through symbolic legitimization and technical tools [...]. On the technical side, Arese offered managers quantitative assessments in an Excel-type computer format, which they were used to using in traditional finance. To legitimize its existence, the argument developed by the agency consisted in presenting extra-financial analysis as a better predictor of a company's health, since it encompasses social and environmental criteria, which are generally left aside by traditional finance".

Now answer the following questions in a few lines:

1. Recall what socially responsible investment and non-financial analysis are (feel free to consult other chapters of this manual).
2. What do financial managers and analysts do?
3. Using the theoretical framework proposed by Michel Callon, which stage of the marketing process is described here?

References

Braudel, F. (1979). *Civilisation matérielle, économie et capitalisme: XVe–XVIIIe siècle. Les jeux de l'échange*. Armand Colin.

Callon, M. (2017). *L'Emprise des marchés: Comprendre leur fonctionnement pour pouvoir les changer*. La Découverte.

Carruthers, B. G. (2015). Financialization and the institutional foundations of the new capitalism. *Socio-Economic Review, 13*(2), 379–398.

Chambost, I., Lenglet, M., & Tadjeddine, Y. (Eds.). (2016). *La Fabrique de la finance*. Septentrion.

Graeber, D. (2011). *Debt: The first 5,000 years*. Melville House.

Keynes, J. M. (1936). *The general theory of employment, interest and money*. Palgrave Macmillan.

MacKenzie, D., Muniesa, F., & Siu, L. (2007). *Do economists make markets? On the performativity of economics*. Princeton University Press.

Weber, Max. *Economy and society* (Vols. I and II). Plon.

Zelizer, V. A. (1978). Human values and the market: The case of life insurance and death in 19th-century America. *American Journal of Sociology, 84*(3), 591–610.

Part II
Financial Actors and Practices

14 Corporate Governance: Shareholders, Employees and Stakeholders

Nicolas Aubert and Xavier Hollandts

Putting Things into Perspective

Why take an interest in corporate governance? It seems to be a secondary economic topic compared to growth, unemployment, monetary policy, fiscal policy or public debt management. In Chapter "Understanding Economic Diversity", we saw that companies have become central players in contemporary economies. The collapse of planned economies has relegated states to the background, with governments intervening primarily to regulate the operation of markets. Against this backdrop, it is crucial to take a closer look at corporate management. The orientation and interests pursued by the company become essential. Should companies pursue only private interests and maximum profit? Can they pursue objectives of common good, or is this incompatible with their nature? Who decides on their strategy? How and to what extent should companies open up to stakeholders and corporate social responsibility (CSR)? Corporate governance provides answers to these questions by determining the economic, strategic and even political orientation of companies.

Learning Objectives

- Understanding the debates surrounding corporate governance
- Identify the main players, processes and levers of corporate governance
- Understanding the link between governance and corporate strategy
- Analyze the role played by employees and stakeholders in governance
- Discovering more inclusive governance models

14.1 Corporate Governance Issues

Businesses have become the dominant form of organization in contemporary economies. Since the first liberal economists of the XVIIIth century, it has been considered that the pursuit of private interest can ultimately contribute to collective well-being. Unfortunately, major environmental and social disruptions have shown that the pursuit of private interests alone cannot maximize collective well-being. The goal of maximizing profit is often difficult to bear for both the company and the community. Tensions can arise between shareholders and other stakeholders over the integration

N. Aubert (✉)
CERGAM, Aix-Marseille Université, Marseille, France
e-mail: nicolas.aubert@iae-aix.com

X. Hollandts
KEDGE BS, Talence, France
e-mail: xavier.hollandts@kedgebs.com

T. Lagoarde-Ségot (ed.), *Ecological Economics and Finance*,
https://doi.org/10.1007/978-3-031-71249-4_14

of extra-financial sustainability criteria such as the United Nations' Sustainable Development Goals (SDGs). Taking these criteria into account entails new costs that reduce companies' profits and/or requires long-term investments that affect their short-term profitability. By analogy with the political system of a state, corporate governance is the equivalent of government. It is the government that decides on major orientations and makes decisions, sometimes arbitrating between conflicting interests. Corporate governance refers to the set of institutions, rules and practices that frame the manager's decision-making power and organize relations with stakeholders, in particular shareholders. Governance thus refers to the political process of stakeholder consultation/deliberation, the control system (verifying that the executive makes and executes the right decisions) and the decision distribution system (who decides what and how). The major decisions that result are of two kinds. First and foremost, they are strategic, providing lasting direction for the company's activities. Decisions are also financial, concerning both the level of performance to be achieved and the distribution of profits. This chapter looks at two different approaches to corporate governance: the shareholder approach (shareholder governance) and the partnership approach (partnership governance). These two approaches are based on different conceptions. The former gives primacy to shareholders' objectives, while the latter emphasizes the role of the company's stakeholders, such as employees and producers. We will highlight the characteristics of the shareholder governance model and underline its limitations in terms of sustainability. We will then examine the partnership approach to governance and alternative modes of governance. We will show that these are more in line with CSR and sustainable development approaches in particular.

14.2 Shareholder Governance and Sustainability

In this section, we begin by presenting the dominant model of shareholder governance that has prevailed since the 1970s. In particular, we detail the arguments that have contributed to its hegemony.

Agency Theory: The Foundation of Shareholder Governance

Corporate governance has been a recurring topic since the 1970s, with the gradual rise of shareholder ownership, its transformation in favor of institutional investors, and the emergence of shareholder engagement and activism. Until this period, corporate governance remained above all a private affair, involving only a handful of people: founders, managers and a few shareholders or investors. They were often close or related, and jurists refer to the notion of *affectio societatis*. Until the XIXe century, companies were both managed and owned by the same people, generally from the same family. The shareholders effectively ran the company. There were no real problems of governance: either because people rarely disagreed with themselves (as in the case of the manager controlling the capital), or because any conflicts were settled within the family circle (family businesses representing the vast majority of companies at the time). Until the end of the Second World War, the family business was the dominant model. Very few companies were listed and opened up their capital. When they did, the capital was generally held by institutional investors, sometimes close to the founders/managers, such as the regional banks. From the 1970s onwards, with the creation of pension funds, companies gradually opened up their capital to an ever-increasing number of shareholders. This financialization of companies and the massification of shareholding (more and more players) were major factors that brought corporate governance to the fore. Between the 1970s and 1980s, more and more companies were listed on the stock market, either because their financing requirements were substantial, or because the cost of financing became more advantageous than bank financing. At the same time, a new economic and financial theory, known as agency theory, was emerging. This theory analyzes governance issues by focusing on the relationship between shareholder and manager. Agency theory emphasizes the need to safeguard shareholders' interests. For this reason, it is also sometimes referred to as *shareholder governance theory*. Among social science theories, agency theory has undoubtedly been the most influential. It emphasizes the fact that information is imperfect, and that this context favors certain actors driven by their own self-interest. In this case, managers are a priori seen as actors in search of a significant room for maneuver (or managerial latitude), and do not necessarily wish to be accountable or explain their strategy or results. At the same time, they seek to increase their remuneration and stay in their jobs. How can we combat these potentially harmful behaviors? The solution identified is to promote independent directors, who would improve the quality and transparency of information, while at the same time being responsible for monitoring management strategy and results, with a view to defending shareholders' interests first and foremost. Agency theory has also made it possible to justify the pre-eminent role of shareholders and to develop management tools geared to their objectives (*economic value added*). The recommendations of agency theory dictate purpose and strategic reasoning, affirming the primacy of shareholders and the need to focus on shareholder value. They guide the structure of the company, proposing to concentrate on those activities likely to generate maximum added value for shareholders. They also inspire the implementation of managerial tools and procedures to maximize profit. With shareholder governance, profit maximization has become an inescapable horizon and a strategic and financial compass governing corporate life.

Reconsidering the Foundations of Shareholder Governance

The shareholder vision of the company is based on the idea that shareholders are the owners of the company and that the company's priority objectives, both strategic and financial, must first and foremost serve their interests. In concrete terms, this translates into decisions in their favor, such as dividend payments or share buy-backs. Beyond these elements of financial policy, other strategic choices can sometimes be guided by purely shareholder objectives: laying off employees when the company is profitable, closing down profitable activities or units, selling off assets and dismantling companies. These decisions are based on the premise that shareholders are the owners of the company. Enhancing their interests would necessarily be tantamount to the common good. This postulate has flourished because it is based on the exceptional dissemination of agency theory. But do shareholders own the company or just their shares? By answering the first part of this question in the affirmative, agency theory ignores the *social interest* of the company.

In French law, the corporate interest (art. 1833 of the Civil Code) is defined as "the interest of the company as a legal entity, distinct from that of its partners and directors".

This is an interest that is superior to the partisan interests of stakeholders, and which must promote the interests of the company above all else. Shareholders therefore have no serious legal basis for being considered the owners of the company. This commonly accepted view is based on fundamental legal errors. By virtue of the company's social interest, shareholder primacy is unjustified. The concept of 'social interest' has not been perfectly defined by legal doctrine, but its contours have been gradually outlined in the wake of the Freuhauf ruling of 1965. Jurisprudence has established that corporate interest necessarily corresponds to a broader and richer vision than a particular interest, and encompasses not only that of the shareholders, but also that of employees, creditors, customers and even the State—in other words, the stakeholders. Thus, in terms of law and jurisprudence, shareholders are not recognized as the owners of the company, and exclusive consideration of their interests is contrary to the notion of social interest.

14.3 Partnership Governance in Support of the SDGs

After describing the shareholder model and its limitations, we propose to study new economic models based on other anthropological conceptions.

Other Anthropological Foundations for Alternative Models

Economic agents also act disinterestedly, through mechanisms such as altruism, giving[1] and gratuity.

Georges Akerlof seems to us to be the economist who best links these anthropological approaches. This Keynesian economist conceptualized the notion of moral hazard (Akerlof, 1970[2]). But he also drew economists' attention to Marcel Mauss and gave economic significance to the exchange of gifts (Akerlof, 1982[3]). To analyze the exchange of gifts, Akerlof examines the reasons why employees work beyond their targets, a situation unthinkable from the point of view of neoclassical theory. The explanation for this phenomenon is explicitly based on the exchange of gifts. Employees who give more of their time expect a counter-gift from their employer, which can take a number of forms: above-market pay, better working conditions or smaller pay differentials between group members. Non-utilitarian approaches therefore call into question contractual approaches to governance. For example, Akerlof's concept of giving helps explain higher wage levels than those that would be achieved by supply and demand alone. These non-market exchanges are present in most social relations.[4]

Employee Participation

In addition to shareholders investing in financial capital, we need to recognize that employees also invest in other capital, namely human capital: their skills, qualifications and ingenuity. Recognition of employees' investment of their human capital should result in their involvement in governance, capital and profits on an equal footing with shareholders.

Shared capitalism is the term used to describe a system in which workers become partial owners of their companies, and thus, in effect, both employees and shareholders. In France, the term "actionnariat salarié" (employee shareholding) is used when employees participate in their company's capital. *Shared capitalism* also includes profit-sharing through profit-sharing bonuses. This model of capital and profit-sharing is highly developed in the United States. Shared capitalism improves perceived (motivation, satisfaction, intention to stay) and actual (absenteeism, staff turnover) working conditions. It is also said to have positive effects in terms of economic and financial performance, as numerous academic studies have demonstrated. These beneficial effects would be the consequence of a long-term reciprocal relationship made possible by the practice of sharing profits and capital with all employees, in line with the theory of gift exchange put forward by Akerlof.[5]

Employee participation in corporate governance means giving employees a seat on their company's board of directors or supervisory board. This type of representation can be referred to as employee governance.[6] In Germany, as in most Nordic countries, supervisory boards include between one-third and one-half of employee representatives. Thus, more inclusive and partnership-based governance can begin with the integration of employee representatives, which shareholder governance excludes in principle. However, this form of representation remains subject to the same constraints as a conventional company. Other forms of governance exist and go

[1] In management and management sciences, we can cite the work by Gomez, P. Y., Grevin, A. and Masclef, O. (2015). *L'Entreprise, une affaire de don. Ce que révèle les sciences de gestion*, Nouvelle Cité, Bruyères-le-Châtel (untranslated).

[2] Akerlof, G. (1970). "The market for 'lemons': Quality Uncertainty and the Market Mechanism". *The Quarterly Journal of Economics*, 84(3), pp. 488–500.

[3] Akerlof, G. (1982). "Labor contracts as partial gift exchange". *The Quarterly Journal of Economics*, 97(4), pp. 543–569.

[4] For an overview of work on giving, altruism and reciprocity, see Kolm, S. C. and Ythier, J. M. (Eds.). (2006). *Handbook of the economics of giving, altruism and reciprocity: Foundations*. Elsevier.

[5] Freeman, R. B., Blasi, J. R. and Kruse, D. L. (2010). *Shared capitalism at work: Employee ownership, profit and gain sharing, and broad-based stock options*. University of Chicago Press.

[6] Hollandts, X. and Aubert, N. (2019). "Employee governance: contribution of employee representation to corporate governance". *Finance Contrôle Stratégie*, (22-1).

even further, both in terms of employee representation and the integration of stakeholder expectations. Cooperative companies are a good example.

Cooperative Governance

According to the official definition of the International Cooperative Alliance, "a cooperative is an autonomous association of persons united voluntarily to meet their common needs and aspirations through a jointly owned and democratically controlled enterprise". In France, this is epitomized by two forms of cooperative: the SCOP and the SCIC. The former places employees at the heart of the company's operations, strategy and governance. The latter represents the archetype of partnership governance, placing stakeholders in the company's project at the heart of governance.

A SCOP (*Société coopérative et participative*) embodies the French model of worker cooperatives. It is a commercial company owned collectively by its employees, which lives and develops in the competitive sector with the same management and profitability constraints as any conventional business. In fact, it operates like any other business. Its differences lie in its governance and the distribution of its profits. In a SCOP, employees hold at least 51% of the capital and 65% of the voting rights. The special features of a SCOP concern the way it is governed. The associates decide on the basis of a democratic rule: one employee (associate) = one vote. This rule, common to all cooperatives, differs from traditional joint-stock companies, where the main shareholders have one vote and voting rights in proportion to the amount of their contributions. Employee-members, on the other hand, have the same power, regardless of the number of shares they hold.

The second distinctive feature is that the cooperative's director and corporate officers are elected by the employee-members. Once again, this is a significant difference from traditional companies, where managers may be the company's main shareholders, or may be appointed and chosen directly by those same shareholders. It is the employees (cooperators) who are placed at the heart of operations, decision-making and governance. This is an alternative model to that of the classic capitalist company. In a SCOP, profits are obligatorily divided into three parts: one part for all employees—in the form of profit-sharing and incentive schemes; one part for associates (some employees are not associates) in the form of dividends; and one part for company reserves. This last part is compulsory and enables the creation of non-distributable reserves which contribute to the company's development by enabling the consolidation of shareholders' equity and investments.

The SCIC (*Société d'intérêt collectif*) is the most recent model of cooperative enterprise in France. There are currently 1060 SCICs, representing 83,000 members and 9700 jobs. SCICs are ideally suited to the development of local projects. For example, nearly seven out of ten SCICs have at least one local authority as a member. SCICs must comply with certain specific rules: heterogeneous membership (multi-company), compliance with cooperative rules (one person = one vote), and disinterested management (operating surpluses must be invested in the business).

The great originality and uniqueness of the SCIC lies in its multi-company concept. Indeed, from the outset, the SCIC must associate three types of members: the employees of the SCIC; the beneficiaries of the goods and services offered by the cooperative (customers, suppliers, local residents, etc.); other types of associates, natural persons or legal entities under private or public law, contributing to the cooperative's activity (companies, associations, craftsmen, volunteers, farmers, local authorities, etc.). The presence of three categories of members makes the SCIC a unique model of partnership-based enterprise. From a political point of view, the SCIC remains a cooperative structure, and the principle of "one member = one vote" is therefore in force, particularly when voting on decisions at the general meeting. SCICs are innovative cooperative structures, founded on a local project, which have built and maintained a genuine partnership-based governance structure. These companies often pursue ambitious social and societal objectives, and provide local solutions in a wide range of fields.

14.4 Conclusion

At the heart of economic theory and business practice, there is a debate between proponents of the shareholder approach and advocates of the partnership approach. The shareholder vision is simple and powerful, but excludes citizens and the planet, and leads to aberrations or significant negative externalities. Alternative governance models differ from the shareholder model, both in terms of the company's objectives and orientations, and in the way governance bodies operate. The partnership approach is certainly more complex, and calls into question the foundations, reflexes and tools deeply rooted in the mental models of players and organizations. The partnership approach presupposes a genuine political and deliberative logic at the heart of corporate functioning and governance. It is a promising way of building a future in which sustainability is at the heart of corporate strategy. The examples presented in this chapter show that it is possible to achieve these objectives without sacrificing economic efficiency.

Activities

Questions for Discussion

1. Why are shareholders often portrayed as the owners of the company?
2. What are the advantages and disadvantages of multi-stakeholder governance?
3. What is the main role of a board of directors?
4. What distinguishes cooperatives from other businesses?
5. Which SDGs are most affected by modes of corporate governance?
6. Is it possible to reconcile economic efficiency with the integration of stakeholder interests?

Mini-case: Danone and Sodiaal: Governance Models in the Production and Sale of Dairy Products

Danone produces and markets dairy and plant-based products, mineral waters, and infant and medical nutrition products. A world leader in its field, it employs over 90,000 people and achieved sales of 27 billion euros in 2022. In 2020, Danone became the first publicly-listed company with a mission to pursue a policy of sustainable development. With its Danone 2030 plan, the company has formulated its strategy in line with the SDGs. In particular, its brand model is broken down into several objectives, such as improving health, preserving the planet and renewing the environment. The "one person, one share" plan aims to ensure that every employee holds one share in the company. This development has been the subject of much comment in the press, which has questioned whether these new objectives can be reconciled with the company's profitability. In 2021, the investment fund shareholder Bluebell Capital sent a letter to shareholders questioning Emmanuel Faber's new strategy at the head of Danone. According to them, Danone had not found "the right balance between shareholder value creation and sustainable development issues". Under Emmanuel Faber's presidency, Danone's share price had in fact lost nearly a quarter of its value between December 2017 and December 2020. In March 2021, the Artisan Partners fund also called for the CEO to step down. Danone's Board of Directors terminated Faber's duties.

Sodiaal is the French leader in milk collection, with 10% of French production, and produces and markets cheeses, milk, cream and butter. It is also present in specialized nutrition, associated ingredients, ultra-fresh and frozen products, and seafood. The company employs over 9000 people and generates 60,000 indirect jobs. Sales are expected to reach 5.5 billion euros by 2022. Sodiaal is a cooperative owned by 16,000 breeders, who elect the 25 farmers who sit on the Board of Directors. Two-thirds of profits are redistributed to members.

The cooperative's main objective is to buy milk from its cooperators, ensuring an identical milk price for all by collecting milk regardless of farm size. At the end of 2020, Sodiaal initiated an employee shareholding plan so that employees can become non-cooperator associates and also own the company. Since 2017, Sodiaal has launched a value creation plan called *#Value* to position the company in the top 5 most profitable dairy companies. Sodiaal has formulated four pillars of its sustainable development such as committing to responsible food and actively contributing to protecting the planet. The system used by Sodiaal and its main competitor Lactalis to set milk prices was heavily criticized in the media in 2018. Sodiaal had encouraged producers to increase milk production at the expense of the selling price. In March 2021, Sodiaal became a majority shareholder in Yoplait, in order to secure outlets for farmers.

Questions

1. What are the main differences between the two companies' governance systems?
2. By consulting their websites, and in particular their latest integrated reports, discuss the differences and similarities between the sustainability objectives of these two companies.

15 Shareholders and Responsibility

Rachelle Belinga and Blanche Segrestin

Putting Things into Perspective

Since the financial crisis of 2008, the influence of shareholders on companies has been severely criticized. Shareholders are accused of imposing a short-termist horizon on companies to serve their own stock market interests, but also of not participating sufficiently in the good governance of listed companies. On the one hand, shareholders intervene too much; on the other, not enough!

To break this deadlock, policymakers and trade associations alike have come up with the same response: shareholder engagement. In its broadest sense, shareholder engagement refers to the way in which shareholders monitor the companies in which they invest, engage in dialogue with them on environmental, social, and governance (ESG) issues, and vote at general meetings.

In this chapter, we will analyze the new responsibilities allocated to shareholders in terms of engagement. We will contextualize shareholder-corporate relations with regard to the history of shareholding and theories of corporate governance, then discuss the new challenges posed by professional investors, and finally examine calls for investor empowerment through shareholder engagement and corresponding theoretical propositions.

Learning Objectives

- Contextualizing shareholder engagement in corporate governance
- Understanding the issues and challenges of share ownership
- Challenging the a priori positive perception of shareholder engagement
- Analyzing and critiquing different shareholder engagement practices

15.1 The Changing Relationship Between Shareholders and Companies

The Origins of Corporate Governance

The first company with a shareholder model of ownership was founded in Toulouse in 1372. To finance the construction of large mills

R. Belinga (✉)
California State University, Los Angeles, CA, USA
e-mail: rachelle.belinga@csun.edu

R. Belinga · B. Segrestin
MINES Paris Tech, Paris, France

T. Lagoarde-Ségot (ed.), *Ecological Economics and Finance*,
https://doi.org/10.1007/978-3-031-71249-4_15

on the Garonne River, local milling families joined forces to create the *Société des Moulins de Bazacle*. They divided up ownership titles, called *uchaux,* which were very similar to today's shares: dematerialized and transferable. What an innovation! Unlike partnerships, shareholders are not liable for the company's actions, debts, or potential losses. This form of company subsequently spread to Europe with the help of colonial ventures, and entered French law under the name of "société anonyme" in 1807. The development of the modern company at the beginning of the XXth century made it the dominant legal form, and shareholders have since been characterized by the free transferability of their shares, limited liability, and voting rights at general meetings. However, the joint-stock company also marks the "erasure of shareholders" (Gomez & Korine, 2009): by protecting shareholders, limited liability keeps them out of the company's operational management.

While law has created a separation between ownership and control, the democratization of financial markets has accentuated this separation. In their seminal work on corporate governance, *The Modern Corporation and Private Property* (1932), Alfred Berle and Gardiner Means noted that the shareholder base of modern American companies at the turn of the century was atomized to the benefit of a multitude of small investors, while a new class of managers monopolized control of the company.

The first theories of corporate governance defined governance as all the mechanisms needed to control these (overly) powerful managers and ensure that companies are properly managed. Agency theory (see Chapter 14), for example, postulates a norm of shareholder primacy: the control of managers must be primarily for the benefit of shareholders. This theory, which has dominated business and legal circles since the 1980s, has nevertheless given rise to much debate. Its detractors not only assert the existence of managerial responsibilities toward companies' other stakeholders, but also hold shareholders partly responsible for the ills of contemporary business.

The Transformation of the Shareholder Base: New Challenges for the Company

In the second half of the XXth century, corporate shareholding underwent a profound transformation. Gone was the classic image of shareholders as isolated and powerless against managerial power. Western companies have now welcomed massive holdings from "institutional investors." These financial intermediaries are professionals in the collection and pooling of savings, such as pension funds and insurance companies, and, according to an OECD report, represent almost 41% of the shareholder base of the world's 10,000 largest listed companies.[1] They are even over-represented in the United States, where they hold 72% of the capital of American companies, compared with around 38% of European companies.

However, financial intermediation does not stop with institutional investors. The latter often call on asset management companies, i.e., investment professionals per se, to manage their assets. By 2022, the asset management market accounted for almost $100,000 billion in assets under management, a sharp increase since 2005, when it accounted for $36,000 billion in assets.[2] These different levels of intermediation constitute a shareholder intermediation chain (see Fig. 15.1), which complicate the link between shareholders and companies.

In this chain, beneficiaries or small savers entrust their assets to a savings collector, often an institutional investor, who either invests these savings directly on the financial markets, or entrusts them in turn to an asset management company.

While some see the rise of professional investors as an opportunity to ensure that management is aligned with shareholders' interests, others have questioned the effects of the influence of these representatives of financial power on the company. Financial intermediaries operate in an extremely competitive environment,

[1] *Source* OECD. (2018). https://www.oecd.org/corporate/Owners-of-the-Worlds-Listed-Companies.pdf.

[2] BCG. (2023). Global Asset Management Report.

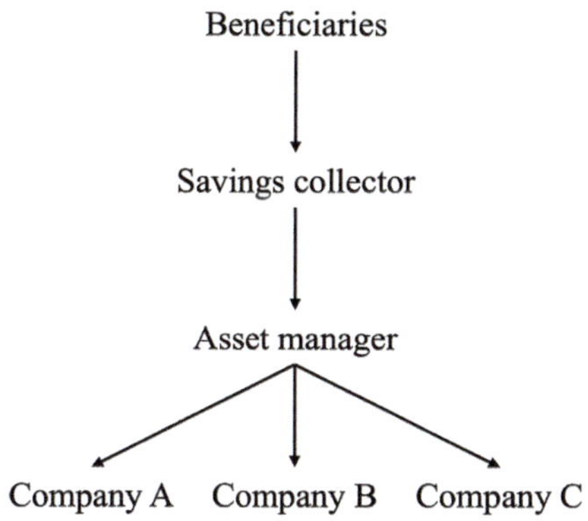

Fig. 15.1 Shareholder intermediation chain (*Source* Adapted from Belinga [2018])

and in order to optimize the performance of their portfolios, some of their investment strategies rely on very short-term investments (from a few weeks to one or two days). A "tragedy of time horizons," according to Bank of England Governor Mark Carney in 2015, which has pushed companies as well toward short-termism. The presence of short-term (long-term) investors often encourages in turn short-term (long-term) managerial practices (Connelly et al., 2010).

At the same time, these investors make an heterogeneous, and potentially contradictory, use of corporate governance. Some observers deplore the lack of involvement most professional investors, who do not contribute to the control of management, while condemning the activism of aggressive hedge funds disrupting corporate governance. For instance, some hedge funds have been known to use empty voting techniques, which enable them to decouple shareholder voting rights from the risk associated with investing in a company (see Box 15.1).

Box 15.1: Perry Corp. Vs. Mylan Inc.

One of the first high-profile cases of empty voting was that of hedge fund Perry Corp. and Mylan Inc. In 2004, Mylan Inc. a pharmaceutical group, planned to acquire its competitor Kings Pharmaceuticals at a very attractive price. This announcement did not go down well with Mylan Inc.'s shareholders, who saw no economic interest in the deal (as it stood). Perry Corp. whose stake in Kings Pharmaceuticals was substantial, had bought nearly 10% of Mylan Inc. shares, but *hedged* this position by buying equity swaps, or derivatives that insured against a fall in the value of Mylan Inc.'s shares. Perry Corp. was subsequently sued by financier Carl Icahn, majority shareholder in Mylan Inc. for influencing shareholders' vote in favor of acquiring Kings Pharmaceuticals, without bearing the risk this represented for the value of Mylan Inc.

Source Hu, H., & Black, B. (2007). Hedge funds, insiders, and the decoupling of economic and voting ownership: Empty voting and hidden (morphable) ownership. *Journal of Corporate Finance, 13*(2–3), 343–367.

Empty voting reveals the risks that investment professionals' opportunistic behaviors can represent for companies.

The transformation of share ownership has therefore redefined the relationship between shareholders and companies. Whereas shareholders used to be portrayed as powerless against the managerial machine that is the modern corporation, professional investors' heterogeneous strategies and expectations are now influencing corporate management, sometimes in damaging ways.

15.2 Defending Shareholder Power

Responsibility Through Commitment

As professional investors pose new challenges for corporate governance, after the 2008 financial crisis, legislators have started to define shareholder "duties".

The UK Stewardship Code and European Directive 2017/828 on long-term shareholder engagement, for example, encourages greater shareholder involvement in corporate governance, but also more transparent "engagement" practices. Shareholder engagement often boils down to putting shareholder resolutions to a vote at general meetings, but professional investors tend to prefer "dialogue," or private discussions with executives, which they see as a more effective and less confrontational engagement strategy.

Shareholder engagement is also seen as an opportunity for socially responsible investors (SRIs) to raise environmental, social, and governance (ESG) issues with companies (see Box 15.2).

Box 15.2: Two examples of shareholder engagement processes

Example 1: BP, Shell, and the climate

In 2013, 75 institutional investors, representing $3.5 trillion in assets under management, formed the Carbon Asset Risk Initiative, a coalition of climate-concerned shareholders. After several years of dialogue with oil companies BP and Shell, coalition members in collaboration with other investors filed shareholder resolutions to improve these companies' transparency on their CO_2 emissions. These resolutions, supported by the management of BP and Shell (an unprecedented feat!), were adopted at the Annual General Meeting by 98.28% of votes cast for BP and 98.9% for Shell.

Source Ceres. (2015). *Carbon asset risk: A review of progress and opportunities.*

Example 2: Verizon and cybersecurity

From 2017 to 2019, 55 institutional investors, bringing together nearly $12 trillion in assets under management, collectively launched a dialogue process with 53 companies within the UN Principles for Responsible Investment (PRI) framework on the subject of cybersecurity. As a result, a report published by the PRI notes an increase of more than 60% in transparency, among targeted companies, about their cybersecurity skills and resources.

This initiative would even have revealed the high level of risk represented by cybersecurity for Verizon Communications, the American telecommunications company, and its customers' data. The company has stepped up its communication on the mechanisms put in place to prevent and manage this risk, such as the creation of a cybersecurity council and cybersecurity training for its employees.

Source UN PRI. (2020). *Engaging on Cyber Security: Results of the PRI Collaborative Engagement 2017–2019.*

In 2015, a study identified 2152 requests for dialogue from investors and estimated the success rate of environmental and/or social engagement processes at 13% over the 1999–2009 period (Dimson et al., 2015).

Cases of successful commitments remain rare, and studies do not specify whether they have had a real impact on company performance. Even when commitments explicitly target ESG criteria, they remain a private initiative at shareholders' discretion. Rather than balancing power among companies' various stakeholders, doesn't shareholder engagement run the risk of reinforcing shareholder power? Between the short-termist activism of hedge funds and other shareholders' ESG engagement, there are two opposing images: that of "good activists", who make a positive contribution to corporate governance, and that of "bad activists," who intend to dictate the course of companies, above all in their own interests (Hill, 2017).

Responsible Shareholder Models

In order to avert the risks associated with shareholder power, three theoretical propositions can offer a starting point for defining a framework for shareholder engagement.

The Habermasian Approach to Commitment

Some researchers suggest drawing inspiration from the ethical philosophy of Jurgen Habermas (see Box 15.3) and question the real capacity of shareholders to represent ESG issues and the interests of other corporate stakeholders, such as employees, suppliers, customers, and civil society as a whole.

> **Box 15.3: Habermas and Corporate Social Responsibility (CSR)**
>
> Jürgen Habermas is a contemporary German philosopher, born in 1929, who has had a major influence on management science. In his work on the ethics of discussion, Habermas examines the processes through which norms governing social order are validated. In his view, these norms are only valid if they are consensual. Their establishment or contestation must then be the subject of collective discussion.
>
> Habermasian approaches have been particularly fruitful in thinking about CSR. For example, they have influenced the way in which companies' dialogue with their stakeholders is assessed. In this respect, Habermasian scholars have proposed an inclusive participation criterion for all stakeholders in order to guarantee the establishment of a valid consensus.
>
> See in particular: Scherer A. G., & Palazzo, G. (2007). Toward a political conception of corporate responsibility: Business and society seen from a Habermasian perspective. *Academy of Management Review, 32*(4), 1096–1120.

For Goodman and Arenas (2015), a Habermasian approach to shareholder engagement then consists of encouraging shareholders to (1) identify the concerns of companies' other stakeholders, (2) facilitate dialogue between companies and their stakeholders, so that the latter can have direct access to management and participate in discussions that concern them, and (3) support at the political level the regulation of dialogues between companies and their stakeholders.

The Habermasian approach to shareholder engagement puts shareholders at the service of other stakeholders. However, this framework remains subject to the goodwill of shareholders and their ability to define ethical commitments.

Universal Ownership

A second possible framework comes from two committed shareholders, Robert Monks and Nell Minows, who, in 1995, observed that most professional investors have such diversified holdings that they participate in the economy as a whole. According to Monks and Minows, they should therefore be natural allies of the general interest, as 'universal owners'.

Universal ownership, however, requires investors to be able to identify and serve the general interest. Who can ensure that their engagement practices are indeed universal, and do not undermine the delicate balance between companies and their other stakeholders? Moreover, financial law stipulates that the only interest that professional investors can serve is that of their clients and beneficiaries. Commonly referred to as 'fiduciary duties', these obligations are designed to limit the risks that financial intermediation may present for beneficiaries, and are often restricted to maximizing fund performance. Many legal experts point out that fiduciary duties are difficult to reconcile with universal ownership. Indeed, if the financial interests of its beneficiaries and clients conflict with the universal public interest, what is a universal shareholder to do?

For universal ownership to be truly embraced by professional investors, legislators would not only have to revise financial intermediaries' fiduciary duties but also establish a legal status for the role of universal shareholders.

Shareholder Involvement in Mission Companies

Rather than assuming the potential benefits of shareholder engagement, a third theoretical framework examines the solutions that enable companies to defend themselves against 'bad activists'. For example, the *Société à Mission* is a legal form recently introduced into French law that protects companies' 'mission' (Segrestin et al., 2020). In its articles of association, a mission-driven company describes its various objectives, including social and environmental ones. Its managers are then responsible for fulfilling the company's mission, above and beyond the interests of shareholders. In this context, shareholders invest with full knowledge of and must comply with the company's bylaws, they can only engage with and evaluate managers within the scope of their mission (see Box 15.4).

Box 15.4: Mirova, an SRI investor with a mission

Founded in 2014, Mirova is a French asset management company specializing in socially responsible investment. A subsidiary of Natixis IM, Mirova managed over 28 billion euros in assets in 2023, invested worldwide. Mirova is also a committed shareholder, particularly involved in ESG issues.

In 2020, Mirova became a mission-driven company, defining objectives based on the positive impact it wishes to have on the companies in which it invests. By adopting this status, Mirova sent a strong signal to all its stakeholders—beneficiaries, customers, Natixis IM and companies alike. Companies, in particular, can anticipate Mirova's objectives when engaging in dialogues, and even draw inspiration from this model to formulate their own mission.

Source https://www.mirova.com/fr/mirova/notre-mission

Although this legal form has only recently been introduced into legislation, it provides an interesting starting point for thinking about shareholder engagement. Mission-driven companies provide a default framework for shareholder engagement. By protecting the company's mission, and its social and environmental strategy, it frames shareholders' engagement possibilities.

15.3 Conclusion

This chapter contextualizes shareholder engagement in terms of the history of relations between companies and shareholders. As a result of the transformation of shareholding in favor of professional investors, companies are facing heterogeneous expectations from their shareholders as well as their at times short-termist and/or opportunistic engagement practices.

This perspective contrasts with that of legislators, who see shareholder engagement as an opportunity for corporate governance and management control. Shareholder engagement is particularly prized by investors as a means of promoting ESG issues within companies. In order to reconcile the promises of shareholder engagement with the risks of strengthening shareholder influence, new theoretical frameworks have emerged for thinking about 'responsible' shareholder engagement.

Activities

Questions for discussion

1. You are a portfolio manager. To offer your clients lower management costs, you invest passively in companies listed on a top stock market index. On a day-to-day basis, you have little or no contact with these companies. Your manager tells you that you need to engage with your portfolio companies on climate issues. Imagine your action plan.
2. One of the companies you have invested in is a mission-driven company whose aim is to develop a sustainable energy supply. You notice, however, that this offer is not affordable for a number of so-called 'developing' countries. What would be your plan as an engaged shareholder to draw attention to the reduction of inequalities and the challenges of climate justice?
3. In corporate governance, executive compensation is the subject of much debate. Some

are now proposing to set a maximum ratio between CEO remuneration and the average salary of employees.

Let us imagine that a socially responsible investor, Actio, makes this proposal its main topic of engagement. During dialogues with companies, Actio asks executives to adopt a compensation policy that defines an 80:1 ratio between CEO pay and the average national salary.

What do you think of this proposal? Discuss its limits from a Habermasian perspective.

Mini-case: BlackRock and Shareholder Engagement

BlackRock is the world's largest asset management company. In 2023, it had over $9,000 billion in assets under management.

Every year, BlackRock's managing director, Larry Fink, publishes a letter to the CEOs of the companies in which BlackRock is a shareholder (most of the world's listed companies!), in which he sets out his priorities and expectations. Although BlackRock has communicated extensively on environmental, social, and governance (ESG) issues in recent years, many of its critics accuse it of promising much but delivering little.

1. Go to the BlackRock website and read Larry Fink's letter to 2022: https://www.blackrock.com/corporate/investor-relations/larry-fink-ceo-lettera. What are the most important themes in this letter?
   b. What does BlackRock expect from the companies it invests in?
   c. What are the possible effects of Larry Fink's letter on the companies in which BlackRock invests?
2. Visit the BlackRock website again, and explore the Investor Stewardship page: https://www.blackrock.com/corporate/about-us/investment-stewardship, including their European market voting policy (https://www.blackrock.com/corporate/literature/fact-sheet/blk-responsible-investment-guidelines-emea.pdf) and their natural capital engagement policy (https://www.blackrock.com/corporate/literature/publication/blk-commentary-engagement-on-natural-capital.pdf).
   a. What are BlackRock's corporate governance priorities?
   b. To what extent do the expectations you identified earlier in the letter to CEOs correspond to BlackRock's engagement initiatives?
   c. Does BlackRock behave like a universal owner? Please explain.
   d. Given its weight in the shareholding of global listed companies, can BlackRock engage with companies without 'pressuring' them?

References

Belinga, R. (2018). *L'engagement actionnarial: De l'industrialisation de l'actionnariat à l'expression de nouvelles responsabilités*. PhD thesis, Paris Sciences et Lettres.

Berle, A., & Means, G. (1932). *The modern corporation and private property*. New Brunswick, reprint Transaction publishers 1991.

Connelly, B., Tihanyi, L., Certo, S., & Hitt, M. (2010). Marching to the beat of different drummers: The influence of institutional owners on competitive actions. *Academy of Management Journal, 53*(4), 723–742.

Dimson, E., Karakas, O., & Li, X. (2015). Active ownership. *The Review of Financial Studies, 28*(12), 3225–3268.

Gomez, P.-Y., & Korine, H. (2009). *L'entreprise dans la démocratie: Une théorie politique de la Gouvernance d'entreprise*. De Boeck (untranslated).

Goodman, J., & Arenas, D. (2015). Engaging ethically: A discourse ethics perspective on social shareholder engagement. *Business Ethics Quarterly, 25*(2), 163–189.

Hill, J. (2017). Good Activist/Bad Activist: The Rise of International Stewardship Codes. *Seattle UL Rev, 41*, 497.

Segrestin, B., Hatchuel, A., & Levillain, K. (2020). When the law distinguishes between the enterprise and the corporation: The case of the new French law on corporate purpose. *Journal of Business Ethics, 171*(1), 1–13.

Can the *Private Equity* (LBO) Industry Rhyme with Ecology?

16

Isabelle Chambost

Putting Things into Perspective

EMI (UK), MEC (Canada), Kmart (USA), Pages Jaunes (France), NewLook (UK), Camaïeu (France), Naf Naf (France), Toys "R" Us (USA), Morrisons (UK), Postmedia (Canada): the business press regularly reports on emblematic restructurings involving companies under leveraged buy-out (LBO).

In 2023, the British Private Equity and Venture Capital Association (BVCA) produced a report to demonstrate how our members' can help to build sustainable businesses fit for the future. What is the reality? This chapter analyzes the *private equity* industry, deciphering the legal and financial mechanisms involved in acquiring companies, and examining the economic and social consequences.

Learning Objectives

- Understand the structure of the private equity industry and the various economic players involved
- Analyze the construction and various mechanisms at work in Leveraged Buy-Out (LBO) structures
- Decipher the mechanisms at work and understand their economic and social consequences at micro, meso, and macro levels.
- Identifying the concept of financialization

I. Chambost (✉)
Conservatoire National des Arts et Métiers, Paris, France
e-mail: isabelle.chambost@cnam.fr

16.1 When the *Private Equity* Industry Acquires Companies via LBO Structures

Once Upon a Time… a Highly Structured Investment System

One morning in November, a private equity fund manager (*General Partner* or GP) proposes a partnership to the head of an insurance company (*Limited Partner* or LP): "You give me 100 euros and I'll grow it for five years. I'll return 308 euros and keep 52 euros. I'll spare you the fees." Such a high rate of return on investment (25%, i.e. $100 = 308\ (1+i)^{-5}$ is not to be refused!

To acquire companies, the manager (*General Partners*) of a private equity (PE) firm sets up a fund with capital contributors (institutional investors, wealthy families, universities, etc.), known as *limited partners* because of their

T. Lagoarde-Ségot (ed.), *Ecological Economics and Finance*,
https://doi.org/10.1007/978-3-031-71249-4_16

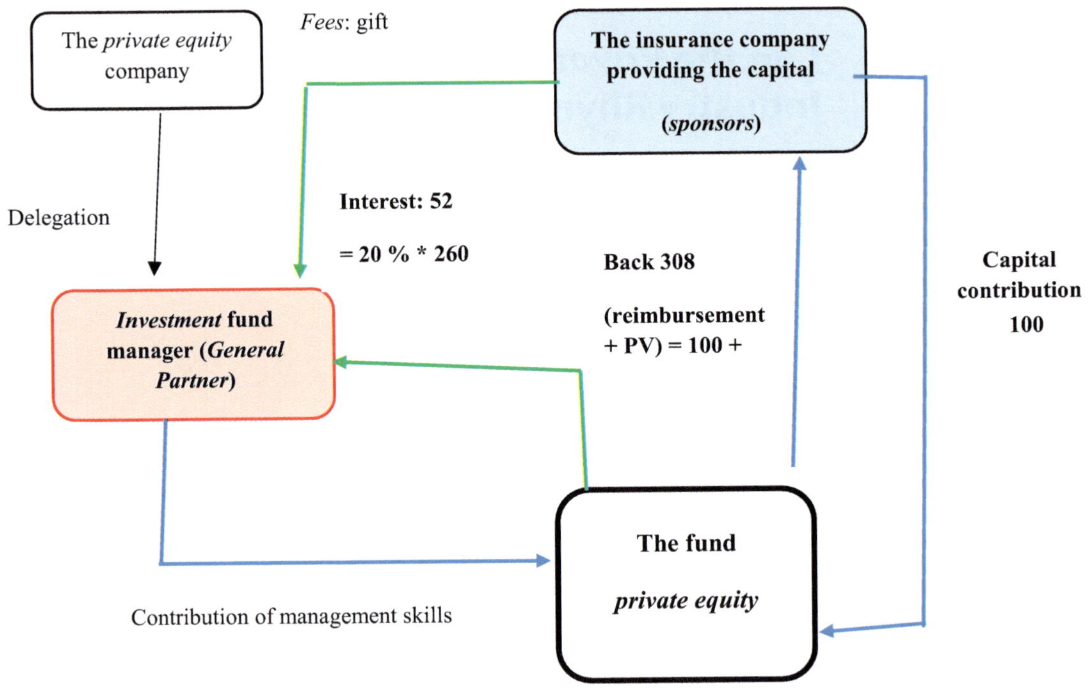

Fig. 16.1 Structuring the investment process: the creation of a private equity fund

limited liability. The *limited partners* contribute almost all the capital (at least 95%), with the manager contributing his or her expertise. The PE manager's remuneration consists of a commission (fees), representing 2% of the capital managed and 20% of the capital gain generated by resale (*carried interest*). This interest can only be paid to the manager if a minimum rate of return (*hurdle rate*) defined by the investors is achieved.

During the investment phase, which generally lasts five years, the fund purchases companies as it goes along. These will be sold five years later, when the fund divests, with the expectation of high capital gains. This five-year holding period is designed to influence company performance (Fig. 16.1).

Investment phase	Divestment phase
Five years	*Five years*

How can these PE managers attract institutional investors to investments that lack the liquidity and information advantages of listed companies?

Private equity managers promise annual rates of return higher than those of the financial markets, ranging, according to the profession, between 20 and 25%, with no precise justification. However, no publicly verifiable information is provided on these rates, which can fluctuate widely.

How can investors have confidence in PE managers, given the risks they are taking and the rates of return they are offering?

The PE managers argue that they are mainly remunerated by a percentage of the capital gains realized, in application of agency theory, according to which, in a situation of incomplete information, incentive (and sanction) mechanisms ensure the loyalty of the co-contractor.

How do PE managers manage to achieve such rates on a regular basis, given the general trend in the economy?

The PE managers have various means of exerting pressure on the company, notably through tax and financial engineering (*Leveraged Buy-Out*), which leads the target company to buy itself, with a very high level of debt (between 50 and 80% of total financing). The aim is to achieve a leverage effect if the borrowing rate is lower than economic profitability. This effect is accentuated by the tax savings generated by interest charges, and amplified by the increase in the debt-to-equity ratio. Last but not least, this industry works hard to inflate company acquisition prices, by creating speculative bubbles to facilitate capital gains when the company is resold (cf. 2.1).

Box 16.1: Illustration of the Leverage Concept

Let us assume that the company's own investment of 1500 euros yields 300 euros before tax, or 240 euros after tax (at a rate of 20%). The rate of return for shareholders would then be 16%. If the investment is made up of 1000 euros in equity and 500 euros in debt at a lower rate than the company's rate of return (i.e. 5% before tax), the company's earnings will fall due to financial costs ($25 = 500 \times 0.05$), but the return to shareholders will rise to 22% (i.e. $(300 - 25) \times 0.8 / 1000$). However, the increased risk inherent in higher debt is not quantified (Fig. 16.2).

Clinic

	December N
Gross operating income/EBITDA	50
Multiple	4
Purchase price	**200**

Clinic

December N + 5	
90	Manager's objectives for N + 5
4	Likely to increase if macroeconomic conditions are favorable...
360	**Resale price**

Fig. 16.2 Performance and capital gain projections for future resale

One afternoon in December, our PE manager (GP) met with the doctor who owns the OLLIONGAIRY clinic, who is close to retirement and wants to sell it. An offer has already been made at 160 (thousands of euros). He is accompanied by his young colleague, who is excellent in her profession but cannot afford to buy the clinic.

"Clinics," explains our manager, "are interesting investments: the population is ageing, and the reimbursement conditions, thanks to the excellence of the French social protection system, open up a wide customer base. In view of the recent acquisitions made by my competitors, I can buy it for 200, i.e. four times its current EBITDA[2] of 50. And I'll be delighted to support this talented young doctor to take part in this operation". "Indeed," says the manager to himself, "I could resell the clinic for 360 in five years' time, based on an EBITDA of 90. The capital gain will therefore be (360–100), of which 80% for the insurance company and 20% for me. With only 100 available, I will borrow 100 at an average rate of 9.8%, repayment of which will be made by the clinic itself."

This story seems impossible.

- Does the law allow the clinic to carry the debt of its acquisition and thus buy itself?
- Will bankers agree to lend an amount at least equal to that contributed by shareholders?
- How can EBITDA grow from 50 to 90 in five years, i.e., at around 11% a year, in line with repayment schedules?
- How can the fund manager ensure that executives achieve these objectives?

[2]EBITDA: Earnings Before Interest, Tax, Depreciation and Amortization.

A Debt-Based System

French law clearly prohibits this: "A joint-stock company may not advance funds, grant loans or give guarantees for the acquisition of its own shares by a third party."[1] In order to circumvent the regulations, the loans granted with a view to the acquisition are not carried by the company itself, but are held by holding companies, which are shareholders in the target company, and will be repaid by the dividends received by the latter. The subsidiary must therefore generate earnings (legal condition) and cash flow (operational condition) (Fig. 16.3).

"To acquire this clinic, it should be possible to borrow 60 in senior debt at a rate of 7% and 40 in junior debt at a rate of 14%," says the manager.

The loans are housed in a cascade of specific holding companies. The least risky loans (*senior debt) are* held by the holding company closest to the target, because their repayment has priority. The riskier loans (*junior debt*) will only be repaid once the senior loans have been repaid, often at the end of the five-year period, thanks to the capital gains generated on resale. They carry much higher interest rates, and their payment may be largely equivalent to the amount of the loan.

More broadly, these arrangements link the company's objectives to those of its shareholders: *private equity* funds thus determine in advance their financial performance objectives for the next five years, on the basis of a debt to which the company must devote the cash flows generated. Debt is thus used to discipline the company.

[1]Article L 225–26 of the French Commercial Code for corporations. We can also refer to the prohibition of abuse of corporate assets…

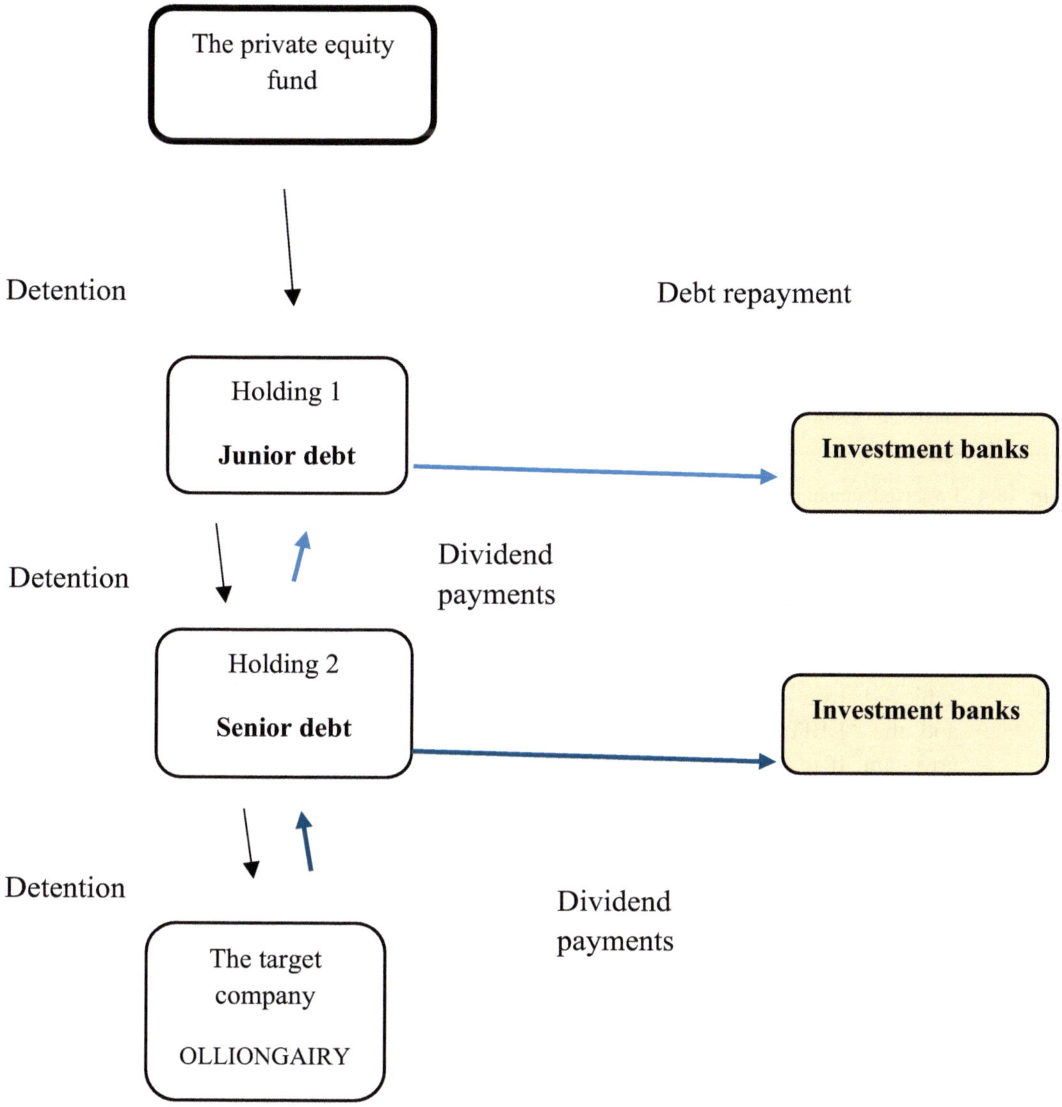

Fig. 16.3 Legal Structure of the LBO Arrangement

Quarterly Business Performance Planning

But even if the banks share among themselves the risks associated with the high level of debt of the acquired company, the risks don't disappear for all that?

Loan agreements will be signed between the company and the lenders, incorporating the need to achieve certain performance indicators (*covenants*) on a quarterly basis. Otherwise, the debt falls due immediately. Covenants are based on the company's ability to pay interest (EBITDA/interest expense), to repay debt (EBITDA/outstanding debt) or to assess the debt burden (debt/equity). They may also contain a prohibition on investment. The company's future is thus planned and codified on a quarterly basis (Fig. 16.4).

	December N	N + 1	N + 2	N + 3	N + 4	December N + 5
EBITDA projections	50	**70**	**80**	**85**	**90**	90
Multiple	4					4
Purchase price	200					360
Debt	**100**	**80**	**60**	**40**	**20**	**0**
Materialization of the 'EBITDA/outstanding debt' ratio in the loan contract		**> 0,8**	**> 1,2**	**> 2**	**> 3**	

Fig. 16.4 Projected annual performance and covenants

For our clinic, achieving an EBITDA of 90 in December N+5 is planned by materializing the EBITDA to be achieved over the five-year period and the "EBITDA/debt outstanding" covenant. If in N+1 the ratio actually achieved is less than 0.45, the entire debt (80) to be repaid will become due immediately.

But corporate life is always full of unforeseen events, and business and results can fluctuate: what happens when commitments can't be met?

This is a situation the fund manager will try to avoid at all costs (see Sect. 16.1.4). If management is struggling to achieve its objectives, he may appoint an advisor, or even replace it. If the covenants are broken, the balance of power shifts in favor of the lenders. The latter will only agree to renegotiate their loans if the fund manager increases the company's capital.

A Singular Codification of the Relationship Between the Private Equity Fund and the Company's Management Shareholders

The young doctor, approached to become the clinic's director and shareholder, had only 10k euros to contribute, taking out a mortgage on her house and investing her father's inheritance. It's not a big deal," says the fund manager. If you meet the targets, you'll be able to buy shares in the company when it resells in five years' time, at a preferential price, and become a majority shareholder." Modifying her initial business plan, the young doctor finally managed, on her Excel spreadsheet, to reach an EBITDA of 90. "Perfect," replied the manager, "let's sign the pact!" "But what pact?" she asks.

The fund manager (PM) signs shareholder agreements with the various categories of shareholders, i.e., contracts setting out their respective rights and obligations. Those signed by the shareholder-managers formalize not only their participation in profits but also their obligations in terms of performance. Failure to achieve the latter results in termination of the contract and dismissal of the shareholder-manager, who then loses his or her financial investment and expectations…

A Company Under Intense Pressure for Five Years

The success of these arrangements depends on the company's ability to pay dividends to cover its debt repayments. This means generating earnings and cash flow (Fig. 16.5).

At a management meeting, the new CFO explains the situation. "Increasing EBITDA from 50 to 90 requires in-depth restructuring. To increase margins, we have to abandon less profitable activities. We have to make redundancies and make our personnel costs more flexible by outsourcing meal preparation and laundry, and by offering nurses the chance to work independently. Nurses' aides will have to be present in the recovery room to limit the need for nurses and doctors. In order to increase our cash flow, we will be increasing the number of advance payments requested from customers, and we will not be investing for five years."

Pressure to increase revenues	**Pressure to increase cash flow**	**Objectives**
Sales figures		Growth in higher-margin activities
(-) Cost of raw materials consumed		Reducing and/or adapting to variations in activity
(-) Committed services		
(-) Personnel expenses		
Gross operating surplus	**Gross operating surplus**	
(-) Depreciation and amortization	(-) Capital expenditure	Discount or cancellation
Net income: legal basis for dividend payments	(-) Impact of timing differences in customer and supplier payments	Accelerate collections and reduce customer payment times
	Net cash flow from investing activities (free cash flow)	

Fig. 16.5 Pressurization action levers

You've forgotten in this diagram that the company has to pay taxes…

Tax optimization is part of the overall scheme.

How do clinic employees and patients feel about this pressure?

The company under LBO becomes a link in a financial mechanism that is totally external to it. This results in a shortening of management horizons, a loss of decision-making autonomy, a distancing of management from the company, which is solely preoccupied with achieving the objectives set out in the shareholders' agreement, and recurring understaffing situations.

> Despite the mild June evening, the mood outside the OLLIONGAIRY clinic is tense. "With the LBOs, we're now concentrating on what pays: cardio, urology, ENT. Everything else has been eliminated," explains a nurse. The focus is always on the company's results. They're obsessed with that." "The new director, who used to be so devoted to her patients, lives in another world," continues a physiotherapist. "We can't take it anymore," sighs an orderly. They've managed to erase the joy of coming to work." "They're selling off our social security, our health to feed shareholders with taxpayers' money," concludes the secretary of the Social and Economic Committee.

Pressure that Often Extends Beyond

At the end of the five-year period, there are several options:

- acquisition by a new private equity fund, known as a secondary LBO (which may become tertiary, etc.), sale to a group or IPO;
- but also the sale as separate lots to other private equity funds and/or, in particular, to vulture funds, which take legal action to obtain repayment of debts on the basis of their initial value, sealing the company's demise.

But can a company survive several LBOs?

Many companies are disappearing and/or being transformed. Some endure, like the French Picard group, which has undergone three successive LBOs. But is it still the same company? What has become of the work collective, and of the public and environmental resources mobilized?

16.2 The *Private* Equity Industry from a Sustainable Development Perspective

Against Financial Stability

The company's resale price depends on a performance indicator, EBITDA, but also on a multiple, which is supposed to reflect the economic vitality of the business sector and macroeconomic conditions (such as the cost of credit). The private equity industry seeks to ensure that multiples rise steadily, fueling price inflation. The boom periods of 1985–1989 (especially in the US and UK), 1995–2000, and 2003–2008 proved to be financial bubbles[3] whose bursting had serious economic and social consequences. The 2008 crisis led to a veritable wall of debt, triggering costly rescheduling and major corporate restructuring and/or liquidation. Furthermore, the European Directive 2011/61/EC of June 8, 2011, on alternative investment fund managers, which was supposed to regulate this field at European level, has been gutted, not least due to lobbying by the City[4].

[3] For further information, please refer to Chapter 11 of this book.

[4] Minutes no. 55, European Parliament Committee on Economic and Monetary Affairs, meeting of September 2, 2009.

Against Inclusive Growth

Contrary to the information provided by national and international associations of *private equity* firms, the impact of private equity on employment is very difficult to quantify, due to the impossibility of knowing how companies would have evolved had they not been acquired by funds, the characteristics of the companies chosen (initially in good financial health) and the impossibility of reasoning on a like-for-like basis if external growth strategies are implemented.[5]

However, as the above developments show, the risks taken by the fund manager are fully transferred—and this is the intrinsic basis of the scheme—to the company's employees (and more broadly those in the value chain)—who can only suffer, through increased suffering at work and/or redundancies. When the company is a benchmark employer, this weakening can extend to a whole employment area.

Inequalities are on the increase, due to the widening gap between different forms of remuneration (capital *versus* labor). The wider sharing of capital gains, sometimes evoked, can only raise the question of increased pressure on employees. More broadly, the gap between aggressive tax optimization and the absence of tangible benefits for the community increases the profoundly unequal nature of such practices. This is all the more true given that the public authorities play a full part in this process through the funding of research (Mazzucato, 2013), as well as through the nature of the sectors that fall under the industry's control (healthcare, education, etc.).[7]

16.3 Conclusions

- The concept of financialization[8] highlights the extent to which profits are captured by financial circuits. In its quest for ever-higher profitability, finance protects itself from the associated risks by mobilizing three types of strategy: (a) an accentuated search for *liquidity* (transforming any asset into a tradable good on a market), (b) the shortening of *management horizons* (driving a very short-termist vision), and (c) the organization of *risk transfer*, both between players in the financial sphere and in the sphere of the social and economic world.
- The *private equity* industry is particularly adept at expressing this concept through the quest for a high rate of return, which can only be achieved at the cost of depleting various existing or future resources. The inherently opaque and asymmetrical arsenal of governance mechanisms in place freezes the company's future for the next 60 quarters. A basic overview by employee representatives, which is mandatory under French labor law, is rarely obtained, even through legal action.[6]
- In essence, therefore, this industry runs counter to the Sustainable Development Goals (SDGs) in terms of economic and social sustainability, financial stability, reducing inequalities, and access to healthcare or education services.

Activities

Question for discussion

- Drawing also on the article "De la finance au travail, sur les traces des dispositifs de financiarisation", *Nouvelle Revue du travail*, n° 3, 2013, https://journals.openedition.org/nrt/1012, identify the risks to the company of

[5] Cf. Bédu & Parlard (2014), who show a positive correlation between company acquisition by *private equity funds* and changes in default risk.

[6] Courts cannot mandate disclosure of shareholder agreements, which are fundamental to understanding the scope of objectives and the constraints attached to them.

[7] https://www.brookings.edu/wp-content/uploads/2021/10/Private-Equity-Investment-As-A-Divining-Rod-For-Market-Failure-14.pdf.

[8] For more on this subject, please refer to Chambost (2013, 2023).

LBO arrangements, distinguishing between those present at the origin of the arrangement and those occurring during the life of the company.

Role-Playing Game

You are a member of the management committee of a French company with over 1000 employees involved in the design, manufacture and marketing of hard/software products and solutions. The company is faced with a disrupted technological environment, a cyclical business highly dependent on economic conditions, and a high turnover of top management. Despite the fall in earnings, the company has always remained economically profitable (as has the Group), but the Group is loss-making due to the weight of interest paid as part of the various LBO packages put in place over the past eight years. The latest LBO is hampering R&D efforts and external growth, and weighs heavily on the financial equilibrium of the company and the Group. Debt is colossal, and debt servicing is out of step with its operational capacity to generate revenues and cash flows.

In the recent period, the difficulties have accelerated, with a breach of covenants at the end of N and the anticipation of difficulties in servicing their debt in June N+1. An ad-hoc mandate procedure was initiated to negotiate with banking and financial partners to adjust senior debt repayment terms and obtain the maintenance of revolving credit lines and bank guarantees. Against a backdrop of tight cash flow, the ad hoc trustee has approached the lenders. However, negotiations were stormy.

Questions

1. As a member of the management committee, what risks do you think the target company faces and what are the potential consequences for management and employees?
2. In this context, how are you positioned and what actions are you taking?

Mini-case

Based on Cédric Durand and Marlène Benquet's article "La financiarisation de la grande distribution" published in 2016 in the *Revue française de socio-économie* (vol. 1, n °16), https://www.cairn.info/revue-francaise-de-socio-economie-2016-1-page-37.htm, you are asked to summarize how the financialization of the Carrefour group took place over the period [1997–2013]. To do this, you will analyze in particular:

- changes in the group's shareholder base;
- the evolution of its performance and strategies;
- the consequences by characterizing the particularities of the financialization process within this group.

References

Bedu, N., & Palard, J. E. (2014). L'impact des LBO sur la défaillance des entreprises. The case of French targets (2000–2010). *Finance Contrôle Stratégie* [Online], 17–2.

Chambost, I. (2013). "De la finance au travail, sur les traces des dispositifs de financiarisation", *Nouvelle Revue du travail,* No. 3. https://journals.openedition.org/nrt/1012

Chambost, I. (2023). Financialization, the private equity industry. In LBOs in T. Lagoarde-Segot (coord.), *Ecological Money and Finance*. Palgrave.

De Esteban, M. (2017). *Vingt feux*. In Gallimard (Ed.), *Le Supermarché des images*. jeu de Paume.

Durand, C., & Benquet, M. (2016). La financiarisation de la grande distribution. *la Revue française de socio-économie, 1*(16).

Epstein, G. A. (Ed.). (2005). Introduction: Financialization and the World Economy. In *Financialization and the World Economy*. Edward Elgar.

Froud, J., Haslam, C., Johal, S., & Williams, K. (2000). Restructuring for shareholder value and its implications for labor. *Cambridge Journal of Economics, 24*, 771–797.

Krippner, G. R. (2005). The financialization of the American Economy. *Socio-Economic Review, 3*, 173–208.

Mazzuccato, M. (2013). *The entrepreneurial state. Debunking public vs. private sector myths*. Demos.

Reinhart, C., & Rogoff, K. (2009). *This time is different*. Princeton University Press.

Crowdsourcing: Citizen Participation (At Last) in Finance!

17

Thibault Cuénoud

Putting Things into Perspective
The opaqueness of the financial markets calls out to us as citizens. The cascade of financial arrangements leaves us perplexed. Is this sector seriously in line with the Sustainable Development Goals (SDGs)? We will need money to finance new, more environmentally friendly activities. This chapter shows that it is possible to involve civil society, and more specifically citizens, in the financing of this energy and sustainable transition, through the *crowdsourcing* process. If the sector is to survive, its players must take greater responsibility for these societal challenges. While many believe that economic, social and environmental issues cannot coexist, the history of finance suggests otherwise. The players in responsible finance—including ethical finance, participative finance (or crowdfunding) and solidarity finance—even if they are all too few in number, demonstrate that an alternative does exist. This type of finance has long incorporated citizen participation and offers real prospects for sustainability in the financial sector

Learning Objectives

- Understanding the basics of *crowdsourcing*
- Identifying *responsible finance* involving citizens (ethical finance/ISR, participative finance/crowdfunding and solidarity finance)
- Defining the organizational aspects of *crowdsourcing* in the financial sector

17.1 *Crowdfunding* in Finance

Thinking about *crowdsourcing* is not a trivial matter for financial organizations. Through the financing they make available to companies, they are driving social change. The societal issues they seek to convey raise the question of the place they may have given—or even left—to citizens. Indirectly, it is the citizen, and therefore civil society as a whole, that is being questioned here. *Crowdsourcing* is a new form of citizen expression and involvement that enables civil society to interact more effectively with organizations. The origins of *crowdsourcing* are associated with the rise of free software. Internet users were able to contribute voluntarily to major projects by gathering large communities of supporters. Today, this form of citizen participation has evolved to meet financial challenges. Social relations have evolved with the advent of the Internet, which has greatly facilitated interaction between communities and organizations.

T. Cuénoud (✉)
Excelia Business School, La Rochelle, France
e-mail: cuenoudt@excelia-group.com

T. Lagoarde-Ségot (ed.), *Ecological Economics and Finance*,
https://doi.org/10.1007/978-3-031-71249-4_17

Citizen communities have contributed to the reappropriation of social debates by civil society.

One of the stakeholders that is increasingly asserting itself is the citizen who, as a consumer, voter or resident, is seeking to take ownership of issues usually left to other representative bodies. Today, it has become easier and faster to intervene as a citizen by simplifying decision-making and coordination mechanisms. Internet technology makes it possible. Civil society, too, has the will to do so. The aim here is to examine the capacity of financial players to modify their practices by integrating citizen dynamics more easily and openly. Interaction with the public is essential to the legitimacy of the financial sector. This interaction can be a source of complementarity in the efficiency of the resources invested. The proximity between citizens and project promoters makes for greater complementarity in the viability of their societal activities (the citizen is also a consumer, a voter, a communicator, etc.). Ultimately, this co-construction of local societal projects can reinforce the efficiency of financial practices, in the sense that information asymmetry is reduced. Unfortunately, a number of 'mainstream' finance studies have sought to justify the separation of financial efficiency from societal efficiency... The damage is manifold: recurrent financial crises, abuses in the allocation of financial investments, opacity of choices, tax optimization, even money laundering...

A number of questions arise as to the viability of the organizational changes implied by *crowdsourcing*. In view of the societal challenges described by the SDGs, it is all the more urgent to (re)demonstrate the societal coherence of a participative and civic-minded approach in the financial sector's quest for greater responsibility. Entrepreneurial finance theories are rarely approached from the perspective of societal issues. However, there are various forms of citizen participation in finance (responsible finance). In the light of crowdsourcing, it is necessary to explain the growing importance of civil society within a financial sector seeking greater sustainability. Is citizen involvement legitimate and relevant in finance? How should it be understood? The answers to these questions should help clarify the link between finance, citizenship and sustainability in the sense of the SDGs.

17.2 What are the Main Problems Facing Entrepreneurial Finance Today?

Against a backdrop of strong tensions surrounding 'classic' capitalist finance (opacity of financial flows, maximization of profits to the detriment of societal issues, systemic risks of international financial organizations, circumvention of national regulations, optimization—even money laundering—of allocated funds...), the sustainability of finance must be questioned. Financing projects with high societal added value is a challenge for mainstream financial theory. Unfortunately, too few theories deal with the construction of indicators to measure extra-financial performance. The financial theory of the firm has been developed essentially for large Anglo-Saxon managerial companies (dispersed shareholding) (see Table 17.1). Major contributions have led to a better understanding of investment choices, methods for valuing financial assets, conflicts between shareholders, managers and creditors, and difficulties in accessing the right information (known as information asymmetry). However, very few of these contributions have focused on financing sustainable activities and the societal issues this might raise. Yet, the SDGs remind us of the importance of finance in the energy and sustainable transition.

A broader analysis of the field of entrepreneurial finance confirms that civil society is not taken into account in financial decision-making. It appears that most of the work carried out over the last 30 years in the field of entrepreneurial finance has focused on the relationship between venture capitalists and entrepreneurs with a view to financing the equity and technological innovation aspects. Although innovation is not necessarily technological in nature, the interaction with civil society has been too little studied.

Table 17.1 Scope and contributions of the main financial theories

Theories	Areas of application	Main contributions
Neoclassical theory	Allows to take investment decisions and measure its value	Fisher, 1930; Markowitz, 1958; Modigliani et Miller, 1958; Fama, 1964; Sharpe, Mossin and Lintner, 1964
Options theory	Allows the evaluation of derivative products and the development of risk management tools	Black and Scholes, 1973; Merton, 1974
Agency theory	Integrate conflicts of interest (shareholders-management-creators), value transfers and incentives	Jensen and Meckling, 1976; Jensen, 1986
The theory of information asymmetries	Financing choices (hierarchical financing, dividends policy...)	Ross, 1977; Myers, 1984; Myers and Maijuf, 1984; Baker and Wurgler, 2002
Institutional theories	Connect financial structures and decisions to external data/factors (Law, political systems, institutional systems...)	La Porta and al. 1997

Source Philippe, H. (2014). "Corporate finance—the proper use of financial theory", *Banking and Strategy*

There is clearly too little room for the search for more sustainable and socially inclusive financing. This leads to a strange situation. On the one hand, civil society is calling for a more sustainable financial sector; on the other, finance research focuses mainly on purely financial issues that are increasingly disconnected from society's realities and expectations.

The capital structure of companies remains an enigma for financial theorists. Two main currents can be distinguished in the literature, based on Modigliani and Miller's (1958, 1963) trade-off theory (optimal debt threshold), and Myers and Majluf's (1984) pecking order theory (POT). According to trade-off theory, corporate financing policy should aim for a debt ratio that offsets the costs and benefits of debt. The costs are linked to the lender's perceived risk of default, leading to a moral hazard problem associated with the lender's inability to determine the actual level of risk taken when investing. In pecking order theory, debt costs are due to the difficulty of obtaining reliable information. The resulting asymmetry of information handicaps the company, which is obliged to incur enormous transaction costs to inform financiers.

Table 17.2 clarifies the different instruments by type of company and stage of development. As you can see, neither theory integrates the specificities of more socially responsible and/or more sustainable governance of entrepreneurs, which are nonetheless part of the challenges of the SDGs. They focus on the level of financial risk and expected profits. Yet it would seem appropriate to reconsider financial and societal risks in the light of current sustainability concerns. Indeed, the SDGs provide a grid of desirable societal gains that could be integrated into their financial theories.

17.3 Understanding Citizen Involvement in Responsible Financial Organizations

On the demand side of sustainable financing, entrepreneurs are faced with several financing options. The first option is for the company to finance itself. If internal financial resources are insufficient, they turn to external financing. Numerous empirical studies on the financing of projects with high societal added value show that these projects make extensive use of committed financiers. These so-called *responsible* financiers—along with ethical finance, participative finance (or *crowdfunding*) and solidarity finance—seek to reconcile their social commitment with their business model (see Table 17.3). The typology of the projects they finance bears witness to this ability to reconcile financial and sustainable issues. It is now recognized that entrepreneurship faces problems of information asymmetry when it comes to financing. However, the involvement of civil society in these financial tools and/or in more sustainable businesses makes it possible to reduce information asymmetries between shareholders, managers and creditors, and to better understand the new expectations of customers who are more respectful of the environment.

The renewal of the financial sector, if it is to be part of a sustainable approach, must be inspired by the SDGs. We've heard all too often of the alleged incompatibility between financial and societal performance. Does this mean that finance can only be "harmful" to humanity, and that it acts to the detriment of today's climate challenges? Clearly, this assertion is false (it is worth looking at the typologies of project owners financed by responsible finance in Table 17.3 to understand that it is possible to reconcile society, the environment and economic efficiency).

To remedy this situation, the involvement of citizens in the sector must be strengthened. The financial sector must not be a sector apart from the rest of civil society committed to the SDGs. The concept of *crowdsourcing* describes these forms of interaction between finance and citizens. *Crowdsourcing* revolutionizes the practices of civil society, which directly, rapidly and collectively challenges these financial players through an *open source* approach (based on direct democracy rather than representative democracy). This type of finance, which claims to be responsible, although still a minority compared to conventional finance, is already interacting with citizens

Table 17.2 Financing instruments by company type and stage of development

Low risk/return		Average risk/return			High risk/return	
Asset-based financing	Other types of loans		Hybrid instruments	Equity securities	Equity instrument	
Loans against collateralFactoringOrder financingStock financingLeasing	Participatory/ BtoB loans	Corporate bondsSecuritizationSecure documents-Seed investment loanPrivateplacement	Subordinated loans/bondsPassive investmentEquity loansProfit sharing rights-Bonds with warrantsMezzanine financing	Platforms specialized in the IPO of SMEs	Investors' contributionsParticipatory financing (equity investment)	Venture capitalOther capital contributions
Accessibility to a wide range of SMEs Particularly interesting for companies with limited (but verifiable) creditworthiness	Compagnies seeking low volumes of financing Businesses without collateral/ with little credit history	Requires a certain size and scale More mature companies with a proven business model	More mature companies, in transition or restructuring High growth compagnies in the early stages of development	Companies with highly structured governance and management systems, who disseminate information widely Companies requiring large capital injections	Early stages of the life cycle Innovative companies, potentially from a wide range of sectors	Knowledge-based industries Later stages of the life cycle

Source OECD (2018), Improving SMEs' access to diversified financing instruments, Plenary session

Table 17.3 Typologies of entrepreneurs financed by *responsible finance*

Responsible finance	Typology of project managers
Equity financing	Safeguarding jobs and businesses are two important themes. Half of the funds generated by participatory financing are directed towards SMEs and mid-sized companies. The social economy comes next, through projects with high added value (humanitarian, cultural…). *Start-ups* also benefit from participative financing (new technological projects mainly aimed at the end consumer). At the margins, we find participatory financing for individual and public authority projects.
Solidarity finance	Solidarity finance is mainly geared towards projects that promote social integration through economic activity. These are companies that combine an economic model with social issues (reintegration through work of people in situations of exclusion: immigrants, the disabled, the long-term unemployed, etc.). This type of financing is also the source of many social innovations in the local and citizen energy transition sector, for example.
Ethical finance/ISR	Ethical finance (or SRI) is more akin to impact finance. The term 'impact' means that the project financed has a positive impact on society. The aim is to use both "classic" financial indicators and "extra-financial" indicators in the financial decision-making process. For example, these financiers might decide to stop financing coal-fired power plants because they emit too much CO_2 and to give priority to financing renewable energies.

and civil society. In the final analysis, there's nothing new here. The search for an ideal form of finance that functions as a common good for society is a historically recurrent theme. What's more, the financial sector ultimately includes a multitude of players and citizens throughout its operating process. All it would take is one more "leap" to see more citizen interaction in the way the financial sector is organized.

Citizen expression in *responsible finance* organizations is all too invisible, as these same organizations do not fully respect the principles of *crowdsourcing* (i.e. greater flexibility, speed and transparency in the collective expression of a crowd, without giving primacy to some citizens over others). Citizen expression will take other forms, such as cooperative advisory committees, or even co-construction for certain projects. Table 17.4 summarizes these existing forms of citizen involvement in responsible finance. However, many researchers consider participatory financing to be an integral part of *crowdsourcing*. According to Jeff Howe (2006), we can speak of crowdsourcing whenever financing enables citizen-contributors and project managers to 'do more' together. However, it remains to be seen whether it really is possible to 'do more' thanks to citizen participation.

17.4 *Crowdsourcing* as a Sustainable Alternative to the Financial Sector

Current citizen involvement practices in responsible finance organizations tend to reflect a representative democracy model rather than a direct democracy model. With this in mind, it is worth enumerating the range of possibilities offered by crowdsourcing. This will enable us to better understand how and why the transformational effect of this concept can be compatible with sustainable finance. Several forms of crowdsourcing exist today, making it possible to tackle simple tasks, solve problems and contribute to creative production. Crowdfunding goes beyond funding by the crowd, by setting up a process of co-construction. A multitude of stages can

Table 17.4 Ways of expressing citizenship in responsible finance

The components of responsible finance	Object	Operating mode	Forms of citizen participation	Forms of *crowdsourcing*
Ethical finance	An approach that integrates extra-financial criteria (environmental, social, ethical and governance) into investment and portfolio management decisions	Socially responsible investment (SRI) funds, which include assets from the most responsible companies according to extra-financial criteria	Influence of NGOs on societal causes (through boycott calls) Influence of individual shareholders on voting at general meetings (particularly with regard to the adoption of non-financial criteria)	Mainly through CSR actions where citizens are considered as relevant stakeholders in the search for the organization's overall performance
Solidarity finance	An approach based on multimedia collections that advocates a demand-driven logic for profound societal change	Activist finance that promotes companies in the social economy. Social solidarity takes precedence over economic rationality	Citizens are represented in the governance (representative democracy) of these organizations (directors in associations, staff and union representatives in employee savings funds, member delegates in mutuals and mid-sized companies, etc.)	*Crowdsourcing* plays an important role in the strategic choices of these organizations (specific assemblies are dedicated to citizen representation in their governance)
Equity financing	This approach is based on raising funds from the general public to finance projects with high social added value (cultural, humanitarian, entrepreneurial, etc.)	Financing that brings together citizens and project owners on an Internet platform facilitated by collaborative social networks	Citizens finance selected projects directly via an Internet platform, without any intermediation	*Crowdsourcing* is one of the tools used to attract and channel citizen funding (when citizens provide advice, opinions, recommendations, etc.)

Source Cuénoud, T., & Karyotis, C. (2020, April). Citizen involvement in responsible finance organizations. *Revue Banque*, n° 843

involve citizens in this co-construction process: publication of the task, pre-selection of the worker, execution of the task, validation and reward… The way crowdfunding works helps us understand how and why the use of crowdsourcing by the financial sector can become an indicator of sustainability. For example, it becomes difficult to implement financial schemes that promote tax optimization or money laundering in a crowdfunding context, given that citizen co-builders are aware of the potential damage these practices cause to society. It also becomes difficult to finance polluting companies in contexts where the selection of projects is made through citizen consultations on a participative platform…

Today, there are two main theories surrounding the concept of *crowdsourcing*. On the one hand, some believe that the crowd only participates financially, and nothing more (as Darren Brabham postulates in his 2013 book, *Crowdsourcing*). Others argue that the crowd has a far greater impact than just funding. This is the view of Jeff Howe (2006), the creator of the *crowdsourcing* concept. The ability of *crowdsourcing* to catalyse the societal relationship between entrepreneurial organizations and citizens suggests that Howe's argument is the most appropriate. The role of social networks (in the processes of communication and involvement in the project) and the communities of citizens that form on them confirm the influence of civil society.

A crowd's contribution can go beyond providing funds for societal causes. The crowd also contributes its intelligence and opinion. They play a major role in disseminating information about the project via networks and providing moral support. It shows an interaction between the type of governance of the organization and the degree of openness to citizens. The citizens who make up the crowd must be able to express themselves and have an impact on the strategy of financial organizations. Table 17.5 summarizes the *crowdsourcing* practices that concern citizens wishing to get involved.

Of course, finance isn't starting from scratch. Crowdfunding practices have already existed for several decades within responsible finance. For example, the governance of solidarity finance is already based on citizen participation. Participatory financing offers specific project opportunities for citizens who wish to get directly involved with entrepreneurs. Ethical finance is no exception, having recognized the role of citizens as key players in the organization at a very early stage (numerous experiments based on CSR practices have emerged in recent years). Jeff Howe (2006) argues that crowdsourcing involves the materialization of four forms of citizen expression (see Table 17.6): *crowd-voting*, *crowd-creation*, *crowd-wisdom* and *crowd-funding*. Each of them raises further questions about the transformational stakes of a more civic-minded and sustainable financial sector.

Table 17.5 *Crowdsourcing* practices

Crowdsourcing: A place where a company publishes a problem and chooses from a range of solutions (e.g. InnoCentive)	**Communities**: Networks where everyone contributes problems and solutions (e.g. open source Linux)	Participation	Open
Expert consultants: Group of practitioners chosen by the company. The company chooses the problem and the solution (examples: KPMG, Capgemini…)	**Consortium**: Private group of participants who decide together on a problem, how to organize the work and select the solution (e.g. IBM partnerships)		Closed
Governance			
Hierarchical structure	Flat structure		

Source Burger-Helmchen, T. (2011). Crowdsourcing: definition, issues, typology. *Management & Avenir,* (1), 254–269

Table 17.6 The four forms of citizen expression in *crowdsourcing*

1. ***Crowd-voting*** is based on the opinion of the crowd. A well-known example is the Danone brand, which solicits the opinion of the crowd for its Danettes in order to choose future flavours.
2. ***Crowd-creation*** implies work by the crowd, in creative or non-creative form, when solicited. For example, the anti-HIV association *Aides* launched a challenge by soliciting the creativity of the community on the eYeka platform, which brings together "a global community of over 320,000 creative individuals from all over the world".
3. ***Crowd-wisdom*** uses the wisdom of crowds, as defined by Surowiecki and Riot (2008): "why the many are smarter than the few, and how collective wisdom shapes business, economies, societies and nations". The Wikipedia website, funded and enriched in content by its citizen donors and contributors, is an example of the wisdom of crowds.
4. Finally, the one we're most interested in, ***crowdfunding***, enables a large number of individuals to become directly involved in financial sector decisions via Web 2.0.

Source Howe, J. (2006). The rise of crowdsourcing. *Wired magazine*

17.5 Conclusion

Should the opening up of crowdsourcing, via the strengthening of civil society in the financial sector, take place at key stages and moments? Crowdsourcing practices are not intended solely to optimize financial risk… Their role is above all to improve societal interaction between funded projects and financial organizations. Involving the crowd at various stages would enable interaction and co-construction, and thus reduce problems of information asymmetry, while reorienting the financial sector towards its true function of financing sustainable projects. Crowds could give their opinion on a new range of more sustainable products, test the new communication envisaged, strengthen the customer base or even benefit from social networks… At this point, we have justified why and how citizens can get involved in finance. We have also highlighted how crowdsourcing can challenge the practices of the financial sector, now and in the future (better management of financial risk thanks to citizen expertise, better visibility of responsible financial tools thanks to the dissemination of information to citizens…). In its quest for responsibility, finance has every interest in renewing itself to strengthen the processes of citizen expression. Citizen involvement deserves to be increasingly tested in the face of the latent sustainability challenges facing the sector. Given the low level of social responsibility of the financial sector as a whole (opacity of flows, tax optimization of investments, financing of carbon exploitation projects, etc.), the transition to greater sustainability will undoubtedly require societal introspection, fostered by lasting civic influence.

Activities

Questions for Discussion

1. Compare and contrast the different forms of responsible finance from the point of view of citizen involvement.
2. To what extent does crowdsourcing challenge existing theories of entrepreneurial finance?
3. Is the involvement of citizens in a sustainable transformation of the financial sector essential to the implementation of the UN's SDGs?

Mini-Case: Sustainable Development Goals (SDGs) 10—*Reducing Inequalities*

Finance can be a source of exclusion for the most vulnerable. The quest for profitability while reducing the financial risk taken can lead to the exclusion of socially innovative projects. And yet, as part of the current energy transition, new forms of activity are emerging. Search the Internet for three innovative sustainable transition projects:

- a green energy innovation project;
- a project on a short production circuit activity;
- a project on new forms of solidarity.

Next, describe the potential contribution of *crowdsourcing* to the financing of these projects, paying particular attention to the risk management dimension.

References

Modigliani, F., & Miller, M. H. (1958). The cost of capital, corporation finance and the theory of investment. *The American economic review, 48*(3), 261–297.

Modigliani, F., & Miller, M. H. (1963). Corporate income taxes and the cost of capital: A correction. *The American economic review, 53*(3), 433–443.

Myers, S. C., & Majluf, N. S. (1984). Corporate financing and investment decisions when firms have information that investors do not have. *Journal of Financial Economics, 13*(2), 187–221.

The Promise of *Crowdlending* in Financing the Agenda 2030

18

Héloïse Berkowitz and Antoine Souchaud

Putting Things into Perspective

"Our innovation is not in financial analysis, even if we do it better than the banks. Our real innovation lies in collective intelligence. [...] We've put sustainable development, the future of the human species and real needs back at the heart of the lending decision" [Head of a *crowdlending* platform].

Crowdfunding is an investment tool that emerged in the early 2000s. Using an online platform enables individuals and companies to directly finance projects presented to them and on which they can interact publicly, in the form of interest-bearing, traceable loans.

This tool therefore encourages the development of direct financing decided by a host of contributors who place their trust in project promoters via an online selection and subscription process that is extremely transparent, fast and very inexpensive.

This chapter aims to analyse the potential impact of this new financing tool to understand whether it carries within it the capacity to transform the financial system in order to achieve the Agenda 2030.

Financing is at the heart of this agenda. It is also an issue that explicitly touches on two of the SDGs: SDG 8.3 (development of VSEs and SMEs) and SDG 9.3 (access to financial services for all businesses).

Learning Objectives

- Understand the usefulness, potential and limitations of crowdlending in financing and implementing the Agenda 2030.
- Understand the similarities, differences and possible partnerships between crowdlending and traditional finance with a view to financing the SDGs.
- Analyse and draw lessons from the French case through the three crowdlending platform models that have been developed there

18.1 *Crowdfunding*: Definition and Purpose

Crowdfunding is a loan underwriting tool operated via an internet platform enabling a group of contributors to collectively choose and lend

H. Berkowitz (✉)
LEST, CNRS, Aix Marseille Université, Aix en Provence, France
e-mail: heloise.berkowitz@univ-amu.fr

A. Souchaud
NEOMA Business School, i3-CRG, École Polytechnique, CNRS, Institut Polytechnique de Paris, Palaiseau, France
e-mail: antoine.souchaud@neoma-bs.fr

T. Lagoarde-Ségot (ed.), *Ecological Economics and Finance*,
https://doi.org/10.1007/978-3-031-71249-4_18

directly to finance identified projects in a traceable way (see Fig. 18.1).

Crowdlending is a sub-category of the larger crowdfunding category, from which it is distinguished by the nature of the financing provided: a loan with interest.

There are several reasons for the emergence of crowdlending, all linked to the development of entrepreneurship.

This tool has thus made it possible to finance development phases or relatively risky types of assets not covered by traditional bank financing, such as the creation of a prototype, intangible assets, working capital coverage or new hires.

Crowdfunding is also characterized by a very high speed of execution, which has attracted many entrepreneurs: only a few days can pass between the submission of a financing request and the receipt of funds in the entrepreneur's account.

Crowdfunding can also be used to run a product-testing campaign, creating a network of individuals and legal entities ready to support the development of the project (investor-customer, investor-supplier, investor-'adjuvant').

The personal risks for the entrepreneur are also limited, as crowdlending loans are not subject to any surety or guarantee. On the contrary, the funds raised are considered as personal contributions by the banks, and can be used as leverage to underwrite traditional bank loans.

However, over and above these assets, which are already substantial on the scale of an individual entrepreneur, crowdlending has singular characteristics that make it a major tool for financing the Agenda 2030 and putting people and sustainable development back at the heart of finance.

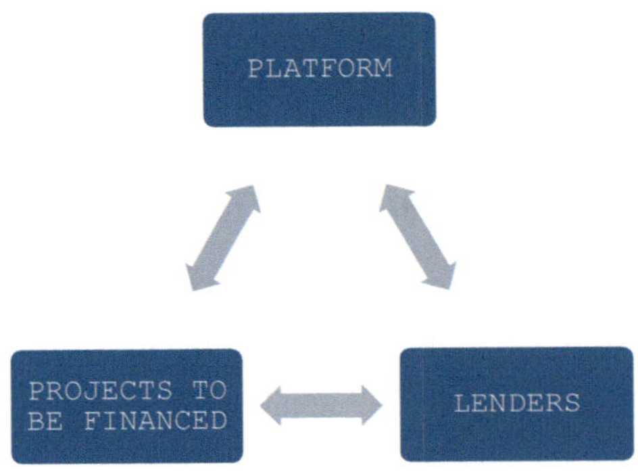

Fig. 18.1 *Crowdfunding* players

18.2 Countering the Distortion of the Banks' Relationship to Risk Through the Principle of Trust and Collective Intelligence

If sustainable development objectives are underfinanced today, this is partly due to the perfectibility of banking support for projects that are part of a sustainable development objective.

Today, banks have adopted a strategy of limiting default risk by only granting loans against guarantees, sureties or collateral that reduce their own risk-taking to a bare minimum.

Anything that seems new or original, anything that is perceived as risky, is not financed. This is the case for sustainable development projects. The human encounter between a banker and an entrepreneur, the long-term relationships that used to take years to forge, are now rarely initiated. The relationship with the public interest has also changed. Banks are just as risk-averse when it comes to projects that serve the public interest as they are to those that do not. The lending relationship has become cold and disenchanted.

That's where *crowdlending* comes in. It can remedy this form of degeneration of the banking profession, and put the human relationship and sustainable development back at the heart of the lending relationship.

Under certain conditions, *crowdlending* could also enable the emergence of a form of collective intelligence in project evaluation, upstream of financing. In a 2017 interview with the authors of this chapter, a manager of a French crowdlending platform explained that "out of the 4,000 people who visit the page of a project to be financed, there are, quite commonly, people with twenty years' experience in the business. The Anglo-Saxons call this 'collective intelligence'. The public interacts with the manager in the form of a public forum. Individuals ask questions and get answers; these answers are public and in everyone's interest".

Crowdfunding also enables the emergence of a form of collective intelligence downstream from projects. First and foremost, it creates a network of supporters throughout the campaign.

However, it's also a collective risk-sharing mechanism that makes default painless for lenders. In fact, individual tickets are of the order of 200 euros, and it is the mass of contributors that makes it possible to finance extremely risky projects with substantial overall amounts. As long as these projects, by virtue of their objectives, meaning and political purpose, enable lenders to feel useful by investing, then the possibility of losing a 200-euro investment is painlessly accepted.

18.3 Recycling Bank Money Creation into Impact Investments

On another level, central banks are now questioning the effectiveness of their traditional intervention tools. Between the creation of bubbles on certain types of assets and the capture of the effects of their policies by intermediaries disconnected from the real economy, the usefulness of central bank tools is clearly being questioned. Discussions on helicopter money and the creation of digital currencies by central banks are now explicitly underway.

However, there is another tool that would enable money creation to be recycled towards impact investments, and that tool is *crowdlending*. It would indeed be possible to create *crowdlending* platforms dedicated to projects that have an impact on achieving the SDGs. A system of partnership between banks and platforms could also be deployed. For example, for every euro lent by the crowd, banks would match two euros from the funds they have on deposit with them.

This is precisely one of the perspectives opened up by the August 2020 UN report entitled "Citizen's money: harnessing digitization to finance a sustainable future".

In France, three very different business models have developed around crowdlending. The study of these models will provide food for thought on the potential of *crowdlending* for financing sustainable development.

18.4 The French Case: Three Coexisting *Business Models*

Lendopolis, or the Ambition to Disrupt Banking Intermediation by Organizing the Expression of Collective Intelligence

The specificity of this first business model (see Figs. 18.2 and 18.3) lies in the central place given to the crowd and the particular care taken in organizing the expression of collective intelligence. Here, contributors are exclusively individuals, with an average ticket of 160 euros per project. For each project proposed for funding, the crowd of private individuals is provided with a description of the project, a three-year forecast certified by a chartered accountant, and a public forum where they can interact with the project owner in complete transparency.

Above all, this crowd has a relatively long and protected period of interaction with the project owner, compared to the other two models. The crowd also benefits from a real ability to decide whether or not to grant the requested funding. Indeed, if the amount initially set as the fundraising target is not reached due to a lack of contributors, the project owner receives no funds.

"If we don't give them [the crowd] information [...], there's no collective intelligence. In the same way that if we don't give the public the means to express themselves about the company via the forum, if we don't give them the means to stop the collection when a negative element appears, we're no longer working with collective intelligence" [Lendopolis CFO].

The platform's role is limited to accepting or rejecting projects, setting the amount of the loan and the interest rate to be paid to individuals, and, above all, organizing the expression of collective intelligence. After the collection, if

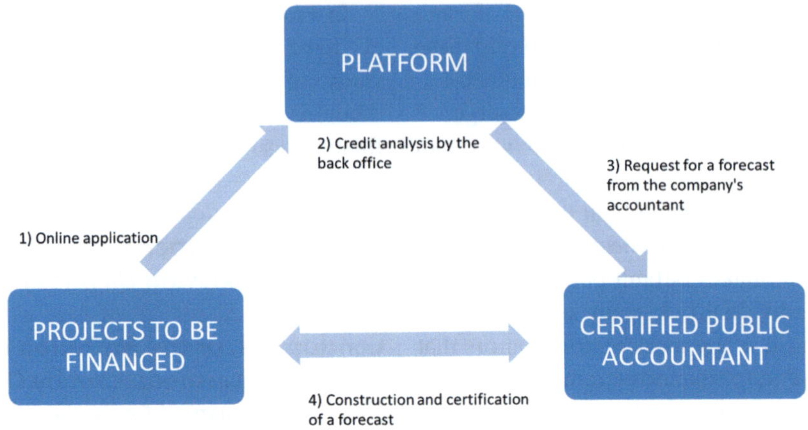

Fig. 18.2 Diagram of the Lendopolis model—phase 1

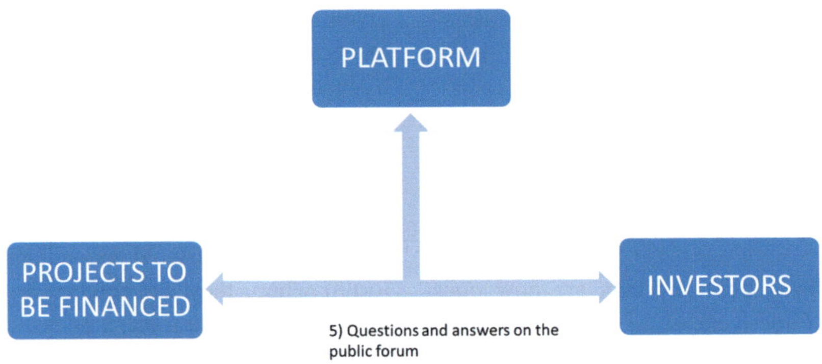

Fig. 18.3 Diagram of the Lendopolis model—phase 2

the project owner defaults, the platform does not intervene, unless the default is linked to a scam that it would not have detected. Apart from this specific case, the default leads to a loss borne by the individual. This remains relatively painless, given the limited amount of average tickets per individual and the legal threshold of 2000 euros per project and per individual.

This business model is driven by people with no previous financial experience, who are philosophically driven by what they themselves call their "faith in collective intelligence", coupled with a desire to put people and simplicity back at the heart of finance.

"There are people who, like [the founder of Lendopolis], believe deeply in collective intelligence, and for whom crowdfunding is almost a philosophical act" [Ministerial advisor].

These leaders are absolutely opposed to any idea of creating a secondary market for debt issued on platforms. They believe that too much complexity in financial vehicles is unhealthy, as it masks risks and alienates citizens from finance. They also see themselves as the only 'chemically pure' representatives of crowdlending, and are initially opposed to any assimilation with the other two models we will now describe.

The Lendix Case: Extending Traditional Finance by Combining Debt Funds with an Investment Fund

In Lendix's business model (see Fig. 18.4), which is organized around a debt fund (i.e. a fund bringing together institutional investors

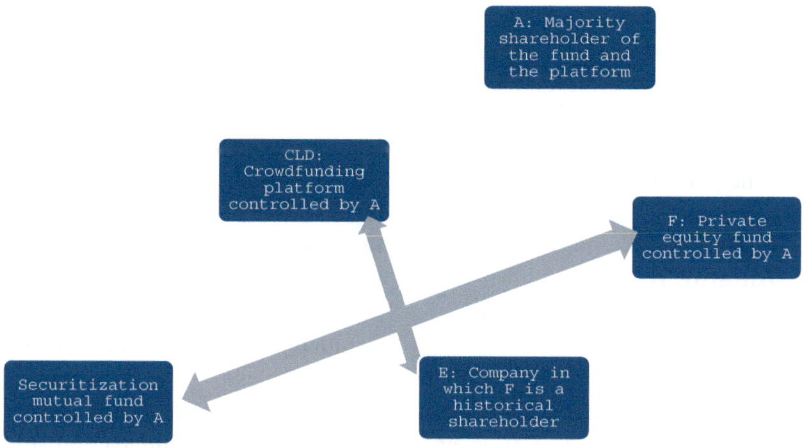

Fig. 18.4 Diagram of the Lendix model

who take on debt together to invest in loans), most of the companies financed have had, or still have, as a shareholder an investment fund, 123 Venture, whose founder is also the founder of Lendix. The teams working on the crowdlending platform are themselves largely drawn from this investment fund.

"The platform relies on the know-how and expertise developed by 123 Venture". [Lendix, *Board* member].

The platform is therefore particularly familiar with the companies it finances, having followed them, via this investment fund, as a shareholder for many years. As a result, the intelligence of the crowd does not appear to be useful, and the credit analysis does not involve any innovation compared with "traditional finance". The analysis is carried out by the platform's own analysts.

"When it comes to credit analysis, we do what all banks do, i.e. we analyse the company's figures, its income statement. At least, that's what we do. We come up with a grade. [Lendix, head of internal control].

The crowdfunding aspect of project financing is also very limited. In this business model, only 10% of loans come from individual contributors. The remaining 90% is provided by institutional investors (banks, insurers and family offices) grouped together in several securitization mutual funds set up by Lendix's directors. These institutional investors take out loans under the same interest rate and maturity conditions as private investors on the platform, but with no limit on the amount. As interest rates are very high on crowdlending platforms, this system enables institutional investors to achieve apparent levels of return that they would not be able to achieve by investing directly, without incurring significant reputational risk. The interest rate and overall loan amount are set by the platform. As soon as a project is put online, it is certain to be financed, because even if no private investor agrees to contribute, the securitization fund will match the full amount requested.

"It's almost an extension of the bank more than a new philosophy since they've created a securitization fund that allows them to provide the entire financing as soon as they've qualified the thing, and mix the institutional people in the securitization fund and the crowd" [Ministerial advisor].

The investment decision is therefore made by the platform, not by the crowd. In addition, the follow-up of companies after the loan campaign is more thorough than in the previous model, notably due to the involvement of institutional investors, who have significant human resources at their disposal. Finally, as in the previous business model, the platform only reimburses contributors who have suffered a default in the event of a scam that it has failed to detect.

The managers of this platform have extensive experience in financial analysis. In their personal capacity, they automatically grant a loan to each project presented on the platform, so as to display an alignment of interest between the contributors and the platform.

The Case of Unilend: Towards a "Euronext" Marketplace for Private Debt

In the 'market place' business model (see Fig. 18.5), the ambition is to create a 'Euronext for private debt', i.e. a place where private debt is continuously issued and traded. This is an extension of the disintermediated finance model:

"Today, the main problem with financial markets is that they are only accessible to very large companies which have the capacity to issue financial instruments, to make very important financial communications and which, through the size of the underlying which they issue, provide liquidity to the market and can therefore be organized on regulated markets, with depth, etc. This does not prevent liquidity crises from occurring. What we're in the process of creating with a platform like Unilend is basically a marketplace, and that's how we see ourselves. Our ambition is to create the equivalent of Euronext for private debt. [Unilend, founder].

First and foremost, there is an important limitation to this ambition. While Unilend can be likened to a primary market for the issuance of private debt, the platform does not yet have the legal capacity to create a secondary market for the continuous resale of debt already issued.

However, compared with the two previous models, the first particularity of this platform is that everything moves faster, thanks to the use of scoring algorithms. As a result, project selection is much more automated than in the two previous examples.

"We interfaced almost thirty databases to enable us, from a simple company ID number, to have a lot of information on the company, such as its payment behaviour, its balance sheet, its history, its privileges, in short a whole bunch of things… precisely to enable us very quickly to reject a huge number of files efficiently without mobilizing staff" [Unilend, founder].

Unlike the two previous business models, the loan interest rate is not set by the platform, nor is it unique to a given project. In fact, the platform gives only one risk rating per project, and each contributor indicates at what rate and for what amount he or she is willing to lend money to the project. Contributors with the lowest rates are served first, until the full amount requested by the project owner is reached. It's a reverse auction mechanism, which means that different rates can be offered to different contributors,

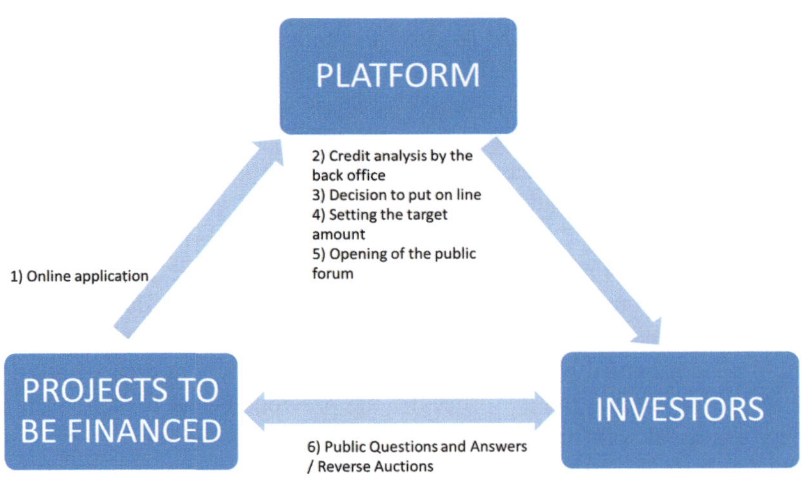

Fig. 18.5 Unilend model diagram

resulting in the lowest possible weighted rate for the project owner.

This business model also features an 'autolend' module for automated loan underwriting. Thanks to this module, fund-raising campaigns often take just a few hundredths of a second from the moment a project is put online to the end of the campaign. This very short time makes it impossible to interact with the project owner, which is essential for the expression of collective intelligence.

This business model also allows legal entities to contribute financially to projects, up to a limit of around 40% of the amounts financed. A special feature of this business model is the public investment bank BpiFrance and a partnership with Groupama Banque, which can finance up to 40% of each project. The company's CEO had a first career in marketing in financial institutions.

18.5 Towards Embedding *Crowdlending* in Traditional Finance with a View to Achieving the Goals of the Agenda 2030

Having analysed these three models, we can now examine whether crowdlending in France has any real potential to lead to better financing of the Agenda 2030 SDGs.

If we start by looking at the volumes involved, one thing becomes clear: crowdlending platforms alone do not have the scale to make a real impact. It is true that we haven't yet witnessed a tidal wave of crowdlending that could replace the banks. Amounts raised through crowdfunding (see Table 18.1) have been rising steadily year on year, but are still too low to really close the financing gap for the MDGs.

(These figures are taken from the barometer published by Financement participatif France).

In the words of a representative of the French Banking Federation whom we interviewed:

"When you look at the amounts [on crowdlending platforms], today we're at less than 300 million [in loans]. So if these loans double every year for ten years, maybe! Last year, French banks produced 240 billion euros in new loans!" [FBF].

It also emerges that the only model to have survived and even developed throughout Europe is that of Lendix, which is part of a logic of embedding with traditional players. It is this model that has the particularity of being structured to benefit from the technical expertise of former investment fund employees, as well as from the long-term relationships these employees have maintained with companies seeking financing. The Lendix model is inclusive in that it enables players in the traditional finance sector, notably banks, insurance companies and asset managers, to join forces within a securitization pool and provide an average of 90% of the financing for projects placed online on the crowdlending platform.

This way of embedding crowdlending with traditional financial players (see Fig. 18.6) seems to be able to create a leverage effect to the benefit of projects with the ambition of achieving the SDGs. Banks see crowdlending as a blessing that can be used to leverage traditional loans, enabling them to lend to their customers without being placed under the Basel prudential framework.

For them, crowdlending also means, in the context of hybrid bank/platform financing, the assurance of risk pooling and painless management of an isolated default on at least part of the overall amount at stake. So, if crowdlending platforms can become an extension of traditional players, particularly banks, the latter will be able to make use of this singular default risk management that they didn't use before, financing non-collateralizable risks at higher interest rates than

Table 18.1 Amounts raised by crowdfunding in France in millions of euros

2015	2016	2017	2018	2019	2020	2021	2022
167	234	336	402	629	1 020	1 880	2 355

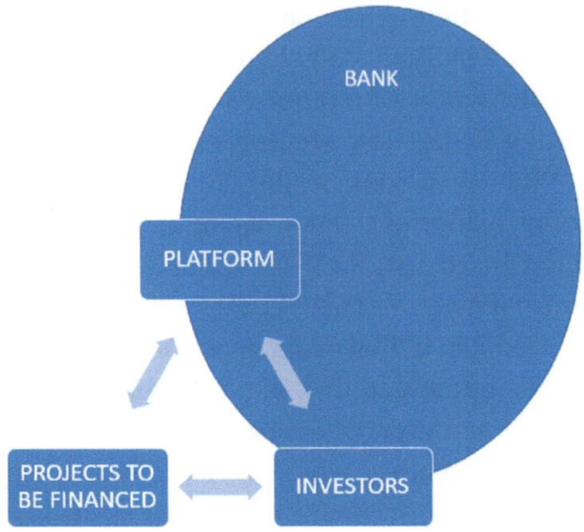

Fig. 18.6 Diagram of how *crowdlending* fits into traditional finance

those they usually apply, and thus enabling better financing of the actions needed to achieve the SDGs.

"As an old-fashioned, almost retired banker, I can say that investing in this platform has enabled us to reconnect with an aspect of our business that we had neglected recently. I'm talking about our local impact. In other words, our human, social and unifying role. Our sustainable action to support meaningful things and unite communities. We're not just machines checking boxes in Basel regulations. We're here to contribute to meaningful, useful projects that are worth taking risks, even if it means losing sometimes. It's not marketing. It shouldn't be. It's a return to the true meaning of the lending relationship" [Bank].

The vision of a representative of the banking industry's union is thus becoming a reality:

"When it comes to current platforms, I see this world converging towards the banks. If I were in a bank's marketing department, I'd be looking to integrate this crowdlending function" [FBF].

18.6 Summary and Conclusion

- In this chapter, we have shown that crowdlending is a credible tool to help put people and sustainable development back at the heart of the credit relationship.
- Crowdlending brings new elements to traditional finance: digitization, speed of execution, absence of surety or collateral, rate levels, traceability, pre-eminence of meaning and locality, pooling of risk between small lenders.
- Under certain conditions, a form of collective intelligence can emerge on crowdlending platforms.
- Crowdfunding seems to offer a way of embedding itself in traditional finance, in order to partially convert the latter to the financing of the SDGs.
- Crowdfunding can help recycle money creation into impact investments in line with the Agenda 2030.
- Through the development of *crowdlending*, we are witnessing the gradual empowerment of a whole range of players, who are acquiring new financial capabilities within their ecosystem and opening up to new financing objectives.

Activities

Questions for Discussion

1. Is crowdlending a way to democratize finance?
2. Which of the three models described in this chapter do you think has the best future?
3. Can a crowd of anonymous people contribute something useful and complementary to financial experts?
4. Is the concept of collective intelligence credible in finance?
5. Is it utopian to think of the SDGs without considering how they will be financed?
6. Are banks doomed to disappear?
7. Should individuals be prohibited from taking financial risks?
8. How can we limit the consequences of a debt default?
9. When a project is already financed, is it still potentially useful to use crowdlending?
10. Can banks partner with crowdlending platforms?

Mini-Case: The Lendosphere Platform

Visit the Lendosphere website (www.lendosphere.com). Browse through the projects already financed and those currently being financed. Also read the FAQ and the platform statistics.

Answer the following questions:

1. To which SDGs do the projects financed on the platform contribute?
2. How many projects have been financed on this platform? For what total amount?
3. How does the platform pay for itself?
4. What interest rates are applied on the platform?
5. Where do we see collective intelligence on the platform?
6. Who regulates this platform?
7. Does this platform offer anything useful or new compared with a bank?

Imagine a project linked to an SDG for which you need to raise 500,000 euros. Prepare a presentation of the project to individuals who lend on the platform.

Social Impact Bonds 19

Catherine Karyotis and Sharam Alijani

Putting Things into Perspective

"Success is not measured by how much money you make, but by the impact you have on people's lives" - Michelle Obama (Democratic Party Conference, September 4, 2012).

A financial system brings together borrowers and lenders of capital funds to finance the economy, and today must play a central role in the ecological, energy, social, and societal transition process. As part of Agenda 2030, the financial market must make up for the shortfall in funding for the SDGs (Sustainable Development Goals): there is a shortfall of between $5,400 and $6,400 billion a year!

This chapter looks at the different financing vehicles, then focuses on social impact bonds. It presents the financial set-up and examines the measurement techniques used to assess the impact of sustainable finance.

Learning Objectives

- Understanding the instruments used to finance the SDGs
- Assessing the role of private, public, and institutional players
- Describing and analyzing Social Impact Bonds (SIBs)
- Questioning impact measurement

19.1 Purpose and Social Benefits of Financial Markets

In September 2023, only 15% of the SDGs have been achieved, and there is a shortfall of between $5,400 and $6,400 billion a year to meet the 2030 Agenda.

Green, social, sustainable, transitional, and social impact bonds are financial products that make it possible to place the market economy at the service of society and the biosphere, provided that finance is re-embedded in the sense of Polanyi (1944).[1]

Public–private partnerships, combining financial and social returns, can finance innovative social or environmental projects, as in the case of Peterborough Prison, which benefited from the first issue of a Social Impact Bond (SIB) in 2010. The bond's remuneration was conditional

C. Karyotis (✉) · S. Alijani
The American University of Paris, Paris, France
e-mail: catherine.karyotis@neoma-bs.fr

S. Alijani
e-mail: salijani@aup.edu

[1] Polanyi, K. (1944). *The Great Transformation*, Reprinted 1983, Gallimard.

T. Lagoarde-Ségot (ed.), *Ecological Economics and Finance*,
https://doi.org/10.1007/978-3-031-71249-4_19

on a reduction in the recidivism rate, which proved to be a success.

The aim of this chapter is to take stock of the support given by financial markets to financing the social and environmental dimensions of sustainable development, highlighting the role of SIBs, as well as the financial risks associated with social impacts. We provide a synoptic overview of bond instruments used to finance environmental and social projects. This is followed by a focus on impact bonds, highlighting the difficulty of measuring impact. Finally, we conclude with the need for effective control mechanisms.

19.2 Bonds: A Public Offering Instrument

The financial market, a long-term capital market, offers a debt security—the bond—that responds to the long-term dimension, a time horizon that is essential to the transition and sustainable development projects of our societies.

Bonds to Finance the Dimensions of Sustainable Development

The financial system, an integral part of the economic system, is essential to the financing of companies, governments and other organizations, but its usefulness will be all the greater if it is conceived in a holistic way, along the lines of the United Nations' *One Health* perspective (see box 19.1).

Box 19.1: One Health—A holistic approach to financial integration

There can be no economic and social prosperity without human health, which in turn depends on the health of the planet. Finance must therefore be part of a global approach with a long-term vision, in order to build a new world.

The United Nations' One Health initiative is an interdisciplinary, intersectoral and integrated approach to the public management of health problems, based on the triptych "human health, environmental health and animal health".

It represents a real paradigm shift: its inclusion in the 2030 Agenda requires changes in the way institutions operate and an adaptation of financing and resource-sharing systems, both in terms of investment distribution and long-term commitment. Lerner et al. (2017)[2] arguing that human public health cannot prevail on a socially and ecologically degraded planet, evoke an Eco Health approach to integrate social and economic factors into any investment decision.

The One Health concept is now taking on its full meaning in maximizing the societal role of finance: social impact bonds enable resources to be allocated to projects to finance the SDGs, which themselves serve people and the planet.

Source https://www.who.int/fr/news-room/q-a-detail/one-health

A bond is said to be sustainable when it makes a positive contribution to the social responsibility objectives of its issuer. So, sustainable or responsible?

Responsible comes from *responsere*, Latin for 'to answer for one's actions and practices' or 'to render an account'. Barbot (2010)[3] speaks of the social responsibility of banks in combating social exclusion and assisting individuals with their financing needs by striking a balance between selling unsuitable loans and refusing to sell; he also speaks of ethical responsibility in

[2] Lerner, H. and Berg, C. (2017). A Comparison of Three Holistic Approaches to Health: One Health, EcoHealth, and Planetary Health, *Front Vet.*

[3] Barbot, G. (2010). L'utilité sociale de la banque en question, quelques réflexions pour l'après-crise, *Vie et Sciences économiques*, 2010/3–4, 185/186, pp. 120–147 (untranslated).

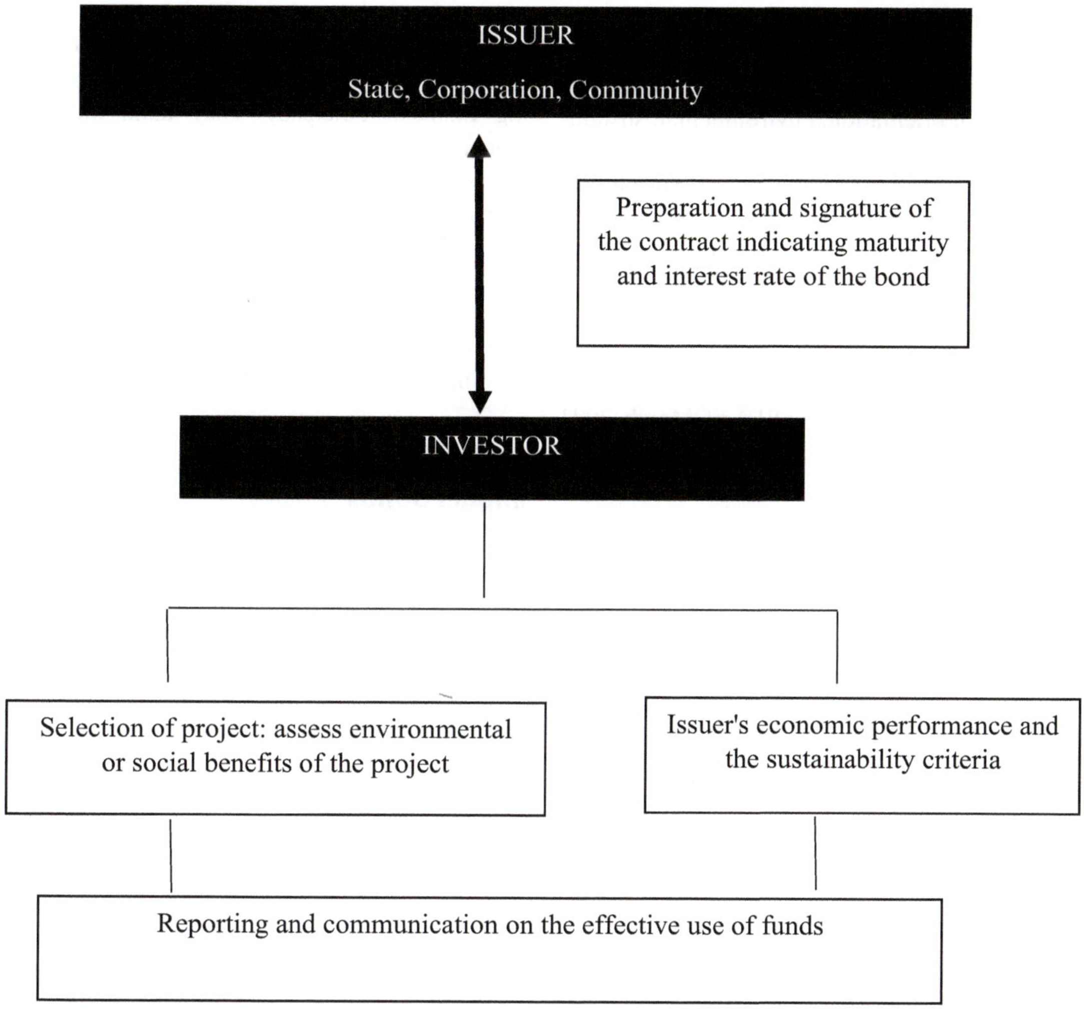

Fig. 19.1 Sustainable bond

combating financial crime and fiduciary responsibility in terms of trust.

According to the United Nations Environment Programme (UNEP), a sustainable financial system is defined as "a system that creates, values and processes financial assets in a way that creates real wealth to meet the long-term needs of an inclusive and environmentally sustainable economy." The sustainable bond meets these criteria[4]: it is issued (see Fig. 19.1) to (re)finance environmental and social projects, defined from the outset by the issuer, who determines the use of funds, project by project, and the objectives to be achieved (reporting and communication).

In France, the *Observatoire de la Responsabilité Sociale des Entreprises* (ORSE) distinguishes between bonds earmarked for environmental and/or social projects, and bonds that enable the issuer to finance its traditional business while being conditional on the achievement of social and environmental objectives, under penalty of a revaluation of its interest rate.

[4]UNEP. (2015), *Report on the financial system we need - Aligning the financial system with sustainable development.*

Supports

Sustainable bonds are classified according to their general orientation: environmental, sustainable and social (see Table 19.1).

Social bonds,[5] green bonds[6] and sustainable development bonds[7] respect international principles of integrity and transparency, without however being subject to regulatory constraint: use and management of revenues, project selection and evaluation processes, and reporting. In the European Union, the Sustainable Finance Disclosure Regulation (SFDR)[8] of March 2021 aims to increase financial transparency and accountability by disclosing information on product sustainability.

The taxonomy takes the form of a list of economic activities and performance thresholds in terms of contribution to six environmental objectives (climate change mitigation, adaptation, water, circular economy, pollution, and biodiversity). The different approaches to sustainable investment can be illustrated in the following diagram (see Fig. 19.2).

Financial products are classified as products without a sustainability objective (article 6), products promoted with social and/or environmental characteristics (article 8) or products with a sustainable investment objective (article 9).

Finally, the European taxonomy,[9] established in 2020, classifies green or sustainable activities to help players (investors, issuers, project promoters) steer investments toward environmentally friendly economic activities in order to avoid greenwashing and make it easier to compare financial products.

It is clear that social impact contracts present a high degree of strategic ambiguity in terms of investor choice and desired impact. Social impact bonds are structured around actions with the aim of improving well-being and equity while ensuring financial efficiency. They build on social innovation policies with the help of institutional actors and public and private resources that seek to increase efficiency and equity in the public economy (European Parliament, 2014; Mulgan et al., 2011). As such, social impact contracts are a lever for accelerating social, economic, and environmental transformation (Alijani et al., 2016; Liebman, 2011; Nicholls & Murdock, 2012).

Impact Investing: The Case of *Social Impact* Bonds

Impact Investing means investing in companies, organizations and funds with the intention of having a social and environmental impact as well as generating stock market performance.

The criteria used to measure impact are additionality, intentionality and measurement.

- Additionality is the direct contribution of an investor to the financing of a project/structure generating positive impact—if another investor had financed the project or structure, would the result have been the same? Additionality can be financial (when financing difficult to obtain on mainstream financial markets) and/or extra-financial (in terms of environmental and/or social impacts).
- Intentionality (what is the investor's intention in financing the project? In what way does this investment exceed the dimension of a responsible investment?) can be apprehended upstream of the investment—*ex ante*—and will be assessed *ex post* via measurement.
- The measurement consists of an assessment of the social and/or environmental externalities.[10]

[5] https://www.icmagroup.org/sustainable-finance/.

[6] https://www.icmagroup.org/sustainable-finance/the-principles-guidelines-and-handbooks/green-bond-principles-gbp/.

[7] https://www.icmagroup.org/sustainable-finance/the-principles-guidelines-and-handbooks/sustainability-linked-bond-principles-slbp/.

[8] https://eur-lex.europa.eu/legal-content/EN/TXT/?uri=celex%3A32019R2088.

[9] https://eur-lex.europa.eu/legal-content/EN/TXT/?uri=CELEX:52021DC0188.

[10] An externality is a benefit (positive externality) or a disadvantage (negative externality) resulting for a third party from an exchange or relationship between other agents. The effect is external to the market and the price system, since it is not compensated for in monetary terms. The impact investor seeks a positive externality or aims to reduce a negative externality; the externality is measured qualitatively and/or quantitatively.

Table 19.1 General typology of sustainable bonds

Bond orientation	Environmental			Sustainable		Social	
Category	*Green Bond*	*Catastrophe bond*	*Transition bond*	*ESG bond*	*Sustainable development bond*	*Social bond*	*Social Impact Contract*
Purpose of financing	Ecological transition	Natural disasters	Decarbonation	Implementing the Agenda 2030	Improved sustainability profile	Social projects (employment, health, education)	Public social actions
SDG	6, 7, 9, 13, 14, 15	1, 2	All			1, 2, 3, 4, 10, 16	
Features	Issuing and reporting on funded projects	Financial protection in the event of a major catastrophe ⇔ Insurance	Issue to finance a company in the process of decarbonization that is not yet eligible for a green bond	Use-of-proceed directly finances ODD projects Or General purpose (finances the implementation of a SDG strategy)	Possible increase in interest and/or repayment if target not reached (penalizing the issuer)	Example: *Vaccine fund* to finance vaccination campaigns	Public actions are financed by public funds, with reimbursement of funds by the public entity plus interest if successful (no reimbursement if unsuccessful)

Source Authors

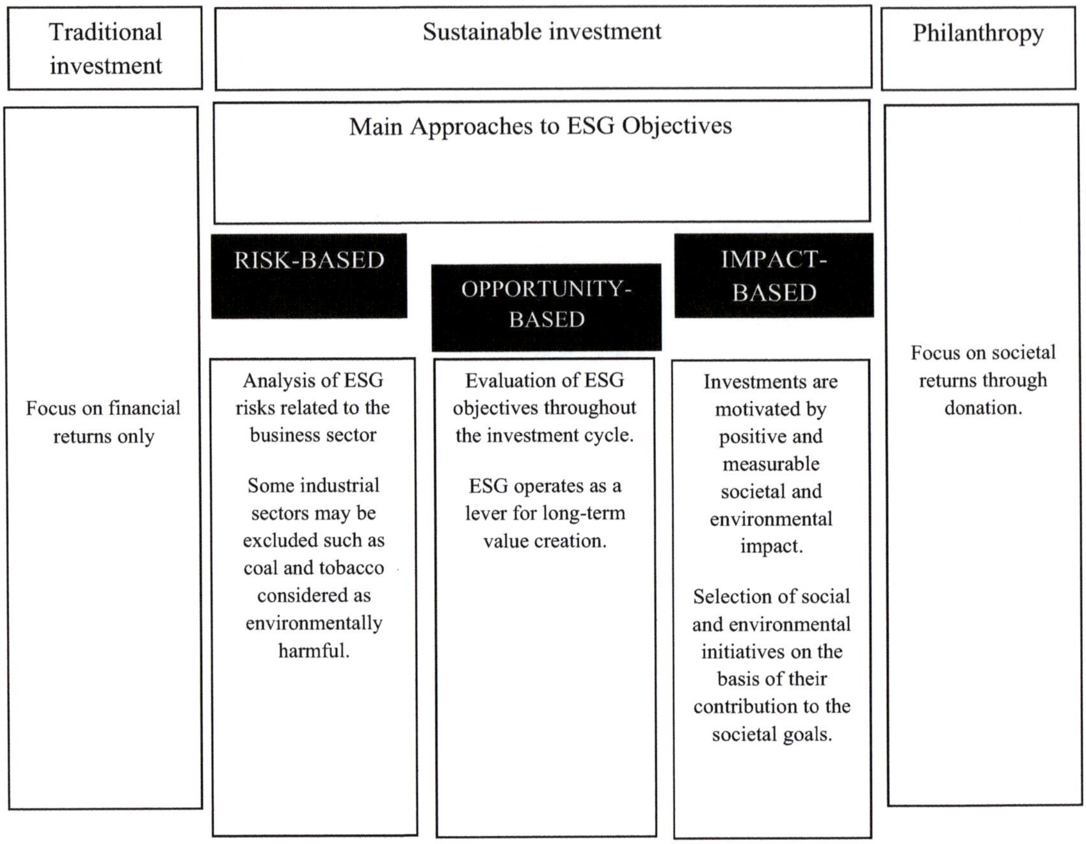

Fig. 19.2 Different approaches to sustainable investment: The sustainable investment model (*Source United Nations Global Compact*)

While the notion of financial return as a measure of value creation is widely used by investors, the importance of additionality needs to be reaffirmed as a means of linking financial performance to societal benefits.

A Social Impact Bond (SIB) or Social Impact Contract (SIC) is a financial instrument that enables private investors to finance social programs with a guarantee of repayment of the capital invested, plus a profitability premium once the social objectives have been achieved.

It is based on a tripartite structure with cooperation between private and public players, a source of value creation (see Fig. 19.3).

The first SIB issue was made in 2010 for Peterborough Prison (UK): £5 million was subscribed by 17 investors, mainly foundations, with the aim of reducing the recidivism rate of offenders by 7.5%. In 2014, an 8.5% drop in the recidivism rate on a sample of 1000 prisoners triggered the first payments in 2016. In 2017, the recidivism rate fell by 9%, 1.5% above target, resulting in capital repayment with a 3% return.

In France, the law of July 31, 2014 created the Social Impact Contract (SIC) to "finance actions that are part of the general development policy of the social and solidarity economy taken on by social players. The mechanism provides for initial financing of the project by a private investor who will be reimbursed by the public authorities in the event of success.[11]"

SIBs can be particularly effective socially oriented instruments for reducing economic and social

[11] *Journal Officiel* of the French Republic, December 30, 2018.

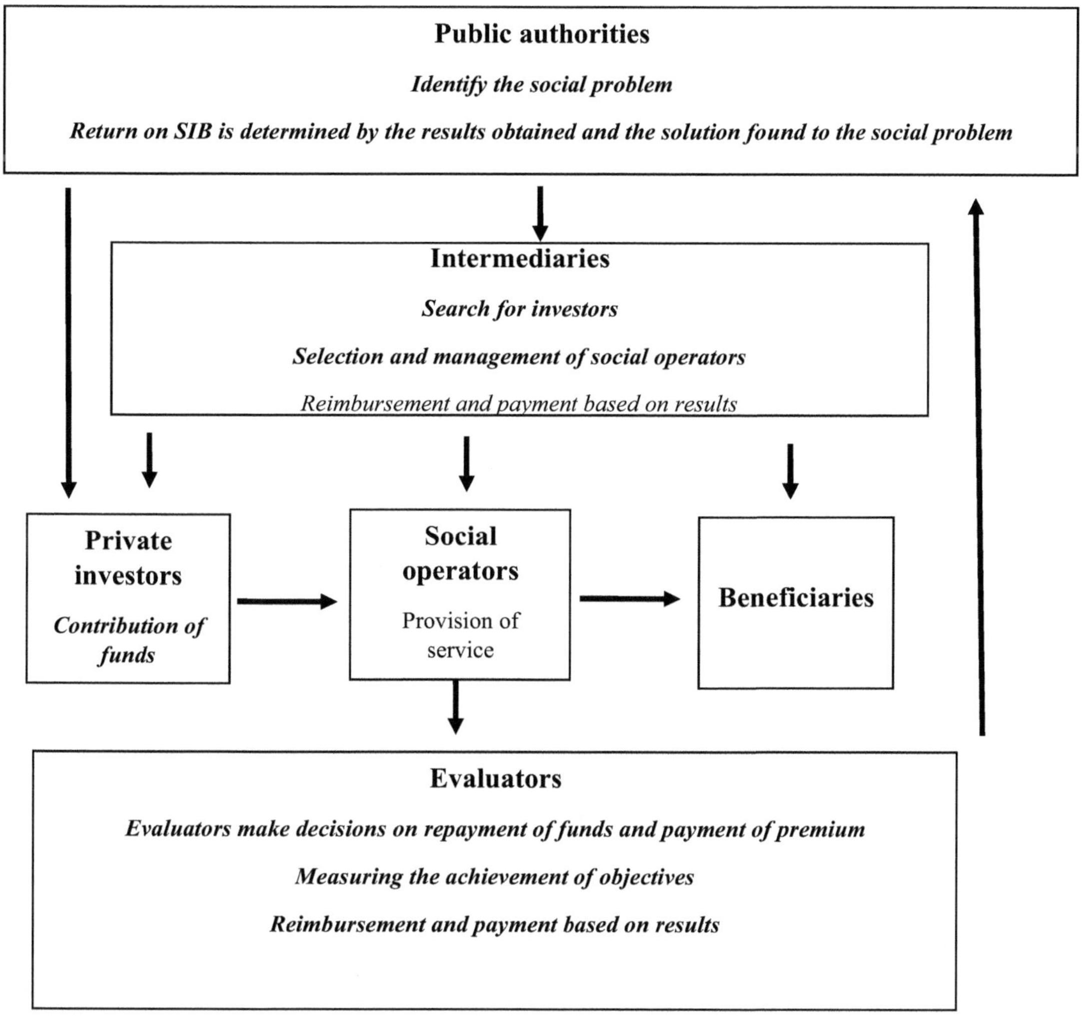

Fig. 19.3 Social impact bond creation process (*Source Authors*)

inequalities caused by institutional inadequacies and market imperfections. By mitigating the undesirable effects of exclusion and poverty, they enable effective public–private partnerships to improve human capabilities, increase social well-being, accelerate economic development and strengthen democracy (Sen, 2018, 2010[12]; Stiglitz, 2012).[13]

19.3 Measuring Social Impact

Various approaches can be envisaged to conceptualize, evaluate, and measure the social impact of SIBs.

The cost–benefit analysis approach focuses on economic value by calculating economic costs, benefits, and utility, but does not provide a complete measure of social impact. Other approaches, such as the 'user preference' approach, take into account the cost of human capital, the opportunity cost, and the cost of non-replacement of resources. In particular,

[12] Sen, A. (2018). *Collective Choice and Social Welfare*, Cambridge: Harvard University Press; Sen, A. (2000) *Development as Freedom*, New York: Anchor Books, Random House.

[13] Stiglitz, J. (2012). *The Price of Inequality*, New York: Norton and Company.

the use of randomized controlled trials (RCTs) can help measure the impact of SIBs. Used in the 1970s to evaluate public policies in various fields (education, health, housing, etc.), RCTs can be used to assess the impact of a specific public policy on targeted populations and beneficiaries. One example is the Anti-Poverty Lab, founded by Banerjee and Duflo at MIT in 2003, which has conducted randomized controlled trial experiments to evaluate public and private investments (Banerjee & Duflo, 2009, 2008[14]).

There are also contingency and willingness-to-pay methods, which are certainly rigorous, but their description of assumptions is contested.

The SROI (*Social Return on Investment*) approach, for its part, is based on estimating the value created for a project's stakeholders, enabling the calculation of a ratio between the sum of social impacts and the total resources mobilized for this purpose. The elements of impact measurement and valuation are more oriented towards the social value created than toward monetary value.

Finally, the cohort or randomization method is based on comparing a population affected by the funded project with a population unaffected by it, in order to measure changes in the former.

19.4 Financialization of Social Services: An Example of a Public–Private Partnership

SIBs are a source of value creation, both societal and financial, as they lead to synergies resulting from shared responsibility between public and private players.

The public sector, now over-indebted, needs private savings, and investors need to give meaning to their investments. The interest of impact investing in general, and social impact bonds in particular, lies in the necessary financing of social action through public–private partnerships.

Le Pendeven et al. (2015)[15] evoke a win–win device for actors:

- The public sector transfers the risk to private investors, without the state withdrawing (if the project fails, investors lose their stake; if it succeeds, the public sector has minimized its investment); it also benefits from regular funding, as it is independent of political power.
- Target populations benefit from curative or preventive actions.
- Private or philanthropic supporters benefit both financially (if the project succeeds) and socially.

SIBs fall within the scope of New Public Management, which aims to bring together players operating in the private and public sectors. The question is whether this could lead to increasing financialization of the social economy.[16] Other products or financial arrangements have fallen into excess, without auguring a similar fate for impact investing, but leading some to raise these excesses: in microfinance, the Mexican institution Compartamos charged interest rates of up to 192%, raising questions about the financialization of this alternative model for financing the poorest.[17] At the same time, the securitization of microfinance has been

[14] Banerjee, A. V. and Duflo, E. (2009). The experimental approach in development economics", *Journal of Political Economy*, 119, 5, pp. 691–726. Banerjee A. V. and Duflo E. (2008), "Mandated Empowerment. Handing Antipoverty Policy Back to the Poor? *Annals of the New York Academy of Sciences*, 1136, pp. 333–341.

[15] Le Pendeven, B., Nico, Y. and Gachet, B. (2015). Social Impact Bonds, A new tool for financing social innovation, Institut de l'Entreprise.

[16] According to Krippner, the predominance of markets over banks, accompanied by the primacy of *shareholder value*, characterizes the financialization of economies, while for Epstein, financialization translates into an increased role for financial markets and their players. Krippner, G. (2005). "The Financialization of the American Economy", *Socio-Economic Review*, 3, 2, pp. 173–208; Epstein G.-A. (2005). *Financialization and the World Economy*, Edwar Edgar.

[17] Karyotis, C. and Alijani, S. (2017). SBI et *Impact investing*: risque de financiarisation du social ou véritable outil? *Revue Banque*, 815, December (untranslated).

accompanied by a shift "from a preoccupation initially focused on the beneficiaries of the policy (populations in difficulty, ecosystems to be protected, children to be cared for, etc.) and the organizations that look after them, to a preoccupation focused on the operators and financial intermediaries who will provide the necessary funds.[18]"

Impact investing must remain true to its mission as a means of financing solutions to social problems. The objective of social well-being, primarily as a preventive measure to address market and institutional failures, must take precedence over the curative dimension of social spending. Robins and Krosinsky (2009)[19] emphasize the need for sustainable finance that goes beyond traditional finance. We need to be alert to the potential abuses and mission drift of impact investing in an increasingly financialized economy.

19.5 Summary and Conclusion

Financial markets can and must finance the social dimension of sustainable development by responding to the SDGs, particularly SDGs 1, 2, 3, 4, 8, and 10. The key points explored in this chapter are as follows:

1. The social benefits of financial markets
2. The need to rebuild finance
3. The need to think finance within and with the *One Health* concept developed by the United Nations
4. Sustainable bonds
5. *Impact investing*
6. Characteristics of a *Social Impact Bond*
7. The need to measure social impact
8. The risk of financialization in the social sector

[18] Chiapello, E., La Financiarisation des politiques publiques, *Mondes en développement*, 2017/2, 178, pp. 23–40 (untranslated).

[19] Robins, N. and Krosinsky, C. (2009). After the credit crunch: The future of sustainable investing, Public Policy Research, December–February 2009, 15, 4, pp. 192–197.

Activities

Questions for Discussion

1. Should an international standard (e.g., ISO) be established to regulate the issuance and reporting procedures for sustainable bonds in general, and SIBs in particular?
2. Can financial markets replace public authorities in financing social services?
3. Should a specific country take the lead in social impact bonds?
4. Is the European social taxonomy useful or futile?
5. Is it necessary to quantify social impact?
6. How can the human factor be taken into account in financial modeling?
7. Real *impact investing* or *social washing*?
8. Are SIBs the instruments of social financialization?
9. How can we ensure the traceability of social financing?
10. Can a social investment fund attract savings from individuals?

Mini-case

Case 1

You are an elected official in a city of 300,000 inhabitants with a high juvenile delinquency rate. You are thinking about a social utility project and are looking for public funding to help you achieve SDG 16. You propose to the city council that it use a social impact contract. Break down your mission as follows:

1. Outline the principles of a social obligation.
2. Explain why and how a SIB is the most appropriate mechanism for combating juvenile delinquency.
3. Refer to the Avise.org website (https://www.avise.org/evaluation-impact-social/demarches-et-methodes/mesurer-decouvrir-les-principales-methodes). Identify key issues and provide arguments for discussing impact measurement.

Case 2

You've been invited to a job interview at the European Investment Bank (EIB) to develop ways of financing SDGs 1 to 6. To prepare for your interview, visit the EIB website and that of a multilateral development bank (e.g. Agence France Développement, World Bank) and answer the following questions:

- What is a multilateral development bank (role, missions…)?
- Propose the best public offering vehicles to meet these expectations for financing the SDGs.

References

Alijani, S., Akgüc, M, Castro Spila, J, Cressy, P., & Deserti, A. et al. (2016). In Terstriep, J. Boosting social innovation's social and economic impact. Boosting social innovation's social and economic impact. (www.simpact.eu), Institute for Work and Technology, Germany.

Banerjee, A. V., & Duflo, E. (2009). The experimental approach in development economics. *Journal of Political Economy, 119*(5), 691–726.

Chiapello, E. (2017). La financiarisation des politiques publiques. *Mondes en développement,* 2017/2 (178), 23–40 (untranslated).

European Parliament. (2014). *Social impact bonds: Private finance that generates social returns*. European Parliamentary Research Service: European Parliament.

Lab, G. O. (2017). *Social impact bonds (SIBs): The basics*. University of Oxford.

Impact Invest Lab. (2020). Le contrat d'impact social de l'ADIE. Etude de cas d'un contrat d'impact social (untranslated).

Karyotis C., & Alijani S. (2017, December). SBI and *impact investing*: Risk of financialization of the social or real tool? *Revue Banque* (815).

Liebman, J. B. (2011). *Social impact bonds: A promising new financing model to accelerate social innovation and improve government performance*. Center for American Progress 9.

Labrousse, A. (2010). Nouvelle économie du développement et essais cliniques randomisés: une mise en perspective d'un outil de preuve et de gouvernement. *Revue de la régulation, 7* (untranslated).

Le Pendeven, B., Nico Y., & Gachet B. (2015). Social Impact Bonds, A new tool for financing social innovation. Institut de l'Entreprise.

Maier, F., & Meyer, M. (2017). Social impact bonds and the perils of aligned interests. *Administrative Sciences, 7*(3), 24.

Moore, M., Frances, L., Westley, R., & Nicholls, A. (2012). *The Social finance and social innovation nexus 1*. Taylor & Francis.

Mulgan, G. Reeder, N., Aylott, M., & Bo'sher. L. (2011). Social impact investment: The challenge and opportunity of social impact bonds. Young Foundation.

Nicholls, A., & Murdock, A. (2012). The nature of social innovation. *Social Innovation*, 1–30. Springer.

Obama, M. (2012, September 4). Democratic party conference.

ORSE. (2021). Panorama des obligations durables (untranslated).

UNEP. (2015). *The financial system we need* report—*Aligning the Financial System for Sustainable*. Development.

The SROI Network. (2012). A Guide to Social Return on Investment.

Warner, M. E. (2013). Private finance for public goods: Social impact bonds. *Journal of Economic Policy Reform, 16*(4), 303–319. https://doi.org/10.1080/17487870.2013.835727

20 The Mutual Bank Model and Sustainability

Charles Daussy and Jérôme Courcier

Putting Things into Perspective

Sustainable Development Goal 17 calls on us to revitalize the global partnership for sustainable development. Because of the complexity and interdependence of the Sustainable Development Goals (SDGs), we need to change the way we work, and enter into a logic of partnership (from the Latin *partitio*, "to share, divide, distribute"), i.e. a logic in which the parties agree to pool their efforts to achieve a common goal

Of all commercial enterprises, the bank is the one that willingly presents itself as the partner of its individual, professional or corporate customers, insofar as it participates in the realization of their projects. The bank performs this very special economic activity, which makes other economic activities possible, because it has been delegated the function of granting credit and creating money. Unfortunately, relations between the two parties are often tense and marked by mistrust, as banks are often criticized for being too cautious, whereas the latter consider that they are obliged to be extremely prudent, given the ratio between the risks they take and the size of their equity capital

However, if the interests of customers and the bank seem irreconcilable, of all the institutions involved, only the mutual banks take a different stance. Insofar as they are owned by their customers, they claim to be structured by the needs and vision of their members, relayed by the presidents of local and regional mutual banks via the boards of directors of these entities. In their view, their cooperative structure creates a community of interest that plays a decisive role in defining the services and products offered by the bank, and in the banking relationship. This is due to the different nature of shareholders in capitalist and mutual banks. This chapter describes the functioning of this alternative model and highlights its contribution to the SDGs.

Learning Objectives

- Understand the need to implement CSR strategies to achieve the SDGs
- Understand the process of integrating CSR into banks' strategies to meet stakeholder expectations through the Weber model

C. Daussy (✉)
NEOMA BS, Mont-Saint-Aignan, France
e-mail: charles.daussy@neoma-bs.fr

J. Courcier
Senior Advisor ESG, KPMG, Courbevoie, France

T. Lagoarde-Ségot (ed.), *Ecological Economics and Finance*,
https://doi.org/10.1007/978-3-031-71249-4_20

- Understanding the specificities of the mutual model in a partnership approach (SDG 17) to achieve all the SDGs

20.1 Mutual Banks: A Model for a Paradigm Shift

According to ICA[1] (2018), the voice of cooperatives worldwide, the cooperative movement is a key player in addressing the SDGs: "Cooperatives are one of the main actors involved in the themes proposed by the 2030 Agenda because these are embedded in their DNA through their principles and values."

SDG 17 is the one in which cooperatives are explicitly mentioned. For the ICA (2018), "the partnership dimension is indeed fundamental to promote the contribution of cooperatives to sustainable development and the SDGs. It is one of the main potential drivers that can significantly improve the contribution of cooperatives".

In the French context, mutual banks were created in the 19th century to finance populations that conventional financing structures considered marginal, either geographically (such as Alsace for Crédit Mutuel in France) or professionally (such as craftsmen and shopkeepers for *Banques Populaires* or farmers for *Crédit Agricole*).[2]

Although mutual banks have been considered banks in their own right since the Banking Act of January 1984, their cooperative values give them a number of specific characteristics that seem compatible with the challenges of corporate social responsibility (CSR).

They follow the seven cooperative principles[3] and share the following common features (according to the ICBA):

1. These are customer-owned entities.
2. They are governed by democratic control: one person, one vote.
3. They are distinguished by their distribution of profits.
4. They are supervised by a central body which, under Article L511-31 of the French Monetary and Financial Code, is responsible for prudential issues such as liquidity, solvency, risk control and development strategy.

As Pierre-Joseph Proudhon's (1809–1865) law of antagonism states, "no more than the opposite poles of an electric battery destroy or confuse each other", the General Manager (representing the central body) and the Chairman of the Regional Bank (representing the members) must strike "an ever-unstable balance, which varies according to the very evolution of the company[4] ", and retain the confidence of both their Board of Directors and the central body, which can dismiss them at any time. Over the last 30 years, for example, Crédit Agricole has had three cases of Regional Bank directors being removed from office.

20.2 Banks and Corporate Social Responsibility (CSR)

CSR and the SDGs

The Need to Align Corporate Social Responsibility with the SDGs

In a first approach to CSR, we can say that, just as the SDGs refer to the common good, CSR policies aim to assess the impact of corporate activities on the environment and society in general.

[1] International Cooperative Alliance.

[2] Today, the Crédit Agricole Group is the leading financier of the French economy, the world's tenth-largest bank in terms of total assets, and the third-largest in Europe. It is also the leading asset manager in Europe (with Amundi), the leading bancassurer in Europe (with Crédit Agricole Assurance) and one of the European leaders in project finance (with Crédit Agricole Corporate and Investment Bank). The Crédit Agricole Group is the bank for almost one in two businesses in France, is present in 48 countries, has 142,000 employees and 52 million customers.

[3] Coop FR (2010).

[4] Theory of property (1862).

There are therefore links between CSR and the SDGs, which can be used to define the priorities of companies' strategic plans.[5] The common good is in fact the "good of the whole", the full development of people within their community, the social and community dimension of the moral good. For Thomas Aquinas (1225–1274), "when one seeks the common good of the multitude, by consequence one also seeks one's own good, for one's own good cannot exist without the common good of the family, the city or the kingdom[6]". From this point of view, for management specialists Alain Desreumaux and Jean-Pierre Bréchet, "participating in society does not mean renouncing one's 'personal good" but, on the contrary, fulfilling it more fully. The quest for the common good is a way for each individual to ensure his or her personal good[7]". Today, to meet the expectations of all its stakeholders, the company must convince them that its performance is in phase with that of its territory, its society, its planet.

While CSR may represent the link between the corporate world and sustainable development, the concept of CSR itself is much older. In its Anglo-Saxon version, it mainly covers the maintenance of public goods or services (infrastructure, schools, police, etc.) that create the conditions for individual success. In its Latin version, adopted by the European Commission, CSR is "the responsibility of companies for the effects they have on society".

Integrating CSR into the strategy of companies—which are partners under SDG 17—will contribute to the achievement of all the SDGs. Let's take a look at CSR and how it can (and should) be integrated into corporate strategy.

Defining CSR

To do this, we can refer to A.B. Carroll's (1979) three-dimensional conceptual model,[8] which states that societal performance is built around the following elements:

1. The definition of social responsibility[9] revolves around four categories of responsibility—economic, legal, ethical and discretionary.[10] Social responsibility answers the question "Do our responsibilities go beyond economic and legal concerns?". In Carroll's model, economic and legal responsibilities are required (i.e., a constrained approach to CSR), ethical responsibilities are expected (i.e., a mimetic approach to CSR[11]: not being responsible on this aspect can have negative consequences such as reputational risk and loss of "license to operate"), while philanthropic responsibilities are desired (i.e., a voluntarist approach to CSR).
2. A list of issues relevant to social responsibility.
3. The company's response to the question: "Are we reactive or proactive in relation to these issues?"

The strategic challenge of putting CSR into practice within a company therefore lies in its ability to meet the expectations of its stakeholders, who are therefore at the heart of the operationalization of CSR and societal performance.

[5] "CSR and the Sustainable Development Goals", CSR Platform, *France Stratégie*, October 2018.

[6] Saint Thomas, D. A. (1860). Summa Theologica, IIa IIae, question 47, article 10, ad. 2, J. Carmagnolle.

[7] Desreumaux, A., Bréchet, J.-P., "L'Entreprise comme bien commun", RIMHE 2013/3 n° 7 (untranslated).

[8] Carroll, A. B. (1979). A Three-Dimensional Model of Corporate Social Performance, *Academy of Management Review*, 4 (4), pp. 497–505.

[9] The term 'societal responsibility' was then used in France to avoid referring solely to the field of employer-employee relations.

[10] Carroll evolved his model in 1991, replacing discretionary with philanthropic, without mentioning environmental responsibility. See Carroll, A. B. (1991). *The Pyramid of Corporate Social Responsibility: Toward the Moral Management of Organizational Stakeholders.* Business Horizons. Elsevier. July–August 1991.

[11] In the Anglo-Saxon approach to ethics (inspired by David Hume), goodness derives from the assent it elicits (I must help someone in need, because that's what's expected of me).

The Stakeholder Approach

R.E. Freeman (1984)[12] defines a stakeholder as "any group or individual who can affect or is affected by the achievement of the organization's objectives". For the author, it's a question of transforming the company without denying the importance of its shareholders, by taking all stakeholders into consideration. The company is thus reconfigured around the following question: "For whose benefit and at whose expense should the company be managed?" (Freeman, 1993[13]). According to this approach, all stakeholders, whoever they may be, have legitimate expectations, and all these expectations have an intrinsic value.

Turning now to the banking sector, we might ask what criteria are used to define CSR in a bank, who the bank's stakeholders are, and how banks integrate CSR into their strategy to meet the expectations of their various stakeholders.

Banks and CSR

CSR Criteria in the Banking Sector

The link between banking and CSR is not obvious, especially if we reduce sustainable development to its environmental component, which is often the case. Yet the impact of banks' activities on their ecosystem (the environment in general) is undeniable.

Weber (2005)[14] identifies three families of CSR criteria in the banking sector. They are summarized by Baret and Chivot (2012) as follows[15]:

1. Internal operations: energy or paper consumption, staff mobility, etc.
2. Investments: equity stakes in responsible projects or pioneering CSR companies (with criteria for rejecting non-responsible projects); SRI[16]; etc.
3. Credit: loans to projects/companies with CSR ambitions (microcredit, social housing or eco-projects); social rating of loans; transparency of credit products; etc.

This more or less corresponds to the three perimeters of the carbon footprint: (1) direct emissions linked to the energy consumption of the company's facilities; (2) indirect emissions linked to the purchase of electricity; (3) other emissions induced by the value chain, whether upstream (suppliers) or downstream (customers).

Let's take a look at the relationships banks develop with their stakeholders.

Bank Stakeholders

According to Freeman, the value of a company results from the combination of a certain number of production factors (or capitals), which can be reduced to six (financial, manufacturing, human, reputational, natural and social capital), and which correspond to as many stakeholders (investors, suppliers, employees, territories, planet and customers). Banks' contractual stakeholders are customers, employees and social partners, shareholders, member-customers and suppliers.

But there are also non-contractual stakeholders with equally legitimate expectations. For example, future employees (through recruitment processes), regulatory bodies, public authorities (governments and parliamentarians), international organizations, networks and think tanks, civil society organizations (especially rights NGOs, consumer, charity and family associations), the media (press, social networks, opinion leaders, etc.) and local populations and communities (territories) all contribute to a company's reputational capital.

[12] Freeman, R. E. (1984). *Strategic Management: A Stakeholder Approach*. Massachusetts, Pitman Publishing Inc.

[13] Freeman, R. E. (1993). Collaboration, global perspectives, and teacher education, *Theory into Practice*, *32*(1), pp. 33–39.

[14] Weber, O. (2005). Sustainability benchmarking of European banks and financial service organizations, *Corporate Social Responsibility and Environmental Management*, 12, pp. 73–87.

[15] Baret, P. and Chivot, M. (2012). Relevance of the Equator Principles as a tool for implementing CSR in the banking sector. AFC Congress, Grenoble, May 2012.

[16] Socially responsible investment.

The banks' strategy will then be built on the more or less proactive responses they provide to the expectations of their various stakeholders. Let's see how banks integrate these responses into their strategy.

Meeting Stakeholder Expectations: Integrating CSR into Bank Strategies

Integrating CSR into banks' strategies should enable them to better meet the expectations of their stakeholders.

Several authors have attempted to model the integration of CSR into bank strategy. Weber (2005) proposes five models of CSR integration:

1. As a reaction of banks following a specific event, either positive or negative;
2. As a new banking strategy: banks are adapting and adjusting their CSR strategy;
3. As a lever for value creation: the banks believe that while a CSR strategy presents risks, it also offers opportunities;
4. As a mission of general interest: the CSR strategy responds to public expectations within a public service rationale;
5. To meet customer requirements: mutual banks are founded on values that set them apart from the rest of the sector. Mutual banks can be linked to this model.

As mutual banks can be linked to the latter integration model, we will examine them using Weber's approach and see how they respond to SDG 17.

20.3 How Are Mutual Banks Responding to SDG 17?

At the customer level, the partnership's owner status has three effects[17]:

1. A compromise between economic and managerial power and democratic power.
2. Better risk control thanks to reduced information asymmetry.
3. Local roots and the establishment of trust-based relationships between management and employee-members.

This enables mutual banks, for example, to take greater risks to support their projects. In June 2006, for example, *Crédit Agricole Nord-Est* agreed to play the role of 'white knight' by buying the Taittinger champagne house, which had been put up for sale by the American company Starwood, in the face of several potential foreign buyers. Eighteen months later, the Taittinger family once again became the company's main shareholder, thanks to an LBO[18] and a capital increase also partly underwritten by a dozen "friendly families".

But it also shows that, as far as investors are concerned, the so-called "member banks" are not free from excesses,[19] which explains their current low share price.

In social terms, mutual banks are hardly any different from traditional banks. Etienne Pflimlin (Chairman of Crédit Mutuel from 1987 to 2010) himself acknowledges this: "We are a consumer cooperative, not a production cooperative; in our model, there is no difference from a traditional company in terms of employee management.[20]"

Nor are mutual banks at the forefront of environmental issues. Crédit Agricole only set up its first sustainable development team in 2002, following the Johannesburg Earth Summit. It only published its first sectoral policies in 2010, after the failure of the international conference in Copenhagen. Similarly, the regional funds only published their first Cooperative and Territorial Pact in 2013.

---

[17] Richez-Battesti, N., Gianfaldoni, P., Gloukoviezoff, G. and Alcaras, J. R. (2006). Cooperative banks and social innovations, *International Review of the Social Economy: Recma*, (301), pp. 26–41.

[18] Leveraged buyouts.

[19] To get out of a highly adventurous investment in the Greek bank Emporiki, Crédit Agricole agreed to lose almost 15 billion euros.

[20] "Les mystères de la gouvernance des banques mutualistes"—January 11, 2008 session of the Vie des affaires seminar at the École de Paris (untranslated).

Hybrid Models: Values Betrayed?

Since the Banking Act of 1984, France's mutual banks have faced a number of challenges: to grow, they have had to finance their international expansion and withstand competition from traditional banks (as well as from their peers). They have therefore adopted a so-called "hybrid" model, i.e. they have turned in part to the financial markets (for example, the Crédit Agricole group, whose central body, Crédit Agricole SA, is listed on the stock exchange, or BPCE with its financing and investment subsidiary, Natixis).

Has the rank-and-file member lost all influence? The example of Crédit Agricole shows that it knows how to make its voice heard. In 2002, Crédit Agricole's regional banks were in favor of a merger with Crédit Lyonnais, so they did not take kindly to Crédit Agricole SA's management refusing to take over the French state's 10% stake by mutual agreement at a price of 44 euros per share. This refusal led the State to put its shares up for auction, and in November they were bought by BNP Paribas at a price of 54 euros. As a result, in December, the Board of Directors of Crédit Agricole SA replaced Marc Bué as Chairman by René Carron, until then Chairman of the national federation and thus representative of the regional banks, and BNP Paribas launched a takeover bid at 56 euros per share, for a total amount of 19.5 billion euros. Similarly, but this time in the opposite direction, following the replacement of Georges Pauget by Jean-Paul Chifflet at the head of Crédit Agricole SA, it was the presidents of the regional banks who, in October 2012, secured the sale by the national structure of the Greek subsidiary Emporiki (acquired in 2006) to another Greek banking institution, Alpha Bank, for a symbolic one euro.

Towards a Risk of "Trivialization"?

As the trend towards mission-driven companies becomes more widespread, some companies with long-standing CSR commitments—in this case, mutual banks—run the risk of loosing their edge. It is therefore becoming increasingly important for these companies to anticipate changes in society's expectations, as well as regulatory developments, in order to continue to differentiate themselves, and for mutual banks to communicate more and better on the values that enable them to differentiate themselves today.

20.4 Summary and Conclusion

- The Agenda 2030 presents the targets to be achieved within the framework of the SDGs with a partnership approach (SDG 17) in which the cooperative movement naturally finds its place.
- The concept of CSR deals with issues of social responsibility (societal responsibility, beyond economic and legal obligations) and the level of responsiveness of companies to these issues.
- The relationship between the banking sector and CSR is not easy to identify. It manifests itself through internal operations, investments and loans (and is assessed in terms of direct or indirect impacts, or impacts induced by the value chain).
- As customer-owned entities, mutual banks are governed by democratic control, have a profit-sharing management system that gives them a long-term perspective, and are organized around a balanced governance system (the "double vision" rule). This enables them to strike a compromise between market pressure (economic power) and the satisfaction of social needs, better risk management (due to less information asymmetry) and a real local anchoring by taking into account the expectations of local stakeholders.
- Compared with shareholder banks, mutual banks are not systematically virtuous, either socially or environmentally.
- What's more, with growing social awareness putting pressure on the financial sector (among others), it's increasingly difficult for banks to stand out from the crowd. There is therefore a real risk of trivialization, and It is becoming essential for mutual banks to

communicate more and more about their values, about what sets them apart, in particular the partnership dimension that defines their contribution to sustainable development and the SDGs.

Activities

Questions for Discussion

1. Defining the stakeholder approach.
2. What's the difference between a primary stakeholder and a secondary stakeholder?
3. What's the difference between a contractual and a non-contractual stakeholder?
4. What are the company's six capital assets?
5. To which stakeholder does each capital correspond?
6. What are the main principles of cooperatives?
7. What are the main differences between mutual banks and capitalist banks?
8. Which stakeholders are represented on the board of directors in the hybrid cooperative model?
9. To which of Weber's (2005) integration models can mutual banks be linked?

True or False?

1. The term sustainable development was first officially used in the Brundtland Report published in 1987.
2. The term CSR was first officially used by H.R. Bowen in his book *Social Responsibility of Businessman* in 1953.
3. CSR is the transposition of sustainable development to the corporate level.
4. SDG 17 specifically concerns cooperatives.
5. Companies need to convince people that their performance is aligned with that of others.
6. Carroll's model distinguishes four types of responsibility (economic, legal, ethical and philanthropic).
7. Share capital represents the company's equity.
8. In a capitalist bank, the decision-making chain for loans lies between the sales department and the commitments department.
9. Customer-induced CO2 emissions account for the bulk of banks' total carbon footprint (scope 3).
10. CO2 emissions from IT data centers account for the bulk of banks' direct footprint (scope 1 and 2).

References

Allaire, G. (2019). The ambivalence of the commons. *Sustainable development and territories. Economics, Geography, Politics, Law, Sociology, 10*(1).

Antona, M., & Bousquet, F. (2017). *Une troisième voie entre l'État et le marché*. Éditions Quae (148 pp) (untranslated).

Coriat, B. (2020). *La pandémie, l'anthropocène et le bien commun*. Éditions Les Liens qui libèrent (untranslated).

Harribey, J. M. (2011). Le bien commun est une construction sociale. Contributions et limites d'Elinor Ostrom. *Political Economy, 1*, 98–112 (untranslated).

Hess, C., & Ostrom, E. (2007). *Understanding knowledge as a commons*. MIT Press.

Ostrom, V., & Ostrom, E. (1977). Public goods and public choices. In E.S. Savas (Ed.), *Alternatives for delivering public service. Toward improved performance* (pp. 7–49). Westview Press.

Perez, R., & Paranque, B. (2012). Elinor Ostrom: The commons and collective action. *Journal of Responsible Organization, 7*(2), 3–10.

Reich, R. (2019). *The common good*. Vintage.

Mermet, Q. (2019). Lorsque l'on parle d'entreprises à mission dans le cadre de la loi PACTE, s'agit-il de RSE? (untranslated) http://www.latribune.fr/opinions/tribunes/la-societe-a-mission-ce-n-est-pas-de-la-rse-835982.html

21 Asset Management and Sustainability. Industry and Regulation

Nicolas Bédu, Caroline Granier and Christophe Revelli

Putting Things into Perspective

In 2022, assets under management amounted to US$98,000 billion. According to BCG's 2022 Global Asset Management Report, this figure is close to the global GDP (estimated at $100,560 billion by the World Bank). One in three assets is managed in a sustainable manner, demonstrating the progressive integration of sustainable finance.

Global sustainable investment assets, 2016–2018–2020 (in thousands of billions of US dollars)

REGION	*2016*	*2018*	*2020*
Europe	12,040	14,075	11,995
United States	8,723	11,995	17,081
Canada	1,086	1,699	2,423
Australasia	516	735	906
Japan	474	2,180	2,874
Total (USD billions)	*22,839*	*30,683*	*35,301*

Source Global Alliance for Sustainable Investment report, 2020.

Like other economic players, asset managers seek to gain market share in a sector governed by specific regulations. This conception of the industry allows us to move away from the vision of investors as isolated entities, and to reveal that their activity is embedded in a set of relationships, rules, and practices. It is these relationships, rules, and practices that we examine here, in an attempt to assess the extent to which they can help achieve the SDGs.

Learning Objectives

- Identify the players in the asset management sector
- Situating the creation of SRI funds within the broader strategy of asset managers
- Analyze the extent to which the current functioning of the financial sector is an obstacle to achieving the SDGs
- Reveal the absence of any strong constraint on the part of the regulator regarding the orientation of savings toward financing the SDGs.

N. Bédu (✉)
ART-Dev, Université de Montpellier, Montpellier, France
e-mail: nicolas.bedu@umontpellier.fr

C. Granier
Chaire Energie Et Prospérité, Paris, France

C. Revelli
KEDGE BS, Marseille, France
e-mail: christophe.revelli@kedgebs.com

T. Lagoarde-Ségot (ed.), *Ecological Economics and Finance*,
https://doi.org/10.1007/978-3-031-71249-4_21

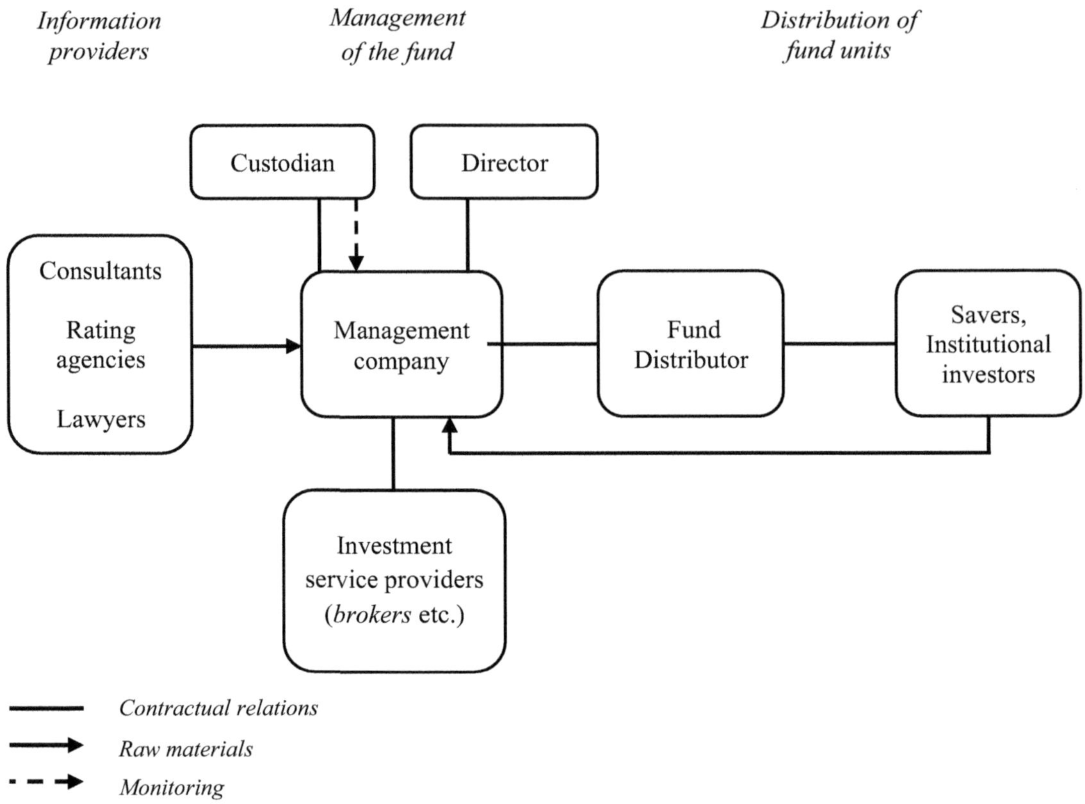

Fig. 21.1 The asset management industry (*Source* authors, adapted from Auvray et al. [2022])

21.1 The Structure of the Asset Management Sector Is Incompatible with the SDGs

Asset Management Players

Asset management, the core business of asset management companies, involves investing money entrusted by households, businesses, governments and institutional investors (insurance companies, pension funds, sovereign wealth funds) in securities or financial assets (shares, bonds, funds, etc.) according to the principles defined by financial theory (see Chapter 22). These companies may be independent entities or subsidiaries of banking groups, insurance companies or conglomerates. For example, Fidelity (a family-owned company) and Blackrock (a widely held company) are large, independent American asset management companies, while France's Amundi and Natixis Investment Managers are controlled by the banking groups Crédit Agricole and Société Générale in the case of the former, and BPCE in the case of the latter.

Around these asset managers are a series of service providers involved in the production process of these services and their marketing (see Fig. 21.1). Upstream, there are data providers, rating agencies, and consultants who collect information on assets. Asset managers can also call on investment service providers, known as brokers, who buy and sell the securities in the managers' portfolios on the financial markets and provide them with sector analyses. Downstream, financial services distributors sell products to end customers.

Competition in the Service of Short-Termism

A Sector Organized Around the Search for Yield

The asset management company's objective is to collect a high volume of savings, its sales depending on the number of management contracts signed. For the same risk, clients entrust the management of their savings to asset management companies that maximize their return (fiduciary responsibility of the asset manager). Each asset manager must therefore ensure that its financial performance does not deviate too far from that of its competitor. Offering a wide range of financial products with different risk/return profiles, in the manner of a supermarket, also makes it possible to meet the demands of a larger number of customers.

In order to offer a high return or a diversified range of financial products, the asset management company may call on suppliers (see Fig. 21.1), whom it selects on the basis of criteria such as production costs, product quality, technological content, or product sophistication. It may delegate the management of part of its portfolio to another manager, because the latter has specific expertise in a particular type of asset, or because it can benefit from economies of scale. Indeed, the fixed cost of gathering information for each security in a portfolio of securities decreases if a larger number of customers have invested in these securities.

This delegation or outsourcing of management mandates also concerns pension funds and insurance companies, which are increasingly turning to asset management companies. The result is increased competition between asset managers to obtain and renew these mandates, exacerbated by the centralization of savings in the hands of a few large financial companies. To avoid losing these 'big clients', asset managers are encouraged to focus on short-term returns. There is therefore a potential time lag between companies committed to the energy and ecological transition and asset managers. For example, the use of new, less polluting production processes may result in lower returns (higher costs, lower productivity, etc.) in the short term, with the gains (cost of reprocessing production waste, increased market share, etc.) only being achieved in the long term.

The Consequences of Financial Sector Concentration and Business Diversification: Too-Big-to-Fail Players

The centralization of savings is linked to changes in the financial sector since the 1980s, with financial liberalization and globalization. The free movement of capital has created competition on an international scale, and financial companies have adopted two strategies to cut costs. The first was to diversify their activities, giving rise to financial conglomerates. By positioning themselves in several business segments (banking, insurance, third-party savings management, etc.), companies benefit from economies of scope, particularly in distribution (marketing of banking, savings, and insurance products within the same network). The second strategy is to merge with or acquire competitors in order to achieve critical mass and benefit from economies of scale.

The implementation of these two strategies has led directly to a high degree of concentration in the financial sector. Asset management is currently dominated by large financial companies with over $1000 billion in assets under management. In addition, many banks now offer insurance products, and many insurance companies have developed bank lending activities: the risks have thus become similar for both types of institutions.

These large financial companies are identified by the Financial Stability Board as systemic players, as their failure could lead to the collapse of the international financial system. What they have in common is that they are large players with little replaceability, whose activities are complex and interconnected with those of other financial and international institutions. These characteristics explain why governments intervened during the 2007–2008 financial crisis to bail out banking and insurance conglomerates that were *too big to fail*. In the USA, for example, insurance giant AIG was temporarily nationalized. In France, the state orchestrated the merger between the *Caisse d'Épargne* and *Banques Populaires* groups, contributing to further concentration in the French banking market.

The dominant position of *too-big-to-fail* financial conglomerates in terms of assets under management and reputation enables them to exert a strong influence on the investment practices of other players. Substantial investments by these dominant players in responsible assets could therefore create ripple effects, i.e., changes in the investment choices of other players and play in favor of achieving the SDGs. The behavior of conglomerates would set the trend and pace of sustainable investment. Conversely, more conservative investment strategies on the part of these players would be likely to create inertia in the allocation of all available savings. The concentration of banking players would then act as a brake on investment in responsible projects.

21.2 Sustainable Finance, an Ecosystem Integrated with Traditional Finance

The Creation of SRI

The first so-called ethical investments appeared at the beginning of the xxth century, based on mainly religious and moral exclusion criteria, such as alcohol, tobacco, pornography, the sale of weapons, etc. These were subsequently replaced by strategies for integrating corporate social responsibility (CSR) and sustainability criteria into investment portfolios. This is the concept of Socially Responsible Investment (SRI), based on decisions taken on the basis of financial and extra-financial analyses.

The SRI market offers specific investment vehicles such as SRI funds. These vehicles take the form of mutual funds in the United States and undertakings for collective investment (UCIs) in Europe. Their main feature is that a buyer can sell the shares he or she has acquired at any time, thereby recovering liquid money.

The SRI market emerged in the 1980s with the development of social rating agencies which, in response to demand from financial players, made it possible to rate companies on their responsible and sustainable practices. This gave rise to environmental, social, and governance (ESG) criteria. The first social rating agencies (KLD in the United States, ARESE in France, now VIGEO, EIRIS in Great Britain, etc.) were able to rate issuers on these criteria and meet asset managers' demand for socially responsible investment portfolios.

Industrial Strategies to Support SRI Fund Offerings

The creation of SRI funds is part of the economies of scope strategy described above, which does not necessarily place the SDGs as the main objective to be achieved. SRI funds are just some of the products in the range of funds offered by asset management companies (equity funds, bond funds, diversified funds, money market funds, and index funds). These products respond to demand from clients who are more sensitive to climate change, or who are looking for new sources of financial performance (assuming that SRI enables better performance than traditional funds, which is not empirically proven). As long as not all asset management companies offer SRI funds in their range, and as long as not all customers want them, these funds will remain niche products.

Box 21.1. SRI fund management strategies

The *best-in-class* approach aims to select the best-rated companies in a sector in terms of ESG dimensions, according to criteria defined internally or by external rating providers (rating agencies, stock market indices). Exclusion (or *negative screening*) consists of excluding companies from certain business sectors, such as arms or fossil fuels, or those that do not respect human rights. The thematic approach favors companies that belong to the sustainable development sector, such as renewable energy production. In contrast to these approaches involving company selection, *activism* or *shareholder engagement* refers to the influence exerted by investors on a company's management through their voting rights and the tabling of resolutions. When this influence is exerted in favor of ESG dimensions, it comes under the heading of socially responsible investment.

Finally, the construction of portfolios for SRI funds and traditional funds is not all that different. It is still based on quarterly information, which favors short-term performance assessment, and therefore behavior geared toward the near future. Finally, it does not call into question the remuneration of fund managers, which remains based on the financial performance of the funds.

The Influence of External Stakeholders

Alongside national and supranational regulators, civil society and individuals can play an important role in transforming the ESG industry through their willingness to invest, their demand for financial products geared toward the SDGs, and citizen actions in favor of ecological and social issues (e.g., climate protests, movements against social inequality, etc.). Finally, in agreement with employees and civil stakeholders, the role of trade unions is also important, if only to push for the integration of sustainable investments into employee savings strategies (most often as a default choice for asset allocation).

Working closely with local communities, non-governmental organizations (NGOs) and associations can act as whistle-blowers when companies fail to meet their commitments to stakeholders. They also lobby political and regulatory bodies through targeted, hard-hitting communication campaigns. In this way, they force companies, public bodies, and financial players to consider the reputation effect as one of the most important to manage and control.

Like NGOs, specialist media (*Novethic, Care News, Sustainable World Media...*) and mainstream media (*The Financial Times, The Guardian, Le Monde...*) also play the role of whistleblowers, helping to promote and democratize sustainability issues in society.

Finally, the academic and scientific sphere can advance sustainability issues from a theoretical and managerial point of view, enabling it to induce behavioral changes in financial players (by advancing their practices), political and influential bodies (political commissions, etc.), or civil society. Teachers also have a key role to play in promoting education geared toward achieving the SDGs.

21.3 Is Financial Regulation Conducive to Sustainable Development?

Financial Stability and Transition

Taking climate change into account is a source of new risks for the financial sector, including physical risks, transition risks, and liability risks.

The increased costs and failures of financial players linked to the implementation of the ecological transition represent a threat to financial stability. For example, regulations heavily penalizing the holding of carbon-based financial assets would lead to a deterioration in the value of investments and in the level of liquidity of securities linked to the oil industry; financial assets (bonds, shares, etc.) issued by companies in this sector would become *stranded assets*. This depreciation would not be limited to securities offered by the oil industry but would affect securities issued by all carbon-intensive business sectors (transport, construction, etc.). It would also extend to sectors whose activities, apparently not very carbon-intensive, depend on those of carbon-intensive sectors (notably the energy sector), generating a cascade of positions. Ultimately, the entire portfolio of financial companies would be affected by the fall in value of the securities making up the portfolio, leading to significant financial losses and jeopardizing financial markets and financial stability. Financial players may therefore have an interest in slowing down the transition to avoid being confronted with this risk too quickly. At the same time, not penalizing high-carbon-emitting activities in the short term does not eliminate the risk of stranded assets in the longer term and increases the difficulty of exiting these activities due to dependence on them, to skills that are difficult to redeploy, etc. It would therefore appear that one of the constraints on financial regulation from an ecological transition perspective lies in the difficult balance between the risks associated with climate change and the imperative of financial stability.

Capital Requirements Based on a Short-Term Approach

The short-termism in investments mentioned above is partly the result of existing regulations. For example, prudential regulations applicable to insurance companies, which are based on those in force for banks, require the holding of sufficient capital to pay claims to policyholders, cover losses and remain solvent in the event of a crisis. The level of capital required depends on the amount of assets under management and their degree of risk. The riskier the assets, and the greater the number of assets in the portfolio, the more capital the insurance company needs. Two strategies are available to the insurance company to meet the prudential target: increase its equity and maintain its securities portfolio, or modify the composition of its securities portfolio so as not to have to recapitalize.

With the first strategy, increasing equity capital comes at a cost (interest and dividends). In practice, insurance companies frequently refinance themselves through subordinated debt, considered as quasi-equity. Creditors of this type of debt demand high interest rates, as the capital they have contributed is only repaid to the lenders after all creditors have been reimbursed, but before shareholders. In order to maintain a level of equity in line with prudential standards without increasing capital, insurance companies can reduce the dividends paid to their shareholders. However, this can lead investors to sell the insurance company's shares and turn to other companies offering higher returns.

Regarding the second strategy, due to the costs associated with the increased capital requirements of holding a high proportion of risky assets, the insurance company may decide to reduce the proportion of risky assets in order to avoid the cost of holding them. However, these assets often include long-run assets needed to achieve the SDGs.

Prudential regulations can have the effect of making investors averse to assets that finance the ecological transition.

A Non-Binding Regulatory Framework

As has been the case in the rest of the financial sector since the 1990s, regulation of sustainable finance relies mainly on *soft law*. This structuring of the regulatory framework is designed to take better account of the needs of players and give them the freedom to interpret the texts, leading to a certain delegation of regulatory power. Its effectiveness is based on market discipline, which is supposed to self-regulate behavior. This approach can be contrasted with the logic of constraint that characterizes hard law. Soft law tends to characterize international law, notably due to the absence of unified governance at the global level. The 'comply or explain' principle, which characterizes the corporate governance codes created in the second half of the 1990s, and which supports the creation of shareholder value, comes under soft law. Adherence to codes is guaranteed by the right to deviate from them. For example, Article 173 of the

French law on energy and ecological transition operates on this principle: financial players must inform their shareholders and customers of the way in which their investment policy takes ESG dimensions into account, and of the means they are implementing to contribute to the energy transition. If they fail to do so, they must publicly explain the reasons, which may prompt the management company's shareholders to sell their shares, and customers to withdraw their savings.

Regulatory practices such as guidelines and recommendations also fall into the category of soft law. For example, the Principles for Responsible Investment (PRI) aim to identify investors who integrate ESG issues into their investment process and to encourage savers, companies, etc. to entrust their money to these investors.

The emergence of standards and labels for financial products is also intended to encourage investment in sustainable projects. These are communication tools that inform customers about characteristics that are not directly observable; their aim is to create confidence among savers. These standards and labels can lead to their widespread adoption, as they intensify competition between players. Existing standards and labels include the European green bond standard, the French *Greenfin* label, and the FNG-Siegel label (Germany/Austria/Switzerland) for investment funds.

Like codes of conduct, standards, and labels are part of a logic of self-regulation and the reduction of information asymmetries with regard to sustainability. These measures are based on a pre-existing taxonomy of green or sustainable activities, enabling investors to identify companies implementing actions or practices in favor of the ecological transition and, more generally, to assess the green footprint of their securities portfolio.[1]

[1] In other words, a company carrying out an activity within this taxonomy is considered a green business.

Political Strategies as a Brake on Regulatory Change

The power of systemic players is reflected in the practice of revolving doors, where staff move from a position within a regulator or central bank to a position within a financial institution, and vice versa. As a result, regulatory changes are influenced by the lobbying of players seeking to protect their interests by blocking new regulation or participating in its development. For example, financial players reacted to plans to introduce a taxonomy of brown activities to accompany the taxonomy of green activities by arguing that such a taxonomy would represent a threat to their own survival and would also have negative consequences for financial stability (due to the presence of securities linked to fossil activities in their portfolios).

Promoting financial stability is not the only reason why governments in developed countries have created a favorable regulatory environment for large financial institutions. The aim of governments is often to promote the development of national players in an internationally competitive environment. Governments have no incentive to modify existing regulations if doing so would reduce the competitiveness of their 'national champions'.

The integration of environmental standards into financing practices will be the result of negotiations between financial institutions and regulators. Given the structure of the sector and the considerable power acquired by the major financial institutions, it is highly likely that any regulatory developments aimed at meeting social and climate challenges will have to take their interests into account.

21.4 Conclusion

- The creation of SRI funds is part of the conventional strategy of asset management companies to broaden the range of funds offered to savers and institutional investors, with the aim of gaining market share;

- The concentration of assets under management in the hands of a small number of players creates inertia in favor of yield-seeking strategies and product range expansion;
- The lack of a binding regulatory framework limits the channeling of savings toward financing the SDGs.

Activities

Questions for discussion

1. What is the role of social rating agencies?
   (a) Assessing the environmental character of company activities
   (b) Playing the role of prescriber by guiding investments
   (c) Produce and sell data to asset managers
   (d) Fulfill the three functions described above.
2. What is a socially responsible investment fund?
   (a) A fund approved by the public authorities
   (b) A fund whose sole objective is to achieve the SDGs
   (c) A fund whose securities portfolio is built on ESG criteria (environment, social, governance)
   (d) A socially responsible investment fund corresponds to the three types of funds mentioned above.
3. Who are the main investors in SRI?
   (a) Institutional investors
   (b) Wealthy individuals
   (c) States
   (d) Hedge funds
4. SRI funds are a type of fund offered by asset management companies such as Blackrock and Amundi to their institutional and retail clients, as part of a strategy to broaden their range. In addition to these funds, they also offer index funds, equity funds, sector funds, and more. What are the objectives of this range extension strategy?
   (a) Attracting savings to maximize assets under management
   (b) Attract savings to maximize fund management fees paid by institutional and retail investors
   (c) Integrating diverse concerns to attract institutional and individual investors
   (d) This strategy meets the three objectives mentioned above

Mini-case

You are the director of an asset management company operating in France and you want to implement a greening strategy for your fund range. You carry out strategic intelligence to establish your strategy. Break down your mission as follows:

a. Competitive intelligence
   Conduct a study of the French savings market (competitors, main customers, subscription, and withdrawal flows).
b. Regulatory watch
   What types of green or sustainable labels exist for funds in France? Are European UCITS directives compatible with a range of green funds? In which country will you domicile your green funds?
c. Supplier watch
   Which player(s) will you contact to obtain information on the ESG dimensions of the companies that will make up the portfolio of your green funds?

Reference

Auvray, T., Bédu, N., Granier, C., & Rigot, S. (2022). *L'Industrie de la finance*. La Découverte (untranslated).

22 Asset Management and Sustainability. Critical Perspectives and Reform Issues

Nicolas Bédu, Caroline Granier and Christophe Revelli

Putting Things into Perspective

"We've long been convinced that our customers, as your company's ultimate shareholders, will win if you succeed in creating sustainable value for all stakeholders."

Extract from Larry Fink's (Blackrock CEO) letter to CEOs (January 26, 2021).

In his annual letter to the CEOs of the companies in which *Blackrock*, the world's largest asset manager, is a shareholder, Larry Fink highlights the climate and carbon objective as the centerpiece of *Blackrock*'s strategy.

However, the reality is quite different. In 2020, *Blackrock* supported just three of the 36 resolutions on global warming at the annual general meetings (AGMs) of listed US companies. It voted against a shareholder resolution submitted to the AGM of Total (of which *Blackrock* is a 6.3% shareholder) calling on the company to align its activities with the Paris Agreement, and financed fossil fuel investments to the tune of €87 billion in 2019.

According to *ShareAction*,[1] 38 of the world's 75 largest asset management companies neglect "the ecological and social damage of their investments." In 2021, Tariq Fancy, former head of sustainable investment at *Blackrock*, denounced the asset giant's lack of action to integrate sustainability objectives into its own investment policies, openly using the term *greenwashing*.

This chapter presents the reasons for the incompatibility between the current financial model in asset management and the objectives defined by the Agenda 2030's SDGs, focusing on the material vision of sustainable finance. According to this vision, sustainability represents an additional risk to be mastered in order to maintain investment cycles and return targets, rather than the main objective to be achieved. We propose ways of transforming sustainable financial asset management into sustainable asset management.

N. Bédu (✉)
ART-Dev, Université de Montpellier, Montpellier, France
e-mail: nicolas.bedu@umontpellier.fr

C. Granier
Chaire Energie Et Prospérité, Paris, France

C. Revelli
KEDGE BS, Marseille, France
e-mail: christophe.revelli@kedgebs.com

[1] https://shareaction.org/wp-content/uploads/2020/03/Point-of-no-Returns.pdf.

T. Lagoarde-Ségot (ed.), *Ecological Economics and Finance*,
https://doi.org/10.1007/978-3-031-71249-4_22

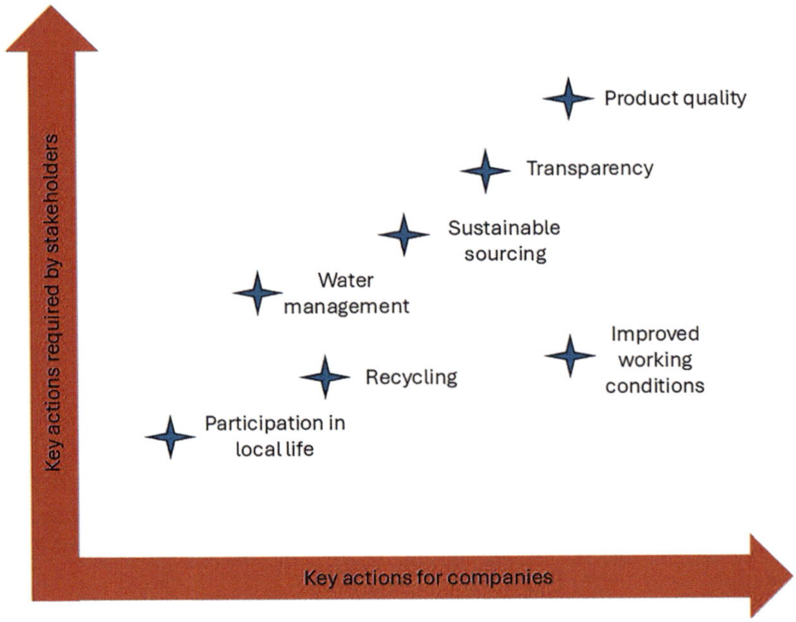

Fig. 22.1 Example of a materiality matrix (*Source* authors)

Learning Objectives

- Identify the theoretical incompatibilities of traditional asset management with the financing logic of the SDGs.
- Understand how the ESG data market works.
- Analyze the development of green/sustainable labels and benchmarks, while explaining their non-alignment with committed, transparent sustainable assets.
- Suggest ways of managing assets in a more resilient way, adapted to sustainability issues.

22.1 A Market Rooted in Financial Materiality

Investors are primarily interested in the financial materiality of an investment, i.e., everything that can have a significant impact on a company, its activities and its ability to create financial value for itself and its stakeholders. It is in response to these expectations that companies have integrated corporate social responsibility (CSR) issues, classifying and integrating them into two-axis matrices that enable them to identify the CSR/ESG (environment, social, and governance) indicators and practices that will benefit them (see Fig. 22.1). These matrices make it possible to "prioritize" sustainability themes, focusing only on those that will have an impact on stakeholders without compromising the company's economic and financial health (corresponding to the upper right-hand part of the matrix, characterized by high interest for both the company and its stakeholders).

These matrices then determine the practices of companies, which are themselves rated by the rating agencies. CSR/ESG policy is thus reduced to a matter of choice and arbitration. This reflects the fact that the financial stakes of economic and financial performance will remain the everything of any corporate strategy, in response to investor demand.

ESG ratings, for their part, are a new signal to investors to prevent the assets in their portfolios from being affected by environmental, social, governance, or business ethics scandals, and losing value as a result of falling stock prices (see Fig. 22.2).

Among investors, some are inclined to divest from companies involved in ESG scandals.

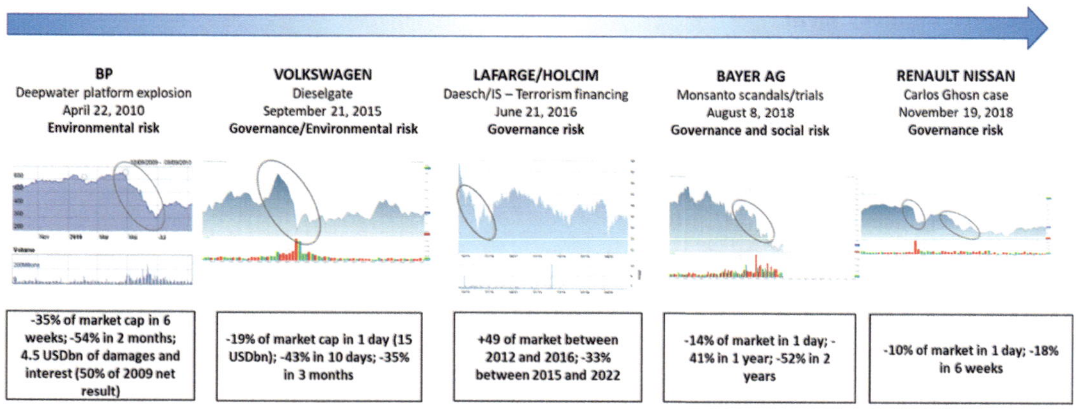

Fig. 22.2 Decline in share prices following ESG scandals (*Source* authors)

Others simply prefer to sell shares because they know the price will fall, which will run counter to their fiduciary responsibility (i.e. managing financial assets for the sole financial benefit of the investor).

22.2 Reasons for the Dichotomy Between Conventional Finance and Sustainability

The Incompatibility Between Traditional Asset Management and the Financing of the SDGs[2]

Since the seminal work of Markowitz (1952), asset management has been defined as the selection of securities using mathematics and statistics. It is based on a trade-off between two types of behavior: (i) a preference for assets with low but certain returns, or (ii) greater risk-taking in the hope of higher returns.

In this context, asset management consists of anticipating future events likely to affect the profitability of an investment, and choosing, from among investments offering the same average return, the one that minimizes the risk of not achieving it. However, this investment logic can hamper the financing of the SDGs, as it puts sustainable investments in competition with non-sustainable ones. To be financed, a sustainable project that is riskier than an unsustainable one must be more profitable. If its expected returns are equivalent, it must be less risky. Furthermore, the expected return on a risky asset is assessed by reference to a market standard. Indeed, the price of a risky asset depends essentially on market performance and the correlation between the profitability of this asset and that of other assets on the market. Consequently, the financing of responsible projects depends on the profitability offered by risky and "non-responsible" assets. Any increase in expected market profitability may discourage investment in responsible assets, since, mechanically, an increase in their profitability will be expected.

Added to this logic is the fact that an asset manager does not invest in a single asset, but in a portfolio of assets. A responsible or sustainable asset will be purchased if, for return levels equal to those of the portfolio, it reduces the portfolio's risk. On the other hand, if the risk of this asset is equal to that of the portfolio, it will only be purchased if its expected return is higher than that of the portfolio. On the other hand, devoting the entire portfolio to responsible projects is not optimal. Responsible projects are often more expensive and riskier than non-responsible ones. The financial securities

[2] For further details, please refer to the first edition of this book.

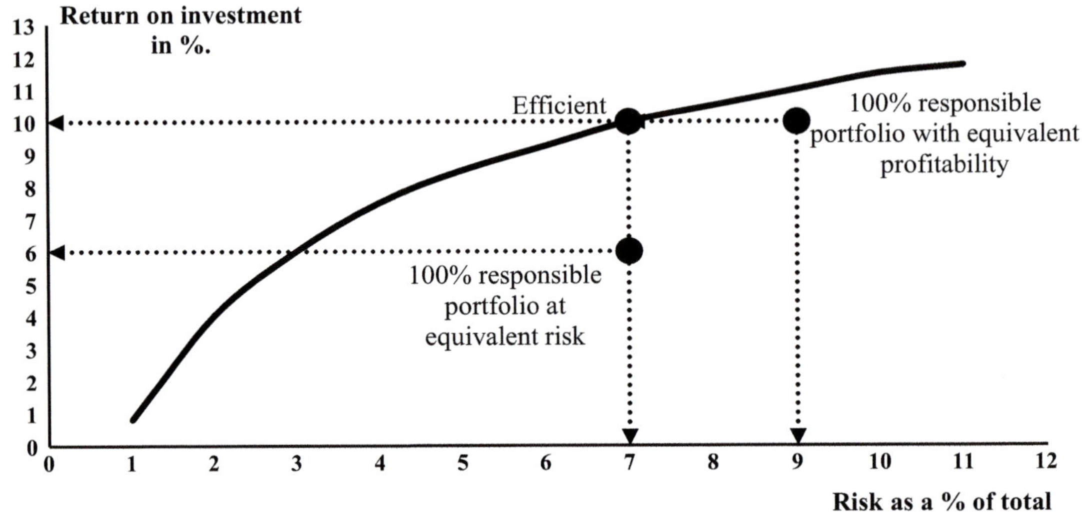

Fig. 22.3 Efficient frontier and responsible portfolios (*Source* authors)

issued to finance them will be more expensive than those used to finance "non-responsible" projects. Consequently, for the same level of risk, the return on financial securities associated with responsible projects will be lower. For an equivalent return, the investor will choose the least risky project and therefore the least risky financial security. If we extend this reasoning to a portfolio of securities, there is no incentive to hold 100% responsible portfolios (see Fig. 22.3).

Beyond the risk-return trade-off, transparency and disclosure of the information needed to make investment decisions are important in traditional asset management.

Portfolio management is therefore a matter of statistics, returns, anticipation of the future, and information. If we reason within this formalized framework, financing the SDGs must be compatible with the portfolio diversification strategy, which implies either an increase in returns on green assets or a reduction in their risks, or a reduction in returns on non-green assets or an increase in their risks.

Financing the SDGs also requires that natural assets be measurable, that it be possible to predict the occurrence of a climate event and its consequences in terms of returns on asset portfolios.

Finally, to perform these calculations, all information concerning the ESG behavior of companies and, more generally, extra-financial criteria must be available.

Sustainability and ecological sensitivity are therefore integrated into financial criteria, rather than the other way around. Finance aims to make everything measurable, by standardizing and comparing initiatives and projects. Yet, while ESG criteria can act as warning signals and encourage the divestment of brown or non-virtuous projects, issues such as the protection of biodiversity or education for all cannot be reduced to a risk-return trade-off.

Box 22.1: Is the Search for Financial Returns Compatible with Achieving the SDGs? The Case of Green Bonds

Like all sustainable finance products, green bonds aim to encourage investors to focus on financial assets behind which there are projects aimed at greater environmental and social sustainability.

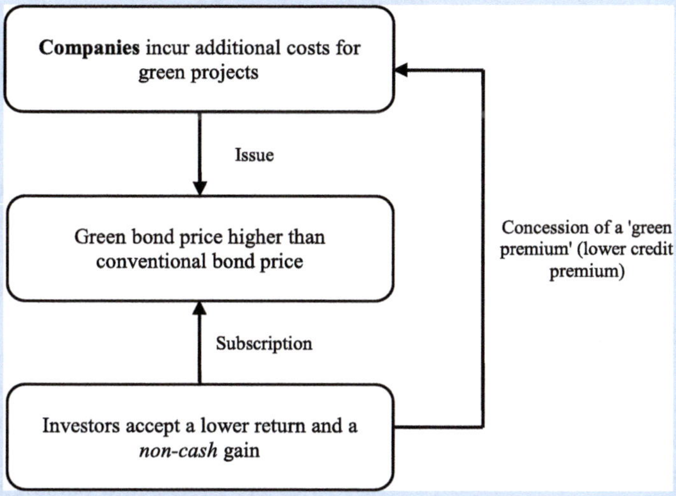

In reality, a green bond is no different from the conventional bond, and is subject to a similar risk/return trade-off. A company's credit risk is assessed on the basis of information drawn from its entire balance sheet, and not from the specific project to be financed. This means that conventional and green bonds issued by the same company will have a similar credit risk. What's more, the investor who buys a green bond is not in a position to oblige the issuer to carry out the green project.

Furthermore, there is no legal difference between the two types of obligation in terms of fiduciary responsibility. Given the impossibility of assessing the non-monetary benefit of financing a green project, paying a green premium to the issuer would be tantamount to failing to comply with the principle of fiduciary responsibility governing the asset management business. Other factors linked to the functioning of the bond market (for example, the way in which purchase requests are aggregated) explain the lack of distinction between the (issue) price of the two types of bonds (see Ekeland & Lefournier, 2021).

Finally, the ability of green finance to finance the SDGs depends on lowering the returns demanded by investors, which is impossible within the current finance framework. As long as brown projects are more profitable, or as long as it is not forbidden to finance such projects, the new green finance instruments cannot be effective.

An ESG Data Market Shaped for Investors

ESG rating agencies operate in an oligopolistic market. Indeed, recent years have seen an explosion in takeover, buyout, merger, and acquisition strategies among ESG rating agencies. The aim of these acquisition strategies is to offer a wider range of data by integrating ESG into their core focus. These include US players S&P Global, MSCI and Moody's, as well as Reuters and Bloomberg.

However, the questions companies have to answer to obtain an ESG rating are not always adapted to their situation. By administering the questionnaires mainly remotely, the rating agencies cut themselves off from the reality on the ground and the complexity of measuring ESG strategy. What's more, they don't provide companies with the support they need to respond effectively. ESG rating is therefore more akin to a trend that companies can display in their branding and communications to reassure and attract investors.

This practice, borrowed from traditional finance, has a number of drawbacks. Firstly, investors form their opinions on the basis of a summary of information, rather than all the information available. Secondly, the commensurability and additionality of extra-financial criteria are questionable. Finally, obtaining a good rating becomes the objective (rather than the extra-financial performance itself).

Benchmarking Reflexes

Like the labels discussed in Chapter 21, so-called green, ESG or sustainable stock market indices have seen record growth in recent years, in response to demand linked in particular to the growth in passive management. These indices enable investors not only to compare the performance of their financial products, but also to encourage companies to be included in them. All the world's financial markets and rating agencies now offer ESG stock market indices. Euronext France, for example, has its own range of indices: CAC 40 ESG and ESG 80.

According to Laermann (2016), around 86% of ESG financial centers and rating agencies offered ESG index ranges at the start of 2016, for a total of around 200 benchmark indices.

Recently, the European Union (EU) created two benchmarks, the *Paris Aligned Benchmark* (PAB) and the *Climate Transition Benchmark* (CTB), which can be used as labels certifying the quality of the process of integrating climate objectives in connection with the SDGs and the Paris Agreements for green indices.

However, these indices do not mean that all the companies in them meet climate targets: the PAB and CTB require an annual reduction in the carbon intensity of the index of 7%, which can be achieved by a balancing exercise consisting of integrating high-emitting companies with low-emitting companies in an investor's portfolio.

22.3 Proposals for Sustainable Asset Management

Speaking a Language of Strong Sustainability

The language used to define ESG criteria and measure sustainable performance needs to be redefined to rebuild a financial and asset management system committed to a strong sustainability principle.

For over 40 years, finance has deployed a plethora of quantitative tools from financial mathematics, stochastics and statistical modeling, creating a complex language. All risk metrics are rooted in a paradigm based on laws of chance and arbitrary probabilities of the future, themselves based on model assumptions of a risk-free real world, which is very quickly confronted with the uncertainty associated with geophysical and terrestrial constraints and the principle of finite resources and limited growth.

It is therefore necessary to rethink the language before thinking about impact measurement, and to integrate all the questions about ecological accounting and the inefficiency of IFRS (*International Financial Reporting Standards*) accounting models, which are part of a material vision of sustainability (what are the effects of sustainable actions on my company?) and which do not protect living and natural capital.

Internalizing ESG R&D

ESG data is mainly in the hands of players operating in an oligopolistic market. They use sustainability for monetary purposes and practice 'volume/cost' strategies. These strategies seek to maximize the volume of companies evaluated with minimum costs (and therefore analysts), and to sell the data at a very high price. They demonstrate an appetite for the financialization of the ESG data market.

One solution for restoring ESG data to its primary role is to internalize ESG research and analysis within asset management companies (buy-side analysts). The latter already have dedicated research and analysis teams, but far too few cover all the companies and institutions in their investment universe. Many asset management companies have implemented a hybrid strategy, bringing ESG research in-house while purchasing external databases. This internalization of research is also an excellent way of controlling data quality and developing diversified methodologies to obtain more robust and independent information. For asset management companies specializing in sustainable and responsible finance, or for smaller players, internalizing ESG R&D is a real challenge, as it can foster the emergence of new investment practices conducive to differentiation from the major asset managers, or even help identify new or more responsible companies.

Repositioning a Micro ESG Perspective in a Macro ESG World

One of the major problems for an asset manager managing hundreds, if not thousands, of billions of euros, US dollars, and hundreds of investment lines in his portfolios is certainly the lack of human and technological resources to engage in such an analysis process, but also the lack of time to devote to it.

Yet meeting stakeholders more regularly to convince them to systematically exercise voting rights at general meetings, to carry out ESG *due diligence*, to regularly update information through frequent audits, and to have the technological resources and information systems to enable these in-depth analyses can only improve overall fund performance. Alongside the need to adopt a more micro approach to investment, asset managers must inexorably return to the long, or even very long term to bring themselves up to speed with the SDGs, and in particular the climate indicators, and thus better align their investment decisions, risk-taking and profit objectives.

Engage in a Comprehensive Impact Process (Intentionality, Uniqueness, Commitment, Measurement)

The question of impact measurement is certainly the Gordian Knot for asset managers today. Regulations are pushing for more explicit, formal and identifiable traceability of impact.

When ESG performance improvement is a formal result of intentional action, the impact is the consequence on the SDGs and on society as a whole, which contributes to improving an overall indicator (see Fig. 22.4).

The notion of uniqueness of impact is a logical consequence of intentionality. Each investment is specific, depending on the characteristics of the company financed, its sector of activity, the geographical area, the local context, the stakeholders, the local regulations, the political risk… In a macro-investment logic and with a large volume of assets under management, it is complex, if not impossible, to implement systematic 'intentionality-uniqueness' strategies. However, that's where the ability to measure impact during investment and at the end lies.

The driving force behind this creation of impact lies in the commitment and intensive activism of shareholders. The creation of impact is generated throughout the investment process by a systematic presence with the company, whether through direct dialogue or the application of voting rights during resolutions at general meetings. The investor must set himself the goal of transforming the company in line with the impact objectives defined at the time of the contract. Of course, an asset manager who has invested in hundreds, if not thousands, of companies will not have the reflex to systematize this process, given that, once again, it is too costly in terms of resources to put in place. However, his power of influence is certainly a key to change (Table 22.1).

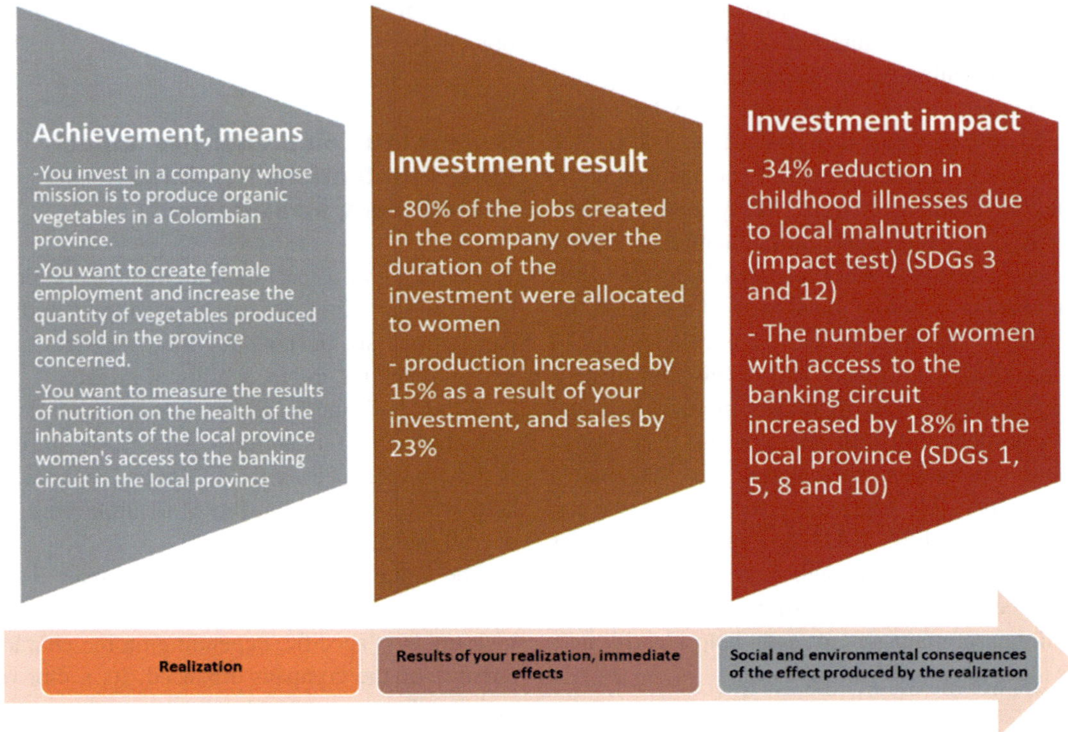

Fig. 22.4 The process of creating impact through intentionality

Implementing Ecosystem-Based Financial Reform

By default, a natural ecosystem is resilient because it combines four characteristics: diversity, risk compartmentalization, regulation, and recycling. Finance as practiced today cannot be defined as resilient, given the absence of the characteristics that define this principle. Financial regulation must therefore work on several fundamental points relating to resilient ecosystems:

- Eliminate the phenomena of concentration, trusts, mega-mergers between players and systems of competition, in order to restore diversity.
- Re-compartmentalize risks and prevent contagion by regulating unregulated markets and securitization.
- Allow the financial economy to circulate within the real economy, close tax havens, apply financial tax justice, and promote the circular economy.

Sustainable finance must then benefit from strong, binding regulation, moving from a voluntary, soft-law framework to a mandatory, hard-law framework that will also form part of a new ESG language.

Activities

Questions for Discussion

1. Define an optimized sustainable asset management strategy.
2. What are the solutions to be implemented at the asset management level to enable a significant contribution to the 2030 Agenda and to bridge the sustainable financing gap

Table 22.1 Resilience principle of a natural ecosystem adapted to current economic and financial systems (adapted from Dron, 2015 and Ulanowicz, 2009)

Natural ecosystem		Economic and financial systems	
Circulation of energy and matter		Circulation of money, liquidity	
Resilience	Regulation (conservation of viable limits, self-correction) = >predator–prey principle	Lack of resilience	Lack of self-regulation (no cap on credit limits, high-frequency trading, derivatives, amplifying compound interest logic)
	Degree of connection, compartmentalization, propagation buffering (risk isolation)		Decompartmentalized finance that connects all domains (accelerated by digital technology) in an instantaneous and universal manner; interconnected and non-diversified actors and systems aiming at the same resource, i.e. liquidity; money making everything that is exchanged substitutable through prices
	Diversity (lower risk of epidemics, no interdependence on resource needs)		Fewer and bigger players (concentration), adopting the same tools, the same rating agencies, the same behavior, having the same objectives (profitability, liquidity), being sensitive to the same signals
	Recycling (looping of cycles) = example: the soil feeds the plants, which die and feed the soil again (virtuous circle)		Actors absorb smaller ones; concentration phenomenon; circulation is not distributed in the network as in an ecosystem (flows are diverted from the investment systems of the real economy, whereas it is the real economy that feeds the financial sector) (non-virtuous circle)

identified by the United Nations and supranational bodies?
3. Do ESG ratings reflect the actual practices of the companies and institutions assessed?
4. Should a financial analyst who takes ESG criteria and the impact of the SDGs into account analyze companies under the same performance prism as analysts who do not integrate these issues? What specific measures should be proposed?
5. Are there ultimately two different asset management activities (with or without integration of SDG and ESG issues) or should sustainable development be a cross-cutting objective?
6. Are the risk assessment methods used in asset management adapted or not to issues related to the SDGs?

7. What is the objective of socially responsible investment (SRI) or "sustainable asset management"? (1: most important; 6: least important.)

Minimize the risk of bankruptcy and thus increase economic profitability
Provide investors with a wider range of products and diversify their assets
Changing the world of finance
Using ESG and the SDGs as levers for financial performance
Enabling the most virtuous companies to be valued and have access to capital
Enabling less virtuous companies to move toward greater ethics and sustainability

References

Dron, D. (2015, February). Pour une régulation écosystémique de la finance. *Annales des Mines - Réalités industrielles* (untranslated).

Ekeland, I., & Lefournier, J. (2021). *The green bond: Theory versus reality* (Working paper, Chaire Energie et Prospérité). http://www.chair-energy-prosperity.org/wp-content/uploads/2019/06/ObligationVerte_Ekeland_Lefournier.pdf

Laermann, M. (2016). *The importance of ESG ratings for socially responsible investment decisions: An examination from a market perspective* (Working paper available on SSRN), https://papers.ssrn.com/sol3/papers.cfm?abstract_id=2873126.

Markowitz, H. (1952). Portfolio selection. *Journal of Finance, 7*(1).

Ulanowicz, R. E. (2009). The dual nature of ecosystems dynamics. *Ecological Modelling, 220*, 1886–1892.

Regulating Practices: A Critique of Neoclassical Theory

23

Marc Lenglet

Putting Things into Perspective

Financial history is punctuated by crises which, cyclically and systematically, raise the question of how to regulate financial actors. Whether we are talking about the October 1987 crash or the *subprime* crisis (2007–2009), crises give rise to regulatory responses that are rarely satisfactory: firstly, because it's illusory to imagine that we can foresee the causes (and therefore the solutions to the problems posed, which are always dealt with a posteriori); secondly, because the theoretical framework mobilized to think about and deploy financial regulation proves inadequate.

Indeed, neoclassical finance is based on a limited number of assumptions (methodological individualism, rationality of actors, and market equilibrium) which seem to take for granted the idea that markets always work better if left to resolve their own crises. Although this approach has been largely deconstructed by the French Regulation School since the mid-1970s, it nevertheless remains dominant. Moreover, while international regulators are now more visible on the financial landscape, they continue to work from the same theoretical foundation: that proposed by neoclassical theory (the standard theory).

In this chapter, we show that another approach to regulation is possible. It would make it possible to use other analytical frameworks from the human and social sciences, and would seriously question what it means to "follow a rule" in the financial field. This would benefit not only the practice of regulation, but also the UN's sustainable development goals.

Learning Objectives

- Taking a critical look at the theoretical framework structuring financial regulation
- Understanding why standard theory offers an inadequate vision of financial regulation
- Defining alternative perspectives for the regulation of financial practices

23.1 The Institutional Emergence of Contemporary Financial Regulation

Since the end of the 1980s, with the general demutualization of stock exchanges, the regulation of financial markets has undergone a number of changes. Within the European Union, the development of financial markets is at the heart

M. Lenglet (✉)
NEOMA Business School, Mont-Saint-Aignan, France
e-mail: Marc.LENGLET@neoma-bs.fr

T. Lagoarde-Ségot (ed.), *Ecological Economics and Finance*,
https://doi.org/10.1007/978-3-031-71249-4_23

of the objectives pursued by the Economic and Monetary Union: the creation of a single currency calls for a common regulatory framework to underpin the deployment of homogeneous financial markets in the European area. The Financial Services Action Plan,[1] created in 1999, was born of the realization that Europe's financial markets were compartmentalized due to the excessive heterogeneity of national legislative systems. Since then, European institutions and market actors have been working steadily to harmonize the regulatory patchwork. Examples include the Regulation establishing a European Supervisory Authority (Regulation 1095/2010),[2] the Markets in Financial Instruments Directive (MiFID, revised 2014)[3] and the Undertakings for Collective Investment in Transferable Securities Directive (UCITS Directive).[4] Outside Europe, it is obviously other institutions that are responsible for drawing up the laws and regulations applicable to financial activities: it is nevertheless worth noting the role played by international institutions (such as the BIS and IOSCO, in particular) in disseminating these regulations which, despite the diversity of the subjects dealt with and the cultural areas concerned, remain homogeneous.

However, the diversity of issues that arise in the context of financial activities makes the practice of regulation much more complex than it might at first appear. Indeed, each market and each activity gives rise to specific practices, making it all the more difficult to take a global approach to the issues that arise in the day-to-day lives of market actors. Confronted with the reality of ordinary life, the abstractions of the law often leave operators at a loss, with complex questions constantly arising: "What type of information can be legally used in *this* specific context?", or "What does it mean to intervene in the market without unduly influencing prices?", or "Is the material organization of the trading room free from conflicts of interest?" These questions, which arise in the day-to-day running of financial activities, used to be debated within communities of practitioners. In the French context, it was the *Compagnie des agents de change* which, until its dissolution in 1988, ensured compliance with the principles of morality and competence required for financial intermediary activities.

The demutualization of stock exchanges has led to the emergence of new actors. In this respect, the French case is exemplary: following the transformation of the *Compagnie des agents de change* into the *Société des bourses françaises* in 1988, and after various institutional changes, the *Autorité des marchés financiers* (AMF) was created by the Financial Security Act of 2003.[5] An independent administrative authority charged with protecting investors and ensuring the smooth operation of financial markets, the AMF works hand in hand with various regulated functions that oversee financial activities within financial intermediaries: internal controllers, compliance officers, anti-money laundering, and anti-terrorist financing officers, and so on. As such, and beyond their supervisory and control missions, these actors contribute to the enactment of rules and standards in specific contexts that are never determined in advance.

23.2 Regulation as a Problem? What Standard Theory Cannot See

The institutionalization of financial regulation and the deployment of new actors charged with issuing standards and monitoring their adoption have not, however, led to the emergence of an alternative regulatory framework. The content of the canonical texts of neoclassical finance raises important questions in this respect: the question of regulation never appears directly in

[1] https://eur-lex.europa.eu/legal-content/FR/TXT/PDF/?uri=CELEX:51999DC0232.

[2] https://eur-lex.europa.eu/legal-content/FR/TXT/PDF/?uri=CELEX:32010R1095.

[3] https://eur-lex.europa.eu/legal-content/FR/TXT/PDF/?uri=CELEX:32014L0065.

[4] https://eur-lex.europa.eu/legal-content/FR/TXT/PDF/?uri=CELEX:32009L0065.

[5] Financial Security Act no. 2003–706 of August 1er 2003.

them, and none of them considers regulation as a *problem* to be constructed. The reason for this is that standard theory, based on the assumption that actors are rational, evolving in a context of known risks and perfect competition, postulates a state of general market equilibrium (see Box 23.1). Proponents of this approach also assume that financial markets are efficient—a property which, as such, guarantees the optimal allocation of resources. From this perspective, regulation should focus primarily on transparency and free access to information, management of conflicts of interest between actors, and differentiated investor protection. In this dominant paradigm, crises are seen as epiphenomena, with regulatory action aimed at re-establishing the system's 'natural' stability.

Box 23.1: Canonical Texts that Don't See Regulation as a Problem

Fifty years after their publication, and in spite of the controversies they generated, the texts that shaped standard theory are still used to justify financial market development choices. Today, they form part of the conceptual foundation shared by market actors and the institutions that set regulatory standards. They are still used in finance teaching programs at universities and business schools.

Fama, E. (1965). The behavior of stock-market prices. *The Journal of Business*, *38*(1), 34–105.

Malkiel, B. G. and Fama, E. (1970). Efficient capital markets: A review of theory and empirical work. *The Journal of Finance*, *25*(2), 383–417.

Markowitz, H. (1959). *Portfolio selection: Efficient diversification of investments*. John Wiley & Sons.

Sharpe, W. 1964. Capital asset prices: A theory of market equilibrium under conditions of risk. *The Journal of Finance*, *19*(3), 425–442.

This work played a major role in structuring neoclassical financial theory, for which the following three assumptions remain essential (Rainelli-Le Montagner, 2006, p. 23):

- **Methodological individualism,** which postulates the possibility of analyzing collective phenomena on the basis of individuals.
- **The rationality of actors**, in the sense of the rationality of *homo œconomicus:* an actor who maximizes his satisfaction by making the best use of his resources.
- **General market equilibrium**, which results from the first two hypotheses.

Moreover, standard theory is highly skeptical of 'excessive' regulation. While recognizing the possibility that actors may develop immoral, unethical or simply fraudulent practices (but without really seeking to *describe* these practices), proponents of standard theory do not see regulation as an ideal solution. They assume that an incentive-based approach is a better way of ensuring proper market regulation. This perspective, which could have been criticized by studies examining the role of laws, rules and other norms specific to the financial sector, has never really been called into question.

This highlights an important semantic distinction that is all too often overlooked: *regulating* may be understood as "ensuring the sustainability of a system, maintaining control over the evolution of a phenomenon" or as "enacting rules and ensuring that they are respected"). Neoclassical financial theory, while purporting to provide a solution to the problem of financial market regulation (i.e., methods for ensuring the sustainability of market equilibrium) *in abstracto*, is at a loss when it comes to defining the specific rules to be put in place *in concreto*. Indeed, knowing which practices to favor or, on the contrary, which to prevent requires attention to context, as well as an understanding of organizations that takes account of their social and cultural heterogeneity. Mainstream financial theory is unable to address these issues, for want of adequate conceptual tools.

23.3 An Inadequate Epistemic Framework

The main problem facing standard regulatory theory is what we call an inadequate 'epistemic framework' (see Box 23.2). On the one hand, standard theory cannot understand the problem of regulation: its conceptual tools do not allow it to make sense of what happens at the level of actors, in real and distinct situations. On the other hand, standard theory is an obstacle to the development of new regulatory frameworks aligned with sustainable development objectives. This section develops this argument by focusing on three specific SDGs: the pursuit of effective, accountable and transparent institutions at all levels (SDG 16.6), inclusive decision-making (SDG 16.7) and the development of multi-stakeholder partnerships (SDG 17.17). These three objectives should enable market actors (investors, intermediaries, regulators) to improve the functioning of financial markets, while taking into account the interests of the stakeholders concerned.

Box 23.2: What is an Epistemic Framework?
By epistemic framework, we mean the framework of knowledge that a given theoretical field is capable of producing. To say that standard theory does not have an adequate epistemic framework to make sense of the problem of regulation means that the type of knowledge that standard theory can produce is not adapted to the type of problem to be solved.

In this respect, Rainelli-Weiss (2015, p. 84) clearly shows that financial regulation is faced with an "epistemic problem": the "social imaginary created around the market world", which has given a preponderant and somewhat disproportionate place to the theory of efficiency, has generated the following situation: "Whole swathes of the financial system are today subject to a deficit of practical as well as theoretical and academic knowledge. This prevents the regulator from confronting the experts [...], who generally represent private interests and have a wealth of tacit experience of how these markets operate, with tangible facts, systematic knowledge and therefore potentially capable of introducing contradiction and fostering public debate."

This inability to address the question of how rules are received by actors is essentially due to the gap between, on the one hand, the concern for modeling (using neoclassical financial economics) and, on the other hand, the use of these models to develop the normative framework required by financial activities—even though these activities are first and foremost rooted in socially situated practices, which are by essence inapplicable to financial theory. Standard theory therefore lacks the means to describe what goes on in practice, as it is far removed from the perspectives deployed by social sciences such as anthropology, sociology, or financial history. These three perspectives take as their object of study the ordinary lives of those who literally "make" the markets. Whether we are talking about commercial offers, financial analyses, or asset valuations, market actors share practices, ways of interpreting reality, and moral codes. These different cultural aspects cannot be ignored.

Given this, how can the three above-mentioned SDGs be translated into the practices of market actors? Probably by starting to describe, and thus recognize, the problems these actors face in their day-to-day activities. This would give us access to the difficulties encountered in the course of market activities, and sometimes even to the ethical dilemmas with which traders, analysts, managers, and other investment bankers are regularly confronted. These dilemmas, which do not necessarily pose intractable problems, could be seen for what they are: practical impasses that more often than not give rise to differences of interpretation. Yet it is only when a rule is interpreted, i.e. *put into practice*, that it takes on its full meaning. Questioning what it means to follow a rule in context therefore means making room for precise, situated, conflictual descriptions, rich in their diversity—in short, it means problematizing regulation: making the actors concerned aware that other perspectives are possible.

Thinking about the issue of regulation in relation to the SDGs would thus mean creating a framework that allows for the expression of divergent points of view and modes of interpretation of the rule according to the situations encountered by each actor concerned. Decision-making that would be more inclusive (SDG 16.7) and involve a greater number of actors (SDG 17.7) would probably also lead to greater efficiency, institutional transparency and, ultimately, greater accountability (SDG 16.6).

23.4 Three Specific Problems

As we explained above, the epistemic framework used by standard theory is inadequate: it lacks the conceptual tools needed to highlight and discuss the specific and very real situations that market actors face in their ordinary practices. The materiality of market mechanisms is at the forefront of these difficulties. The dominant approach develops models and tools that provide access to financial reality but underestimates the complexity of this reality. The limits of the neoclassical approach to regulation are manifold. Broadly speaking, we can distinguish three levels:

- Firstly (a), the *structural advance of practice over theory*: the appropriation of practices by market actors means that it is always too late to assess any aspect of a routine, even when it has been expressed in a legislative framework. The law, translated into detailed procedures, always needs to be interpreted, and this is done in practice. These elements are not taken into account in standard theory, whose object is reduced to abstract concepts.
- Secondly (b), the *absence of any socio-political consideration in the theorization of markets*: this can no doubt be understood from the point of view of financial theory, but it cannot be satisfactory, since it is precisely financial theory that provides the main framework for the elaboration of regulation. This incapacity also refuses to see the extent to which financial markets are, above all, diverse social constructs, structured by formal and informal institutions, more or less recognized, accepted and codified by agents.
- Finally (c), the *monolithic nature of the concepts used*: methodological individualism (whereas a market is made up of relationships between agents), the supposed rationality of agents (whereas this is lacking in many situations) and the general equilibrium of markets (whereas this equilibrium is the result of a construction and cannot be considered intrinsic) are the dominant principles on the basis of which neoclassical financial theory claims to structure the reality of markets (see Box 23.1).

Standard theory is intellectually flattering and undoubtedly convenient for actors as a shared language, but it does not address the regulatory challenges facing market players. The recurrent use of these concepts, for example during consultations with market actors as part of the legislative and regulatory effort, does not allow other approaches to have their say.

23.5 A *Perspectivist* Alternative

To remedy these shortcomings, we develop below the idea of a *perspectivist* approach to regulation. Perspectivism refers to the idea, developed in various philosophical doctrines, that reality is made up of the sum of the perspectives that can be developed on it (see Box 23.3). This approach is now commonplace in many areas of the social sciences and is also indirectly present in stakeholder theories. However, it has not yet found its place in financial theory.

Table 23.1 Two approaches to regulation

	Standard theory	Perspectivist approach
The role of the actors	Neutrality of actors, conceived as rational individual agents	Involvement of actors, conceived as the authors of a specific perspective necessary to the construction of reality
Relationship to reality	There is an objective reality that is independent of the actors	Reality doesn't exist apart from the actors who make it up
The role of context in rule interpretation	Minor or almost non-existent	Central
Interpretation(s) produced	Unique and structured by neoclassical theory	Multiple and structured by each point of view

Box 23.3: What is Perspectivism?

Perspectivism generally refers to a set of philosophical doctrines for which reality is constituted by the sum of possible perspectives—in other words, reality is expressed through the multitude of points of view we have on it. This idea was notably developed by Leibniz in the XVII th century, then by Nietzsche in the XIXth century, before being more widely disseminated in various social sciences (anthropology, sociology, history). Advocates of perspectivism reject the idea that there can be an objectivity of reality outside given situations—whether by situation we mean a specific cultural context, or the expression of a necessarily subjective point of view.

Unlike the neoclassical approach, a perspectivist approach to regulation would not rely on a dominant explanation supported by a single theoretical framework. On the contrary, a perspectivist approach to regulation would recognize that understanding, appropriating, and implementing a rule necessarily implies acknowledging the situated, partial and biased character of the actor who describes, enunciates, or deploys it (see Table 23.1). Contrary to the dominant approach, which is based on the postulate of an objective reality, the perspectivist approach to regulation accepts the idea that both the context and the nature of the actors involved play a decisive role in the act of regulation. This is not, of course, to give in to relativism, but rather to recognize that there can be no epistemic absolutes in regulation—and that the expression of perspectives lies at the heart of the ethical dilemmas that arise in the normal course of financial activities. Access to these dilemmas requires descriptions, each offering a possible interpretation of the meaning of a rule in a given context: it is then up to the actors concerned to accept the interpretations thus co-constructed.

The dominant epistemic framework, which today constitutes the main (not to say only) reference point for financial actors, locks up epistemic space (see Box 23.1). It prevents the expression of conceptual and practical alternatives to the problems posed by the regulation of financial activities. Questioning the practical consequences of what it means to 'follow a rule', by redeploying some of the existing mechanisms, would instead make it possible to identify multiple alternative perspectives, which today are neither heard nor developed. Deploying a different perspective on regulation would, in particular, enable access to the SDGs mentioned in this chapter: for there can be no effective, accountable and transparent institutions (SDG 16.6), inclusive decision-making (SDG 16.7), or development of multi-stakeholder partnerships (SDG 17.17) without recognition of the stranglehold of standard theory on the imagination of market actors—a theory which we have seen is incapable of thinking through the problems to which regulation must be able to respond.

However such a change of perspective on financial regulation cannot be achieved without a major revision of the epistemic framework from which the activity is thought and deployed. This change, analogous in every respect to that required by the transformations linked to climate change, calls for a Copernican revolution on our part, which must undoubtedly begin in the academic field.

23.6 Conclusion

- This chapter shows that standard theory offers an extremely limited approach to financial markets, which are regarded as systems in equilibrium, with regular crises considered as epiphenomena.
- Several approaches have criticized this vision of markets, notably by giving greater importance to the question of legal systems. Yet these approaches remain dependent on the epistemic framework deployed by neoclassical finance, due to the adoption or redeployment of its concepts.
- On the contrary, taking the SDGs into account implies deconstructing the dominant financial theory and developing an alternative epistemic framework—which we have very briefly called 'perspectivist': more inclusive, open to differences, and rooted in the description of the practices of all those who make markets.

Activities

Questions for Discussion

1. To be as effective as possible, should financial regulation be based on a single paradigm?
2. Why does standard theory contain so little on market regulation?
3. What is the main objective of the perspectivist approach to regulation?
4. What are the advantages of perspectivism in financial regulation?
5. What are the limits of perspectivism in financial regulation?
6. How does the perspectivist approach help to achieve the SDGs 16.7 and 17.17?
7. Why is the compliance function important?
8. Why is attention to context important in regulatory practices?
9. Can all financial practices be regulated?

Mini-case

Visit the AMF website (https://www.amf-france.org) and read the sections presenting the AMF. Then answer the following questions:

1. What elements of the vocabulary used by the AMF explicitly refer to the dominant paradigm (standard theory)?
2. Which of the three SDGs mentioned in the chapter does the AMF refer to?
3. How, in your opinion, could the AMF rely more on these three SDGs? Argue with specific examples.

References

Rainelli-Le Montagner, H. (2006). Financial theory on ethics: Reasons for silence. *Finance & the Common Good*, *24*, 20–27.

Rainelli-Weiss, H. (2015). Problèmes et enjeux de la régulation financière. *Cités*, *64*(4), 77–86 (untranslated).

Further Information

Chambost, I., Lenglet, M., & Tadjeddine, Y. (Eds.). (2019). *The making of finance: Perspectives from the social sciences*. Routledge.

Lenglet, M. (2017). Coding, decoding, recoding? Normative orders and the stakes of financial regulation in the era of algorithmic trading. *Revue Française De Gestion, 43*(269), 147–162.

Lenglet, M. (2021). Algorithmic finance, its regulation and Deleuzian jurisprudence: Some remarks on a necessary paradigm shift. *Topoi. International Journal of Philosophy, 40*(4), 811–819.

Lenglet, M. and Taupin, B. (2017). The rise and fall of the compliance function. A perspective on internal control in banking and finance. *Comptabilité—Audit—Contrôle*, *23*(1), 11–40.

Ethics, Risk and Sustainability: A Theological Perspective

24

Elias Erragragui

Putting Things into Perspective

In his book *Commerce des promesses*, Giraud (2014) reminds us that a claim is never just a promise of future payment. Even if we take all possible precautions and guarantees to ensure the debtor's solvency, we cannot absolutely guarantee the occurrence of a future due date, which is by nature *uncertain*. Faced with this obvious fact, the concept of "risk-free assets", the cornerstone of modern financial theory, raises epistemological and ethical questions. Assuming the existence of risk-free assets is tantamount to asserting that the future is predictable, and that creditor default scenarios are simply eliminated from the realm of possibility. In a perfectly transparent deterministic world, where the future is known with certainty, ethics would be of little importance. However, the uncertain nature of economic activity calls for a normative reading of economic risk. Islamic finance provides a framework for the representation of economic risk, shaping behavioural archetypes and modes of regulating market exchanges that differ from the conventional framework. In Islamic economic morality, risk is seen as an unavoidable social cost, a kind of 'common evil', comparable to Ostrom's notion of the 'common good'.[1] This common evil must be assumed collectively and equitably, rather than being the object of systematic transfer or rejection—the risk being that the illusion of a risk-free asset may bias long-term investment decisions to the detriment of the SDGs.

Learning Objectives

- Understanding the function of risk-free assets in modern finance
- Critically examine the theoretical underpinnings of risk-free assets
- Analyse the role of social representations in shaping the risk avoidance ethic
- Examine the contributions of traditional representations (philosophical and theological) linked to the remuneration of risk
- Understanding the implications of the risk-free rate concept in the evaluation of sustainable investments
- Discuss the contribution of Islamic finance to the development of alternative models

E. Erragragui (✉)
Al Akhawayn University, Ifrane, Morocco
e-mail: e.erragragui@aui.ma

[1] Ostrom, E. (1990). *Governing the commons: The evolution of institutions for collective action*. Cambridge University Press.

T. Lagoarde-Ségot (ed.), *Ecological Economics and Finance*,
https://doi.org/10.1007/978-3-031-71249-4_24

24.1 Risk-Free Assets

The Relationship Between Risk and Profit

Risk critically shapes the field of financial decision-making, enabling investors to weigh up the prospects of expected gains. The risk incurred and the expectation of gain are communicating vessels that structure the representation of financial exchanges (see Box 24.1), so that the financial sector appears as a centre for the processing, purification and distribution of risk (Walter, 2010).

Box 24.1: The Risk/return Trade-off

Let us suppose you have 100 euros to invest and you can choose between two projects run by two companies, A and B, both of which promise you a 10% return. However, company A is very solid financially, while company B is much more fragile. Why would you invest in company B and take on more risk for a comparable return?

To convince you to invest with it, Company B will have to offer you a higher return than Company A, say 15% instead of 10%.

The investment trade-off can be summed up as follows: more risk means more return.

The introduction of the risk-free rate as the basis for assessing the profitability of any investment has changed traditional representations of risk, making it possible to conceive of the decoupling of profit and risk.

Genesis of Risk-Free Assets

Theoretically, a risk-free asset is defined as a financial security that provides the same payment regardless of the state of the world. In his seminal paper on the capital asset pricing model, Sharpe (1964, p. 431) defines a risk-free asset as one whose "standard deviation of return is zero and whose expected return is equal (by definition) to the pure interest rate". In other words, it is predicted that the issuer of such an asset will always be able to meet its financial obligations. The notion of the risk-free rate, described as a "mysterious object",[2] was originally a mathematical construct devoid of any economic foundation. In practical terms, risk-free assets are assimilated to information-insensitive assets, used as collateral and based on a perception of security independent of any fundamental analysis. Since Mehra and Prescott published their article 'The (equity) risk premium—a puzzle' in 1985, practitioners have been using the government bond rate of the most developed countries[3] as a proxy for the risk-free rate. At the end of 2022, the global stock of risk-free assets was estimated at $69,500 billion. The use of credit ratings issued by trusted third parties leads to a concentration of issuers in the most visible and informationally efficient markets, foremost among which is the United States, whose sovereign debt alone accounts for over 43% of the stock of sovereign securities (see Fig. 24.1).

Trusted Third Parties and Conflicts of Interest

The problem with credit ratings is that they all emanate from private bodies subject to conflicts of interest. The absence of fundamental analysis targeting issuers and the unreliability of trusted third parties create an illusion of security, which is the "original sin" behind the concept of risk-free assets (see Box 24.2).

Box 24.2: Dagong's View of Risk-Free US Assets

Doubts about the bias of US agencies have been expressed by some international observers, who question the viability of US debt. In the aftermath of the

[2] El Karoui,N. (2012). Un univers risqué-neutre, *Risques*, N° 92 (untranslated).

[3] Ten years in France for the OAT or in Germany for the Bund, and 30 years in the United States.

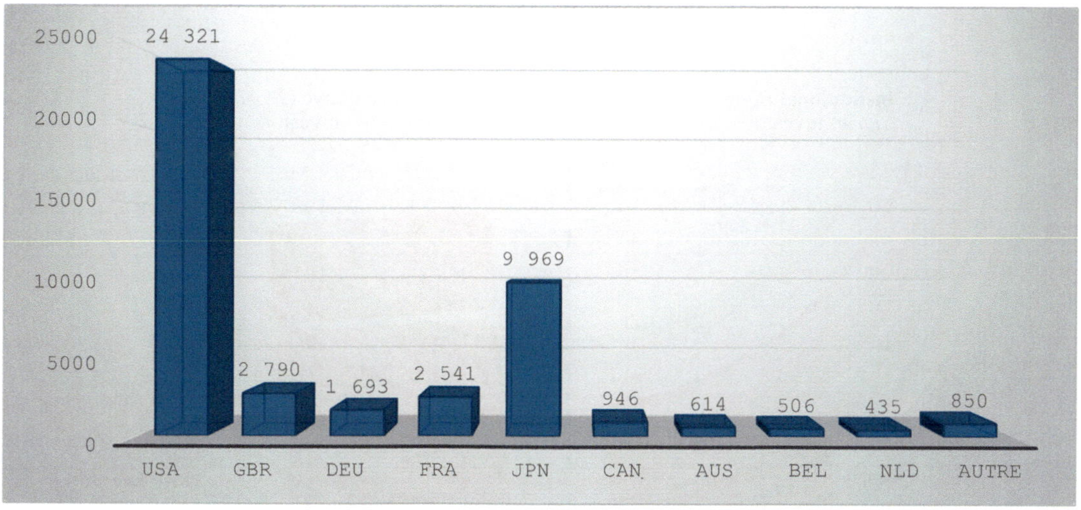

Fig. 24.1 Geographical breakdown of sovereign debt on Q2 2021 (in billions of dollars) (*Source* World Bank, 2021)

2009–2012 sovereign debt crisis, Chinese rating agency *Dagong* expressed doubts about the sustainability of US debt in light of the federal government's severe fiscal imbalances. In particular, *Dagong* noted that between the start of the *subprime* crisis in 2008 and the end of 2012, US debt had risen by 60%, while tax revenues had fallen by 2.9%. The significant depreciation of the dollar caused by the Fed's money creation policy prompted *Dagong*, back in 2013, to downgrade the US credit rating to A -, then to BBB+in 2018 following a drop in tax revenues.

Theoretical Implications of Risk-Free Assets

Risk-free assets are the starting point for many models used in finance to calculate the profitability of a stock or industrial project. Since the seminal work of Markowitz (1952), risk-free assets have been used to assess the profitability of risky portfolios. The principle is that the return on a "risky" asset cannot be lower than the return on a risk-free asset. The assumption is that the greater the additional risk, the higher the excess return on the asset. This principle is one of the foundations of financial theory. The *Capital Asset Pricing Model* (CAPM), introduced by Treynor (1961, 1962), Sharpe (1964) and Lintner (1965), provides an estimate of the rate of return expected by the market for a financial asset as a function of its exposure to the risk of the market portfolio (see Box 24.3).

Box 24.3: The CAPM

The CAPM is based on the assumption that the total risk of a security is divided between systematic risk, which is unavoidable, and non-systematic risk, which can be reduced through diversification. A stock's total risk is measured by its standard deviation, while its systematic risk is measured by its beta, which measures the stock's co-movement with the market:

$$\beta i = \mathrm{Cov(Ri, Rm)/Var(Rm)} \quad (24.1)$$

where Cov(Ri, Rm) is the covariance of stock (Ri) and market (Rm) returns, and Var(Rm) is the variance of market returns.

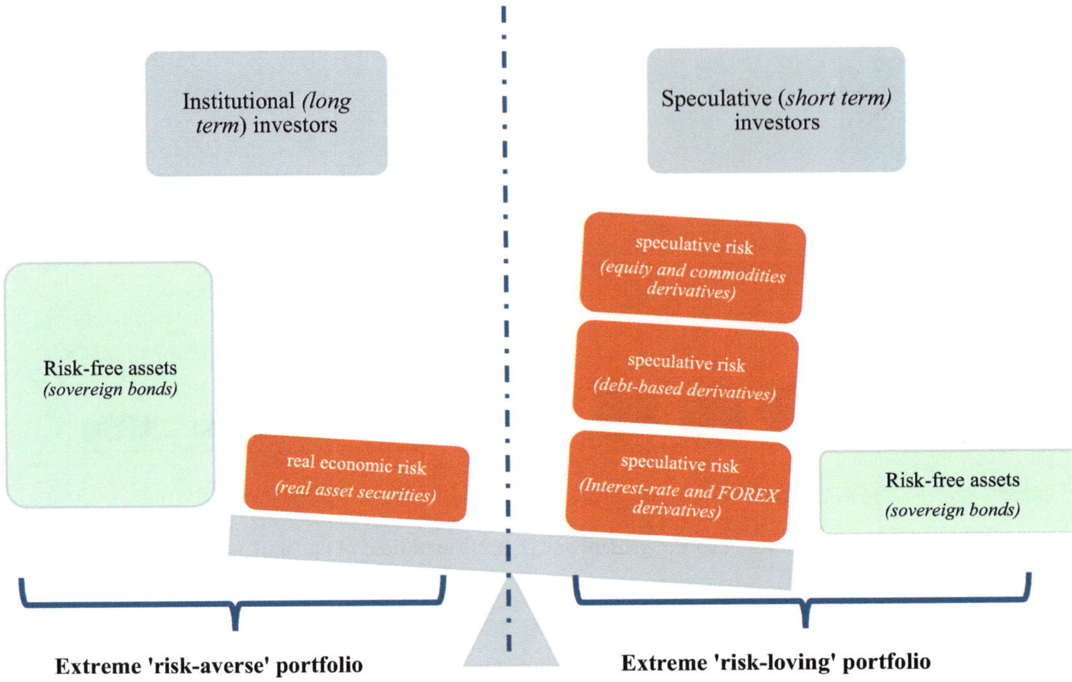

Fig. 24.2 Institutional investors' low appetite for real economic risk Fig. 24.3—institutional investors' low appetite for real economic risk (*Source* author)

The CAPM's "expected return" is then a function of:

- the measure of the asset's systematic risk, i.e. the non-diversifiable risk noted βi (asset beta);
- the expected market return, noted E (Rm);
- of the risk-free interest rate (usually government bonds), denoted Rf.

$$E(Ri) = Rf + \beta i.(E(Rm) - Rf) \quad (24.2)$$

In Eq. (24.2), [E (Rm)−Rf] is the risk premium, i.e. the additional return required by investors when they buy a diversified market portfolio, rather than the risk-free asset.

According to CAPM, investors are rewarded on the one hand according to the opportunity cost (Rf) of investors who would have bought risk-free bonds, and on the other hand in relation to the risk premium (βi (E (Rm)−Rf)) associated with the security. One of the main implications of CAPM is that it establishes the possibility of a permanent risk-free return as the basis for arbitrage in a financial portfolio.

Towards an Ethics of Risk Denial

The risk-free asset hypothesis initially poses an epistemological problem that runs counter to scientific knowledge, which distinguishes between events with zero probability and negligible events. Financial science voluntarily assumes this mathematical approximation for modelling purposes. Walter (2010) speaks of a "conceptual deficiency" that has the effect of eliminating the understanding of risk to the point where financial practitioners believe that risk can be eliminated. These shortcuts in logical reasoning highlight the ethics that presided over the formation of modern financial science, and in particular *homo economicus*' desire for an almost mechanical mastery of a probabilistic future. This 'original sin' translates into a dissociation between risk and return. As recent practices such as synthetic securitization[4] and the use of hedging instruments demonstrate, risk management is legitimized by the principles of risk avoidance and systematic risk transfer. This normative choice, made to the detriment of other principles such as risk pooling, illustrates the ethical positioning chosen by the designers of these tools.

The Arrow–Debreu model of competitive equilibrium (Arrow & Debreu, 1954), however, states that efficient sharing of economic risk requires that it be distributed among participants according to their risk tolerance. Setting a risk-free asset as the benchmark for measuring returns on all other assets, including equity returns, has the effect of introducing an artificial floor into the price structure of the real sector of the economy and into all financial decisions. The resulting system has become one of risk transfer or *risk avoidance,* rather than *risk sharing* which would allow for healthier dilution.

The permanent trade-off in favour of risk-free assets therefore generates a negative externality with regard to the real economy, which is inherently associated with risky assets. The perverse effect of the illusion of security produced by risk-free assets on institutional investors is illustrated by their strong preference for sovereign bonds to the detriment of real economy assets (equities, private debt) (see Fig. 24.2). Yet history has repeatedly shown that risk-free assets can, on the contrary, carry risks. During the Great Depression, many countries whose sovereign debt was considered risk-free went bankrupt, including the United States in 1933.

24.2 The Remedies to the Chimera of Zero Risk: Towards an Ethics of Risk Reward

The representation of risk in monotheistic traditions contrasts with the modern perception of risk as something to be avoided, transferred or even eliminated. The principled framework of Islamic finance, following in the footsteps of ancient monotheistic and philosophical traditions, provides an example of this traditional representation of risk. At this point, it is interesting to return to Aristotle's interpretation of interest as remuneration for lending. For him, interest illustrates the impossibility of applying a quantitative reading to an object whose nature cannot be reduced to a quantitative measure. The nature of money justifies the fact that the fruit of its use cannot be included in the category of the product of money. He thus opposes the practice of interest, perceived as an unnatural increase in wealth, and lays the groundwork for a distinction between a monetary object, the *medium*, instituted by convention, and an object that is natural in essence, and alone capable of generating a fruit (*τοκος* in Greek).

While in the Christian West, the separation of secular and religious powers has helped to detach economic discipline from its moral anchor, in the Islamic tradition, the representation of economic and commercial practices remains embedded in normative prescriptions. Islamic thought, in condemning usury in favour of a just and shared gain, is closer to the scholastics, whose arguments echo the texts of Islamic jurisprudence widely disseminated and translated in the Andalusia of the XIth century (Guéranger, 2009).

The key point of Islamic commercial law is the balance (*iwad*) between counterparties, embodied in the two legal maxims: no remuneration without risk (*al-ghorm bil ghonm*) and no profit without risk of loss (*al-kharaj bil daman*).

[4] In a synthetic securitization, a bank buys credit protection on a portfolio of loans from an investor. This means that, if a loan in the portfolio defaults, the investor reimburses the bank for losses incurred on the loans in the portfolio, up to a maximum equal to the amount invested.

This balance is formalized by the principle of profit and loss sharing (PLS), which constitutes the 'DNA' of Islamic financial contracts. By agreeing to share risks with the manager/entrepreneur, the capital provider reinforces mutual cooperation *(ta'wun)*.

Although modern financial theory agrees on the principle of a positive relationship between risk of loss and return, the imposition of a minimum compensation threshold for the provision of financial capital, independent of any economic risk, seems incompatible with this cardinal principle.

The payment of an interest rate perceived as a rent remunerating the use of monetary capital is therefore incompatible with Muslim ethics, as it is assimilated to *riba*[5] (see Box 24.4).

Box 24.4: Prohibition of Riba

Etymologically, the word *riba* (masculine Arabic noun) comes from the verbs *rabâ* and *arbâ*, meaning 'to increase' and 'to make increase' something from itself. Its prohibition, like the Christian canonical ban on usury, is based on the dual assertion that time belongs to God alone and cannot be the object of a commercial exchange, and that money in itself does not create wealth.

The use of an interest rate established *ex ante* as an indicator of the expected return on capital is therefore excluded from the Islamic principled framework. Nevertheless, some modern theorists argue that if Islam requires all profit to be associated with risk-taking, then the possibility of loss resulting from the uncertainties of time must be able to give rise to fair compensation. They therefore justify the principle of discounting future income according to the risk associated with the time element involved. The use of the discount rate in the evaluation of future wealth reflects, at the same time, the value we attribute to the well-being of future generations. In a way, it determines the trade-off between economic agents' preference for the present or for the future. A discount rate freed from its anchorage to the risk-free rate can therefore contribute to renewing models for evaluating sustainable investments. Indeed, the epistemological problem posed by the interest rate requires discounting models to be better anchored in real economy indicators, by replacing the risk-free rate with the GDP growth rate or inflation, for example (Khan, 1991). Since inflation affects any investment regardless of risk, the risk-free rate can be replaced by the inflation index, on the assumption that an investor has a minimal interest in preserving the purchasing power of his financial capital while expecting a substantial gain.

With this in mind, the asset pricing model equation could include inflation in place of the risk-free asset and be formulated as follows:

$$E(Ri) = Inf + \beta i.(E(Rm) - Inf)$$

where $E(Ri)$ *is* the expected return of a stock, $E(Rm)$ is the expected return of the market portfolio and βi is the stock's beta. The inflation indicator Inf can be approximated by using the consumer price index (CPI), the wholesale price index (WPI), a basket of selected products, or even a basket of currencies.

24.3 Focus on a Risk-Free Financial Instrument: *Sukuk*

Main Characteristics of *Sukuk*

As risk-free assets are a concept and an instrument that does not comply with Islamic law, the purchase of sovereign bonds by Islamic portfolio managers is prohibited.

The alternative offered to these investors focused on the creation of a hybrid instrument, the *sukuk*, in line with the principle of profit and loss sharing. Often referred to as Islamic bonds, *sukuk* are generally issued by *special purpose vehicles* (SPVs) set up by sovereign or corporate borrowers and which have a fiduciary function (see Fig. 24.3).

[5] Translated as 'interest' or 'usury' by some legal experts.

GPSR Compliance

The European Union's (EU) General Product Safety Regulation (GPSR) is a set of rules that requires consumer products to be safe and our obligations to ensure this.

If you have any concerns about our products, you can contact us on ProductSafety@springernature.com

In case Publisher is established outside the EU, the EU authorized representative is:

Springer Nature Customer Service Center GmbH
Europaplatz 3
69115 Heidelberg, Germany

Batch number: 10371059

Printed by Printforce, the Netherlands

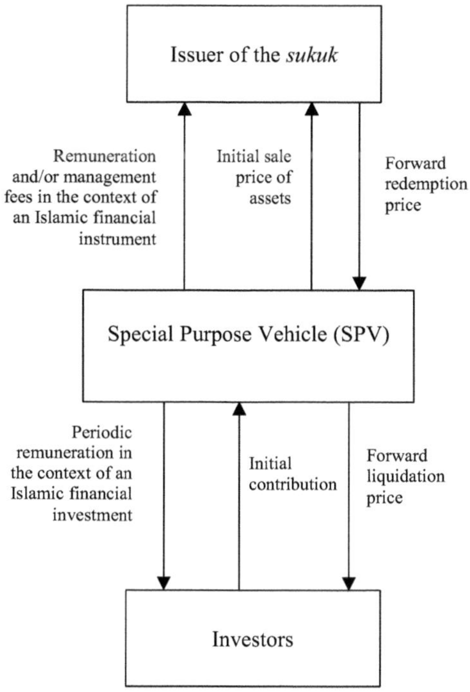

Fig. 24.3 Generic representation of financial flows in a sukuk structure (*Sources* Jouaber-Snoussi [2012] and author)

Are *Sukuk* Risk-Free Assets?

Like bonds, *sukuk* are financial products with a fixed maturity. However, there are several features that distinguish these two types of securities:

- Income: *sukuk* income differs from coupons in that, in line with the principle of profit and loss sharing, holders' remuneration must be indexed to the income streams associated with the underlying asset. It cannot therefore be considered fixed and guaranteed.
- Risks: *sukuk* holders are exposed to specific risks. The PLS principle exposes the holder to a higher counterparty risk, since in the event of a loss or lower-than-expected return, the counterparty cannot be held liable.

Integrating Environmental Risks into *Sukuk*?

Like green bonds, green *ṣukuk* can be used to finance investments in SDG-compliant projects (see Fig. 24.4). What distinguishes green *ṣukuk* from other *sukuk* is the nature of the underlying assets financed, which can include projects with a positive environmental impact.

Green *ṣukuk* therefore represent a new asset class that lies at the intersection of Islamic and socially responsible investing (SRI) (Paranque & Erragragui, 2016).

Sukuk and Sustainable Development: What are the Prospects?

A crucial question then arises: how can sustainable projects be better valued in the arbitration of public funding? The question of the fair valuation of a future societal benefit or damage arises in a very immediate way for various issues such as global warming, the sustainability of infrastructures, the exploitation of natural resources, the preservation of biodiversity, or even in the debate on GMOs. The lack of consensus on the choice of discount rate creates a situation in which operationalizing the concept of sustainable development becomes perilous. Depending on whether the discount rate is 0.5% or 3% per annum, the avoidance of damage estimated at 10 euros in 100 years' time would only be appreciable through its discounted cost, which would be of the order of 6 euros… or 19.8 cents! The longer the valuation horizon, the more crucial the choice of discount rate. A high risk-free rate will mechanically increase the discount rate of future cash flows, leading to a minimization of impacts (see Box 24.5).

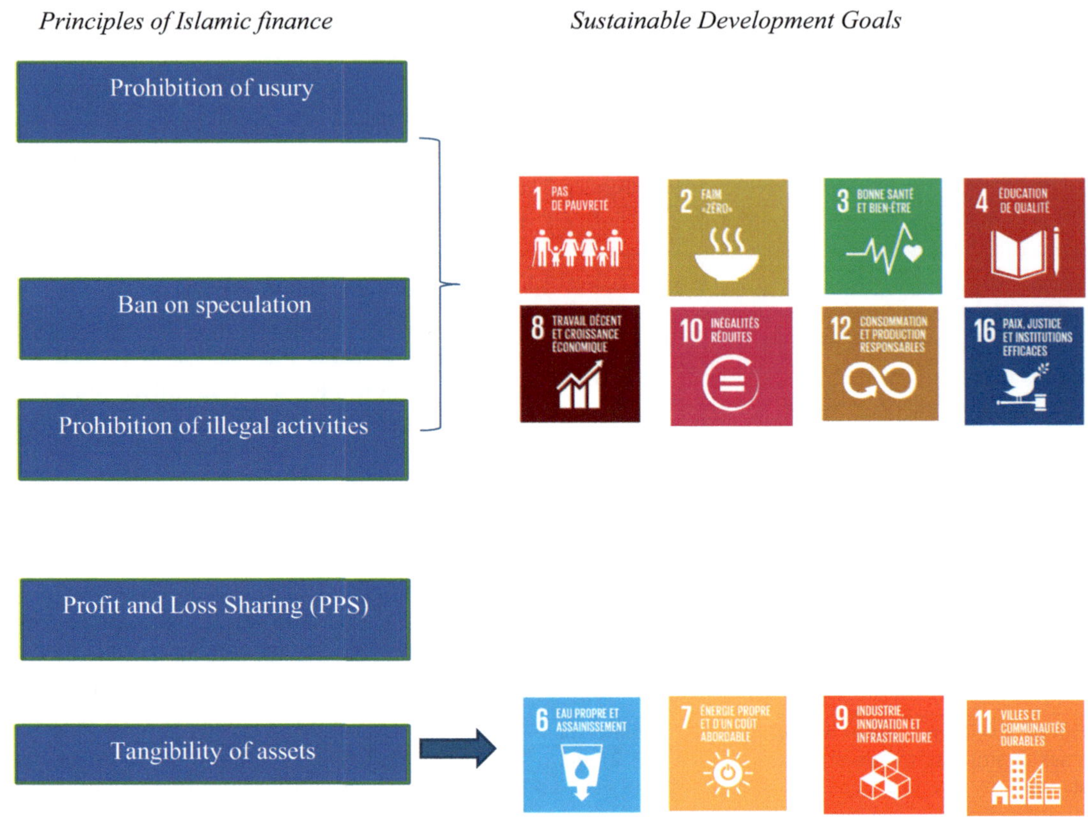

Fig. 24.4 The impact of Islamic finance principles on the SDGs (*Source* Standard and Poor's [2016][6])

Box 24.5: Illustration of the Effect of the Discount Rate in Assessing Future Carbon Costs

In 2008, economist and future Nobel Prize winner Nordhaus estimated the discounted damage of a tonne of CO_2 released into the atmosphere in 2013 at eight dollars, putting the cost of a 6 °C temperature rise by 2100 at 10% of global GDP. Using a much lower rate of 1.4%, Stern arrives at a price of $85, reducing the assessment of this same cost to 80%. The consequence of these differences in assessment is that, in one case, the damage appears so high that emission reduction policies become a priority.

The hypersensitivity of very long-term financial flows to the chosen discount rate makes it difficult to rationally assess the financial trade-offs involved in major public investments. A high discount rate, synonymous with a preference for the present, leads to the renunciation of major investments for future generations. Public investments financed by bond issues come up against a financial trade-off in which the risk-free asset is the stumbling block: how can we justify public investments, which certainly have a strong social impact, but whose financial return would be lower than the risk-free rate?

An alternative vision of the remuneration of financial capital, based on ancient traditions, which would consider that the remuneration of a zero risk can only be zero, would make it possible to overcome this stumbling block. The logic of society is that the provision of capital for the common good, whose repayment would

[6]The report is available at https://www.eticanews.it/wp-content/uploads/2016/04/Islamic-Finance.pdf.

be guaranteed by the State, should not be subject to any expectation of return other than the social benefits it is intended to provide. By rethinking the risk-free rate, ecological public investments could be freed from a financial constraint created ex ante, the theoretical underpinnings of which appear more than questionable. An in-depth academic debate on the coherence and relevance of an arbitrage based exclusively on a postulate as questionable as that of the risk-free asset should make it possible to envisage other bases for evaluating sustainable investments.

24.4 Summary and Conclusion

- The concept of a risk-free asset suffers from theoretical weaknesses that bias investment decisions.
- Ancient philosophical and religious traditions are opposed to the idea of a guaranteed, risk-free return on financial capital, which is considered unnatural.
- The Muslim tradition is opposed to the modern representation of a risk that should be transferred or eliminated, in favour of a concept of risk that is mutualized and assumed collectively.
- The hypersensitivity of future cash flows to the discount rate means that the valuation of sustainable investments depends largely on the risk-free rate used.
- By rethinking the risk-free rate in discounting models, future ecological costs can be better understood.
- Green *ṣukuk* represent a new asset class alternative to risk-free assets whose aim is to address sustainability concerns.

Activities

Questions for Discussion

1. How is financial risk represented in contemporary financial theory?
2. What do you think is the most relevant argument to illustrate the theoretical and conceptual inadequacy of the risk-free asset?
3. In the modern financial landscape, which practice best reflects the logic of risk transfer?
4. What is the bias introduced by using the risk-free rate in the CAPM to assess the performance of an investment?
5. What are the economic consequences of institutional investors' excessive preference for risk-free assets?
6. How do ancient traditions help to shed light on the theoretical limits of the risk-free asset concept?
7. Why is the risk-free rate a problem when evaluating sustainable investments?
8. What indicators can be used as alternatives to the risk-free rate in discounting models? Justify your answer.
9. To what extent can *sukuk* be considered a relevant financial instrument for financing sustainable development?

Mini-case

The French government plans to participate in the financing of an offshore wind farm along the Côtes d'Armor coastline, comprising the installation of 62 wind turbines that will produce the equivalent of the consumption of 850,000 inhabitants. Total investment in the project amounts to 15 billion euros. The lifetime of the wind farm is estimated at 50 years, after which the turbines will have to be dismantled at an estimated cost of 1 billion euros.

In return for this investment, the French government will be able to buy a kilowatt of electricity at a price 30% below the current market price.

The wind farm will generate annual cash flow of €550 million over the life of the project.

1. Estimate and compare the NPV of the project using the formula PV = a[1 - (1 + r) -n]/r (which calculates the present value of a series of constant annuities (a) over a defined period (n)) using the following two discount rates (r):
   a. the first r is based on the 20-year French Treasury bill rate (which you can find on the Banque de France website) plus a 2% risk premium.

b. the second $r = 1.2\%$ is based solely on the average level of inflation over the last ten years, with no premium (the risk of the project being neglected in relation to the expected environmental benefit).

2. Comment on the effect of the chosen discount rate on the project's valuation.

References

Books

Giraud, P. N. (2014). Le Commerce des promesses. Petit traité de finance moderne. *Media Diffusion. Chapter, 1*, 11–32 (untranslated).

Guéranger, F. (2009). Islamic finance: An illustration of ethical finance. *Dunod. Chapter, 1*, 7–19.

Articles

Arrow, K. J., & Debreu, G. (1954). Existence of an equilibrium for a competitive economy. *Econometrica: Journal of the Econometric Society*, 265–290.

Jouaber-Snoussi, K. (2012). Les sukuk, in *La Finance islamique*. La Découverte, 2012, 95–112 (untranslated).

Khan, M. F. (1991). Time value of money and discounting from an Islamic perspective. *Review of Islamic Economics,* 1(2), 35–45.

Lintner, J. (1965). Security prices, risk, and maximal gains from diversification. *The Journal of Finance,* 20(4), 587–615.

Markowitz, H. (1952). Portfolio selection. *The Journal of Finance,* 7(1), pp. 77–91.

Paranque, B., & Erragragui, E. (2016). Islamic investment versus socially responsible investment: Lessons from comparison. *Finance reconsidered: New perspectives for a responsible and sustainable finance (Critical studies on corporate responsibility, governance and sustainability, Vol. 10)* (pp. 355–383). Emerald Group Publishing Limited, Bingley.

Sharpe, W. F. (1964). Capital asset prices: A theory of market equilibrium under conditions of risk. *The Journal of Finance, 19*(3), 425–442.

Treynor, J. L. (1961, August 8). Market value, time, and risk. *Time, and Risk.*

Treynor, J. L. (1962). *'Jack Treynor's 'Toward a theory of market value of risky assets'*. Available at https://papers.ssrn.com/sol3/papers.cfm?abstract_id=628187

Walter, C. (2010). The ethics of finance after the Brownian virus. *Finance Bien Commun,* 1, 10–20.